The changing European firm

Throughout Europe, governments have acted in accordance with the conviction that a larger and uniform market would enable greater economies of scale and the growth of large corporations. This is seen in terms of the spread of multinational, US-style companies, enforcing a uniform type of firm across countries.

The contributions to this volume, in contrast, show how the nature of firms is embedded in the larger societal context of nations, preventing the spread of a homogenized firm-type across European countries. It becomes clear that researchers should locate the firm in the social context in which it is rooted, rather than looking to economic science to explain a 'non-ideal type'.

Areas covered by the contributors include the comparison of typical firms in Denmark and Finland; the limited transformation of large enterprises in Hungary; and an analysis of supply networks in Britain and Germany. These essays and discussions of the variations in the nature of the firm in Europe by leading European researchers provide new insights into how national patterns develop and are reinforced.

Richard Whitley is Professor of Organizational Sociology at the Manchester Business School.
Peer Hull Kristensen is Associate Professor at the Copenhagen Business School.

The **European Science Foundation** is an association of its 56 member research councils, academies and institutions devoted to basic scientific research in 20 countries. The ESF assists its Member Organizations in two main ways: by bringing scientists together in its Scientific Programmes, Networks and European Research Conferences, to work on topics of common concern; and through the joint study of issues of strategic importance in European science policy.

The scientific work sponsored by ESF includes basic research in the natural and technical sciences, the medical and biosciences, the humanities and social sciences.

The ESF maintains close relations with other scientific institutions within and outside Europe. By its activities, ESF adds value by cooperation and coordination across national frontiers and endeavours, offers expert scientific advice on strategic issues, and provides the European forum for fundamental science.

This volume arises from the work of the ESF Scientific Programme on European Management and Organizations in Transition (EMOT).

Further information on ESF activities can be obtained from:

European Science Foundation
1 quai Lezay-Marnésia
F-67080 Strasbourg Cedex
France
Tel. (+33) 88 76 71 00
Fax (+33) 88 37 05 32

The changing European firm

Limits to convergence

Edited by Richard Whitley and
Peer Hull Kristensen

London and New York

First published 1996
by Routledge
11 New Fetter Lane, London EC4P 4EE

Simultaneously published in the USA and Canada
by Routledge
29 West 35th Street, New York, NY 10001

Phototypeset in Times by Intype, London
Printed and bound in Great Britain by
Clays Ltd, St Ives, plc

British Library Cataloguing in Publication Data
A catalogue record for this book is available from the British Library

Library of Congress Cataloguing in Publication Data
A catalogue record for this book has been requested

ISBN 0–415–12999–0
ISBN 0–415–13000–X (pbk)

Contents

Contributors

Professor L. Czaban, Manchester Business School, University of Manchester, Booth Street West, Manchester M15 6PB, United Kingdom.

Dr Tor Halvorsen, Dept. of Sociology, Universitetet I Bergen, N-5007 Bergen, Norway.

Professor J. Henderson, Manchester Business School, University of Manchester, Booth Street West, Manchester M15 6PB, United Kingdom.

Dr Ad van Iterson, FdEW, University of Limburg, NL-6200 MD Maastricht, The Netherlands.

Professor O. Korsnes, Dept. of Sociology, Universitetet I Bergen, N-5007 Bergen, Norway.

Professor Peer Hull Kristensen, Copenhagen Business School, Institute of Organisation and Industrial Society, 23B Blagaardsgade, 2200 Copenhagen N, Denmark.

Dr Christel Lane, Faculty of Social and Political Sciences, University of Cambridge, Free School Lane, Cambridge CB2 3RQ, United Kingdom.

Professor Kari Lilja, Helsinki School of Economics, Runeberginkatu 14–16, 00100 Helsinki, Finland.

M. Mayer, Warwick Business School, University of Warwick, Coventry CV4 7AL, United Kingdom.

R. Sakslind, Dept. of Sociology, Universitetet I Bergen, N-5007 Bergen, Norway.

Professor Arndt Sorge, Humboldt-Universität zu Berlin, FB Sozialwissenschaften, Unter den Linden 6, 10099 Berlin, Germany.

Professor Risto Tainio, Helsinki School of Economics, Runeberginkatu 14–16, 00100 Helsinki 10, Finland.

Dr Richard Whittington, Warwick Business School, University of Warwick, Coventry CV4 7AL, United Kingdom.

Professor Richard Whitley, Manchester Business School, University of Manchester, Booth Street West, Manchester M15 6PB, United Kingdom.

Dr Graham Winch, University College London, The Bartlett, Philipps House, Gower Street, London WC1E 6BT, United Kingdom.

1 Variations in the nature of the firm in Europe

Peer Hull Kristensen

INTRODUCTION

The growing interdependence of European economies has been seen as encouraging the standardization of firm type and structure across Europe. Examples are the development of the Single European Market (SEM) in the European Union and the growth of cross-national alliances and investment. Throughout Europe, governments have acted in accordance with the conviction that a larger and uniform market would enable greater economies of scale and the growth of large corporations. Most European states have taken action to facilitate their own industries' adaptation to these new conditions by supporting mergers and acquisitions so that firms would speed up their restructuring and move faster towards the 'ideal type', which is believed to be universally valid. In many political discourses such steps are believed necessary in order to confront the Japanese and American challenges.

However, it is not easy to reach agreement about which 'ideal type' of firm is most preferable. Many authors seem to be of the opinion that the multi-divisional, diversified corporation as institutionalized in the USA is competitively superior, especially when favouring the establishment of the ideal type through mergers and acquisitions. However, after having made expensive experiments with that type of organization, many industrialists have begun to favour sticking to 'core businesses', and some revitalization of the 'integrated corporation' seems to follow. A third camp, inspired by the organization of Japanese industry, has discovered the advantages of outsourcing. While buying in some business units, they began selling off others, initiating a process that would take them away from the two ideal types of firms that have dominated post-war debates.

Simultaneously, the structure of small- and medium-sized firms in the 'Third Italy' started to attract attention, as this region demonstrated improving prosperity at a faster rate than any other region in Europe. Still, however, many governments throughout Europe continue to act from the conviction that establishing large corporations is the only way to take advantage of the Single European Market. Mass seems to be critical, not least because European governments imagine that this will enable their own firms to meet competition from foreign multinationals. Convergent views still dominate, as multinationals are believed to spread best practices across European countries, or even globally, thereby enforcing a uniform type of firm across countries. It seems as if convergence follows as much from convictions among political bureaucracies as from market selection.

The contributions to this volume, in contrast, show how the nature of firms is embedded in the larger societal context of nations so that, despite conjunctural political reforms and prevalent market forces, a uniform firm-type is very unlikely to spread across European countries. In this introductory chapter we discuss the arguments in this debate and present an integrated overview of them. The first section presents the theoretical arguments in favour of a universal ideal firm-type. In the second section, we use some of the material in this volume to explain why the M-form corporation may be conceived as a particular firm-type, which owes its efficiency to the distinct American social and institutional context in which it became established. Finally, in the third section, we combine the contributions of this volume into a preliminary framework in order to explain why firms are constituted and develop differently in various nations.

THE SEARCH FOR A GENERAL ECONOMIC THEORY OF THE EVOLUTION OF THE FIRM

Mainstream textbook economics conceives of the firm as just a set of cost and revenue schedules together with an objective function, anticipating the firm as a profit-maximizer. In his 1991 Nobel lecture, Coase was very critical of the current state of orthodox theories of the firm:

I have called the result 'Blackboard economics'. The firm and the market appear by name but they lack any substance. The firm in mainstream economic theory has often been described as a 'black box'. And so it is. This is very extraordinary given that most resources in a modern economic system are employed within firms, with how these resources are used dependent on administrative decisions and not directly of a market.

(Coase, 1991a: 229)

But why are treatises on the nature of firms not easy to put on the 'blackboard' or into textbooks? It is certainly not because economists have not tried to deal with the question. Coase's article of 1937 is just one attempt among many between the First and Second World Wars when European economists and social researchers were discussing the challenge from the American corporations. Nor is it because economists who have addressed the problem were considered to be of low scholarly status. However, while Alfred Marshall's early work, *Principles of Economics*, has had a profound impact on economic thought in the twentieth century, his 1919 *Industry and Trade* had little effect on the set of core ideas defining the science of economics. The same phenomenon may be observed with another famous British economist, E. A. G. Robinson, who became famous for his work on monopoly, while his earlier work from 1935, *The Structure of Competitive Industry*, had been neglected by and large.

Though Marshall's ability to make generalizations and theoretical abstractions cannot be questioned, his 1919 enquiry is dominated by the question of how the organization of industry differs from one country to another, and how economies of scale and competitiveness are achieved by different institutions in different countries. This led him to the conclusion that if Britain was to meet the challenges of the American corporations, she had to build on her current organization of industrial districts composed of small and medium enterprises (SMEs), which would have to develop a more coherent division of labour in order to achieve the necessary cost reductions. A belief in one universal solution to how industry can be organized would be very difficult to deduce from Marshall's later work.

Robinson (1935) considered the same problem, but instead of enquiring how various countries had achieved this goal, he directly asked: What does 'the optimum firm' look like? He provided the following analysis:

> The optimum firm is likely to result from the ordinary play of economic forces where the market is perfect and sufficient to maintain a single firm of optimum size. . . .
>
> The forces which determine the best size of the business unit, assuming that the market is sufficient to absorb the whole

production of at least one firm of optimum size, may be divided into five main categories: Technical forces, making for a technical optimum size; managerial forces, making for an optimum managerial unit; financial forces, making for an optimum financial unit; the influences of marketing, making for an optimum sales unit; and the forces of risk and fluctuation, making for a unit possessing the greatest power of survival in the face of industrial vicissitudes.

(Robinson, 1935: 16–17)

With these propositions in place, Robinson's book ought to have been just a first step in the completion of a theory of the firm, ready to be presented on the blackboard. But it was not, which is easy to understand from his own analysis that demonstrates how low the probability is that 'optimum' in one aspect is in equilibrium with optimum in the other aspects. In discussing how these disequilibria can be reconciled, Robinson suggests a 'palette' of different organizational forms, which comes very close to the complexity of industrial organization that Marshall had demonstrated for very different reasons. Consequently, from the methods of reconciling optima-differences, a whole range of different organizational forms emerges for firms, dependent on the circumstances of the given industry.

While both Marshall's and Robinson's analyses recognize complexity and diversity as to how firms can be organized, they share the conviction that the *raison d'être* of firms is that they enable a division of labour. The more this division of labour can be improved, the lower the costs. They share the image of Adam Smith's pin-factory, and their line of argument follows this logic,[1] which is reproduced in nearly all textbooks and is one of the nicest stories to tell from the blackboard at any undergraduate course in economics. Division of labour not only leads to dexterity so that the whole action becomes automatic and therefore cost-saving. It has a very human aspect, too in that it allows individuals to specialize in tasks for which they are specifically gifted. For this reason large firms are better than small firms:

> It is a waste to employ a skilled craftsman on work that a child might equally well do; it is a waste to employ a skilled accountant on work which a typist ought to be doing. In a large firm, a skilled man can be kept all the time employed on work which requires all his abilities. In a small firm, he may spend much of his day on tasks which a less skilled and cheaper worker could equally well perform.

(Robinson, 1935: 21)

This type of reasoning has been widely accepted among Marxists as well as mainstream economists, who see the firm as enabling a 'team' of workers to allow for a more productive division of labour than atomistic producers can achieve. With an increasing division of labour firms must integrate what technically can be separated into individual tasks. Thus, by necessity they will tend to grow larger.

In his article of 1937, Coase clearly distanced himself from this view:

> The 'integrating force in a differentiated economy' already exists in the form of the price mechanism. It is perhaps the main achievement of economic science that it has shown that there is no reason to suppose that specialization must lead to chaos. . . . What has to be explained is why one integrating force (the entrepreneur) should be substituted for another integrating force (the price mechanism).
>
> (Coase, 1991b: 25)

Coase's answer was that when transaction costs can be reduced more than the costs involved in organizing teams of workers, firms may operate more effectively than markets.

Transaction cost economics, as inspired by Coase, has greatly helped reformulate approaches. Since Coase, this school of economics has defined the firm with considerable clarity:

> We can best approach the question of what constitutes a firm in practice by considering the legal relationship normally called that of 'master and servant' or 'employer and employee'. . . . it is the fact of direction which is the essence of the legal concept of 'employer and employee'. . . .
>
> (Coase, 1991b: 29)

The firm is seen simply as an alternative coordinating mechanism to the market and is defined over and against the market:

> Evidently there are at least two coordinating mechanisms: within markets the price system signals (decentralized) resource allocation needs and opportunities; but firms employ a different organizing principle – that of hierarchy – whereupon authority is used to effect resource reallocations.
>
> (Williamson, 1991: 3)

With the concept of transaction costs in place, it is easy for Coase to determine the optimum size of a firm:

When we are considering how large a firm will be the principle of marginalism works smoothly. The question always is, will it pay to bring an extra exchange transaction under the organizing authority.... But it is clear that the dynamic factors are also of considerable importance, and an investigation of the effect changes have on the cost of organizing within the firm and on marketing costs generally will enable one to explain why firms get larger and smaller. We thus have a theory of moving equilibrium.

(Coase, 1991b: 30)

With this elegant conclusion it is understandable that Coase's theory of the firm has attracted widespread attention from economists. Suddenly, 'organizational phenomena' can be related to economics in a coherent way. But Coase's conclusion has also made it possible to readdress the question of how the 'optimum' firm evolves. Williamson's 1975 book is a beautiful argument as to how organizing costs have been reduced by inventing new organizational forms which enable firms to expand continuously:

Starting with the assumption that in the beginning there were markets, progressively more ramified forms of internal organization have successively 'evolved'. First peer groups, then simple hierarchies, and finally the vertically integrated firm in which a compound hierarchy exists have appeared.

(Williamson, 1975: 132)

The last stage is the creation of a multi-divisional (M-form) structure, which reduces the costs of organizing arising with the growth in size and complexity of the unitary form (U-form) of the vertically integrated corporation. Essentially, the argument is that by creating new levels of authority in a hierarchical manner, organizations can deal with shirking, free-riders, opportunism, and partisan interest and thus monitor the organization so as to reduce the costs of organizing. Williamson has created a theoretical framework and argument that underpins Chandler's (1977) historical record of the rise and evolution of the American corporation.

But Williamson goes further than that. Rather than just dealing with the M-form as a heuristic device, he is eager to determine what the optimum form of the M-form involves:

(1) the identification of separable economic activities within the firm; (2) according quasi-autonomous standing (usually of a profit centre nature) to each; (3) monitoring the efficiency performance of each division; (4) awarding incentives; (5) allocating cash flows

to high yield uses; and (6) performing strategic planning (diversification, acquisition, and related activities) in other respects.

(1975: 149)

The hierarchical principles of the M-form are strongly contrasted with the loosely defined holding company and it is stated that planning and operational matters should be carefully separated also at this structural level. Williamson cannot conceal his admiration of the M-form, though he admits that, in the future, organizational innovations may be possible and even probable. One thing, however, will not change:

while evolutionary change is to be expected, the hierarchical decomposition principles on which the M-form is based is [*sic*] very robust. In his discussion of adaptive corporate organization, Beer observes: 'The notion of hierarchy is given in cybernetics as a necessary structural attribute of any viable organism. This is not surprising to us, although its theoretical basis is profound, because all viable systems do in fact exhibit hierarchical organizations.'

(Ibid.)

The great advantage of the concept of hierarchy as an attribute of the firm, is that it allows us to think of the firm as an entity, an acting unit, 'the economic agency', because it is able to enforce the centralized decisions of the 'head' on the 'body', from owners over managers to workers. Furthermore, it enables us to take for granted a distinction between the internal world of the firm and the external world. The hierarchy, however, in Williamson's world did not evolve this way as harmony prevails. Rather, it is exactly because hierarchy makes it possible to resolve problems of opportunism, free-riderism and shirking among various actors within the firm that organizations evolve through the mentioned stages. Hierarchy, thus, evolves not only as the result of the external market forces and competition, but as the consequence of the 'internal logic' of organizing (see also Abrahamsson, 1986).

NATIONAL VARIATIONS: DIFFERENT INSTITUTIONAL CONTEXTS SHAPE DIFFERENT FIRM-TYPES

In their contribution to this volume, Mayer and Whittington focus on the diffusion of this model of the multi-divisional corporation.

They demonstrate that the idea has been tremendously successful. Rooted in the work of a large number of Harvard scholars, it has had a major impact on modern ideas of management, institutionalized not only in managerial education but also in transnational consulting firms. In Europe, thus, the M-form organization mode has become the blueprint for organizational design. And yet Mayer and Whittington show that it is very unclear to what extent the M-form has been really followed and put into practice in Europe. Many large firms stick to the holding company form, despite the very unclear organizational relations between the various organizational units. They also suggest that the success of the M-form in the USA may be explained by particular circumstances there, so that it developed in that country not because it was universally effective but due to the development of American institutions. Such a viewpoint has recently found increasing acceptance also among American scholars (see, for example, Fligstein, 1990), and even Williamson (1993) has recently 'dropped earlier universalistic claims on behalf of the M-form. . . . Theory finally allows the Japanese *keiretsu* to be as effective as the American multi-divisional.'

The comparative differences in institutional contexts and characteristics of economic actors are systematically discussed by Whitley in this volume. From Whitley's point of view the American M-form would develop where firms have to internalize risks and have difficulties in developing linkages with other economic actors. It happens 'in economies where the state remains aloof from economic coordinating and risk-sharing, and the banks likewise are remote from the activities of particular firms', while other organizational forms may evolve where firms can 'develop obligational relationships between enterprises and reciprocity is a strongly established norm'. Whitley advocates the point of view that 'ways of structuring the coordination and control of economic activities are the outcome of different paths to industrial capitalism and associated differences in dominant institutions, such as the state and the financial system.'

If we re-examine Williamson's original synthesis (1975) from Whitley's point of view it becomes obvious that institutional specificity plays an important role even in Williamson's argument. Two specific institutions are particularly salient in his book. First, the multi-divisional form with a strong coordinating apex at the top is particularly efficient as it enables the firm to deal with the capital market, rather than the credit-based system that we find in some continental European countries. The M-form is designed to benefit the principal with adequate information if the principal is a mass of stock-owners, and short-term profits are the guiding principle. The argument is that the chief executive of the M-form company will perform the controlling role on behalf of the investors. On the other hand, in a credit-based system, where banks are directly represented on boards, as in both Germany and France, the holding company form may be an effective forum for discussing projects between business units and external financiers, i.e. for creating the kind of consortium necessary to initiate new investments in relation to which many separate actors are involved and business units and external stakeholders do not see themselves as components of portfolios. Similarly, having organized mutual ownership between different, but friendly business units, the Japanese *keiretsu* is rather a forum for horizontal negotiations among a number of stakeholders that cannot easily be ordered hierarchically. To coordinate their businesses they must engage in some of the painful processes characterizing peer groups, which Williamson originally deemed inefficient from a trans-action cost perspective.

Whitley's discussion makes us aware of how difficult it is in various countries to identify economic actors, if we stick to either the Coase/ Williamson hierarchical employment contract or to the Penrosian concept that 'firms' are areas of authorized communication. Neither financial holding companies, French industrial groups nor the Japanese *keiretsu* may be defined as 'the firm' from such a perspec-tive, because the units composing these groupings often plan their actions independently of the larger group. In this perspective the M-form as idealized by Williamson is a very special case, rather than being a representative form of federal organization.

Secondly, in arguing in favour of the universalistic hierarchical principle of organizing, Williamson strongly based his thinking on the existence of company-wide 'employment contracts' and 'internal labour markets'. For very different reasons, and in highly different institutional contexts, such a situation seems primarily to have existed in the USA and Japan. In Europe, major variations can be observed from one country to another. For example, in countries with strong craft unions it is not possible to set up company-wide 'contracts'. Different groups of workers are subject to national regu-lations, which set (serious) limits to the allocation of different groups of people to idiosyncratic jobs. Further, it is characteristic of 'internal labour markets' that skills are attributed to the individual company, rather than to a profession or group of workers in the larger society. While firms in the former situation are free to allocate workers to predetermined jobs in a hierarchical order, the latter situation implies that they have to try to make jobs attractive to certain types of workers who establish their identity from a larger institutional and social context. Expansion of educational institutions has in general favoured a development from the former to the latter situation, and in countries with strong apprenticeship traditions combined with school-based training (as in the famous dual system of Germany), the effects of this on worker-discretion has long been well known.

If American firms and enterprises tend to be hierarchical without complications due to a general firm-wide employment contract, the explanation is probably that during industrialization and the growth of large corporations, firms were managed by a core group of highly skilled staff, simultaneously recruiting a very heterogeneous labour force that had migrated from many quarters of the world with very different backgrounds. Skill and discipline could most easily be institutionalized as part of, and remain with, the managers of the organization, to be hierarchically imposed top-down on newly recruited workers. Scientific management, no doubt, was a needed and very helpful social innovation in the USA. Further, we would also expect hierarchy to be a less difficult concept to comprehend in a system of industrial relations, where individual strategies of exit, rather than collective strategies of voice and loyalty, dominate among different groups of workers.

In contrast, in most continental European countries employees did not and could not act as individualistically as is generally taken for granted in the American context. Consequently, employers did not deal with atomistic individuals, but rather faced collectives and groups of employees that had accumulated organizing capabilities, which could be used to secure entire groups a place in the status hierarchies and help them achieve discretion in playing their respective roles within different parts of the hierarchy. In many countries, of which Germany is most famous due to its law on co-determination, the reallocation of jobs between groups thus cannot be decided without a formalized negotiation among the parties involved.

It is obvious for these reasons that within a different institutional and social context it will not be as easy to reconcile problems of shirking, free-riderism, and opportunistic behaviour by establishing the different hierarchical organizational forms suggested by Williamson. But the need for reconciling such problems may also be less urgent. It is a well-known fact that groups establish themselves through norms and create world-views which codify certain behaviour as honourable and other forms of behaviour as unworthy.

These group norms, and the internal discipline of groups in many countries, reconcile informally what needs to be formally addressed in the American context. Consequently, the trajectory of finding institutional innovations to the problems of organizing firms may differ in important respects from one country to another. For these reasons we suggest that Williamson's classical contribution of 1975 should be seen as a synthesis of the American experience and historical development of the firm, rather than a universally valid theoretical contribution.

Turning to firms in other national contexts, however, involves more than just evaluating how firms were institutionalized in different ways. We see at least two additional complications. First, in many European countries the processes of institutionalizing firms did not at all follow the sequence from markets, via peer group organizations and simple hierarchies to the vertically integrated and finally M-form company. Many firms were created large either by state action or through the initiatives of large bank groups. Second, the problems which firms have to reconcile in Europe may be very different from those in the American setting. Opportunism, shirking and free-riderism are much more difficult in countries where people and economic actors are less mobile and social ties are more lasting than is the case in America.

It is well known that the large French and German corporations challenging the British industrial leadership at the end of the nineteenth century did not emerge as a result of a competitive game gradually leading to the existence of oligopolies through centralization and concentration of capital or competitive reduction of transaction costs. Rather, they were the outcome of dedicated and concerted action by banks of the crédit mobilière type and the state in an effort to meet the challenge from Britain (Marshall, 1919 and Gerschenkron, 1991 (1952)). These firms were born large and allocated an important role in the plans for national industrialization. Having powerful players among their initiators, i.e. the banks and the state, it is also quite evident that challenges from national competitors, should they have emerged, would have been met with strong regulatory powers. German cartels were efficient in reconciling problems of competition and cooperation and made it very dangerous for customers and suppliers to engage in the type of opportunistic behaviour which Williamson sees as a major explanation for the need to reduce transaction costs through large hierarchies. It could be said that 'hierarchical' authority went far beyond the individual firm, leaving a very limited role to the market and its forces.

This process of industrialization with strong state and bank involvement is observed in the contributions on Belgium and Finland in this volume. Ad van Iterson demonstrates how the central state initiated large managerial and holding companies in Wallonia, while in Flanders small family-owned firms emerged as a continuation of the traditional lives of craftsmen and farmers. Combined, they established a 'dual' structure, which is still characteristic of Belgium. The Wallonian large corporations were soon transformed into holding companies and they have actively used this form to stabilize the system by gaining financial control which enables them to monitor companies. Looking for explanations of why the system has been so stable and unchanging, Ad van Iterson asks us to search for an explanation in 'the preferences and traditions of the French speaking, mainly Brussels' haute bourgeoisie'.

In the Finnish case, Lilja and Tainio demonstrate that the state not only played an active role in institutionalizing large firms within the pulp and paper industry but also that today banks and the state serve as mediators of cooperation between large firms within this sector, enabling these firms to engage in highly risky processes of growth. The large Finnish pulp and paper firms are not large primarily because they have engaged in processes to reduce transaction costs. Rather, the logic of vertical integration is reversed. Paper and pulp firms occasionally have to engage in huge investments, which may provide them with plants that immediately create excessive capacity. In order to protect this initial investment against reducing profitability, they must then engage in investments that utilize the increased production of pulp by building speciality mills for paper etc., thereby gradually developing the more diversified type of firms, which they say is so typical of Finland. Finnish firms can be seen as large hierarchies, but a closer look reveals that they are not designed to enable the firms primarily to counter opportunism, shirking and free-riderism. Their primary nature is concerned with improving operations and technically maintaining huge capital investments. Within large Finnish corporations workers and middle-managers enjoy an autonomy comparable to the situation in Denmark (Dobbin and Boychuk, 1994). But whereas the job-autonomy of Danish skilled workers is rooted in the social conditions of a group, the Finnish job autonomy is rooted in a codified education, which structures the labour force at different levels to take on the responsibilities and duties defined by the needs of the 'large machine' of the paper and pulp industry.

Furthermore, it is obvious from Lilja and Tainio's contribution that workers benefit very handsomely in economic terms by improving existing processes. As a consequence of this monitoring system it is often the workers who initiate activities in the wider 'hierarchy'. It could be argued that 'opportunism' is governed to benefit both the company and the worker which is also the case in Japanese manufacturing (Sabel, 1993). Whereas in Japan workers within the *nenko* system tie their career to a specific firm, in Finland both managers and workers tie their lives to the operation of a specific mill. The destiny of both groups depends on how skilful they are at making improvements on a given investment. Both groups are subordinated to the 'machine' and the machine is seen as benefiting the developmental trajectory of the entire nation. It would be difficult to identify the American employment contract in Lilja and Tainio's contribution. The needs of the machine, so to speak, authorize and legitimate decisions, and to make sense of the machine, firm organization has taken the shape of a strong engineering meritocracy. Finally, it may be difficult to understand the principles of social regulation within Finnish pulp and paper mills without recognizing that it is strongly integrated with the entire community in which it is located. Consequently, it becomes impossible to violate the rules in one sphere without violating those of the other.

In neither of these cases does the corporate hierarchy arise as a solution to experienced transaction cost problems. Such firms were created large and their organizational form seems to have been remarkably stable. Composed of large plants, often located in small communities, the community often helped the plant regulate behaviour, making little room for opportunism, shirking and free-riderism, and therefore reducing the need for some of the modern American attributes of 'advanced' hierarchies. In many such mill communities, informal regulation among peer groups based on community ties allows even large plants to function with very simple and 'flat' hierarchies in which the regulatory modes only develop a few of the attributes of bureaucracy. This may also serve as a hypothetical explanation of the fact that the social space of managers is remarkably smaller in continental Europe than in both the UK and the USA (Gordon, 1994).

It seems that the costs of organizing are especially high in the Anglo-Saxon world (USA, UK, Canada and Australia). One reason for this difference may be that in continental Europe community ties, group and inter-group regulations take care of many of the problems that occur in corporations located in more 'footloose' societies. This may also be one of the reasons why European firms encounter problems when they expand beyond their normal locality, as they try either to duplicate their home-organization or to install the American M-form. The results of the mergers and acquisitions of the last couple of decades have shown the limitations of such expansion in most cases.

While large plants established through the coordinated action of the state, banks and industrialists in small communities may explain very well why there is no reason to invent new organizational forms to defy opportunism, shirking and free-riderism, it is much more difficult to explain why small firms have persistently played a major role in industrial production in continental Europe. Particularly during the 1980s it became clear (Sengenberger *et al.*, 1990) that rather than heading towards extinction, SMEs were expanding and playing an important role in making such regions as Emilia Romagna, Baden Württemberg and Western Jutland successful (Piore and Sabel, 1984; Pyke *et al.*, 1990; Pyke and Sengenberger, 1992). According to Williamson such firm structures ought to undergo radical changes due to the enormous transaction costs involved. Porter, on the other hand, argues in his original contribution (1980) that there are enormous gains at stake for firms that can 'overcome fragmentation'. How come, then, that some of these regions in Europe have been able to deal with opportunism, shirking and free-riderism without making use of the organizational solutions offered by Williamson?

Ad van Iterson suggests in his contribution to this volume that the SMEs in Flanders regulate their business by a strong dynastic tradition. They succeeded – and still succeed – in 'keeping it all in the family', avoiding the use of salaried managers from outside. Furthermore, they have relied almost entirely on the local labour market for workers, from whom they perhaps expect loyalty, nourished by chauvinistic sentiments. This strategy allowed them to continue with a flat hierarchy, regulated more through paternalistic principles than by relying on modern bureaucracy. Ad van Iterson additionally suggests that, as is also the case in many explanations of the Italian industrial districts, the Catholic family has played a major part in the SMEs' ability to survive up to now. From the Flanders example the suggestion seems to be that small firms have survived as simple hierarchies in which family ties have been able to solve some of the difficulties involved in regulating their mutual relations.

From the vast amount of literature on the Third Italy, we know that it has taken much more to create the social fabric in which relations within and among these small firms are embedded. Specialization on related industries making use of the ties and social norms of these small communities, makes it possible to cooperate across family boundaries. An extensive use of associations (e.g. CNA) helps organize managerial and accounting facilities, supporting directly small firms' ability to deal with the state authorities and the banks; however, it also makes the firms' economic situation remarkably transparent to customers and suppliers, thus reducing the uncertainty involved in doing business with strangers. Furthermore, in Emilia, SMEs lose the right to membership of the CNA if they employ more than 20 persons. Therefore, for institutional reasons they tend to increase their transaction costs if they grow. The solution to this problem is, of course, to comply with the rules formally by inventing informal ways to undermine them. One way is to establish new firms co-owned by an ever-changing combination of persons. Consequently, in Italian districts, shirking and opportunism lead to the expansion of the mass of small firms and the number of entrepreneurs that from their birth as entrepreneurs belong to a peer group constituted in such a way that free-riderism is a poor strategy.

In the search of firm-types in the Danish setting, Peer Hull Kristensen can neither attribute the strong role of SMEs in Denmark to Catholic family traditions, nor to the associational logics of the Third Italy. He shows how the institutionalized behaviour of craft-workers have helped establish 'reputational linking' as a regulatory principle within and among Danish firms. His argument is that the worker must gain a good reputation if he is to continue to belong to a team of good reputation. Firms, especially of the 'skill container type', must themselves try to gain a good reputation if they want to recruit such work teams and aim to receive increasing orders from other skill containers and 'project coordinators'. Kristensen constructs an interactional logic for the entire system, which helps to explain why a system of small firms may grow without the single firm involved needing to develop in size. In a way this system is an example of a stabilized peer-group structure in which the need for coordinated action is taken care of in the sequence following the building of transactional relations.

The system suggested by Kristensen is a very simple resolution to problems of opportunism and shirking. It probably only works under a situation of quite narrow and closely knit social ties, i.e. in the context of a small and very stable community – be it a region or an industry sector dominated by a strong sectoral craft ethos. However, without, for instance, associations to monitor members' behaviour, institutions for setting standards, etc., the system may quickly be destroyed by external shocks. This may explain why such a system disappeared from Copenhagen during the 1930s, while it was reborn in the agricultural areas of Western Jutland after the Second World War (Kristensen, 1992). However, nothing seems to indicate that Denmark's system of small firms is losing its competitive power. According to Kristensen the system is composed of equally powerful 'skill containers' and 'project coordinators', i.e. a modernized form of putting-out system. Rather, the system has proved its strength during the volatile period since 1975.

In all the cases cited so far, the general theme is that patterns within and between firms become fairly stabilized once they have been established. The nature of firms seem to be reproduced – possibly in a non-identical way, as suggested in Arndt Sorge's contribution. Yet this pattern seems to survive even during periods of radical change. This was the case during the Allied occupation of Germany, when the Allies tried to give Germany a more liberal, i.e. Anglo-Saxon, constitution. Banks and industries seem to have interacted during this period in such a way that the German pattern could continue – both in respect to SMEs and to the large corporations. That the same stabilization of the pattern of firms may be possible in Eastern Europe despite very radical ideologies in favour of liberalism may come as a surprise to most observers. However, this is exactly what Whitley, Henderson, Lengyel and Czaban argue in favour of in their article on the limited transformation in Hungary. Despite radical 'changes in forms of property and increase in competition' since 1988, these changes have only had 'a limited impact on the structure and activities of leading economic actors there'.

This discussion of how firms have evolved in various countries shows that very divergent dynamics are at work among firms in different countries. We would suggest that even if a certain form of formal organization were implanted in all the cases mentioned, prevalent forms would work through the informal organization so as to change the whole functional mode of the firm within each country. At this moment, at least, it seems impossible to identify an 'ideal firm type' towards which European countries are converging, despite the serious attempts made in many European countries to imitate the American M-form through politically initiated processes or by adding new institutions to the present social fabric favouring such convergence. Rather, what can be observed is that a given type of firm within a specific national system deals with global challenges by adjusting in particular ways, seeking help from existing national institutions, thus reinforcing national patterns and, in part, changing their meaning.

Arndt Sorge's contribution to this volume develops this argument by reinterpreting the 'societal effect approach' in terms of processes and dynamics, all adding up to the suggested evolutionary process of non-identical reproduction. National types of firms and their institutional context change, but because the process of change happens through and by nationally patterned relations and interactions, nothing ensures convergence.

TOWARDS A FRAMEWORK FOR INVESTIGATING THE EVOLUTION OF FIRMS IN THEIR NATIONAL CONTEXTS: THE SOCIOLOGY OF THE FIRM

This section outlines a theoretical framework for explaining how firms are constituted differently in different countries. The causes of these differences are seen here as sociological and historical in the manner outlined by Berger and Luckmann (1967), i.e. firms are part of the set of institutions by which the social construction of reality takes place. This view sees the firm as produced by social actors in their struggle for resources and autonomy. Simultaneously the firm becomes structured in its distinct national way by gradually developing ways of regulating interaction among the groups it brings together.

Approaching the constitutional processes in this way rejects deterministic processes, be they technological or through the market, that have traditionally been seen as producing firms. We think that recent debates among economists point in the same direction. Sidney Winter (1991) has tried to clarify the very heterogeneous debate among economists by categorizing it along four 'contemporary paradigms in the theory of the firm' (ibid.: 186 ff.). Within a rational perspective, Winter distinguishes working paper orthodoxy from textbook orthodoxy, while within a perspective of bounded rationality the two paradigms are evolutionary economics and transaction cost economics. The focal concern for textbook orthodoxy and evolutionary economics is production, while working paper orthodoxy and transaction cost economics focus on exchange. Compared to textbook orthodoxy, there is no doubt that the three emerging paradigms offer a rich framework for investigating differences among firms and industrial organization in different countries. Working paper orthodoxy seeks to investigate differences in the relationship between principal and agent, whether that be among owners and managers or between managers and workers. It would include comparative differences in incentives, information and control systems and how contractual relations are shaped. It attempts to characterize the total monitoring system and its dynamics. Transaction cost economics guides us to investigate different 'modes of governance', market and hierarchy being only two extreme possibilities, as suggested by Williamson in his later writings, allowing for such governance systems as networks, clans and business groups as the Japanese *keiretsu*. Finally, as evolutionary explanations are said to reflect the continuity between past and present ('some antecedent condition existed, and the state of affairs now observed reflects the cumulative effect of the laws of change operating on that antecedent condition' (Winter, 1991: 187)) it is obvious that if industrialization was initiated differently among countries, different trajectories may evolve for the evolution of routines and skills, seen to constitute the genetic programming of firms and technologies in Nelson and Winter's (1982) framework.

But the primary aim of these three alternative paradigms has not been to develop frameworks and analytical guidance for comparisons across countries. The debates have been dominated by critiques of the original textbook orthodoxy and new universalistic theories seem to evolve focusing on certain aspects rather than theories aiming at sharpening our understanding of the contextual constitution of firms and evolutionary processes as they are channelled by distinct institutional frameworks in various countries. Recently, some of the more flexible representatives of the three emerging paradigms are developing ideas that point in the same direction as this volume, though confined by their respective paradigms. One of the most severe limitations to this new debate may be that investigations of national differences are focused upon some a priori defined theoretical questions, while serious attempts to position the constitution of firms within the larger process of a socially constructed reality are neglected. As is emphasized in Kristensen, Lilja and Tainio's coordinated introduction to the Finnish and the Danish case-studies in this volume, it is not possible to identify 'the social place of firms' and the very nature of firms within different national contexts, if we do not grasp – or at least aim to grasp – the social totality in which the firm acts and develops. From this perspective, it would improve our understanding to work with all three emerging paradigms of economic theory, rather than limiting ourselves to a single one.

The contributions to this volume focus upon empirical issues and try to identify patterns of behaviour within a contextual whole. Many contributors have guided their investigations by using Whitley's (1992a,b) systemic perspective. This framework, however, rather than being a fully developed theory, is a systematization of explanatory causes which have been observed at work in different countries. In one country we may explain why firms differed from the American pattern in a specific way by attributing this to distinct institutional/societal effects, while in other countries different types of institutions were at work. Each contributor supports his thesis that in order to be institutionally effective – and not only effective in terms of market competition and technology – firms organize to match the institutional fabric of a country.

The material included in this volume, however, enables us to do more than simply reconfirm Whitley's former contributions. From the essays it is possible to induce an improved systemic framework for the comparative sociological analysis of the forces constituting firms in societies. The framework we propose has emerged from a synthesis of what in this volume are seen as constituting factors for firms. Simultaneously, we also see it as a further development of what has been proposed by researchers such as Maurice *et al.* (1986) and Granovetter (1985, 1992), which we see as a continuation of a sociology which can be associated with Weber's *General Economic History* (1961) and Herbert Blumer's *Industrialization as an Agent of Social Change* (1990). In Arndt Sorge's contribution to this volume, this line of thought is explicated further, partly in contrast to other approaches. The proposed framework is summarized in Figure 1.1.

Throughout the contributions to this volume there runs a general message: the social division of economic roles varies significantly between nations. This is implicit in the contributions on Finland, Denmark and Belgium and is made explicit in the papers in the third section of the volume. At an analytical level we think that the social division of economic roles corresponds with the economist's concept of the social division of labour. At this level it is possible to cross the line between universal discourses on economic theory and, on the other hand, the sociological explanation of how firms are constituted within national social formations.

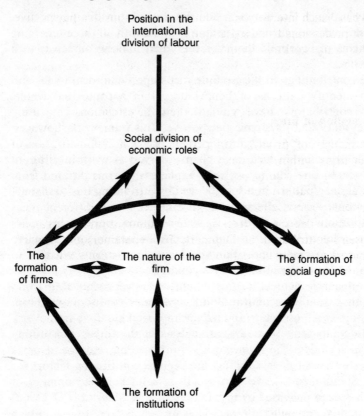

Figure 1.1 The national construction of the firm

The social division of economic roles is constituted through the entire social process of a country. Patterns of group formation and interaction reach into political spheres besides purely economic relations, are rooted in historical traditions and carry with them, and depend on, cultural capabilities. Narrow economic processes are embedded in this larger social process, but it is also from this larger social process that we can explain why various kinds of groups engage in industrial and economic activity, as the economic process is just one of the expressions of this larger process (see Blumer, 1990; Granovetter, 1985, 1992). Even Adam Smith conceived of this larger social process behind 'the social division of labour', which we think can be better expressed as leading to a 'social division of economic roles'. As Smith pointed out, its roots were 'habit, custom and education' (Smith, 1970: 120), while 'by treaty, by barter and by purchase' such interpersonal relations are established that enable different professions to concentrate on their speciality.

In this framework we propose the social division of economic roles to be constituted by two mutually dependent spheres: the formation of firms, and the formation of social groups.

The formation of firms

The formation of firms is defined by the interactive strategies between firms within a country. In using the term 'formation of firms', we stress that firms perform roles interdependently, and it is from this interactive totality that activities receive their meaning and attitudes are established. A clear example of how the formation of firms may define special roles specific to different firms is given in Kristensen's contribution on Denmark. Skill containers and project coordinators are mutually dependent for their existence. Without a widespread system of subcontracting skill containers, project coordinators could not evolve, while the craft tradition within skill containers would not have been able to develop into a modern industrial economy without having project coordinators coupling them to different markets. This way of separating activities makes it obvious that roles are defined in a way that enables skill containers to engage in many rather than a single value chain. Simultaneously the skill container role may be related to other firms in such a way that it is possible for an individual firm to organize the firms, with which it is interacting, through reputational links into a totally new value chain, which is then organized for a specific project. A foreign firm engaging in business with these two firm-types will find that the Danish business partner, though most often a very small firm, is able to solve problems far beyond preconceived demands. When dealing with a skill container the foreign firm may have supplied a part that is very flexible and that is produced in many variants, and when dealing with a project coordinator the foreign firm may discover that such a firm is able to provide entire new products or complicated turn-key projects, though their size is very limited indeed. They can play this role only by being part of the formation of firms, which play mutually cooperating roles in shifting tasks. All this happens in a very informal way, making it very difficult for foreign firms to exercise normal control over businesses. Neither complicated juridical contracts, nor sophisticated calculations of costs, plays an important part in creating exchanges. They may experience firms as very technically oriented 'horse-traders', which are able to provide a given product in many variants dependent on the price that the customer is ready to pay.

In contrast, such circumstantial negotiations are not the rule in the Finnish formation of firms. Small independent firms acting on their own are rare exceptions, partly because the players among the formation of firms are corporations, or rather vertically integrated, relatedly diversified companies, that have been authorized by the state and large banks to act on behalf of Finnish society and its future development in a way that is established through negotiated planning. Most formerly independent firms have been integrated into these vertically integrated enterprises, which they tend to represent in dealing with foreign firms. The system works smoothly and very effectively when providing goods that have been developed through careful, often long-term planning, within the realm of vertically integrated firms. The value chain, so to speak, is clearly defined and carefully improved in a systematic way. Foreign customers rarely experience the vaguely defined projects found in Denmark. Terms of trade are basically dependent on such issues as number of items or batch size and exchange rates. Finnish firms can act in a very powerful way and often engage in foreign acquisitions and direct investment, because of this formation of the firm community.

In his comparison of the organization of construction projects in the UK and France, Graham Winch gives a very illustrative account of how economic roles are composed very differently among firms in the two countries. Though a construction project necessarily has to follow a universal sequence of phases, this sequence does not imply a standardized division of labour between different actors. Precisely because the composition of actors and the formation of firms differ between the two countries, the whole process is organized very differently. From this it follows that it is impossible to know in advance the role of a main contractor or a project management firm within a country, before the entire composition of roles in a given country has been investigated. Winch enables us to see that the entire construction process, rather than being just administered differently, is of a very different nature in the two countries, creating in turn buildings of very different qualities and costs. But the different composition of roles within the construction process also has consequences for comparative advantages on the international market. British architects and engineers are powerful both in defending their home territory and engaging in international projects, while French contractors are able to capture markets abroad, while defending their internal market.

Christel Lane approaches one of the classical and recurrent themes concerning industrial structure or the formation of firms: supplier relations between large and small firms. She asks whether both British and German firms are adapting to the Japanese pattern of obligational contracting. In answering this question she shows how different are the roles played by the two types of firms within the two nations. One consequence, of course, is that the two types of actors can only approach the Japanese ideal by initiating two very different processes of development. While in Germany national institutions have supported SMEs to develop skills and technical ability, and therefore to play a technically highly sophisticated role towards large outsourcing German firms, the institutional isolation of British SMEs has made them so weak that they have been forced to become 'sweatshops' for their larger customers. When large British firms want to change their relations to subcontractors, they face a firm formation which simply lacks the Japanese type of supplier. Lane's contribution is also significant because she underlines the importance of the wider institutional system in determining which roles are established between firms, and how institutions empower large and small firms differently in different countries. But the institutional formation of a country not only does that; it also affects the ways in which these roles can be enacted *vis-à-vis* other roles. According to Lane, supplier relations may be regulated in such a way that economic power relations are equalized, making it much easier for the powerful and the powerless to act as partners, as in the German case. Consequently, Germany's profile on the international market as a high-quality producer of standardized goods is strongly rooted in the combined efforts of SMEs and large firms; as is Britain's low price and quality profile.

By imposing particular 'rules of the game' between firms, the institutional formation of a country may do much of the work of selecting among legitimate and illegal actions and strategies, and thus directly help establish certain roles. In some countries the legal framework of firms is even more important for creating the mutual roles. Fligstein's (1990) analysis of the impact of the Celler–Kefauver Act on the corporate community in the USA after 1950 is well known. The legal definition of firms belonging to the category of *Handwerker* in Germany simply makes it impossible for large German corporations to take over and to dominate the entire SME sector (Streeck, 1992). In Italy legal obligations and rights differ between firms according to whether they employ more or less than 20 employees. For this reason it has been much easier here than in other countries to organize SMEs in associations of different political orientations along criteria of size. Consequently, in both Germany and Italy SMEs have had a much more profound impact on defining their own role *vis-à-vis* the large corporations than in the Anglo-Saxon world, where SMEs have had their role ascribed by the community of large corporations, resulting in the performance by SMEs of a number of residual roles.

Whereas most conceptualizing about industrial structure has been formulated within the framework of competition among atomistic firms, the examples in this volume rather express how different firms may complement each other in a process of both competition and cooperation. Recent discoveries of how the interaction between sub-suppliers and large assembling firms in Japan combined compose a hierarchy in which sub-supplying firms may engage in 'careers', developing from simple sub-supply to responsibility for entire sub-systems, illustrate what may be discovered from investigating the formation of firms more carefully than economic theories would tell us to do. Monitoring the relations between firms of different types within the Japanese firm formation according to an overall goal of rapid productivity improvements thus enables Japanese exporting firms to make very fast improvements (Sabel, 1993), when a specific product has proven that it is becoming a 'star'. No wonder that Japan has developed an economic role that frustrates most other countries with stakes in emerging mass-produced goods sectors.

The formation of social groups

The second element of the social division of economic roles is the formation of social groups. To most philosophers and political economists there is no doubt that industrialization and the establishment of a capitalist regime mean that capital and labour become established as two antagonistic classes. With the centralization and concentration of capital, and with the restless advance of technology, a managerial class emerges between these two classes. The formation of social groups consisting of owners, managers and workers seems to be the uniform outcome of industrialization and the rise of the modern corporation. Universalistic economic thinking then provides norms for how these three roles must be performed in a certain way in order to enable the economic process to maximize output and income.

How these three roles can be performed to the greatest benefit to the maximizing agent, usually stockholders, is the object of principal–agent thinking. However, many philosophers and social scientists have argued in favour of one group against the others. For many years Marxists urged the necessity of overthrowing owners of capital in order for the productive forces to advance more rapidly, while social democratic reformers rather thought of limiting the power of owners and enlarging economic democracy. Veblen was also against owners, i.e. the leisure class, which he saw as preventing engineers from advancing the productive 'machinery' to such a state that it becomes possible to feed everyone. Joseph Schumpeter saw the owner-entrepreneur as the only group that would stand on the doorstep of the factory to defend capitalism, which he clearly saw as being eroded by 'socialism' in the form of large corporation and managerial bureaucracies assisted by the critical discourse of intellectuals.

We do not want to deny that this categorization of major social groups can be identified in any capitalist economy. Or rather that in any society it is possible to classify social groups according to the roles postulated by universal schemes of capitalism. However, we do think that it is less than enlightening to assume that economic organizations regulate this set of roles in a uniform way across countries. Even if we accept the three roles as a preliminary classification, we will discover that at the time of industrialization the relative power among the three groups strongly differed across various countries.

This is partly because they had to make compromises of very different types and state agencies intervened in very different ways, which meant that the rules and institutions which encapsulated the future drama were very different. Furthermore, the groups representing the three roles, organized as collectives in highly different ways, and for that reason they were able to conduct very different fights for enlarging their social space. The rights and privileges, the world view and the institutionalized career path which a recruit to one of the groups would follow differed from country to country. In some, élites became clearly established, not least through their association with the state, while in others élite formation became more fragile after the end of feudalism. Groups that are classified identically across countries experienced very different histories and learned very different lessons from practice. They do not share myths that help them define their identities and a sense of honour which effects how and what social space they will fight for. Groups of the same type will have different fears and hopes from one country to the other.

Maurice *et al.* (1986) have made us sharply aware of how different it is to be a manager in Germany compared to France. We know that workers' behaviour differs depending on whether they must remain with a specific company, or enjoy freedom to move horizontally from one firm to another. We also know that there are huge differences involved in how unions combine, and what assistance they offer their members. Consequently, they encounter different levels of loyalty if they need to fight for their cause against industries or the state. Previous battles may have made them influential in shaping institutions that advance their interests in one respect or another, and this may become a decisive factor for their course in a new situation. In some countries, belonging to a group restricts individual members' social mobility, while in others the group has been able to fight for such social space that individuals can cross group boundaries, for example allowing a worker to play his role in such a way that he changes to the role of a manager, if not an owner of his own SME.

The various groups that play universal roles of owners, managers and workers, are simply not identical across countries. They are empowered differently by institutions in the various countries and they do not occupy similar social spaces. Agents in any country may be opportunistic, try to shirk and even to be free-riding towards their principals in any country, but what they can shirk about, and what is defined as shirking, differ. So does the nature of their opportunism because they are able to strategize with very different means and from very different situations. In some countries, the only route to advancement in social space lies in shirking, while in others it is possible to follow an institutionalized career trajectory, which brings individuals from the lower strata to the higher.

In some countries owners have been able to form a dominant coalition with engineers (see Noble, 1977 on the USA) encapsulating industrial skills within the higher levels of enterprise hierarchies, leaving a very limited role to the workers indeed. In other countries, such as in Germany and Denmark, industrial skills have continuously been offered to workers through apprenticeships and schools, enabling this group to play a much more profound role in shaping the industrial space. Halvorsen, Korsnes and Sakslind in their contribution on Norway show how the engineering profession was constituted very strongly through state institutions and industry. Being able to advance their role through state bodies, they have been able to greatly enlarge their social space by convincing the state to finance large applied research institutes. Simultaneously, the engineers have been able to service social democratic visions of state-owned firms in such a way that today private ownership in Norway plays a much lesser role than in most Western societies. Veblen's country of origin thus seems to have neutralized the destructive role of 'the businessman', i.e. speculative ownership, and been able to engage in much more long-term engineering projects than most countries.

One of the lessons from Norway is that the importance of the engineers within the individual firm is dependent on the larger context in which engineers operate. Engineers become important because they may connect a firm to the formation of institutions in which the engineers operate through personal and professional ties. But this holds even for the organization of continuous relations between firms within the formation of firms. Professional ties between engineers function as channels through which firms may establish exchanges. Consequently, interactions and exchange between firms will tend to be dominated by technological issues, rather than purely economic calculations and juridical contracting, thereby advancing the engineering profession to an even more dominant position. As indicated already, the social democratic movement in Norway has seen the engineering profession as an ally in its project to industrialize Norway. For that reason reformers who spoke in favour of establishing an institutional formation to advance the skills of workers themselves have preached to deaf ears. Consequently, workers' careers in Norway are seldom role-transcendent, hierarchies are more steep, and the number of managers per worker is higher than in the other Nordic countries (see Gordon, 1994 and Dobbin and Boychuk, 1994), but not nearly as high as in the Anglo-Saxon world.

In the British case, we might say that Veblen's worst fears have come true. The ownership role has been highly affected by a capital market system making industrial enterprises dependent on short-term profits to satisfy stock markets. Partly for that reason accountants play a crucial role within the managerial hierarchy. No wonder, then, that price negotiations have become the main issue in dealing with sub-suppliers, leading to technologically incapable and sweating SMEs in Britain.

The formation of social groups thus interacts with the formation of firms. Relations between firms are mediated through dominating groups within the country. Economic relations are, as Granovetter said (1985, 1994), embedded in social relations. We have very few studies on how different professional groups relate. However, it seems quite obvious to us that it is over very different matters that the discourse among accountants results in interpersonal friendship or enmity, than it is among engineers. Consequently, to function in a skilled way means very different things in Britain compared to Norway, while in France firms will have much easier access to industrial groups, the state and financial institutions by recruiting presidents from one of the *grandes écoles*.

In Norway, France and Britain the groups playing the dominant role also furnish the highest positions of the hierarchical ladder of firms. In Denmark, however, this is not the case, according to Kristensen's contribution. There the horizontal mobility of skilled workers enables them to establish numerous contacts with colleagues in other enterprises. As these horizontal movements gradually bring them up the hierarchical ladder of firms, it is at the lower levels of the hierarchy – among foremen and production managers with apprenticeship backgrounds – that interactions are looked after. Owners, often with an apprenticeship background, workers and middle mangers thus squeeze the role of chief executive officers (CEOs) from all sides. The managerial class is relatively powerless within the formation of social groups.

These remarks are only an initial discussion of what is involved in understanding the formation of social groups. We have tried to indicate differences among countries in the positions of owners, managers and workers. However, each of these groups is living in a larger context of social groups and their ability to form coalitions with groups outside the industrial sphere may influence their power *vis-à-vis* the two other groups. Without engaging in cooperation with farmers in railway towns in the countryside, Danish skilled workers and craftsmen would never have been able to achieve such a strong role in larger enterprises and factories. Had the pulp-and-paper workers in mill communities in Finland not been tied through family bonds to the neighbouring farmers who own the forests that the mills process, it is unlikely that the same worker-aristocracy would have evolved.

From this perspective both Britain and the USA represent the exception rather than the rule. Enclosures in the countryside of England left not only the would-be factory worker without land, they also destroyed the group connections that they had enjoyed. Atomization of the labourer was not an effect of industrialization, but it meant that industrialization structured the conditions for shaping a new group identity, predominantly through the union movement. Immigrants to the USA were even worse off. Their atomization was radically underlined by the fact that they came from different countries and spoke different languages. Industry, so to speak, was unique in giving them their group identity. In most other countries workers were not atomistic individuals. Rather, they belonged to traditional groups which connected in order to create a social space for themselves *vis-à-vis* other groups and/or group coalitions. As we have learned from the proto-industrialization debate, it was often in the fight for social space or simple survival that such groups engaged in industrial projects. In many countries the leap from the small family farm to the SME is a very short one, enabling the farming father to see in his sons' enterprises a continuation of his own world-view.

This discussion points towards a very crucial issue in determining the nature of firms in different countries. It was often non-industrial classes that struggled for social space or survival by means of industrial firms. In the Danish case it is obvious that the cooperative establishments of the farmers enabled them to industrialize. In these organizations authority rested with the peer group, and the 'firm' became one of the most important means of enabling the social group to stay organized and become a strategic actor in the struggle over the design of the entire formation of institutions, the 'firm' being just one element of a larger institutional complex. In Emilia Romagna, as demonstrated by Piore and Sabel (1984), SMEs were intensively established when communist craftworkers were black-listed by the large enterprises of north-western Italy during the cold war. What is unusual in both Denmark and Third Italy is that groups of humble status initiated industrial firms for reasons which are difficult to include in economic discourses. Rather, it is usual to see much more powerful groups – landowners, merchants, the state, or engineering associations – in the role of entrepreneurs. In these normal cases élite groups have used the formation of industrial firms as a means to protect their élite status, whereby it becomes a central concern how élites may keep their distance from productive activities and still maintain control over firms' strategies, i.e. the principal–agent problem.

Thus, there are no self-evident actors who enable nations to adapt to changes in the extent and nature of markets and in technology, thereby establishing within the individual nation an optimal reflection of the division of labour made universally possible at a given moment. Rather, as we have seen, historical development has led to the definition of a social division of economic roles specific to each individual nation. Changes in international markets and technologies provide these role-holders with challenges and opportunities and, dependent on their position in each nation, they can act differently. However, their strategies follow less from the challenges and opportunities of the global setting than from their position within national systems. There is no doubt that because the important role-holders are different in each nation, the nature of global challenges and opportunities will be defined differently between nations. Finally threats to dominant role-holders in one nation may be perceived as opportunities by the dominant role-holders in other nations.

The sociological view of the firm

With this in place, we can now turn to the nature of the firm from a sociological point of view. First, from an institutional point of view we see the firm as an arena which is defined *vis-à-vis* the other parts of the institutional formation of a nation. The state may, as in Finland and France, ascribe a very direct and strong role to firms and corporate groups in developing the economy, while in others, for example Denmark, the firm is seen less as a core institution (see also Whitley, 1994). Dependent on the social space which the firm occupies within the formation of national institutions, the state and other institutions may be more or less eager to have a say about how the evolutionary processes of the firm are regulated. Germany and Britain, in this respect, show very different behavioural patterns. Whereas changes mean recodifying formal rules in Germany, in Britain new managerial ideas gain acceptance more easily, but are also much more volatile and dependent on persons and successive managers.

Within organization theory it is usual to conceive of the organization as enacting its environment (Pfeffer and Salancik, 1978; Weick, 1979; Cyert and March, 1963). We think that it is possible that, in some nations, the state has furnished the firm with such regulatory power that it becomes constituted as a coherent actor, but we suggest that this is rare. Within the framework developed above, the firm is rather seen as being constituted between the larger formation of firms and the formation of social groups, and not least by the way these two formative spheres have combined in shaping a division of social roles. In most countries the firm is, as is the case also of most democratic states, more generally a battleground where different social groups fight for social space. The power of each competing group, however, is not determined solely by its ability to become part of the dominating coalitions within individual firms. Each group transfers power from the larger formation of social groups and has rights and codes of behaviour which are defined through the economic roles it occupies within the larger societal framework. Social life within a business firm in a condensed form thus reflects or represents the larger social framework. This becomes very explicit in any comparison of the roles managers play in Germany and Britain. It is obvious that their behaviour reflects demands which stem from how the formation of social groups has been institutionally founded, and thus has given them different identities. To supervise a German skilled worker demands technical competence from managers, while in Britain the demands are less clear and usually take on the use of economic incentives. It is also obvious that organizational innovations in Britain and Germany will have to address very different problems, because the two types of organizations will create very different problems when facing the same global challenges. Therefore, the ontology of organizational forms and the evolution of the firm will take very different paths.

Secondly, individual firms operate in the context of the larger formation of firms, and it is within this realm that the particular role selected by the individual firm must be decided. As in football, the best strategy for the individual player comes from reading the strategies and operational routines of all the other players. Furthermore it is important to enact such a persistence in behaviour (i.e. in decision rules) that it enables the other players to use the focal player in the roles which this player has chosen to play (Axelrod, 1980). The kind of opportunism, which is so important in Williamson's argument for transaction costs, presupposes that a given set of firms are not dependent on mutually lasting relationships and exchanges. Most nations, however, have been shaped in such a way that they enforce lasting relationships and in these cases opportunistic strategists recognize this in such a way that much of the transactional costs associated with anonymous market-players do not occur. The players are forced to reveal their identity, not least for their own good.

Aoki (1984) has suggested that we view the firm as a space in which a cooperative game takes place. In his terminology, originating from Marshall, within the firm there is a constant bargaining process by which the different groups associated with the firm have their interests satisfied according to customs and fairness. According to Aoki the most efficient organization of the firm is not necessarily established where managers take on the role of 'surrogate shareholders', but rather where they are able to carry out strategies that mediate the needs of various groups (shareholders, workers, suppliers, customers, etc.). To us this perspective can be seen as an elaboration of Chester Barnard's (1938) concept, that the social function of the executive is to devise solutions, when interactions between different groups within the informal organization lead to conflicts between these groups. What is essential, in our view, is that the group life of the larger formation of social groups within a nation enters into the firm, primarily by creating an informal cooperative system. Firms, as formal organizations, may prosper from this cooperative game by being able to develop such policies and create such formal settings that enable coalitions of groups to realize 'their careers at work' or 'world-views' (Sabel 1982).

The conflicts and collaborations between groups associated with a firm are not, though, unregulated and solely dependent on managers' abilities to act as referees (Aoki, 1984) or supreme courts (Barnard, 1938). Past conflicts and their resolution become codified and institutionalized and rules are developed, so that a specific governance system emerges which reflects, in part, the specific nature of conflicts arising from a distinct national formation of social groups. Accumulated rules and solutions constitute the means by which managers are able to both define and enact the collective will. In this perspective, the firm may be conceived as a 'constitutional system' (Knudsen, 1993; Sabel, 1991) where the different groups 'subject themselves to a series of procedures for making collective decisions and dividing the joint outcome of their collaboration' (Knudsen, 1993: 26). This idea originates from Selznck (1968), who from this perspective conceived 'bureaucracy' as one form of constitutional order. Sabel (1991) made us aware that many other forms may be possible. The constitutional order metaphor also enables us to conceive many federal forms of organizations as part of the formation of firms of a nation and, therefore, how they mutually shape their roles by interacting.

At this moment, however, comparative research about how firms from different countries have developed different constitutional orders is less than systematic. Partly because our age has been so preoccupied with imitating American practices, we have omitted the task of studying the existing constitutional orders and governance systems that exist in different European countries. However, rather than jumping to entirely new constitutional orders and finding totally new governance systems when firms and groups are faced with new challenges, we find it much more probable that they will use the tools already at hand in attempts to develop new policies that enable firms to recreate dominant coalitions of groups, facilitating cooperative strategies towards new situations.

THE FIRM AND ECONOMIC EVOLUTION: CONCLUSION

It follows from what we have said so far that there are strong reasons why the concept of the firm has had such difficulties in being formalized in economic textbooks as a well-determined 'ideal type'. Rather than blaming economic science for this omission, we think it is crucial for social researchers to locate the firm in the social context in which it is embedded. This, however, raises a new set of problems. As economic evolution is basically an outcome of actions of collectivities, and as the firm is one among the major collectivities of Western societies, it follows that the economic evolution of nations should be studied from the perspective of how firms evolve within the context of national formations of firms, national formations of social groups and national formations of institutions, amongst which the firm is just one element of many. The dynamics going on within all these formations, when challenges from international competition and global technology arise, are more than complicated.

Economic role-holders will develop a variety of strategies towards the Single European Market, and so will different groups. Some firm types within a country's formation of firms will benefit from these changes, while others will be less favoured. Strategies within all the social realms mentioned in Figure 1 will thus be activated. However, we firmly believe that in devising these strategies, firms, groups and economic role-holders will have to work with what is at hand, thereby reinforcing beneficial group alliances, reasserting those parts of the institutional formation that enable such strategies to succeed by using them more intensively. Arndt Sorge (1991) has shown how the challenge from information technology has been met in different ways by French and German firms. French firms, for instance, have developed comparative advantages in custom-built CNC (computer numerically controlled) machine tools, while Germany has gained particular competencies in providing universal CNC machine tools. In other essays in this volume we learn about different ways of dealing with such problems in ways in which distinctive national patterns develop and are reinforced.

NOTE

1 So much was this followed by Robinson that he attributed the inefficiency
and reduced scale of English firms of the day to the 'uneconomic' taste
for variation in products among English consumers. Robinson concluded:
'It is, as Adam Smith told us, the extent of the market that limits the
division of labour, and it is you and I who determine the extent of
the market. It was, we all know, "the rolling English drunkard made the
rolling English road". It is the contrary English customer who has done
most to make the contrary English firm' (Robinson, 1935: 176).

REFERENCES

Abrahamsson, B. (1986) *Varför finns organisationer? Kollektiv handling,
yttrekrafter och inre logik*, Stockholm: Nordstedts.
Aoki, M. (1984) *The Cooperative Game Theory of The Firm*, Oxford:
Clarendon Press.
——, Gustafsson, B. and Williamson, O. E. (eds) (1990) *The Firm as a
Nexus of Treaties*, London: Sage Publications.
Axelrod, R. (1984) *The Evolution of Cooperation*, New York: Basic Books.
Barnard, C. I. (1938) *The Functions of the Executive*, Cambridge, Mass.:
Harvard University Press.
Berger, P. L. and Luckmann, T. (1967) *The Social Construction of Reality*,
New York: Anchor Books.
Blumer, H. (1990) *Industrialization as an Agent of Social Change*, New
York: Aldine de Gruyter.
Chandler, A. D. (1977) *The Visible Hand. The Managerial Revolution in
American Business*, Cambridge, Mass.: Harvard University Press.
Coase, R. H. (1991a) 1991 Nobel Lecture: 'The institutional structure of
production', in Williamson and Winter (eds) *op. cit.*
—— (1991b) (1937) 'The nature of the firm', in Williamson and Winter
(eds) *op. cit.*
Cyert, R. M. and March, J. (1963) *A Behavioural Theory of the Firm*,
Englewood Cliffs, N.J.: Prentice-Hall.
Dobbin, F. and Boychuk, T. (1994) 'Job autonomy and national management
systems: evidence from seven countries', mimeographed manuscript,
Princeton and Duke University.
Fligstein, N. (1990) *The Transformation of Corporate Control*, Cambridge,
Mass.: Harvard University Press.
Gerschenkron, A. (1992) (1952) 'Economic backwardness in historical per-
spective', in Granovetter and Swedberg (eds) *op. cit.*
Gordon, D. M. (1994) 'Bosses of different stripes: a cross-national perspec-
tive on monitoring and supervision', *American Economic Association
Papers and Proceedings* May: 375–9.
Granovetter, M. (1985) 'Economic action and social structure: the problem
of embeddedness', *American Journal of Sociology* 91(3): 481–510.
—— (1992) 'Problems of explanation in economic sociology', in Nohria and
Eccles (eds).
—— and Swedberg, R. (eds) (1992) *The Sociology of Economic Life*,
Boulder, Colo.: Westview Press.

Homans, G. (1950) *The Human Group*, New York: Harcourt, Brace and Jovanovitch.

Knudsen, C. (1993) 'The competence view of the firm: what can modern economists learn from Phillip Selznick's sociological theory of leadership', typescript, forthcoming in R. W. Scott and S. Christensen (eds) *Advances in the Institutional Analysis of Organizations: International and Longitudinal Studies*, London: Sage.

Kristensen, P. H. (1992) 'Industrial districts in West Jutland, Denmark', in Pyke and Sengenberger (eds) *op. cit.*

Marshall, A. (1919) *Industry and Trade*, London.

Maurice, M., Sellier, F. and Silvestre, J.-J. (1986) *The Social Foundations of Industrial Power: A Comparison of France and Germany*, Cambridge, Mass.: MIT Press.

Nelson, R. and Winter, S. G. (1982) *An Evolutionary Theory of Economic Change*, Cambridge, Mass.: The Belknap Press of Harvard University Press.

Noble, D. F. (1977) *America by Design. Science, Technology and the Rise of Corporate Capitalism*, New York: Alfred A. Knopf.

Pfeffer, J. and Salancik, G. R. (1978) *The External Control of Organizations*, New York: Harper and Row.

Piore, M. J. and Sabel, C. F. (1984) *The Second Industrial Divide*, New York: Basic Books.

Porter, M. E. (1980) *Competitive Strategy*, New York: The Free Press.

Pyke, F. and Sengenberger, W. (eds) (1992) *Industrial Districts and Local Economic Regeneration*, Geneva: IILS.

——, Becattini, G. and Sengenberger, W. (eds) (1990) *Industrial Districts and Inter-firm Co-operation in Italy*, Geneva: IILS.

Robinson, E. A. G. (1935) *The Structure of Competitive Industry*, Cambridge: Cambridge University Press.

Sabel, C. F. (1982) *Work and Politics*, Cambridge: Cambridge University Press.

—— (1991) 'Constitutional ordering in historical context', in F. W. Scharpf (ed.) *Games in Hierarchies and Networks*.

—— (1993) 'Learning by monitoring', mimeographed paper, Cambridge, Mass.: MIT.

Selznick, P. (1968) *Law, Society and Industrial Justice*, Berkeley, Calif.: Russell Sage Foundation.

Sengenberger, W., Loveman, G. W. and Piore, M. J. (eds) (1990) *The Re-emergence of Small Enterprises*, Geneva: IILS.

Smith, A. (1970) *The Wealth of Nations*, Harmondsworth: Penguin Books.

Streeck, W. (1992) *Social Institutions and Economic Performance Studies of Industrial Relations in Advanced Capitalist Economies*, London: Sage Publications.

Weber, M. (1961) *General Economic History*, New York: Collier Books.

Weick, K. E. (1979) *The Social Psychology of Organizing*, Reading, Mass.: Addison Wesley.

Whitley, R. (1992a) *Business Systems in East Asia*, London: Sage.

—— (ed.) (1992b) *European Business Systems. Firms and Markets in their National Contexts*, London: Sage.

Whitley, R. (1994) 'Dominant forms of economic organisation in market economies', *Organization Studies* 15: 153–82.

Williamson, O. E. (1975) *Markets and Hierarchies: Analysis and Antitrust Implications*, New York: The Free Press.

—— (1991) 'Introduction', in Williamson and Winter (eds) *op. cit.*

—— (1993) 'Transaction cost economies and organizational theory', *Industrial and Corporate Change* 2(2): 107–56.

—— and Winter, S. G. (eds) (1991) *The Nature of the Firm. Origins, Evolution, and Development*, New York: Oxford University Press.

Winter, S. G. (1991) 'Competence and the corporation', in Williamson and Winter (eds) *op. cit.*

Part I

Structure and agency in the social construction of European firms

2 The social construction of economic actors

Institutions and types of firm in Europe and other market economies

Richard Whitley

INTRODUCTION

The organization of firms and markets varies significantly across Europe, as many recent analyses have demonstrated (e.g. Lane, 1992; Lévy-Leboyer, 1980; Lilja *et al.*, 1992), and new patterns are emerging in the developing market economies of East-Central Europe (e.g. Stark, 1992). These varied ways of structuring the coordination and control of economic activities are the outcome of different paths to industrial capitalism and associated differences in dominant institutions, such as the state and financial systems (Cox, 1986; Hart, 1992; Whitley, 1992b; Zysman, 1983). An important aspect of these differences in forms of economic organization concerns the nature of firms as economic actors. Rather than converging on a single type, such as the diversified multi-divisional managerial hierarchy described by Alfred Chandler (1977, 1990), it is clear that European economies continue to exhibit considerable variations in the sorts of collective entities that coordinate economic activities and how they do so (Mayer and Whittington in this volume). The autonomous and strongly bounded Anglo-Saxon corporation is only one form of economic actor found in Europe, and one that has not been dominant historically, nor is becoming so today. Relatedly, the ways in which these different kinds of economic decision-making units compete and cooperate in markets also vary, and cannot be reduced to a single idealized state of 'perfect' competition similar to 'efficient' markets in financial claims (Lane in this volume). It is therefore important to consider how 'firms' vary across Europe, and the critical relationships which have helped to establish these contrasting kinds of economic actors, and which continue to maintain their distinctive characteristics.

To do this we need to identify those critical characteristics of firms as economic actors which vary significantly across market economies. We also have to consider the major features of social institutions that influence these characteristics, and how they do so. Accordingly, in this paper I first outline the major ways in which economic actors differ and then identify the primary features of their institutional environment that together help to account for these variations. Subsequently, I suggest how these key institutional features affect the sorts of economic actors that become established in different economies and consider some implications of these relationships for the emerging firms and markets in Eastern Europe.

THE NATURE OF ECONOMIC ACTORS AND THEIR KEY CHARACTERISTICS

In considering how firms vary across market economies as separate decision-making units, it is important to clarify the particular way in which economic actors are conceived and understood. They are the combination of both the collective organization which transforms human and material resources into productive services in distinctive ways, and the primary unit which decides which resources to organize and how a firm will grow and develop. It is the locus, then, of both managerial and entrepreneurial services in Penrose's terms (1959: 31–5), and excludes purely financial holding companies which invest in a range of businesses on a portfolio basis. The key differentiating feature here is whether there is any administrative coordination of sub-units' activities and plans, especially financial decisions, and their inclusion in the same area of authoritative communication (*cf.* Barnard, 1938; Penrose, 1959: 19–22). Thus, while investment trusts may constitute important centres of economic power in an economy, they are more financial organizations than industrial and commercial ones, and operate as holders of financial claims rather than as organizers of resources adding value to them through administrative coordination. Of course, if the managers of such trusts do become involved in the organization of economic activities, as opposed to simply trading financial assets, then the trusts develop into Penrosian firms.

Firms, then, are not just centres of economic power in this view, but rather combine allocative decision-making with the authoritative coordination of economic activities, which adds value to human and material resources through the collective organization of work. The units of economic action being compared across economies here are those organizations which collectively integrate particular kinds of resources in distinctive ways and generate added value to them. It is the sort of organization that authoritatively selects and controls economic activities which is the focus of concern. This is not to say, of course, that concentrations of economic power in financial holding companies are unimportant in comparing market economies, but this view separates such largely financial institutions from those firms which constitute the primary unit of economic action that organizes the transformation of resources into productive services. Indeed, some significant differences in the characteristics of such firms can be explained in terms of variations in the organization and policies of financial institutions.

In practice it is not always easy to identify the boundaries of such administrative structures or to locate the crucial unit of decision-making power. French industrial groups, for example, often combine quite large businesses which make many decisions themselves, just as the constituent, legally separate firms in Chinese family businesses (CFBs) are sometimes managed by non-family members who are able to take operational decisions themselves (Bauer and Cohen, 1981; Hamilton and Kao, 1990; Mayer and Whittington in this volume; Redding, 1990). Such subsidiary organizations could, then, be considered to constitute separate managerial entities. The critical issues in considering such cases – and the general phenomenon of 'network' organizations in East Asia (Hamilton *et al.*, 1990) and in European industrial districts (Pyke *et al.*, 1990; Lazerson, 1988) – are whether activities and plans are coordinated, formally or informally, and where the decisions about the nature of activities to be undertaken and changes in these, are made.

For example, one of the key factors limiting the pace of firms' growth in Penrose's formulation is their inability to expand in all feasible directions at the same time because of the limited availability of managerial services for new activities at any one moment (Penrose, 1959: 48–9). This means that critical decisions have to be made about which opportunities to pursue and which to ignore. Where subsidiaries are not entirely free to make such decisions on their own, but some coordination takes place between them, or the central authority decides, the key unit of economic action is the group as a whole, rather than each sub-unit. Thus, the CFB is the major unit in the private sector in Taiwan, Hong Kong and elsewhere in South East Asia because the owning family – particularly the founding patriarch – typically takes these sorts of decisions and subsidiaries are rarely able to plan new activities without central authorization (Redding, 1990; Silin, 1976). Conversely, the post-war Japanese inter-market groups rarely act as the decision-making authority for constituent firms; rather, these corporations exert considerable autonomy over major plans and paths for expansion, although they may exchange ideas and enter into joint ventures with other group members (Clark, 1979; Fruin, 1992; Gerlach, 1992; Hamilton *et al.*, 1990; Orru *et al.*, 1989). So, it is the dominant unit of strategic decision-making and coordinated planning which is the focus of comparison here, rather than the individual organization concerned with day-to-day operational issues.

However, it is important to note here that, as the examples of the Chinese family business and Danish 'skill containers' (Kristensen in this volume) suggest, managerial coordination and control of economic activities are variously connected to entrepreneurial decision-making across institutional contexts. As many of the contributions to this book show, the hierarchical integration of these functions in a single, strongly bounded organization, similar to the Chandlerian multi-divisional corporation, is only one type of firm – and not a common one at that – which has become institutionalized in Europe, and there are many different ways in which managerial and entrepreneurial services can be effectively coordinated. First of all, as the Italian industrial districts and similar phenomena indicate, coordination of economic activities can be achieved in quite different ways in different circumstances, and authoritative, hierarchical coordination is by no means always superior. Secondly, the primary location of entrepreneurial decision-making need not lie at the apex of managerial hierarchies but may be shared between different groups and organizations, so that identifying a single source of economic agency becomes quite difficult – as in perhaps some of the larger French industrial groups (Mayer and Whittington in this volume). It is therefore an important part of the comparative analysis of the firm to identify the different processes by which varied linkages between managerial coordination and entrepreneurial resource allocation and control become established, reproduced and changed to constitute 'firms' in different ways in different societies.

Considering economic actors in market economies in this way suggests a number of important ways in which they vary as the result of institutional differences. First of all, there are significant variations in the sorts of activities and resources they coordinate and control. Relatedly, the nature of the managerial competences which give firms their distinctive character, and which provide the basis for their competitive advantage, can differ across economies, as well as, of course, across sectors. This aspect is connected to firms' preferred growth patterns and how they develop their resources and services. These characteristics can be summarized as being concerned with what firms, as organizations characterized by authoritative communication patterns, coordinate and control: the nature of their skills and resources and how these change. Secondly, there is a range of what might be termed 'governance' issues. These concern the sorts of groups and interests which dominate firms' decision-making processes, the dominant objectives pursued and how managerial and entrepreneurial services are combined or separated in firms. As units of economic action, firms vary in how they are 'governed' and in the major influences on decision-making in different institutional contexts.

Considering first the sorts of resources and activities controlled by leading economic actors in market economies, these can vary along a number of dimensions, perhaps the most obvious of which concerns their degree of similarity and specialization. Richardson (1972) has distinguished activities that are similar and which use the same 'capability' of a firm, from those that are complementary and utilize dissimilar capabilities. By capabilities he means any combinations of knowledge, experience and skill that provide some competitive advantage for firms, and suggests that these capabilities tend to be specialized since firms will, *ceteris paribus*, prefer to expand in directions where their particular capability generates comparative advantage. Complementary activities are those which represent different phases of a production process – and so need to be coordinated – but draw on separate skills and competences. Thus ceramics manufacturers rather than electrical engineering firms usually specialize in fabricating porcelain insulators, and retailers often focus on distributing a wide range of different products, rather than being integrated with manufacturers of a particular product sector, such as clothing. However, the extent of firm specialization, and the means by which coordination of complementary activities is achieved, differ between market economies, as the contrasting cases of Denmark and Finland by Kristensen and Lilja and Tainio in this book clearly demonstrate.

Specialization in a particular set of capabilities is often taken to be the inverse of diversification as defined in terms of the variety of product lines and SIC codes. However, as Richardson points out, a conglomerate could specialize in taking over failing companies, rationalizing them and subsequently reselling them. Their managerial capability is then more a matter of restructuring and rationalizing ability, than linked to particular product sectors and technologies, just as some venture capitalists might claim an expertise in selecting promising new ventures, rather than in funding innovatory projects in particular business areas. Furthermore, as Penrose (1959: 107–9) demonstrates, the meaning of diversification is inherently ambiguous and cannot be reduced simply to the variety of product lines, because the significance of each set of products will differ for each firm. For example, a firm may specialize in developing a particular technology, which leads them to manufacture many different kinds of products, as Canon has done in moving from cameras to photocopiers (Hamel and Prahalad, 1990). Where, on the other hand, different product lines are made with different technologies in different ways, clearly diversification has increased and the firm is less specialized.

The crucial point about specialization here is the extent to which managerial and technological capabilities – in a broad sense, including the service sector – vary significantly so that economic actors authoritatively coordinate different kinds of expertise and knowledge within the same organization. It is diversification of capabilities which is the key characteristic here, rather than of products, so that firms are more diversified and varied in the kinds of activities and resources they control when they combine different skills and knowledge which enable them to carry out dissimilar – and sometimes non-complementary – activities. These skills and knowledge include, of course, marketing and distribution programmes, so that moving into radically different markets with novel kinds of customers and methods of reaching them requires the development of new capabilities and so diversification. Even more dissimilar capabilities are involved when manufacturing companies move into quite different service sector activities, as when Hong Kong cotton-spinning companies developed surplus land and became active in property development (Nishida, 1991; Wong, 1988).

A basic contrast can be drawn, then, between economies which encourage and manifest a high degree of diversification of capabilities and activities within economic actors – understood as Penrosian firms – and those where firms specialize more in particular, closely related capabilities. In those latter economies, complementary activities are coordinated through various forms of cooperation or through arm's-length market contracting, and so the typical size of leading firm tends to be smaller than in the former case. Japanese car manufacturers, for instance, are much smaller in terms of employees than their US counterparts because of the extensive use of subcontracting (Cusumano, 1985; Fruin, 1992, Sako, 1992). Verti-

cal integration may involve the development of new capabilities –
as when Ford integrated backwards into steel manufacturing – but
is often the result of technological developments which enable
complementary activities to be coordinated more effectively internally than through cooperation with suppliers or customers. It may
not, then, always involve diversification of capabilities, although full
integration of an entire production and distribution chain is likely
to require considerable variety of skills and knowledge.

This characteristic of economic actors can be summarized as the
degree to which economic actors coordinate different kinds of capabilities through some authority system. The small, specialized production units found in the Italian industrial districts clearly represent
one extreme, while the highly diversified conglomerate operating in
heavy industry, light industry, construction, retailing and financial
services – such as some of the largest Korean *chaebol* (Amsden,
1989; Steers *et al.*, 1989; Whitley, 1992a; Zeile, 1992) – are at the
other end of the continuum. In between are the relatively specialized
Japanese *kaisha*, the vertically integrated German enterprise and
the Anglo-Saxon diversified multinational.

This dimension is related to the preferred pattern of growth of
economic actors in different economies. This can either be incremental and closely tied to current capabilities, or more radical and
discontinuous, involving the acquisition or development of quite
different skills. While many firms may prefer to expand through
developing their particular capabilities, in some economies it may
be easier to seize growth opportunities through acquiring new
expertise by buying other firms and/or recruiting different kinds of
skills from the external labour market. Kagono *et al.* (1985), for
example, contrasted US and Japanese firms in terms of their strategic
or incremental patterns of change and, in general, it is worth comparing economic actors' ability and willingness to radically alter
their capabilities.

Although associated with the variety of capabilities managed
within firms, such that narrowly specialized firms are unlikely to
consider rapid qualitative shifts in their activities and skills, the
example of some Chinese firms in Taiwan and Hong Kong shows
how specialization can be combined with rapid shifts from, say, wig
production to making plastic flowers to toy manufacture (Redding,
1990: 219–22). These small firms avoid being tied to a particular
product line or technology by concentrating in sectors with relatively
simple and labour-intensive machinery, which can either be rapidly
adapted to new products, such as sewing machines, or can be

amortized over a short period so that they can be scrapped when better opportunities arise in novel areas. In a sense, these CFBs specialize in flexibility and adaptiveness, rather than in a particular technological capability or product sector, and so can change their activities quite radically and quickly. Conversely, firms that are vertically integrated and combine complementary, different capabilities may be firmly committed to a single sector and reluctant to shift resources and activities to quite unrelated and novel ones. It is useful, then, to make this distinction between these two dimensions for contrasting the variety of activities and capabilities coordinated by economic actors over time.

Turning to consider characteristics of governance structures, these are often linked to ownership patterns and the relationships between different kinds of shareholders and other major groups of stakeholders. Frequently discussed in terms of the separation of ownership from managerial control over economic actors, the issues here concern the nature of the groups dominating decision-making and the strategic choices of economic actors, and the interests they represent and reflect. These may be family owners, executives of banks and other business partners, salaried managers or, more likely, varied combinations of these. Differences in such groups are linked to variations in economic priorities and preferences and in the logic governing the evaluation of firm performance and success.

One of the major ways in which the governance of economic actors varies across economies is the extent to which they are embedded in a number of interdependent relationships with other major actors – such as banks, state agencies, suppliers and unions – or are able to act largely autonomously as 'islands of planned coordination in a sea of market relations' (Richardson, 1972: 883). In the former case, firms are components of networks of relationships in which their ability to act independently is restricted by their ties of mutual obligation and dependence to various stakeholder groups which often are represented on supervisory boards or similar oversight bodies. In the latter, they function more in isolation, at arm's length from key associates, and their top managements are able to make decisions as separate, discrete collective actors.

The most obvious example of interdependent economic actors is the post-war Japanese members of inter-market groups who are typically embedded in both horizontal – i.e. inter-sectoral – networks and vertical ones (Dore, 1986; Gerlach, 1992). However, this sort of interdependence also occurs in Europe, and often includes representatives of the labour movement, as we see in Germany and some of the Scandinavian countries (Herrigel, 1989; Lilja *et al*., 1992; Streeck, 1992). Other important groups which structure firm type and behaviour in Europe are professional élites, such as engineers in Norway (Halvorsen *et al*. in this volume), and intermediary associations. An important subdivision of this type of economic actor is between those that are interdependent with non-industrial actors, such as the banks and the state, and those which have linkages with sector-specific actors, such as suppliers and customers. The former are less tied to particular fields and activities than the latter which are, perhaps, the most restricted in their ability to pursue discontinuous policies and expansion plans. The obverse of this lack of autonomy, of course, is the ability of economic actors to share risks and develop cooperative links with members of their networks. The more isolated firms, on the other hand, internalize risks to a much greater extent and cannot count on the support of financial institutions or similar actors, since their interests are not coordinated. Anglo-Saxon economies typically develop these kinds of isolated enterprises whose controllers are usually separate from other groups, and whose boards rarely contain representatives of long-term business associates which are mutually locked into each other's destinies. Although, of course, networks and cooperative relationships do develop in these economies, they are rarely so institutionalized, recurrent and reciprocal as in other economies, and are additionally subject to the much stronger market for corporate control (Lawrisky, 1984; Lane, 1992 and in this volume). This characteristic can be summarized as the isolation of economic actors from other organizations and agencies.

A second important characteristic of the governance of economic actors is, of course, who, or which group, dominates decision-making and control. In particular, do owners play a major role in the direction of the enterprise, or do they substantially delegate this, in effect, to salaried managers? A further distinction can be drawn here between owners who delegate much control to managers but who can, and do, intervene on major strategic issues, and those who treat their investment largely as a component of a diversified portfolio of financial assets. The latter are more likely to sell their shares when firms underperform, than to become involved in changing managerial direction and personnel. They are, therefore, the most remote group of owners from the control of economic actors, but, because of the liquid secondary market in issued shares in economies where this sort of ownership is prevalent, the strong market for corporate control ensures that managerial élites focus on the interests of portfolio shareholders and their investment managers. This dimension, then, can be summarized as the degree of delegation of control over economic actors to non-owning managers, but the varied patterns of ownership also need to be borne in mind when considering the priorities and interests dominating strategic decisions. Family-dominated top management clearly represents the least delegation of control, as found in the CFB, in Korea and in some Latin European countries; bank-dominated ownership and voting rights in credit-based financial systems represent greater degrees of managerial control, as in many German, North European and Japanese enterprises, and the capital market-based economies of the Anglo-Saxon world grant considerable autonomy to managerial élites, subject, of course, to the demands of portfolio investors. In this last situation, entrepreneurial decision-making is usually located at the top of firms' hierarchies, but these firms are dependent on the verdicts of remote, impersonal and uninvolved financial institutions focusing on purely financial returns.

These characteristics of governance structures of economic actors are related to the sorts of dominant objectives pursued by the controllers of firms, and the criteria by which they judge success. In the traditional theory of the managerial firm (e.g. Marris, 1964), growth goals were seen as dominating profit-maximization ones, usually on the grounds of salaries and other rewards being tied to firm size. An additional factor encouraging the pursuit of large size in capital market-based financial systems was its connection with increased security for top managers, although this safeguard now appears less convincing, after the merger booms of the 1980s.

In practice, growth is typically pursued by most firms, subject to a profits constraint, both for competitive reasons and because managerial skills develop and generate increased resources for new activities (Penrose, 1959). However, the extent and type of growth goals do differ across market economies, as does the significance of the profits constraint. For example, in South Korea, and perhaps post-war France and Italy, the dominant role of the state and the high level of business dependence on the state have, together with other factors, encouraged the pursuit of very large size and dominant position in a variety of markets, with only a very limited profits constraint (Amsden, 1989; Janelli, 1993; Whitley, 1992a). In Japan, on the other hand, firms pursue market share goals and seek to grow in size within their sector, partly because of the hierarchical nature of the 'society of industry' (Clark, 1979), and also as a result of the complex networks of mutual dependence between firms, suppliers, customers, banks, employees and other organizations which restrict unrelated diversification but lead to strong collective interests in expansion (Abegglen and Stalk, 1985; Fruin, 1992; Gerlach, 1992). Profit constraints may be more significant here than in Korea, but they are less strong than in the Anglo-Saxon economies because of the weakness of the market for corporate control. In other kinds of bank-dominated economies where firms are closely tied into large banks but are not so embedded in sector-specific obligational networks as in Japan, growth goals are likely to be dominant because increased size implies greater demand for banks' services (Zysman, 1983), although profit constraints obviously are strong enough to ensure that loans can be serviced. Such growth may be more diversified than in Japan, but where employees have a strong influence, as in Germany, growth through radical diversification is unlikely if it is perceived to be a threat to current skills and capabilities. Similarly, where firms have developed close links with the state, banks and important economic groups such as forest owners and engineers in Finland, they are unlikely to move quickly into quite different markets and technologies (Lilja and Tainio in this volume).

In contrast, where firms are much more isolated, and owners operate as portfolio holders and/or managers at arm's length from the companies they invest in, the pursuit of growth goals – and hence managerial rewards and power – is limited by the market for corporate control and the need to meet the targets and expectations of the capital market. Dividend pay-outs and growth in share prices are here more significant measures of corporate performance than growth *per se*, and those financial objectives are indifferent as to how profits are made. Effectiveness in these sorts of firms, then, is more a matter of achieving financial objectives than market share goals, and large size without sufficient rates of return on capital employed to pay significant dividends is unlikely to appeal to shareholders. Because the owners of these companies do not have any other connections to them, and so only benefit from the direct rewards of holding their shares, they have a very narrow interest in them, and one which, furthermore, is typically easily traded in the securities market.

Finally, family-owned and controlled businesses may experience limited growth because of a reluctance to share control and a desire to increase family wealth rather than firm size. Where firms are viewed more as the means to enhance family prestige through the acquisition of wealth, than as separate organizations, profits may

well be more important than growth *per se*, especially if owners feel
politically insecure and large size is seen as attracting unwanted
scrutiny from the state, as in Taiwan and many other countries
where the CFB is strongly developed (Gold, 1986; Greenhalgh, 1984,
1988; Redding, 1990). This does not imply that all family-controlled
firms will restrict growth, but that, in particular circumstances they
may do so more than other kinds of firms and will concentrate on
areas where direct personal control can be maintained. Thus, the
dominant industries in Flanders and Wallonia reflect the different
priorities of owners, as well as their links to the state and major
holding companies, in different regions of Belgium (van Iterson in
this volume).

These examples suggest that a simple way of comparing and
contrasting dominant objectives of economic actors is in terms of
their pursuit of growth and large size with varying degrees of profit
constraints. While the preferred direction of growth also varies
significantly across market economies, especially with regard to its
focus on a particular sector, it is the extent to which growth goals
are subject to strong profit constraints which summarizes many of
the important differences in firms' objectives discussed above. This
dimension, together with the four considered earlier, constitute five
summary characteristics for comparing economic actors across institutional contexts, which are listed in Table 2.1. They vary as the
result of differences in dominant institutions during and after
industrialization which structured the sorts of economic actors that
became established and which flourished in different countries. Critical features of these institutions will now be discussed briefly, before
considering how they are connected to characteristics of economic
actors.

Table 2.1 Characteristics of economic actors

A. Nature of activities and resources coordinated and controlled
  1. Diversity of activities and capabilities coordinated through authoritative communication.
  2. Extent of radical discontinuities in activities and capabilities over time.
B. Governance structures
  1. Isolation of economic actors from other organizations and agencies.
  2. Delegation of control to salaried managers.
  3. Dominance of growth goals with weak profit constraints.

INSTITUTIONAL INFLUENCES ON CHARACTERISTICS OF ECONOMIC ACTORS

In considering the major institutions affecting the kinds of firms that develop in different countries, those governing the development of, and conditions of access to, key resources are obviously central. Thus, institutions and organizations concerned with the provision of capital and of varied kinds of labour power can have a major influence over firms' policies and structures, as can the terms on which these resources become available. Relatedly, the system governing the allocation and transfer of private property rights and the powers of owners is clearly central to the functioning of market economies, as are the structure and policies of the state as a whole. Finally, institutions governing trust relations, conceptions of personal identity and loyalty, and the acquisition and use of authority to obtain compliance, have important implications for how owners and managers organize firms and for their relations with each other.

These broad institutional areas can be compared and contrasted along a considerable number of dimensions across societies, as the numerous studies of, for example, industrial relations systems in Europe indicate (Baglioni and Crouch, 1990; Crouch, 1993). There are, however, a limited number of institutional features which together help to explain the major differences in characteristics of economic actors found across European and other economies. These can be summarized in terms of the nine sets of institutional influences listed in Table 2.2. Other features are important in

Table 2.2 Institutional features affecting characteristics of economic actors

---

A. *Cultural conventions*
  1. Strength of institutions governing trust relations and extra-family collective loyalties.
B. *State structures and policies*
  1. Extent to which state dominates economic system.
  2. Level of state risk-sharing with private economic actors.
  3. State support for intermediate associations and inter-firm cooperation.
  4. Formal regulation of market boundaries, entry and exit.
C. *Financial system*
  1. Credit-based financial system.
D. *Labour system*
  1. Significance of labour movement in strategic decision-making.
  2. Centralization of bargaining and negotiation.
  3. Collaboration in skill training and certification.

understanding variations in the organization of markets and in the organization and control of work, but here we are concerned with those most directly influencing the nature of economic actors.

First of all, the overall extent to which social institutions provide a reliable foundation for extending trust to business partners, employees and other groups is an important influence on the level of inter-firm collaboration and tendency to delegate in an economy. While there are important differences in how competence, contractual and goodwill trust (Sako, 1992) are developed in different cultures, the key feature here is the strength of the social institutions generating and guaranteeing trust between exchange partners in general. In particular, the extent to which owners of property rights, and their economic actors, feel able to rely on institutionalized procedures when making business commitments is a crucial factor in the development of cooperation within and between firms, and in the perception and management of risk (*cf.* Zucker, 1986). Where such procedures are weak or judged unreliable, personal and particularistic connections become especially important in organizing exchange relationships (cf. Redding, 1990).

Allied to the strength of institutions governing trust relations in many economies is the way that collective loyalties are organized and, in particular, the extent to which commitment can be generated among employees to collective entities on a non-personal basis is a critical factor in the development of large organizations that continue to coordinate economic activities over managerial generations and personnel changes. The establishment of a distinctive corporate persona and culture which is not tied to the characteristics of particular individuals, and which constitutes the focus of employee commitment, is clearly much easier in a culture where collective loyalties are not restricted to families and family-like connections (Hamilton and Kao, 1990; Numazaki, 1993). Weak collective loyalties beyond the immediate family are often combined with weak institutions governing trust relations in many cultures, and have similar consequences for the sorts of economic actors that become established. In considering differences in characteristics of economic actors, they can usefully be combined into a single institutional feature: the strength of institutions governing trust and non-personal loyalties. Where they are weak, authority also tends to be personal and paternalistic, which additionally limits the reliability of formal procedures for controlling the delegation of authority and decision-making.

A further aspect of the organization of collective loyalties which is particularly important for the constitution of firms in Europe is the significance of horizontal occupational groups, especially skill-based ones. As Halvorsen *et al.*, Kristensen and Winch demonstrate in this volume, such groups are important economic actors in many European countries and structure the sorts of firms that develop in particular sectors. As intermediary associations they limit the extent to which large firms can, and arguably need to, manage standardized company-wide labour markets for all employees in the Chandlerian multi-divisional mode, and play a significant role in structuring their internal division of labour. Firms in such countries cannot function as isolated, strongly bounded, discrete economic actors pursuing individual objectives autonomously from other social groups.

Turning to consider the major features of state structures and policies which affect economic actors, four summary ones seem especially significant. First, the cohesion and power of the state in society as a whole, when combined with a commitment to coordinate economic development, is a key variable feature of all market economies. When this is strong it leads to high levels of business dependence on the state and therefore to high levels of political risk among firms, as in South Korea over the past several decades (Kim, 1988; Whitley, 1992a; Woo, 1992). A second, but often connected, feature of state policy is the willingness of state agencies to share risks with private enterprises, as in the early stages of industrialization in many European countries, or alternatively to remain aloof from economic actors' decisions. Third, states vary considerably in their support and encouragement of intermediary associations of economic actors and their general toleration of cooperation between firms. Corporatist forms of intra- and inter-sector organizations differ considerably across Europe, largely as a result of state support or discouragement, and have important consequences for the nature of economic actors. A final significant feature of state policies in market economies is the degree of formal regulation of market entry and exit, including labour markets. This affects the mobility of resources and flexibility of firms as we can see in comparing many continental European countries with Anglo-Saxon ones (Lane and Mayer and Whittington in this volume).

Financial systems also differ on a number of dimensions, but the key feature is whether capital is mobilized and allocated through large and liquid capital markets or through large financial institutions which become locked into the fates of their customers, summarized by Zysman's (1983) contrast of capital market and credit-based systems. Although there are important differences between credit-based financial systems, and the distinction is not always clear-cut and easy to draw (as in the case of the Netherlands, cf. van Iterson and Olie, 1992) the basic contrast between these two broad sets of systems has quite strong implications for firms and markets and is a key feature of the institutional context for economic actors.

Finally, the key features of the labour system for characteristics of economic actors are the ability of the labour movement to influence decision-making, especially when it is organized along sectoral lines, the centralization and integration of bargaining procedures and the extent of collaboration in the provision and certification of training. The influence of trade unions on corporate priorities is important because it can affect the ability of employers to change the nature of the activities and capabilities they coordinate, and because it generally limits owners' and managers' autonomy and increases employer–employee interdependence, as is clear in Kristensen's analysis of Danish 'firms' in this volume. Centralization of bargaining is likewise significant because it encourages employers to cooperate with each other and, over time, often with trade union federations, so that they develop interdependent linkages with each other and become locked into particular patterns of cooperation and competition. Related labour market institutions that also increase sectoral commitment are cooperative systems of training which integrate employers, unions and state agencies, as in Germany and some other continental European countries (cf. Maurice *et al.*, 1986).

These nine features of the institutional environment combine to generate varied characteristics of economic actors across market economies, although many connections between institutions and the nature of firms are strongest at the extremes of the dimensions, rather than being continuously positive or negative. For example, where institutions governing trust relations are weak, it is unlikely that property-right owners will delegate full control of firms to non-family managers. However, it does not follow that strong institutions always lead to full delegation to salaried managers, especially in economies where banks' influence over strategic choices is strong. Accounting for particular characteristics of economic actors in an economy, then, typically involves a number of institutional features which function interdependently, as will now be discussed.

INTERDEPENDENCES BETWEEN INSTITUTIONS AND CHARACTERISTICS OF ECONOMIC ACTORS

Considering first the diversity of activities and capabilities coordinated by leading economic actors, this usually increases as the result of internalizing risk and of difficulties in developing linkages with other economic actors. Thus, highly diverse economic actors tend to develop in economies where the state remains aloof from economic coordination and risk-sharing, and the banks likewise are remote from the activities of particular firms. In other words, economies characterized by arm's length relationships between major institutions and essentially adversarial relations between organizations are likely to encourage higher levels of diversification than those with more integrated and interdependent institutions. Conversely, where it is easier to develop obligational relationships between enterprises and reciprocity is a strongly established norm, firms are more likely to restrict their radical diversification into related fields. Thus, diversified multi-divisional firms are more likely to be developed in Anglo-Saxon economies than in most continental European ones, as Mayer and Whittington show.

Credit-based financial systems, where banks and other financial institutions develop close links with particular firms as they become locked in to them, are also likely to limit unrelated diversification. This is because risks are shared and because banks invest in the development of knowledge of, and skills in, the particular industries of their clients and so will be reluctant to undertake further investment in unrelated areas. Banks may also be unlikely to believe that firms can manage quite different kinds of activities and will exercise more veto power over such moves than over expansion in present or related business areas. Additional constraints on unrelated diversification arise when firms are embedded in strong-sector specific associations and linkages. Thus, where bargaining, training and similar activities in labour markets are governed by strong institutions at the sector level, firms will find it more difficult to pursue high levels of diversification than when such institutions are weak or nonexistent, as in the Anglo-Saxon economies. Similarly, state support for intermediary trade associations, employers' federations and tolerance of inter-firm coordination and cooperation will limit diversification because sectors are more likely to be governed by industry associations and formal and informal conventions limiting both entry and exit (Lane, in this volume).

There is, however, one situation in which state coordination and risk-sharing may well increase diversification. This is when business dependence on the state is very high and the dominant risk for firms is to lose state support. Here, firms may undertake considerable unrelated diversification as a way of limiting the risks attached to failure in any one area of business, especially where they are subject to state targets and sanctions. This is particularly probable when the state has encouraged investment in new areas and has provided much of the capital required, as in South Korea (Amsden, 1989). Although risks may be shared with the state in this instance, they are still considerable and are dominated by the fear of losing access to cheap credit and other political favours. Thus, unrelated diversification is most likely to be a feature of market economies in which:

1 state support is either very low or else dominates large firm strategies;
2 there are few strong intermediary associations;
3 financial institutions are remote from particular firms;
4 sector-based institutions governing labour market activities are likewise weak.

Similar factors affect the degree of radical change in activities and capabilities coordinated by economic actors. The more embedded are firms in particular networks of mutual dependence with other employers, banks, unions and other major institutions, the less easy will it be for them to alter their major sector of activity, divest resources and acquire new ones. Conversely, the more autonomous they are from trade associations, sector-based bargaining and training institutions and employers' federations, the more straightforward it is to change business areas and core competences. Additionally, strong trade unions are likely to inhibit radical shifts in resources and skills, since they will resist the devaluation of their members' expertise. In economies where institutions and organizations are interdependent and develop close ties of mutual obligation, then, economic actors are likely to focus on specific sectors of activity and not engage in radical changes of direction. Rather, strategic development will be incremental and closely related to current strengths and capabilities, as in Japan (Kagono *et al.*, 1985). Similarly, firms in the more 'corporatist' European states are unlikely to operate as portfolio-holders, buying and selling subsidiaries for short-term gains because they are members of complex networks which cannot easily be changed and, often, because there are legal barriers to rapid entry and exit. Thus, large firms in Belgium, Finland and

Germany tend not to change sectors radically or to dispose readily of major business units when short-term market conditions deteriorate (van Iterson, Lane, and Lilja and Tainio in this volume).

Flexibility in resources and skills, on the other hand, is likely to be encouraged when both capital and labour are highly mobile and there are few, if any, strong institutions linking firms together. State indifference to economic coordination and development needs, together with antagonism to inter-firm cooperation and collaboration, will emphasize the isolation of economic actors and adversarial, predatory relations between them. Large, liquid capital markets, weak trade unions, fragmented bargaining and training systems and weak intermediary associations such as trade associations and chambers of commerce, together facilitate flexible and rapid responses to changing market pressures by radically changing the nature of resources and skills coordinated by economic actors (Campbell *et al.*, 1991; Lane, 1992).

Turning to consider governance structures, it is clear that the autonomy and independence of economic actors will be greater in market economies where the state does not play a significant coordinating role and does not support the growth of intermediary institutions or inter-firm cooperation. Equally, capital market-based financial systems do not encourage close links between banks and firms and joint risk-sharing, so that economic actors tend to be more isolated in economies with large capital markets than when the financial system is credit-based. Autonomy is also encouraged when bargaining and training are decentralized and left to the initiative of individual firms. Finally, where there are few institutions governing trust relations which can be relied upon, and collective loyalties are focused on the immediate family, owner/managers are unlikely to share control of firms and will limit commitments to other economic actors, except in cases where family-like linkages exist (Hamilton *et al.*, 1990).

Similar considerations affect the extent to which owners delegate control over economic resources to non-family managers. In societies where trust is predominantly personal, loyalties are kinship-based and authority relations are largely paternalist, owners are unlikely to trust managers who do not have close personal connections and obligations to themselves, and so will prefer to retain substantial levels of control within the family (Redding, 1990). Another factor affecting the delegation of control is the degree to which owners, or their agents such as trust banks, are able to sell their shares on a large, liquid capital market. If owners and lenders are locked into particular economic actors, they are less likely to delegate full control to managers than if they operate largely as portfolio managers. Thus, banks and other financial institutions in credit-based financial systems are more involved in strategic decision-making, and in the direct monitoring of managers' performance, than in capital market-based ones. They thereby take on more of the entrepreneurial function in these societies than do banks in capital market-based financial systems. It could also be argued that family control will be significant where owners are locked into ownership of particular shares and where the state dominates the economy. High levels of political risk, as in post-war South Korea and perhaps France, limit delegation because of the need to ensure compliance with state demands and to maintain secrecy.

Political risk also encourages strong growth goals because firms compete for state support and attention in this situation and size is a major factor in both gaining assistance and in limiting the likelihood of withdrawal of support. Growth is also often facilitated by a strong state role in coordinating economic development and in sharing investment risks because of the preferential access to subsidized credit provided by the state. Thus rapid expansion can be achieved through cheap loans without risking family capital and existing assets. This typically requires a credit-based financial system in which the state plays the leading role in allocating scarce capital (Zysman, 1983). Family control of large firms is thereby facilitated since growth is funded by debt rather than equity and so is much more significant in France and South Korea than elsewhere (Amsden, 1989; Bauer and Cohen, 1981; Mayer and Whittington in this volume).

Credit-based systems also encourage growth goals, because banks and other intermediaries become locked into particular customers and develop a multiplicity of linkages with them. Since they are interdependent with particular firms, it is in their interests to encourage growth so that they can provide more loans and other services on the basis of their initial commitment. If they own shares themselves, or act as trustees, the return on these investments is only part of the total return from all the services they provide, and so share price growth and dividends are not so crucial to them as they are to portfolio managers in capital market-based financial systems. Additionally, banks have to develop specialist expertise in particular fields and markets in order to competently judge investment proposals and demands for loans. Once acquired, these skills have to be used so that further growth is encouraged. Similar arguments apply to strong trade unions where their interests also imply an emphasis on growth goals, especially where the workforce is effectively locked into particular employers and employer–employee interdependence is high, as in post-war Japan (Clark, 1979).

These connections are summarized in Table 2.3, where particular 'values' of the institutional features are emphasized because these are most likely to affect the characteristics being considered. Low levels of state risk-sharing, for example, are likely to encourage internalization of risk and diversification, but the reverse relationship is by no means always likely to occur because of the high levels of political risk when coupled with a dominant state. In any particular empirical instance, of course, these institutional features function interdependently and may, on occasion, have conflicting implications. For example, the credit-based financial system in France may have restricted the degree of unrelated diversification and the isolation of firms, but the strong state antipathy to intermediate associations coupled with a willingness to play a major role in economic coordination and direction has focused firms' attention on political risk and state priorities, and weakened linkages between firms.

Turning to consider how this framework could be applied to the emerging firms and markets in Eastern and Central Europe, it is important to note that the present period of transformation is characterized by a number of contradictions and conflicts between particular features of dominant institutions, and so clear conclusions about the kinds of economic actors that will become established in particular economies are difficult to draw. For example, in most post-state-socialist societies the level of confidence in formal institutions governing trust and loyalty is low, and so firms rely extensively on informal networks when making commitments and limit the extent and scope of commitments to business partners, employees and other economic actors. However, the continued involvement of state agencies and state-controlled banks in the ownership and management of many – if not most – enterprises means that state risk-sharing and state–business relations remain significant, as is demonstrated by Whitley *et al.* in this volume. Thus, most large firms are not yet isolated and do not behave like either Anglo-Saxon corporations or CFBs. However, in the informal sector and where independent entrepreneurs have established a significant presence, these sorts of economic actors and flexibility-focused strategies may well dominate, subject to the extent of formal regulation of markets,

Table 2.3 Connection between institutions and economic actors

Institutional features	Characteristics of economic actors				
	Diversity	Discontinuous change	Isolation of firms	Delegation	Dominance of growth goals
Weak institutions governing trust and loyalties	+	+	+	−	−
Low state risk-sharing	+	+	+		+
Dominant state				−	+
Formal regulation of markets	−	−	−		
State support for intermediate associations	−	−	−		
Credit-based financial system	−	−	−	limited	+
Strong labour movement		−			+
Integrated, centralized bargaining	−	−	−		
Collaboration over training	−	−	−		

the power of trade unions and the nature of the bargaining and training systems.

In analysing the consequences of linkages with other economic actors, local and national state agencies, etc. for enterprises' strategic priorities and choices in Eastern Europe and elsewhere, it is important to bear in mind that conflicting managerial factions attempt to use these connections to bolster their own positions before, during and after privatization. Depending on the relative strength of banks, trade unions, local labour organizations and other groupings, and the skills of different managers in gaining their support, the policies of individual enterprises will vary. For example, in some Polish firms, the local workforce has been able to exercise a veto power on restructuring proposals, thus limiting the enterprise director's ability to break up the organization into separate units (Konecki and Kulpinska, 1995; Thirkell *et al.*, 1993), whereas in one Hungarian case a new director elected with strong trade union support was removed by a coalition of senior managers and state agencies. In the present highly volatile situation in most East or Central European countries it is obviously difficult to be confident about the sorts of alliances and factions which will emerge within the leading enterprises, and the kinds of policies they will try to pursue, but it does seem clear that dominant coalitions will continue to depend on support from powerful external organizations, such as different kinds of national and local government agencies, banks, business partners, various forms of labour organization and foreign firms, for some time, and their priorities will reflect these connections, as is reflected in Whitley *et al.*'s contribution to this book. The extent of decentralization of decision-making to subsidiary business units and of fragmentation of vertically integrated enterprises will depend, for instance, on the interests of these allies, and their relative power, as well as on market positions and the quality of suppliers.

Additionally, the present institutional features are changing as the result of political shifts within each country and external economic pressures. While these changes are probably going to be most noticeable in affecting privatization processes (Henderson *et al.*, 1995), they will also affect the structure and operation of the financial system, the extent to which corporatist connections between institutions and élites develop and the organization and control of labour markets. At the moment, it seems unlikely that Anglo-Saxon-style capital markets will develop, or that the state will retreat to a purely regulatory function as in the UK and USA, and so large enterprises will probably not evolve into Anglo-Saxon-style diversified cor-

porations. Similarly, the likely limitation of deregulation of labour
markets, and the continuation of current forms of training and certification of skilled workers, will restrict the isolation of large firms
and their radical diversification into new areas, although this may
differ between countries according to the extent of deregulation.

A key question about the transformation of East European economies, then, is how far the deregulation and separation of firms,
banks and state agencies will go and, relatedly, to what extent
informal networks based on personal connections and obligations
will provide an alternative foundation for inter-firm alliances and
collaboration. The more economic actors are isolated from each
other and from state support, and the more labour and capital
markets are deregulated, the more likely it is that firms will focus
on short-term survival through reducing commitments to staff and
trading partners, and perhaps seeking external investment and partners where that seems feasible. Where banks and/or the state remain
owners and/or controllers of firms, on the other hand, and labour
markets remain quite regulated, economic actors will be locked into
their present sets of activities and capabilities and will be unlikely
to diversify radically or to change their business sector. Assuming
such enterprises survive the current transformation, they will follow
growth strategies with only limited profit constraints because their
major allies and stakeholders will favour those priorities, as discussed above. It should also be borne in mind that the high level of
enterprise debt and low availability of investment funds in most
former state socialist countries severely limit investment in new
machinery and hence changes in product lines and markets.

Given the current levels of uncertainty and change, it seems probable that owners and creditors will only delegate limited powers to
managers and will continue to be involved in day-to-day decision-
making in most large firms. Centralization of control will therefore
remain high. This is even more likely in the small firm sector where
entrepreneurs have few, if any, formal institutional sources of support and risk-sharing. Furthermore, when appointing top managers,
it is reasonable to expect banks and other owners to rely on personal
knowledge and trust, rather than formal qualifications or previous
experience. This reliance on informal and personal connections
means that when key stakeholders change, so too will top managers,
even if their policies remain roughly similar. Thus, the changeable
political environment is likely to lead to considerable volatility in
top management positions, although other senior managerial personnel may remain more stable because of the lack of an external

labour market in managerial skills and the historical pattern of each large vertically integrated, enterprise dominating separate sectors, as is clearly the case in Hungary (Whitley *et al.* in this volume). Overall, then, the general pattern of economic organization in most East-Central European economies seems likely to combine large, various vertically integrated, enterprises enmeshed in networks of banks, suppliers, customers and state agencies with small and medium-businesses specializing in particular market areas and searching for short-term advantages. As long as the large firm sector remains closely tied into the formal banking sector and to state agencies – both national and local – it is unlikely to diversify into unrelated businesses, especially if organized labour is influential. While, then, some parts of these large enterprises may be sold off or closed down, they are not likely to shift their core economic activities. Where the state and banking system do withdraw support and connections, though, and labour and other markets are substantially deregulated, we would expect a greater extent of change in economic activities and capabilities, and perhaps a break-up of vertically integrated combines into much smaller and more specialized units coordinating their inputs and outputs largely through personal obligation networks.

CONCLUSIONS

The variety of types of economic actors in European and other market economies is closely connected to differences in patterns of industrialization and in dominant social institutions. Focusing on the nature of economic actors as Penrosian firms, their key characteristics can be summarized under two headings: the nature of activities and capabilities coordinated through authority structures, and the nature of the governance system controlling them. The five characteristics identified as central to the comparison of the sorts of leading enterprises that have become established in different European and other economies summarize the major ways in which these vary across institutional contexts as distinct units of economic coordination and control.

Differences between types of economic actors are linked to variations in the dominant institutions governing trust, loyalty and authority relations, as well as the state, financial and labour systems. Combinations of specific features of these institutions help to account for the particular kind of firm that has developed in each country, although, of course, the influence of any one institutional feature can be offset by that of other ones, as in the case of some Central European countries. For example, Lilja *et al.* (1992) have shown how the particular combination of certain features of the Finnish state, financial, education and labour systems can explain the distinctive characteristics of the leading forest sector firms in Finland. These institutional features structure the nature and degree of risk to be managed by economic actors, and also the preferable ways of dealing with it. They also encourage certain kinds of ownership patterns, and inhibit the establishment of others. This means that radical changes in the sort of economic actor that dominates particular economies are unlikely without major institutional changes, and even then the historical pattern will influence the ways such changes occur, as Stark (1992, 1993) has discussed in his comparison of privatization processes in East-Central Europe.

REFERENCES

Abegglen, J. C. and Stalk, G. (1985) *Kaisha, The Japanese Corporation*, New York: Basic Books.

Amsden, A. H. (1989) *Asia's Next Giant*, Oxford: Oxford University Press.

Baglioni, M. and Crouch, C. (eds) (1990) *European Industrial Relations*, London: Sage.

Barnard, C. (1938) *The Functions of the Executive*, Cambridge, Mass.: Harvard University Press.

Bauer, M. and Cohen, E. (1981) *Qui gouverne les groupes industriels?*, Paris: Seuil.

Campbell, J., Hollingsworth, R. and Lindberg, L. (eds) (1991) *The Governance of the American Economy*, Cambridge: Cambridge University Press.

Chandler, A. D. (1977) *The Visible Hand*, Cambridge, Mass.: Harvard University Press.

—— (1990) *Scale and Scope*, Cambridge, Mass.: Harvard University Press.

Clark, R. (1979) *The Japanese Company*, New Haven, Conn.: Yale University Press.

Cox, A. (1986) 'State, finance and industry in comparative perspective', in A. Cox (ed.) *State, Finance and Industry*, Brighton: Wheatsheaf.

Crouch, C. (1993) *Industrial Relations and European State Traditions*, Oxford: Clarendon Press.

Cusumano, M. A. (1985) *The Japanese Automobile Industry: Technology and Management at Nissan and Toyota*, Cambridge, Mass: Harvard University Press.

Dore, R. P. (1986) *Flexible Rigidities*, Stanford, Calif.: Stanford University Press.

Fruin, M. (1992) *The Japanese Enterprise System*, Oxford: Oxford University Press.

Gerlach, M. (1992) *Alliance Capitalism*, Berkeley, Calif.: University of California Press.

Social construction of economic actors 65

Gold, T. B. (1986) *State and Society in the Taiwan Miracle*, Armonk, N.Y.: M. E. Sharpe.
Greenhalgh, S. (1984) 'Networks and their nodes: urban society on Taiwan', *The China Quarterly* 99: 529–52.
—— (1988) 'Families and networks in Taiwan's economic development', in E. A. Winckler and S. Greenhalgh (eds) *Contending Approaches to the Political Economy of Taiwan*, Armonk, N.Y.: M. E. Sharpe.
Hamel, G. and Prahalad, C. K. (1990) 'The core competence of the corporation', *Harvard Business Review* 68: 79–91.
Hamilton, G. and Kao, C. S. (1990) 'The institutional foundations of Chinese business: the family firm in Taiwan', *Comparative Social Research* 12: 95–112.
——, Zeile, W. and Kim, W. J. (1990) 'The network structures of East Asian economies', in S. Clegg and G. Redding (eds) *Capitalism in Contrasting Cultures*, Berlin: de Gruyter.
Hart, J. A. (1992) *Rival Capitalists*, Ithaca, N.Y.: Cornell University Press.
Henderson, J., Whitley, R., Czaban, L. and Lengyel, G. (1995) 'Dilemmas of state economic management: contention and confusion in the Hungarian route to industrial capitalism', in E. Dittrich *et al.* (eds) *Industrial Transformation in Europe*, London: Sage.
Herrigel, G. (1989) 'Industrial order and the politics of industrial change: mechanical engineering', in P. J. Katzenstein (ed.) *Industry and Politics in West Germany*, Ithaca, N.Y.: Cornell University Press.
Janelli, R. L. (1993) *Making Capitalism: the Social and Cultural Construction of a South Korean Conglomerate*, Stanford, Calif.: Stanford University Press.
Kagono, T., Nonaka, I., Sakakibara, K. and Okumara, A. (1985) *Strategic vs. Evolutionary Management*, Amsterdam: North Holland.
Kim, E. M. (1988) 'From dominance to symbiosis: state and *chaebol* in Korea', *Pacific Focus* 3: 105–21.
Konecki, K. and Kulpinsk, J. (1995) 'Enterprise transformation and the redefinition of organizational values in Poland', in E. Dittrich *et al.* (eds) *Industrial Transformation in Europe*, London: Sage.
Lane, C. (1992) 'European business systems: Britain and Germany compared', in R. Whitley (ed.) *European Business Systems*, London: Sage.
Lawrisky, M. L. (1984) *Corporate Structure and Performance*, London: Croom Helm.
Lazerson, M. H. (1988) 'Organisational growth of small firms: an outcome of markets and hierarchies', *American Sociological Review* 53: 330–42.
Lévy-Leboyer, M. (1980) 'The large corporation in modern France', in A. D. Chandler and H. Daems (eds) *Managerial Hierarchies*, Cambridge, Mass.: Harvard University Press.
Lilja, K., Rasanen, K. and Tainio, R. (1992) 'The forest sector business recipe in Finland and its domination of the national business system', in R. Whitley (ed.) *European Business Systems*, London: Sage.
Marris, R. (1964) *The Economic Theory of 'Managerial' Capitalism*, London: Macmillan.
Maurice, M., Sellier, F. and Silvestre, J. J. (1986) *The Social Foundation of Industrial Power*, Cambridge, Mass.: MIT Press.
Nishida, J. (1991) 'The Japanese influence on the Shanghaiee textile industry

66   *Structure and agency*

and its implications for Hong Kong', M.Phil. thesis, University of Hong Kong.
Orru, M., Hamilton, G. and Suzuki, M. (1989) 'Patterns of inter-firm control in Japanese business', *Organization Studies* 10: 549–74.
Penrose, E. (1959) *The Theory of the Growth of the Firm*, Oxford: Blackwell.
Pyke, F., Becattini, G. and Sengenberger, W. (eds) (1990) *Industrial Districts and Inter-Firm Cooperation in Italy*, Geneva: ILO.
Redding, S. G. (1990) *The Spirit of Chinese Capitalism*, Berlin: de Gruyter.
Richardson, G. (1972) 'The organisation of industry', *Economic Journal* 82: 883–96.
Sako, M. (1992) *Prices, Quality and Trust*, Cambridge: Cambridge University Press.
Silin, R. H. (1976) *Leadership and Values. The Organization of Large Scale Taiwanese Enterprises*, Cambridge, Mass.: Harvard University Press.
Stark, D. (1992) 'Path dependence and privatisation strategies in East-Central Europe', *East European Politics and Societies* 6: 17–51.
—— (1993) 'Recombinant property in East European capitalism. Organizational innovation in Hungary', paper presented to a conference on Economic Transformation in Central and Eastern Europe, held at the WZB, Berlin, 24–25 September.
Steers, R. M., Shin, Y. K. and Ungson, G. R. (1989) *The Chaebol*, New York: Harper and Row.
Streeck, W. (1992) *Social Institutions and Economic Performance*, London: Sage.
Thirkell, J., Scase, R. and Vickerstaff, S. (1993) 'Enterprise strategies and labour relations in the context of marketisation', unpublished paper presented to ESRC East–West Initiative Workshop on The Enterprise in Post-Communist Societies, London, 26–27 November.
van Iterson, A. and Olie, R. (1992) 'European business systems: the Dutch case', in R. Whitley (ed.) *European Business Systems*, London: Sage.
Whitley, R. (1992a) *Business Systems in East Asia: Firms, Markets and Societies*, London: Sage.
—— (1992b) 'Societies, firms and markets: the social structuring of business systems', in R. Whitley (ed.) *European Business Systems: Firms and Markets in their National Contexts*, London: Sage.
Wong, S.-L. (1988) 'The applicability of Asian family values to other socio-cultural settings', in P. L. Berger and H.-H. M. Hsiao (eds) *In Search of an East Asian Development Model*, New Brunswick, N.J.: Transaction Books.
Woo, J. (1992) *Race to the Swift*, New York: Columbia University Press.
Zucker, L. (1986) 'Production of trust: institutional sources of economic structure, 1840–1920', *Research in Organisational Behaviour* 8: 53–111.
Zysman, J. (1983) *Governments, Markets and Growth: Financial Systems and the Politics of Industrial Change*, Ithaca, N.Y.: Cornell University Press.

3 Societal effects in cross-national organization studies

Conceptualizing diversity in actors and systems

Arndt Sorge

INTRODUCTION

The purpose of this paper is to give a general introduction to the theoretical foundations underlying organizational treatments of cross-national diversity in organization, vocational education and training, business strategy, industrial relations and technical change. Key notions in organization studies revolve around 'actors' and 'systems' (Crozier and Friedberg, 1977). It therefore comes as no surprise that some treatments of cross-national diversity are actor-centric, whilst others centre on systems as principal locations in which cross-national diversity is rooted.

The next two sections outline a framework for accommodating such different approaches to the analysis of cross-national diversity, and show how these fit into a more general theory. I then put forward the theoretical core of the societal effect approach in terms of general social and organization theory as one way of developing a systemic approach that allocates an important role to actors. Examples will be given to show how the approach works in the practice of cross-national empirical comparisons.

Whilst it has been suggested that the societal effect approach neglects socio-organizational change, I will try to demonstrate that it can accommodate change extremely well, and shall attempt to explain how it occurs and where it leads to, in different societies. The implication is that existing societal and actor structures, or 'constructions' of actors and systems, produce different paths of social, economic, political and even technical change. The final section of the paper traces the consequences that this conceptualization has for the convergence and divergence of business structures and practices between societies.

SOCIETAL EFFECTS AND CROSS-NATIONAL DIFFERENCES

To suggest that making cross-national comparisons constitutes a very complex task would be the understatement of the year. To describe and explain cross-national differences adequately, one would have to present an encompassing treatment of:

• the 'construction' of actors, consisting of the programming of actors' minds in the form of values and preferences, and of the way actors imagine, and make sense of, system design;
• the design of organizational systems, including structures, norms, rules of the game and other institutionalized regularities; this includes their implications with regard to individual actor mentality;
• causal influences, either way, and relative autonomy, between the construction of actors and the design of systems;
• the social, political, economic and psychological architecture of a society, as the sum total of external reference points which orientate the behaviour of both actors and systems;
• the way in which the dynamic development of organizational outcomes is different or similar in one society compared to another.

Organizational outcomes can be sub-divided into two major types. Direct organizational outcomes consist of organizational goals and economic results, while indirect outcomes consist of structural and processual properties of organizations. The reason for this distinction is that organizations try to achieve goals and standards of performance (direct outcomes), but this is not the only result of their efforts. A manifest or latent consequence of what they do is to change their own structures and processes (indirect outcomes).

It will be obvious that the development of such an encompassing approach on an empirical basis is daunting. The amount of detailed and coordinated research work required, even for a treatment of a small number of societies, would be overwhelming. Practical difficulties of coordination of concepts and methods, making resources available and motivating researchers over a long period, get in the way. Scholars require a certain pragmatism to narrow down an unwieldy perspective of study, adopting more limited approaches which have the advantage of being practically feasible. Thus, they opt for more specific, one-sided approaches which represent imperfect approximations to a comprehensive challenge, each approach in its own way. It is also clear that there is a temptation to generalize the one-sided conceptual basis of either approach more than is warranted, in which case pragmatism obtains an ideological extension. The point is, however, that this is perfectly natural, as long as we are aware of such limitations and are prepared to relativize them. Over-extended generalization of limited approaches is a normal fact of life. It is not harmful but productive, if it serves a specific purpose: a controversial discussion of countervailing approaches can alert us to possibilities of contradiction which are dialectical – they stand for complementarity of approaches within a larger body of theory. This points the way to the formulation of a more general theory.

ACTORS, CULTURALISM AND STRUCTURALISM

Let us then focus on one possible narrowing-down of the more general and complex framework into a more single-minded and handy-to-use approach. This would be to base research and theory-building on the category of the actor. Actors are human individuals or a whole collectivity which may be defined by either common characteristics (quasi-groups) or integrated social interaction. Individual and collective actors typically feature what may be called a 'programming of the mind', arising from socialization processes which are similar for members of the collectivity. There are various possible commonalities that can be imagined: early childhood socialization may have a distinctive pattern in a society; education at school is different in different countries; working careers are again different, and they exert a socializing influence on the human mind although they are not necessarily labelled as education or training. In every example, a socialization process of a specific form and with a specific content contributes to the formation of an individual identity that is typified by a particular mode of operation of the individual mind. In exemplary fashion, this approach is found in the work of Hofstede (1980).

The cornerstone of the approach is the actor. Hofstede also showed that actors feature a particular correspondence between the general programming of the mind and more specific mental programmes with regard to what he called 'work-related values'. The latter refer us to characteristics, not only of actors but also systems. They contain an imagination of desirable and undesirable organization structures and methods, preferred and contested organization outcomes.

On the basis that culture means a specific programming of the mind, this approach may be called culturalist. According to Hofstede, the effect of culture becomes extended, from the level of the individual mind to characteristics of organization systems and other structures. Individual mental programming has an influence on the selection of system characteristics; the individual must choose between alternative system characteristics, in conformity with its own values and preferences. Such system characteristics will, in turn, stabilize or reinforce a specific programming of the individual mind. The feedback cycle will, furthermore, predispose actors and systems to go in the direction of specific organization outcomes, notably particular self-referenced outcomes. A universal management principle, for instance management by objectives, will be adapted to existing mental progammes and related system characteristics, thereby acquiring a specific application – or even non-application – within the actor-and-systems constellation of the society in which it is implanted.

Further examples can be mentioned and have been demonstrated by Hofstede. Whether in the case of delegation or centralization of authority, individual versus group work, number of levels in the hierarchy of authority, the strength of the position of superiors, methods of motivation to work, communication patterns or other organization practices – every time a plausible link between mental programmes and system characteristics can be demonstrated in cross-national comparisons. This tends to confirm strong causal influences between actors' and system properties. However, the approach also builds on the open systems concept, since mental programmes are shown to be rooted in wider socialization processes, in the society-at-large and they are definitely open to change. Hofstede has extensively documented such instances of what he called value changes. Actors are shown to confront obstacles, restrictions and opportunities; this makes them adapt the selection of system characteristics to match given mental programmes and system properties.

However, Hofstede would be the last to claim that mental programmes evolve completely autonomously. He would admit that feedback loops may go either way, and they may be equally strong in both directions. Yet, through the conceptual focus on the actor and the preferred research method of individual value surveying, the approach is slanted towards a particular form of methodological individualism. This form is continuously on the look-out for mental programmes to match system characteristics, actor-and-system constellations, and the outcomes which they generate. The mental programmes of actors always matter.

The opposite point of view would be that the mental programme does not always matter, but system characteristics do. The generation of organizational outcomes would be seen to rest, in the first instance, on system characteristics. These may or may not have given rise to an adaptation of mental programmes. This would be a secondary matter. The main point is that different 'rules of the game' make individuals move in different directions, even if their mental programming were to be the same. It may well be that different rules of the game provoke an adaptation of individual mental programmes, through a process of learning about context-specific factors associated with success (such as physical well-being, social recognition, professional and social advance and personal development).

Such an approach when, for instance, faced with organizational outcomes in Japan compared with other societies, would play down the role of Japanese culture. Proponents of such an approach would argue that the specificity of Japanese practices resides in a different construction of professional careers, labour markets (lifetime employment), payment systems, industrial relations, etc. They would argue that if Europeans and Americans were to be transplanted into a Japanese-type context, they would generate the same organizational results. They would do so because the institutionalized context of Japanese society makes them act this way, rather than because their values are the way they are. Outcomes would therefore have to be traced back to institutionalized rules of the game. The plausibility and empirical corroboration of this approach are rooted in the fact that actors adapt to institutionalized systems, no matter what their specific values are. Indeed, they tend to adapt to institutionalized opportunities and constraints even though these may run counter to their values.

This approach is very structuralist, which can be taken to represent the opposite of a culturalist approach. Structuralism is very much in evidence in industrial sociology or, more narrowly, sociological cross-national comparisons. It is forever on the look-out for system characteristics as factors that are at the root of organizational outcomes, whether mental programmes are adapted in due course or not. The evidence in favour of structuralism is by no means weaker than that in favour of culturalism. A study comparing attitudes and social rules in similar US and Japanese enterprises by Lincoln and Kalleberg (1990) came to the result, surprising to many but methodologically well substantiated, that work commitment is not larger in Japanese workers, if measured as an individual mental attribute. Differences in organizational outcomes are explained by different rules of the game, rather than ascertainable individual mental differences. The authors do show how enterprises have to some extent adapted in congruence with cultural predilections, as they call it, but the main factor is the design of system characteristics, the role of culture being considered to be indirect and additive.

I will not develop, here, a strong structuralist counter-programme to a culturalist programme. That would not be in the interest of authors such as Lincoln and Kalleberg, either. Instead, I will try to summarize an approach with strong structuralist foundations and a conceptual basis broad enough to take on board many culturalist analyses. The idea is that the gap which, in a purely nomothetic framework, would exist between different sorts of reductionism – looking for causes within the mind of the actor or, conversely, in properties of supra-individual systems – can be bridged in the manner indicated by Giddens (1986), through what he called 'structuration theory'. This is no more and no less than an erudite explication of how actors and systems constitute each other reciprocally. This eliminates the chicken-and-egg problem by simply declaring that:

• it is silly to quarrel about the order of causality or precedence between chickens and eggs;
• every chicken has hatched from an egg;
• chickens cannot reproduce except via eggs;
• the reproduction of chickens never occurs in an identical way;
• the historical variation and evolution of chickens occurs because the interposed egg does not simply recreate properties of the mother hen.

(The argument neglects cocks and their contribution, in order to comply with recent pressures to choose language and metaphors that help redress the traditional imbalance in favour of the masculine gender.)

Within organization theory, a similar dialectical approach had been proposed by Crozier and Friedberg (1977). Whereas use of the term 'dialectical' evokes fears of intellectual hair-splitting, let it be clear that the purpose of this exercise is merely to make a more refined explication possible of what is, basically, a common-sense notion on which, one would hope, we can all agree.

SOCIETAL EFFECTS AND CROSS-NATIONAL DIFFERENCES

A succinct and understandable introduction to the societal effect approach has been written by Rose (1985), a sympathetic outsider who has brought out its essence. The classic statement of the approach is found in Maurice *et al.* (1982), on the basis of a Franco-German comparison reported in greater detail in Maurice *et al.* (1977). This studied four principal dimensions (and, more recently, a fifth) of the wider social, economic and political spheres of society:

1 the organization of work and of the enterprise;
2 human resources, education, training and socialization;
3 industrial and sectoral structures, and relations between such industries and sectors;
4 labour markets, as the sum total of events and arrangements which constitute the exchange of labour power for an equivalent, such as intrinsic satisfaction, social affiliation or money;
5 technology.

Each of these four dimensions can be subdivided into a **structure** and a **flow** aspect. The structural aspect refers to 'stocks' and properties which characterize the composition of an aggregate of people or of a system. The flow refers to additions and subtractions which occur with regard to a dimension over a certain period of time. The interesting thing is that structures and flows are not set apart. A flow – for instance labour market mobility between enterprises – has a clear structure, being decomposed into relative shares of types of labour, differentiated by age, experience, specialism, education and training and other salient variables. Inversely, a structure has to be characterized by flows, since it is never completely stable. The identity of the structure over time cannot be limited to those elements that remain stable over a period of time; it also includes a relatively stable pattern of addition and subtraction, i.e. of flows.

Any system and subsystem can be said to transform inputs into outputs. Such transformation processes therefore also suppose flows, and these have structures. There are flows of information, materials, semi-manufactured inputs, people, experience, knowledge, competence and other things, and these are all structured in ways that have to be described. Now, the identity of an actor and a system is not constituted by a minimum of flows, i.e. not by a restriction of change. Instead, it reposes in an equilibrium of flows. This means that the system maintains an equilibrium in two different ways. First, despite the 'departure' of people, knowledge, information, etc., new additions are integrated into existing structures and interpretations. Second, truly novel structures and interpretations give rise to a 'rewriting' of the system's history, which creates at least a semblance of identity over time. In these two different ways, structures are reproduced in a non-identical fashion, and the identity of systems and actors comes to rest on this non-identical reproduction. Paradoxical as this may sound, it is a basic fact of social life.

The authors of the societal effect approach do not really use the notion of equilibrium because they would not consider equilibrium a necessary or normal condition of any kind of system. Disequilibria are considered normal and pervasive. They show that countervailing forces – such as stability and change – hold each other in place. This may warrant the theoretical notion of system equilibrium, because even in situations of social 'disequilibrium', such as revolts, revolutions, upheaval, malfunctioning of institutions, civil war, power struggles, etc., the changes that occur, and the imbalances that exist, tend to reproduce patterns which therefore have to be considered stable.

The *organizational dimension* has structures like formal and informal organization structures, of both hierarchical and functional kinds. On the flow side of the dimension, we find primary and secondary transformation processes which transform inputs into outputs. This transformation will be familiar from the theory of sociotechnical systems.

The *human resources dimension* has, on the flow side, personnel flows across stages of education, training and socialization more generally. The latter includes job changes, since even a succession of jobs without a manifest training purpose has a definite socialization effect. On the structure side, there are professional structures, the apparatus (schools, instructors, teaching methods, etc.) dedicated to training, and the educational system of a society, both inside and outside enterprises.

The *industrial–sectoral dimension* includes, on the structure side, the subdivision of an economy into sectors and industries, the subdivision of industries into enterprises of different types (differentiated according to size, age, dependence, etc.). On the flow side, we get transactions of commodities and goods between industries and sectors, including ideas and informations, rather in the manner of an input–output table. There are also flows of enterprises which leave and enter industries.

The *labour market dimension* has structures such as organisms, contractual, informal and statutory rules, which govern flows in the transaction of labour power. Professional structures also have to be included here, under the structural aspect, since they affect the supply of and demand for labour. Such professional structures also form part of the human resources dimension, which is, in a way, next to the labour market dimension.

More recently, a *technical dimension* has been added; this comprises structural characteristics of physical artefacts, of their mode of development, design and employment, plus flows of information, knowledge and experience which constitute and change technology. Innovation comes under the flow aspect of the technical dimension, being concerned with additions to, and subtractions from, structures of technical experience and knowledge.

The intention is not to define, once and for all, a rigid decomposition of the society and the economy into subsystems. The above categorization can easily be supplemented, for instance by capital markets. It can also easily be differentiated and changed round in any other way. The precise structure of the subdivision is not central; it has been derived in a fairly pragmatic way. Proponents of the societal effect approach do not think that dogmatic classifications which are sometimes proclaimed as basic to disciplines, are very helpful. The important thing is to grasp the relations between events, arrangements, structures and flows, *across* any classificatory scheme. This means that it is important to explore the societal aspect of any social, economic and political phenomenon we are concerned with. The notion of society, then, is distinctive for embracing the whole range of institutionally differentiated social, political and economic spheres. The societal effect is concerned with lateral, reciprocal, relations between any subdivided systems or spheres of society. What happens in a specific sphere, be it technology, social stratification, labour markets, enterprise organization, etc., has to be explained with reference to a set of cross-relations with other spheres or dimensions. And such an explanation is considered approximately complete if the cross-relations it adduces touch on the largest possible number of differentiated subsystems and spheres.

Through these cross-relations, there is what the American sociologist Talcott Parsons termed 'interpenetration', meaning that the economy has a social and a political subsystem, and similarly for any other category. In the terminology of the societal effect approach, this is referred to as reciprocal *encastrement*, which denotes the fact that any 'separate' sphere of political, social, economic and technical life also forms part of every other sphere.

In essence, it is therefore impossible to keep spheres of human life apart; through the reciprocal interpenetration of spheres, a societal effect is ever-present. Let us then look at what the approach has to say about the cross-relations. In addition to the cross-relations already mentioned, between spheres of human life, there are two other types: cross-relations between actors and systems, and between actor–systems constellations at different points in time. Let us first deal with cross-relations between the dimensions described above, as one possible way of categorizing major components of economy and society.

The first central tenet of the approach is that characteristics along any of the four dimensions mentioned above, are related to specific, parallel characteristics on every other dimension. This means that specific patterns of work organization and enterprise structures are linked with specific patterns of human resource generation, of industrial and sectoral structures, and of industrial relations. What happens on one dimension has implications for what happens on the other dimensions. If a society, for instance, shows a tendency to deepen the hierarchical differentiation of enterprises, there will be a related differentiation with regard to human resources and in industrial relations structures, and it will also be related to the importance of concentrated industries in that society. The implication is that such characteristics are specific for a society, and the identity of society is constituted through the reproduction of such characteristics.

This is the more static aspect of the approach, which tries to summarize features that are relatively stable over time. These can, in essence, be formulated following a more nomothetic logic of theory-building: if work is organized in a particular way, this will be interdependent with related human resources, industrial–sectoral and industrial relations patterns. Note that one-way determination or causality are not implied, but rather reciprocal interdependence between dimensions of social, economic and political life. Some readers have suggested that, for instance, vocational education and training patterns 'explain' organization characteristics. But this is not the way the approach is to be understood. Its proponents insist on interdependence rather then dependence. But the societal effect analysts do not pretend to put in place a new kind of 'grand theory'. Rather, they see themselves as developing an approach based on different 'grand theories' rolled into one. Neither do they see themselves as developing just another 'theory of the middle range', which can be translated as nomothetic theory represented by interlinked 'if A, then B' statements.

This takes us to the second basic tenet: that actors reproduce characteristics on any dimension of society and the interrelations between such dimensions. This happens because structural properties and rules of the game, i.e. the 'systems' properties, tend to load individual 'choices' that actors make, in a specific way. It also happens because the actors learn to see particular 'choices' as generally favourable, and develop a specific 'programming of the mind'. In contrast with the culturalist perspective, the emphasis is on the interactive relationship between systems characteristics and mental programming. But the interactive relationship may be marked by both correspondence and opposition: faced with hierarchical organization patterns, the actors may learn to internalize corresponding assumptions and find them legitimate; but they may also develop a dislike for them, and try to evade them at the same time as trying to comply with them. This means that expressed value preferences and manifest behaviour may both converge and diverge. Under this tenet, the emphasis is on the complementarity, or mutual affinity, of opposites. Here, we see dialectical rather than nomothetic theory-building at work.

The example of Japanese workers given by Lincoln and Kalleberg (1990) and mentioned above, illustrates the point about complementary opposites. The Japanese do not view the company more favourably than the Americans, but the social rules of the game load their behavioural 'choices' towards manifest company loyalty, even if they hate it. Similarly, surveys tend to show that German workers in no way attribute greater importance to the work ethic, work discipline and the centrality of work in life; indeed the reverse is usually true. Yet, the cliché is widespread that Germans work hard and maintain work discipline. Is this all nonsense? Germans work comparatively fewer hours per year, on average, and have less working years per life than in most other countries; this would suggest that at least part of the cliché is nonsense.

On the other hand, company studies do show work discipline in operation. However, its persistence is due to the construction of social relations in the work-place and the employment sphere, which is also reflected in the 'mental map' of the individual, of legitimate and advantageous expectations, forms of behaviour and outcomes. The simple fact is that Germans tend to hate work and yet comply with the ground rules of the work-place because they appear legitimate. This may culminate in a love–hate relationship as a frequent phenomenon. Anyone who has seen Germans work will find the interpretation entirely plausible.

Neither the mental mappings of individuals, nor their values, nor the systems characteristics to which they attach, nor the relations between them, can ever be free of conflict or contradictions. This shows the limitations of a nomothetic approach, and also of a perspective which stresses the 'static' side of the societal effect. Conflicts and contradictions exemplify the necessity of using, in addition, a dialectical perspective. This stresses that openness and the natural properties of systems in the wider sense account for an ever-present tendency to change and modify, in ways that transcend the relatively stable patterns put forward in the first two tenets, of the societal effect approach. This transcendence has an uncomfortable habit of blurring nomothetic statements that were meant to be so beautifully precise and general.

We then come to the third tenet, which defines the reproduction of characteristics on every mentioned dimension, and of their inter-relations, as non-identical. Thus, although open and natural systems properties imply erratic, or at least unpredictable, variations in the course of evolution, the approach says that such changes develop the continuity of characteristics at the same time as breaking it. Let us take a simple example. Until the mid-1960s, the prevalence of greater numbers of skilled workers in German factories had gone hand-in-hand with much more restrictive access to selective secondary education; more young people went into apprenticeships, rather than going to selective secondary schools. In France, when access to selective general education was more open, fewer people went into apprenticeships or vocational education.

The example may be taken to imply a simple nomothetic logic: if selective secondary education in Germany is expanded, this will mean greater convergence with French patterns, and a concomitant reduction of apprenticeship as a major socializing arrangement. That would have been change, but change to be expected on the basis of a nomothetic proposition alone. But since life does not work this way, what happened in Germany was different. To be sure, there was not simply a haphazard or accidental deviation from 'relatively stable' patterns. What Germany got was an increase of secondary education *before* apprenticeship, such that increasing numbers of ex-grammar school and secondary modern or secondary technical school (*Realschule*) leavers went for apprenticeships. The change was that the starkness of the choice between selective education and apprenticeship training had been reduced, but earlier patterns had been reasserted since apprenticeship continued to be an attractive education and training choice. Change and continuity are therefore united in the non-identical reproduction of previous patterns. France has since greatly increased the status and quantity of vocational education, but mainly through the upgrading of vocational schools and diplomas. It has improved the attractiveness of vocational education by giving it *baccalauréat* status and by other measures. Even so, apprenticeship training has continued to dwindle. Thus, France has asserted the particularity of its own education and training arrangements in a way which is parallel but different with regard to Germany.

Convergence between France and Germany did not come about, for a specific reason. The novel education and training arrangement is distinctive for a creative combination of old and new patterns; there was no mechanical shift along a known continuum of 'choice'. It is the new combination that is novel, rather than the sheer rate of increase in secondary education. This insight can be generalized. In the societal effect approach it lays the basis for the view that true 'convergence' hardly ever takes place, since any change tends to consist of non-identical reproduction; we are not in reality dealing with change upon a continuum of nomothetically established alternatives.

Let us now go through a number of findings in the light of the societal effect approach and start with the simpler, more nomothetic side, to expound the first major tenet of the approach. We had tried to sum up comparative findings on France, Germany and Britain, by a set of three law-like statements which focused on the interdependence of the organizational and the human resources dimension (Maurice *et al.*, 1980: 80ff.).

1 The higher the practical professionalization of workers, technical employees, and supervisors and managers, the less technical and authoritative tasks are split off from shop-floor roles and organized into differentiated jobs, and the less such activities are differentiated internally in the white-collar area.

This relationship explains how different measures for job specialization, organizational differentiation and professionalization in the three countries are obtained. France features the highest amount of specialization and differentiation, and the smallest amount of practical professionalization; Germany has the smallest amount of specialization and differentiation, and the highest amount of practical professionalization; Britain comes in between. The explanation could be extended into the interdependence with other dimensions, but this is left out to be brief, not because it is of lesser importance. Contrary to many clichés, the professional autonomy of shop-floor production workers is most developed in Germany, and production management therefore more technical than authoritarian.

2 The higher the training and competence discrepancy between production and maintenance components of the shop floor, the higher the separation between production and maintenance activities and careers.

This combined organizational and human resources effect is strongest in Britain. This society has brought forth a characteristic difference between the autonomous maintenance craftsman and the production worker as a more restricted and less responsible worker. The effect lays the basis for functional, human resources and career differentiation higher up in the pyramid of the enterprise, between the line and staff personnel, functions and careers. This 'lateral' differentiation is very strong in Britain, intermediate in France and smallest in Germany. As a result, managerial authority is most isolated from technical responsibility in Britain, whereas the two are most intimately linked in Germany. The British manager is more of a pure, or general, manager, whereas the German manager is more of a technical (or commercial, or administrative) leader. Leadership implies joint involvement in similar tasks, whereas management means a separation of operative and managerial tasks. Such findings can be summarized through the final hypothesis:

3 The greater the human resources and career differences between line management and the experts, the greater also are the differences between line management and specialist functions.

Such differences between societies are recreated, even in the midst of technical and economic change. In all the three countries, in the period after about 1977, computer numerically controlled (CNC) machine tools were introduced in factories on an increasing scale. This made it easier to combine automation with productive flexibility, and to let shop-floor workers share in work planning and programming tasks, than under previous forms of automated metal-cutting. Yet the precise impact of such new machines depended less on the potential of the technology itself and more on the continuation of previously existing characteristics on the various dimensions. German companies accordingly exploited the potential for 'shop-floor programming' of machine-tools more purposefully than British companies (Sorge and Warner, 1986), and French companies continued earlier patterns of hierarchically more differentiated human resource generation, work organization and internal labour markets (Maurice *et al.*, 1986). This happens because of the type of non-identical reproduction of actor–systems constellations that was put forward. There are changes, to be sure. French companies went over to a policy of recruiting and training a higher calibre of metal worker, but in addition to less-trained workers, and this boiled down to a maintenance of the received hierarchical differentiation patterns. Similarly, British companies invested more in the skilling of direct production workers, but this went more into more restricted 'company skills', rather than the broader apprenticeship skills which are linked to maintenance of craftsman status.

The relevance of the societal effect approach in the midst of dynamic change is also illustrated by the differential evolution of the French and the German machine-tools industries. Actor systems constellations prepared the German industry better for developing and manufacturing universal, flexible CNC machines and control systems, giving them a better position in the machine-tool market and leading to a better outcome in terms of market share and employment. The French machine-tool industry entered a severe crisis and shed employment on a larger scale, after a series of redundancies, bankruptcies and take-overs by competitors from abroad. Interestingly, the French manufacturers that survived or did better were those which produced more single-purpose CNC machines. The French industry had previously featured more manufacturers of single-purpose machines already, whereas the German industry had previously been stronger in universal machines.

Therefore, a successful outcome in each country was marked by different types of success: In Germany, there was success through the manufacturing of universal machines, but in France through the manufacturing of single-purpose machines of a more specialized kind. And this was valid both before and after the introduction of CNC as a major metal-cutting innovation.

All this attests to the reproduction of societal patterns, even where an oncoming innovation is basically similar, and although a great deal of technical, industry structure, human resource and organization changes are in evidence. The simple fact is that such changes are not the same in every society, even when we are dealing with technical changes. Rather than simply being confronted with technical changes, societies 'breed' specific sets of technical challenges and solutions. In this way, technology becomes a factor which is endogenous to society, rather than a supposedly exogenous or independent variable.

Another interesting case of the working of the societal effect in a dynamic perspective is represented by a Franco-Japanese comparison of machine-tool makers and users. In the French case, the linking of electronic controls with mechanical equipment and processes was slower and more precarious, in view of the practice of separating jobs, functions, competences and industries, and the more inferior status of the machine-tools industry in many respects. In contrast, the Japanese practice of mixing professional experience of different types, within the internal labour markets of firms and industrial groups, and the absence of status differences between industrial sectors and professional bases, made for a quick move into the 'mechatronic age', a specifically Japanese term to refer to the amalgamation of electronic controls and mechanical production processes (Maurice *et al.*, 1988).

Even if this Franco-Japanese comparison brought forth differences which are similar to the Franco-German comparison in the machine-tool industry, this is not to suggest at all that German and Japanese institutions and practices resemble each other more closely. For instance, the German inter-firm labour market for engineers is well developed, whereas there is no inter-firm labour market for engineers in Japan. Germany has a strongly developed notion of professional specialism, generally valid apprenticeship (training methods, contents, exams and certificates) and practically oriented education, whereas Japan has the opposite on all counts. But on the basis of totally different institutional regimes, Germany and Japan achieve something which turns out to be more difficult in France: to stabilize technical people in technical functions over a longer part of their career, on the basis of reward structures, a common and overlapping basic qualification, the role of continuous learning, and a continuous human resource dimension.

In France, the human resource dimension and the organizational dimension are more segmented, both laterally and hierarchically; career mobility and rewards promote an escape from technical specialism into generalism and management. The Japanese engineer is more of a multi-specialist, the German engineer a specialist who extends his domain into other specialisms, and the French engineer is a potential generalist who tries to escape the specialism in which he initially finds himself. Hence, German enterprises have a propensity to be 'mechatronic' which is not too far from that of the Japanese firms, but on the basis of radically different education, training, labour market, industrial and organizational systems. In contrast, French firms are either electronically or mechanically based, and a forward integration of mechanical firms and professions into electronics is more precarious.

THE SOCIETAL PRODUCTION OF ORGANIZATIONAL DIVERGENCE

All these examples reiterate the point that organizational outcomes are quantitatively and qualitatively different from one society to another. This holds true both for direct outcomes (the nature of precise organizational goals, and the extent and the way in which such goals are achieved), and for indirect outcomes, which are represented by the simple or reflexive reproduction and change of actor–systems constellations. For instance, it is clear that the average French machine-tool manufacturer has become more different from the average German and Japanese competitor after the advent of a basic technology which is the same, and after the development of a market situation which is very international. Manufacturers in different countries have carved out different slices of a global market, with different measures of success. In France, manufacturers of universal flexible machines have died or were taken over; in Japan, makers of universal standard machines have boomed and, in Germany, such makers have maintained their position.

More recently, the importance of societal settings has also been documented for the patterns which specifically apply to research and development departments in the electronics industry. Multi-specialism in Japan appears to favour market and production-oriented applied research and development. Multi-specialism seems to be related to very transient (or non-existing) boundaries between occupational specialisms and knowledge domains, which can be seen to reduce the autonomy of disciplinary basic research.

Conversely, fragmentation of organizations and of careers, and engineering generalism in France, appear to favour a high calibre of basic research and development which is more de-coupled from production implications and marketing concepts. Hence, internationalization of competition and the advent of a similar basic technology may imply that enterprises in different countries develop different strengths and weaknesses, focus on different market segments and localize different functions in different countries.

There is, of course, 'institutional learning', whereby firms in one society try to emulate 'best practice' from another country, within a pervasive 'globalization' trend (Mueller, 1994). But an important countervailing tendency remains strong, which prevents global emulation of best practice leading to the adoption of identical practices and structures. Even when firms and societies do learn from each other internationally, they will usually achieve comparable direct outcomes in ways which are institutionally different. This is illustrated by the contrast in the institutionalized methods employed by the Japanese and German firms to 'mechatronize'. In the Japanese case, the internal labour market and inter-professional job chains are central; in Germany, professionalized multi-specialism and an inter-firm labour market remain important.

What kinds of outcomes firms achieve, and how much success they have in which market segment or activity, is then explained by the society in which they are embedded. The same point was made for the evolution of the automobile industry in the major manufacturing countries. There has been a process of market segmentation; which kinds of manufacturers did well in which kinds of segments is explained by the societal setting in which they were already placed. Of particular importance are, again, the dimensions of organization, human resources, the labour market and industrial structures (Streeck, 1992: chap. 6).

To sum up this particular point, the societal effect approach argues that internationalization and universal technical change lead to different outcomes in each society, within an intensification of the international division of labour. How this division of labour develops we can only explain if we refer to societal characteristics that are relatively stable, even in the midst of change. This change triggers development of societal specificity, rather than bringing about convergence between societies. That is also the clear message which the approach offers to all those who think that European integration will reduce the differences between individual European countries. Such a message suggests that the societal effect approach will continue to be topical and inform new research into cross-national differences. It will be central to an exploration of emerging new sectoral, industrial and functional profiles of different countries.

The approach suggests a likelihood of societies becoming more different in their industrial and activity portfolio, because they are already different in the institutionalized construction of their systems. Internationalization of economic activity and technical innovation, and institutional differentiation of societies are, therefore, two sides of the same coin. But the approach also suggests that, to the extent that societies and firms try to achieve similar direct outcomes, the international learning which takes place precludes direct transfer of institutionalized practice. If direct outcomes are to be similar, the systems and actors needed to achieve them have to be constructed in ways that accommodate the systems and actors that are already there.

Whichever way you turn it, institutional (indirect outcome) and direct outcome convergence are fundamentally incompatible. Either you assimilate institutions cross-nationally, or you assimilate performance with regard to direct outcomes. There is a trade-off between them, and usually, neither option is a very good idea in the real world.

REFERENCES

Crozier, M. and Friedberg, E. (1977) *L'acteur et le système*, Paris: Editions du Seuil.

Giddens, A. (1986) *The Constitution of Society*, Berkeley and Los Angeles, Calif.: University of California Press.

Hofstede, G. (1980) *Culture's Consequences. International Differences in Work-related Values*, Beverly Hills, Calif. and London: Sage.

Ishii, T., Ito, M., Kameyama, N., Lanciano, C., Maurice, M., Nohara, I., Silvestre, J.-J., Yahata, S. and Kudo, T. (1991), 'Innovation: Acteurs et organisations. Les ingénieurs et la dynamique de l'entreprise. Comparaison France-Japon', Tokyo and Aix-en-Provence: Laboratoire d'économie et de sociologie du travail and Japan Institute of Labour, research report.

Lincoln, J. R. and Kalleberg, A. L. (1990) *Culture, Control and Commitment. A Study of Work Organization and Work Attitudes in the United States and Japan*, Cambridge: Cambridge University Press.

Maurice, M., and Sorge, A. (1989) 'Dynamique industrielle et capacité d'innovation de l'industrie de la machine-outil en France et en RFA', Aix-en-Provence: Laboratoire d'économie et de sociologie du travail, document 89-1.

Maurice, M., Sellier, F. and Silvestre, J.-J. (1977) 'La production de la hiérarchie dans l'entreprise. Recherche d'un effet sociétal', Aix-en-Provence: Laboratoire d'économie et de sociologie du travail, research report.

Maurice, M., Sorge, A. and Warner, M. (1980) 'Societal differences in organizing manufacturing units. A comparison of France, West Germany and Great Britain', *Organization Studies* 1: 59–86.

Maurice, M., Sellier, F. and Silvestre, J.-J. (1982) *Politique d'éducation et organisation industrielle en France et en Allemagne. Essai d'analyse sociétale*, Paris: Presses Universitaires de France.

Maurice, M., Eyraud, F., d'Iribarne, A. and Rychener, F. (1986) 'Des entreprises en mutation dans la crise. Apprentissage des technologies flexibles et émergence de nouveaux acteurs', Aix-en-Provence: Laboratoire d'économie et de sociologie du travail, research report.

Maurice, M., Mannari, H., Takeoka, Y. and Inoki, T. (1988) 'Des entreprises françaises et japonaises face à la mécatronique. Acteurs et organisation de la dynamique industrielle', Aix-en-Provence: Laboratoire d'économie et de sociologie du travail, research report.

Mueller, F. (1994) 'Societal effect, organizational effect and globalization', *Organization Studies* 15: 407–28.

Rose, M. (1985) 'Universalism, culturalism and the Aix Group', *European Sociological Review* 1: 65–83.

Sorge, A. and Warner, M. (1986) *Comparative Factory Organization. An Anglo-German Comparison of Management and Manpower in Manufacturing*, Aldershot: Gower.

Streeck, W. (1992) *Social Institutions and Economic Performance. Studies of Industrial Relations in Advanced Capitalist Economies*, London: Sage.

4 The survival of the European holding company

Institutional choice and contingency

Michael Mayer and Richard Whittington

INTRODUCTION

This chapter focuses on a relatively unchanging feature of the European business environment – the industrial holding company. Loosely structured and typically diversified, the holding company is a bit of an oddity. Theoretically, it is economically far inferior to its rival, the classic multi-divisional. The holding company is nearly extinct in the United States, and long-predicted for extinction in Europe. Nevertheless, the holding company survives. One purpose of this chapter is simply to document this curious and neglected form. A second is to address some of the intriguing theoretical challenges posed by the survival of such an apparent anachronism.

The challenges concern both sides of the 'universalist' and 'societal-contingency' divide (Clark and Mueller, 1994). For the 'universalists', the continued vigour of the European holding company flies in the face of claims for the universal superiority of its more coordinated rival, the multi-divisional form. It seems that the multi-divisional's advantages may be more context-specific than once was thought, linked to the local features of the American business system in which it originated. Universalist claims on behalf of the multi-divisional need to be qualified. The relative success of holding company and multi-divisional forms depends on the peculiarities of local institutional environments.

But the pattern of holding company survival across Europe poses some awkward questions for 'societal-contingency' theorists as well. These theorists (Sorge, 1991; Whitley, 1994) have stressed how economic organization varies according to local institutional environments, with effectiveness depending upon fit. The need for effective local 'fit' supposedly determines the predominant form of organization in each environment. The problem for 'societal-contingency' theorists is that patterns of business organization in Europe are simultaneously overlapping and fragmented. In particular, as we shall show later, significant minorities of holding company forms remain in all three of France, Germany and the United Kingdom. What are the features in common that can sustain these holding company forms across quite widely differing national economies and cultures within Europe? Moreover, given that multi-divisional firms now compete widely in Europe, how is it that holding companies are able to coexist with them within the same distinct national economies? National economies in Europe seem both to be more internally diverse and to have more in common than most existing societal-contingency accounts can easily explain.

In explaining the survival of the European holding company, we will propose a 'societal-choice' account that stresses the plurality of means and ends involved in economic organization. We will suggest that institutional environments contain certain kinds of actors – the state, entrepreneurs and families – that may prefer and support holding company forms of organization in defiance of apparent economic rationality. These kinds of actors are more or less active in all advanced economies, and it is due to their presence that holding companies survive in greater or lesser numbers in different national systems. The societal-choice account, then, is one that is sensitive not only to dominant patterns of business organization in particular societies, but also to minority forms that cross-cut national business systems. Such a perspective is particularly appropriate to the complex plurality of European economies.

This chapter begins by introducing the Harvard studies of large European businesses by Channon (1973), Pavan (1976) and Dyas and Thanheiser (1976). Their universalistic claim was that the new diversified multi-divisional form would drive out all alternative forms, especially the holding company, just as it had in America. However, as the following section makes clear, recent surveys of big business in Europe have consistently demonstrated the survival of a significant minority of holding companies. In the next section we examine in detail three of these surviving holding companies, considering them in the light of both societal-contingency and societal-choice approaches. Both approaches have something to add, but none the less we conclude by arguing for greater recognition of the societal-choice approach. Not only can this more pluralistic perspective account better for the existence of minority forms across borders, but, we argue, it provides a much richer appreciation of institutional environments than those perspectives that stress only conformity.

THE HARVARD ACCOUNTS OF STRATEGY AND STRUCTURE IN EUROPE

For Chandler (1962), the emergence of the diversified, multi-divisional form was the final chapter in the evolution of modern American capitalism, superseding the era of single-business functional firms and ramshackle holding companies. Like many theorists of the time (cf. Kerr *et al.*, 1960; Hickson *et al.*, 1974), Chandler drew radically universalist conclusions: all advanced economies were bound to follow the same route as American business, albeit with differing starting points and velocities according to their precise historical circumstances. Britain, for instance, was slow to adopt the multi-divisional form because of its dominance by family owners who were over-attached to loose holding company arrangements (Chandler, 1990). None the less, the overall trend amongst advanced economies seemed clear for Chandler (1982: 17): 'in the post-war years, the governance of European and Japanese groups have [*sic*] become more similar to the American M-form'. There was 'convergence in the type of enterprise and system of capitalism used by all advanced industrial economies for the production and distribution of goods' (Chandler, 1992 [1984]: 156).

The first systematic evidence for this convergence had been the Harvard studies of Channon (1973), Dyas and Thanheiser (1976) and Pavan (1976) of the top 100 firms in each of Britain, France, Germany and Italy. The trend in all four countries over the post-war period seemed ineluctably towards the multi-divisional, with the rival functional and holding company forms gradually ceding ground. At the end of the 1960s, though, Europe still seemed to be behind America, where the multi-divisional penetration had reached 77 per cent, against 70 per cent for Britain, and around 40 per cent for both France and Germany (Rumelt, 1974; Dyas and Thanheiser, 1976). The Harvard researchers accounted for this by the persistence of family ownership in Europe and the lack of effective competition.

To understand the place of the multi-divisional next to older forms such as the functional and holding forms, we need to define our organizational types carefully. The distinction between the functional form and the multi-divisional is easy, the former being highly centralized around key functions, the latter decentralized into business units (see Figure 4.1). More difficult is to distinguish the two more

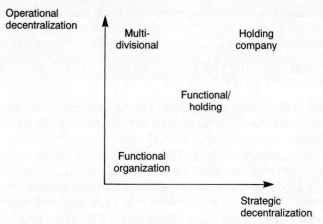

Figure 4.1   Organizational types

decentralized forms, the supposedly anachronistic holding company and the allegedly more efficient multi-divisional.

For Chandler (1962), as for Williamson (1975: 288), the essential characteristic of the multi-divisional was the separation of operating and strategic decisions, with operating matters decentralized to divisions ('quasi-firms', in Williamson's terms). Strategic control over the portfolio as a whole, however, is retained firmly at the centre. By equipping itself with an élite staff and rigorous reporting systems, and by detaching itself from operational responsibilities, the general office of the multi-divisional is supposed to suppress subsidiary management opportunism and to decide strategy and control performance rationally and objectively (Williamson, 1985). The multi-divisional is decentralized operationally, centralized strategically. As is clear from Chandler's very title *The Visible Hand* (1977), Williamson's (1985: 284) conception of the M-form as an internal capital market, and Scott's (1973) insistence on the internalization of market mechanisms, these authors tend to attribute to the multi-divisional form the same frictionless, transparent rationality as is claimed for the invisible hand of the market itself.

The characteristic of the holding company, by contrast, is that the centre's strategic control over subsidiaries is personal, provisional or partial.[1] Although this did not preclude excellence at the operational level, for the original Harvard researchers this lack of objective, systematic central control over subsidiaries was a critical problem. The Harvard researchers' accounts of these European holding companies were, by business school standards of hierarchical rationality, fairly shocking. By contrast with the firm visible hand of the multi-divisional form, in the holding company top management's grip appeared blind, weak, confused or partisan – blind, because lacking either systematic and rigorous financial reporting systems or adequate headquarters staffs to monitor and intervene; weak, because confronted by entrenched, baronial business managers or inhibited by significant external shareholdings at subsidiary level; confused, because unable to rationalize hosts of historically acquired subsidiaries into coherent strategic business units capable of yielding corporate synergies; and finally partisan, because top management is either constituted by favoured cliques or dominated by the business managers themselves, bargaining between their own sectional interests (see particularly Channon, 1973: 98, 105, 138, 168, 177–8, 189, 191, 208; Dyas, 1972: 153–5; Thanheiser, 1972: VII, 48–54). In 1970, between around a quarter and a third of British, French and German top industrial firms were still clinging to this apparently irrational and anachronistic model of organization (Channon, 1973; Dyas and Thanheiser, 1976: see Table 4.1 below).

In the USA, by contrast, Rumelt (1974) found only 2.4 per cent of his sample still had pure holding company structures by 1969. Unless the European holdings changed, it was plain to the Harvard researchers that market forces would soon sweep away these apparently unprofessional anachronisms. Top management in Europe would have to disentangle itself from operations; managerial professionalism should replace patronage and politics; management information should be systematic and comprehensive; clusters of partly owned subsidiaries should be rationalized into coherent divisions. Bruce Scott (1973: 142), who supervised the four Harvard studies, made a direct Darwinian analogy, comparing the arrival of the American multi-divisional in Europe to the introduction of the weasel in New Zealand: in the face of this new import, uncompetitive European forms of organization, such as the holding company, were as doomed to extinction as the kiwi. Here, we think, the Harvard group was too bold.

INSTITUTIONALIST EXPLANATIONS FOR THE EUROPEAN HOLDING COMPANY

Two decades after Scott's dire prediction, the European holding company still seems far from extinct. Table 4.1 compares the proportions of holding companies found in various recent studies of large firms in France, Germany and the United Kingdom. The

Table 4.1 Proportions of holding or functional/holding companies in various studies of large European firms

Study	Year	France	Germany	UK
Channon (1970)	1970			23%
Dyas and Thanheiser (1976)	1970	33%	27%	
Cable and Dirrheimer (1983)	1980		31%	
Hill and Pickering (1986)	1981?			16%
Hill (1988)	1984/5?			16%
Schmitz (1989)	1965–85		13%	
Ezzamel and Watson (1993)	1985/6?			31%
Pugh *et al.* (1993)	1988/90	20%	8%	0%
Geroski and Gregg (1994)	1993			18%

pattern is certainly confused by the widely different definitions, methodologies and samples used in these studies, with some probably less sensitive to holding companies than others. However, it does seem safe to conclude from this table that something looking remarkably like the holding company is still at large in Western Europe.

What explains this incomplete triumph of the weasel-like M-form over the European kiwi? It cannot simply be that the penetration of the multi-divisional is sectorally dependent, as Chandler (1962) himself suggested and others have considered since (Hollingsworth *et al.*, 1991). While this might account for surviving pockets of functionally organized firms, sectoral arguments do not deal with the holding company, which is typically diversified. Sectoral arguments are also strained when the holding company's survival in Europe is contrasted with its virtual disappearance in America (Fligstein, 1990, found only four holding companies amongst the top 100 US industrials in 1980). Some appeal to institutional differences appears inevitable.

As we suggested at the start, institutionalist arguments come in two main varieties. 'Societal-contingency' approaches (Sorge, 1991; Sorge and Warner, 1988; Whitley, 1994) suggest that firms in particular national economies may adopt certain distinctive ways of behaving which, although different from foreign competitors' behaviour, may still be effective because they fit well with features of their local institutional environment (labour markets, financial systems and so on). As in traditional contingency theory, effectiveness depends on fit with critical contingencies, but here country contingencies may override more universalistic industry or technological factors. The result is that the dominant patterns of business organization may vary widely from country to country, 'business system' to 'business system' (Whitley, 1991). Within a particular business system, however, there may be strict limits on internal deviance (Whitley, 1992).

A different view – which we might call a 'societal-choice' one – is one which again emphasizes local institutional features, but which also allows for more pluralistic motives and outcomes within a particular country or system. In this 'societal-choice' view, institutional environments contain actors with other sources of power and rationality than those simply of competitive capitalism. These actors might include the state (Hollingsworth and Streek, 1994), families (Granovetter, 1994) or even banks (Palmer *et al.*, 1987). In many societies, these actors may be powerful enough to choose and support for their own reasons uneconomic enterprise behaviour over long periods of time (Granovetter, 1992; Whittington, 1992). It is according to the local balance of powers and policies amongst these actors that particular countries will be characterized by distinctive long-run mixes of enterprise behaviour.

In analysing the three cases that follow, we shall make use of both societal-contingency and societal-choice perspectives. The importance of the societal-contingency perspective is that it has drawn attention to influential institutional difference between countries. Whitley's (1991, 1994) insight into different financial, ownership and managerial systems within Western economies is one that we shall particularly exploit. None the less, the problem of the surviving European holding company is not an easy one for societal-contingency theorists to grasp. Their interest is in explaining how dominant patterns of business organization vary from country to country. Here, though, we are concerned with a tenacious minority of holding companies surviving in a range of countries. Indeed, the cases we shall examine come from two countries – France and Germany – which societal-contingency theorists have specifically juxtaposed.[2]

Thus the problem of the European holding company seems to require a more pluralistic explanation than that provided by societal-contingency theory (cf. Räsänen and Whipp, 1992). In France, Germany and the United Kingdom, there still survives a significant number of holding companies, all apparently capable of coexisting with the common dominant form, the multi-divisional. It seems that particular institutional factors may support, to a greater or lesser extent, a minority of holding companies in a range of advanced economies. As minorities in such diverse economies, it is unlikely that those holdings simply represent effective fits with national business system requirements.

It is here that a societal-choice approach, pluralistic in ends as well as means, can help. While societal-contingency theorists have emphasized the different means by which institutional environments may facilitate a distinctive form of behaviour, ends are assumed to be the same: their bottom-line still remain effectiveness. By contrast, the societal-choice approach recognizes not just the diversity of institutional resources, but also the plurality of rules that might guide and inspire enterprise behaviour (Whittington, 1992). Powerful actors – entrepreneurs, families, states – may choose strategies and organizational arrangements that suit their own purposes, even at the cost of economic effectiveness. In this societal-choice account, the holding company survives according to the powers and objectives of diverse local actors within a particular society.

The following sections, therefore, will explain the survival of the European holding company in the terms of both societal-contingency and societal-choice theories. This dual perspective extends the explanation to include economically ineffective as well as effective local economic behaviour. The next section introduces certain institutional features in common between France and Germany, but distinctive from the United States, and considers how these institutional features relate in detail to three particular holding company cases.

INSTITUTIONAL ENVIRONMENTS AND BUSINESS ORGANIZATION

Institutional environments are critical to the development and priority of particular forms of business organization. Other commentators have demonstrated already how the American multi-divisional was originally the product of a specific legal regime that suppressed cartel behaviour and gave growth and profit-orientated managements little alternative but to pursue diversification and internal efficiency through multi-divisionalization (Fligstein, 1990; Hollingsworth, 1991). In this account of the surviving European holding company, however, we shall lay the emphasis on institutionalized differences in financial systems.

Continental Europe differs significantly from the United States in the structure of its financial markets and corporate ownership and control (Scott, 1991; Albert, 1991). The first obvious difference is the relative importance and activism of the state in the ownership and control of business enterprise. The United States is, of course, a 'free-enterprise' society, in which public enterprise accounts for only 1 per cent of all value-added, employment and gross capital formation (US Survey of Current Business). By contrast, in France – a traditionally *dirigiste* economy – the state accounts for 18 per cent of business activity, while even in Germany this proportion is 11 per cent (CEEP, 1993). In other words, the state remains a powerful actor in these two European economies, with direct control over the choices of a significant minority of firms.

But even within the private sectors, American and European systems differ markedly. The United States has long possessed large and effective stock-markets. Because shares are easily tradable, ownership tends to be fairly diffuse (Demsetz and Lehn, 1988; Fligstein and Brantley, 1992) and firms are strictly disciplined by the market for corporate control (Jensen and Ruback, 1983). The result has been the emergence of the modern professionally managed enterprise, where ownership is separate from managerial control. Berle and Means (1967) found that by as early as 1930, in nearly 90 per cent of the top 200 American enterprises, no individual or group owned all or even a majority of the shares, and that in around half this population, owners had ceased to be involved in management. Chandler (1990) likewise emphasizes how the great managers of the period – Sarnoff of RCA, Watson of IBM and Walter Chrysler of Chrysler – had tiny stakes in the companies they ran. More recent data suggest a continued separation of ownership and control, with the largest five shareholders controlling less than 20 per cent of the stock in just under half of Demsetz and Lehn's (1988) sample of large US firms, and entrepreneurs representing less than 5 per cent of corporate presidents in Fligstein's (1990) group. In the United States, then, management is thoroughly professional, free of substantial family ownership interests and always conscious of the penalties for underperformance. As Chandler's (1990) account emphasizes, these professional managers should be ready and able to undertake the substantial corporate rationalizations necessary for transition to the multi-divisional form.

In Continental Europe, however, financial systems are very different. Stock-markets are less efficient and ownership and control are still closely connected (Scott, 1991). In Germany, Ziegler (1984) estimated that 37 per cent of the 259 largest firms in the late 1970s were still privately owned and controlled, with a further 21 per cent state-owned. At the end of the 1980s in France, 28 per cent of the top 180 industrial and commercial corporations were under 'active' family control, with a further 16 per cent under 'passive' family control and 13 per cent under state ownership (Leser and Vidalie, 1991). According to Bauer and Bertin-Mourot's (1992) analysis of the top 200 firms in each of France and Germany, 34 per cent of French chairmen/chief executives, and 27 per cent of German, had significant ownership connections, either as founders of their firms or as members of shareholding families.

Thus Continental Europe is still quite remote from the conditions in which the original multi-divisional was born. Of course, as the societal-contingency theorists would point out, the French and German environments do differ between themselves in certain important respects – for instance in state centralization and the role of the banks (Lane, 1992; Sorge, 1993). However, the essential point here is that both countries remain characterized by a significant minority of powerful actors – entrepreneurs, families and the state – whose direct influence on economic enterprise has hardly any equivalence in the United States. These actors are likely to have substantially different motives and resources to those of American professional managers. State- or privately controlled firms are under significantly less external pressure to adopt efficiency-maximizing internal organization than professionally managed US corporations, always under fear of sanction by the market for corporate control. They may of course have different interests – state enterprises in the area for industrial policy, private enterprises in continued autonomy and steady dividends. Just as were the personally controlled firms of prewar Britain (Chandler, 1990), therefore, these state or privately controlled firms may both choose and sustain economically sub-optimal holding company structures for long periods of time. Exactly how powerful shareholders actually do choose to organize will be explored in the three French and German case-studies that follow.

HOLDING COMPANIES IN CONTEMPORARY EUROPE

This section draws upon early findings of a study intended to update the original studies of Channon (1973), Dyas (1972) and Thanheiser (1972) by examining the strategies and structures of large British, French and German industrial corporations. By working with similar samples and the same methods and concepts, we aim to develop measures of corporate diversification and organization structure amongst modern-day large European businesses exactly consistent with those of the original studies. The end result should be a continuous picture of trends in strategy and structure in the three countries between 1950, the starting date of the Harvard research, and today. We should thus be able to tell the extent either to which Western Europe has converged on any single organizational form – for example the multi-divisional – or to which countries have been able to cling on to characteristically national patterns of strategy and structure over this long post-war period.

Here we are not able to present systematic statistical comparisons of strategy and structure in the three countries. At the time of writing, the work in the United Kingdom had only just started. What we do have, however, is a wide range of mini-cases drawn from interviews and documentary sources on the strategies and structures of large French and German companies. These provide abundant materials with which to explore holding company structures as they exist in Europe today.

We have seen that there are effectively two kinds of institutionalist explanation for the survival of the holding company in Continental Europe. The 'societal-contingency' approach would propose the holding company as an effective adaptation to local conditions. 'Societal-choice' theorists, on the other hand, would emphasize how powerful actors might prefer to retain a holding company style of management for their own reasons, even at some cost to economic effectiveness. This section, therefore, will take three companies, examining them in some detail both to demonstrate how these supposed anachronisms still work and to consider the theoretical reasons for their survival. All three companies are large industrials, active in a wide variety of sectors and competing in international markets. As Table 4.1 earlier demonstrated, these three cases are far from unique.

The Financière Agache group is a contemporary French holding company apparently fitting the 'societal-contingency' approach. As the inset indicates, the group is a long way from the internally transparent, rational and hierarchical order of the multi-divisional. The head office is too small to impose policy from above, and its oversight is complicated by the independence of its main subsidiary's financial systems. The group Président-Directeur Général,[3] Bernard Arnault, has not removed himself to the lofty level of strategy, but is actively involved at various subsidiary levels (Dior and LVMH). There are substantial external ownership stakes, potentially capable of blocking significant strategic moves, and family owner-managers remain important. Related activities are only slowly being integrated into the coherent divisions called for by theory.

Financière Agache

Financière Agache is the highest-level managerial unit in a cascade of financial holdings and subholdings that include such famous names as Christian Dior, Bon Marché and the various components of the LVMH group (including Louis Vuitton, Givenchy, Christian Lacroix, Moët et Chandon and Hennessy). The group as a whole had a consolidated turnover in 1993 of FF27,000m. (60 per cent overseas), making it the thirty-third largest industrial company in France.

One level higher than Financière Agache is the personal holding company of Bernard Arnault, the creator of the group by a series of daring acquisitions during the 1980s. However, at no level does Arnault hold complete ownership: indeed LVMH, which accounts for 80 per cent of employees, is only 46 per cent owned by a subholding far removed from Arnault's own ultimate holding (see Figure 4.2). Arnault himself has depended on minority shareholders at various levels for the capital to support his newly constructed empire – most notably Guinness, Worms and Crédit Lyonnais.

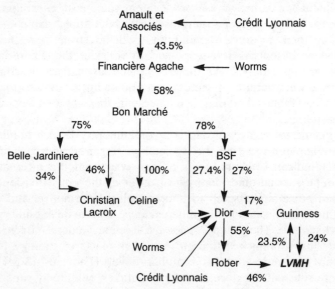

Figure 4.2   Financière Agache

Source: *Challenges*, December 1991

Although highly successful, managerial practice within the Financière Agache group departs somewhat from the multi-divisional ideal. The company describes itself as 'a federation of small and medium-sized enterprises'. At the Financière Agache level, there is a Direction des Ressources Humaines, which oversees personnel policy, especially regarding management development, for the group as a whole. Otherwise, there is little standardization imposed from this level. LVMH operates separate financial reporting and treasury functions from those of the rest of the group, in no sense depending on Financière Agache. Within LVMH itself, clusters of subsidiaries are only gradually being coordinated – the seven main champagne brands not coming under a common managing director until 1994 – with members of the original owning families still prominent in management positions and retaining considerable shareholder rights. For example, in 1994, Arnault brought the perfume company Guerlain into the group, but left the owning family with a slight majority in the new subsidiary, with management control and with a 12 per cent share of the Christian Dior subholding. Subsidiaries owned at various levels are integrated only partially into coherent divisions: thus on the couture side, Celine and Christian Dior remained outside LVMH's couture operations, Christian Lacroix only being transferred in 1993.

Control and coordination are typically direct and informal, largely ensured by Bernard Arnault himself. Arnault is chief executive not only of his ultimate personal financial holding company (Arnault et Associés), but also of Christian Dior and LVMH. All subsidiary chief executives are brought together for bi-monthly meetings of the Comité d'Information et Renseignements Généraux, presided by Arnault himself. Also, every two months, there are meetings by 'secteur' (not divisions), again presided over by Arnault personally. Arnault is not supported by a large head-office staff at group level (Financière Agache has 30 people; above this he operates a small personal 'cabinet'). In principle, synergies are negotiated voluntarily between subsidiaries, according to the opportunities that come to the attention of either Arnault or subsidiary presidents at any of their formal or informal interactions.

Principal sources: interviews; Kerdellant, 1992; Servan-Schreiber, 1990; *Figaro*, 21 October 1991: 3–8; *Challenges*, December, 1991, 30–1; July–August 1994: 32–7.

Financière Agache's management has been extraordinarily successful, its entrepreneurial head having built up from scratch a global luxury goods group in the space of a decade. Like several other acquisitive French entrepreneurs during the 1980s, Arnault financed his expansion not simply by appealing to the stock-market, but by sharing ownership with sympathetic external allies brought in at various levels (Crédit Lyonnais, Worms, Guinness). The result is an empire over which his allies allow him day-to-day control, at a price considerably cheaper than complete ownership at each level would have required.

It was on exactly this kind of financial engineering that Lévy-Leboyer (1980) blamed the survival of the French holding company for so long. However, within the French context, the practice is not necessarily ineffective. In the absence of well-developed financial markets, the holding company serves a capital-raising function, as well as the capital-allocating function stressed in the multi-divisional. Cascades of holdings and subholdings, each bringing in external minority shareholders, can play an important role in raising capital without losing substantial control (Couret and Martin, 1991). This diffuse pattern of ownership may have considerable overall economic benefits: what might be lost in terms of complete hierarchical control in such holdings may be compensated for by the additional scope for the vigour and rationalizing drive of dynamic but capital-short entrepreneurs. The complex ownership of Financière Agache, far from being the simple encumbrance that theorists of the multi-divisional might expect, in fact gave Bernard Arnault the means necessary to achieving his strategy. From a 'societal-contingency' point of view, Financière Agache may represent an effective adaptation to the constraints of local financial systems.

Röchling, on the other hand, corresponds better to a 'societal-choice' view. This German family-controlled conglomerate is similar to Financière Agache in having a small headquarters, independent financial systems, partial ownerships and growth by acquisition (see inset). In these respects, it has all the characteristics of a typical holding company. However, here the divided ownership structure imposes clear barriers to efficiency, and it is not evident that the company is achieving any compensating rationalization of German industry. The Röchling family's concern not to dilute its control has blocked the merger of related businesses from the GmbH. The group appears prepared to accept this handicap, despite its relative exposure to overseas competition. In this case, family interests have enforced a choice of organization that overrides concerns for overt economic effectiveness.

Röchling

The Röchling group is Germany's forty-seventh largest industrial company, with a turnover in 1993 of 5,859m. Marks,
around a third earned overseas. The group has a long history,
starting in the steel industry in 1881 and close to first the
Kaiser and then Hitler in successive world wars. During
the 1950s, President Adenauer encouraged it to take control
of the major armaments manufacturer, Rheinmetall Berlin AG.
Since the 1980s, the company has exited steel and acquired an
array of subsidiaries, stretching from defence to communi-
cations, measuring equipment and plastics.

The group is in fact made up of two main entities. The Gebr.
Röchling KG (*Kommanditgesellschaft*, a limited partnership) is
an exclusively family concern, made up of around 150 Röchling
family members. Next to this there is also the Röchling Industrie Verwaltung, a GmbH (limited liability company), in which
outside shareholders own about half of the capital but have
no voting rights. Each of the two companies owns its own set
of subsidiaries, though the two share top management. The
majority of subsidiaries are securely owned, the most important exception being the Rheinmetall defence company which
is only owned $66\frac{1}{2}$ per cent. Rheinmetall represents roughly
60 per cent of the size of the group as a whole, and itself
controls a further group of subsidiaries, several of which are
themselves only partly owned.

Subsidiaries have always been allowed a great deal of
autonomy. The head office is only 35 strong, with four *Prokur-
isten* responsible for corporate law, contract law and property,
technology and technical education, and finance and personnel.
Strategic intervention by the centre is reported to be 'sehr,
sehr minimal'. Reporting and accounting systems are not standardized or integrated in any way. Subsidiaries are 'managed'
principally by influencing senior management appointments:
'wir führen über Personen'.

Röchling's subsidiaries are not fully integrated into divisions,
branches effectively being collections of businesses for presentation purposes. There are no divisional offices. Rationalization
of overlapping groups is impeded not only by the light managerial hand, but by the complexities of the ownership structure.
Thus the rationalization of two subsidiaries serving the same

automobile industry customers has been stymied by ownership of one by the KG and the other by the GmbH. No solution to this divided internal ownership has yet been found.

Principal sources: interview; *Handelsblatt*, 16 June 1994: 12 and 18 June 1993: 19; *Die Welt*, 16 June 1994: 14; Gierke, 1994.

The French oil giant Elf-Aquitaine before privatization illustrates a different set of social priorities. Here separation into coherent divisions and a substantial headquarters was not enough to ensure smooth multi-divisional operation (see inset). Long-established divisional heads, family managers, partial ownerships and independent financial systems all constrained the group's capacity to impose overall strategic control from the centre. In practice, Elf behaved like a holding company. If not economically optimal according to theory, this loose organizational structure was sustainable because of its fitting political objectives. Under state ownership, the company was to some extent conceived of as an instrument of industrial policy, closely connected to the interests of the Mitterand presidency. At the beginning of the 1980s, the independent Atochem branch had been at the centre of the socialists' restructuring of the French chemical industry, while a decade later the investment policy of Le Floch Prigent – known as 'Pink Floch' – served to create a set of interlocking shareholdings, securing crucial parts of French industry from hostile takeover. The stake in the textile company Biderman was taken to help rescue a major employer and the largest French company in the sector. The absence of any significant industrial logic behind these participations was confirmed by the reversal of the investment strategy by privatization. Up until that point, though, the French state appeared to prefer the flexibility of Elf's holding company style to the constraints of multi-divisional centralization.

The cases of Elf and Röchling, therefore, illustrate a 'societal-choice' interpretation of organizational strategies and structures. These two companies were as they were precisely because powerful actors – the family or the state – wanted them that way and, moreover, could afford to keep them that way. Over long periods of time, they have chosen to sacrifice some degree of economic effectiveness in favour of their own interests.

Financière Agache, on the other hand, appears to correspond more to the 'societal-contingency' view, according to which the group's complex structures were in fact effective responses to local capital market failures.

Elf Aquitaine

Elf is the largest company in France, and until 1994 was majority-owned by the French state. At the point of privatization, it had three main businesses – hydrocarbons, chemicals and health – each organized as *branches*. This structure was established by Le Floch Prigent, the new group Président-Directeur Général arriving in 1989, and was designed to promote more coordination of the previously autonomous exploration-production and refinery-distribution branches. Le Floch Prigent also cut the size of his executive board in half by ending the dual representation of each *branche*, thus reducing the voice of the operating businesses at this corporate level. The centre was supported by 600 headquarters staff, including a substantial planning group.

On the face of it, therefore, Le Floch Prigent presided over a fairly conventional multi-divisional structure, one which he has shown he could rearrange. In fact, however, the businesses still retained a great deal of autonomy, especially the African operations (overseas turnover accounted for 40 per cent of the total), chemicals (Atochem) and health (Sanofi). To take the example of Sanofi, the *branche* was actually an independently quoted company, of which Elf owned a proportion fluctuating around 50 to 60 per cent. Its chief executive, Dehecq, was the founding MD in 1973, and has seen three group heads come and go over the lifetime of his power. He has his own personal team of managers surrounding him, and there are very few managerial transfers between Sanofi and the parent. Dehecq was just one of three entrenched *branche* heads that Le Floch Prigent left in place when parachuted into Elf in 1989. A graduate of a minor provincial engineering school, Le Floch Prigent was very much an outsider amongst a top management team dominated by graduates of the élite Polytechnique and Ecole des Mines schools, most of whom had known each other since starting in the company at the original Lacq oilfield.

Powerful as *branche* heads might be, they themselves did not necessarily have complete control over their subsidiaries. Within Sanofi's own beauty division, there were a string of partial ownerships and independent managements: at Yves Rocher, voting control still rested with the family and Didier

Rocher, son of the founder, was chief executive; at Nina Ricci, where Elf held 55 per cent of shares, the company was still run by the son-in-law of Robert Ricci; at YSL, taken over in 1993, the previous owner and Yves Saint-Laurent himself were guaranteed continued managerial control of the 'couture' side of the business. In 1994, the chief executive of the beauty division as a whole resigned in protest against the final success of the centre in imposing a common accounting system on the diverse subsidiaries.

Le Floch-Prigent exercised a vigorous and personal investment policy outside the ambit of his executive board. By 1993, he had acquired around 400 holdings, representing about 8 per cent of the company's total assets. These holdings included significant stakes in such unrelated companies as Suez and Générale des Eaux. Often these acquisitions appeared motivated by political or friendship reasons, as in the case of the FF800m. invested in failing textile group Biderman. After the departure of Le Floch Prigent, the new chief executive declared that this investment policy would be reviewed, with the intent of disposing all non-strategic holdings.

Principal sources: interview, *Figaro*, 21 February 1994: 3–6; *Les Echos*, 7 March 1994: 15 and 18 October 1993: 9; *L'Expansion*, 7/20 October 1994: 10–11, 112–16.

The point of the three cases is not, of course, to adjudicate between theories – 'societal-choice' scoring two, 'societal-contingency' one. The cases are intended to give some depth to the persistent survey finding that the holding company still survives in Europe. Together they show just how distant from the Harvard ideal many contemporary European organizations remain, and help to illuminate some of the reasons why that might be. In large part, the reasons are institutional. European capital markets and ownership structures have not yet converged with those of the United States. The market for corporate control does not exercise the same discipline for maximum financial returns that it may in America, and the rules and resources by which owners act are far from simply capitalistic. So long as these institutional differences remain, there will be a role for the holding company in Europe.

CONCLUSIONS

The European holding company has proved to be far more robust than the Harvard group originally expected. Competitive market forces have not forced complete convergence on the universalistic ideal, the multi-divisional. According to the surveys, the holding company survives to a much greater extent in Europe than in the United States. The cases have shown how downright peculiar some of these surviving holding companies can be.

The survival of the holding company in Europe and the relative failure of the multi-divisional support an institutional rather than universalist approach to economic organization. But now the question is: what type of institutional approach? The various types of societal-contingency perspective associated with Sorge (1991) and Whitley (1994) offer only partial explanation for the holding company's survival. These theorists have persuasively countered the universalists by highlighting the importance of institutional factors, such as different financial systems, in explaining distinctive patterns of organization within particular business systems. By and large, though, the holding company slips below their threshold, marginalized by a concern simply for dominant and effective national patterns of organization. The holding company is a minority; it is not unique to any particular country and may be rather ineffective financially. None the less, it remains.

It is unnecessarily restrictive to confine institutionalist analysis to the dominant and effective patterns of organization in particular business systems. The case of the European holding company suggests the potential of a societal-choice perspective that can accommodate the deviant and the ineffective. Being alive to all the kinds of power and motive at work in a society, a societal-choice perspective is sensitive to different mixes of economy activity within a particular national system. If Europe does show some degree of convergence on a particular form of organization, the multi-divisional, then the index of difference at this level is not so much variety in dominant forms of organization, but distinctive mixtures – more or less multi-divisional, more or less holding companies. It is a pluralistic perspective concerned, with deviation rather than conformity, that can most fully capture the different degrees of national resistance to international trends.

Moreover, a societal-choice approach can capture more comprehensively all the richly idiosyncratic behaviour that institutionalist and comparative research into business enterprise is beginning to turn up. The societal-contingency theorists impose an unduly narrow appreciation of institutional environments by focusing only on those elements with which local business has achieved effective fit. It is important to assert, contrary to much social theory of twenty or thirty years ago, that advanced industrialized societies do differ between themselves in effective economic behaviour, but it is a pity to hide from view those organizations which cling to their own ways for their own reasons. The case of the European holding company reminds us that economies contain actors – the state, entrepreneurs, families – which are willing and able to resist the simple dictates of economic efficiency for long periods of time. Enterprise is motivated by plural rules, enabled by plural resources (Whittington, 1993).

The great promise of comparative research, therefore, is to illuminate the variety of institutional factors important for all kinds of economic activity, not just those contributing to economic effectiveness. Often, these institutional factors may be like submarine mountain ranges that rise above the surface only at certain points, but which none the less continue across and beneath other territorial waters. For the social scientist concerned chiefly with dominant patterns, only the peaks will be visible; but for economic actors immersed in the complex reality, even submerged institutions will have consequence, as reefs or as anchorage points. A pluralistic approach will capture more of the richness of institutional environments, as well as getting closer to the real complexities of change and choice that face the managers engaged in them.

NOTES

1 It is important to note that the type of holding company with which we are concerned is distinct from that of purely financial or portfolio holding companies such as Suez or the Société Générale de Belgique (see Daems, 1978; van Iterson, 1994). The Harvard notion implies some sort of management structure, however weak (Dyas, 1972: 86). The functional/holding form mixes a functional organization around a core business with a periphery of relatively unintegrated subsidiaries (Channon, 1973: 15).

2 Whitley (1994) describes France as a 'state-coordinated' system, Germany as a 'collaborative' system; Sorge (1991) characterizes French business organization as highly segmented hierarchically and laterally, Germany as much less so.

3 The Président-Directeur Général (PDG) in France is the rough equivalent of a British executive chairman.

REFERENCES

Albert, M. (1991) *Capitalisme contra Capitalisme*, Paris: Editions de Seuil.
Bauer, M. and Bertin-Mourot, B. (1992) *Les 200 en France et Allemagne*, Paris: Hiedrich and Struggles.
Berle, A. and Means, G. (1967) *The Modern Corporation and Private Property*, New York: Harvester.
Cable, J. and Dirrheimer, M. J. (1983) 'Hierarchies and markets: an empirical test of the multidivisional hypothesis in Germany', *International Journal of Industrial Organization* 1: 43–62.
CEEP (1993) *L'Enterprise publique dans la Communauté Européenne*, Brussels: Annales CEEP.
Chandler, A. D. (1962) *Strategy and Structure: Chapters in the History of American Enterprise*, Cambridge, Mass.: MIT Press.
—— (1977) *The Visible Hand: the Managerial Revolution in American Business*, Cambridge, Mass.: Harvard University Press.
—— (1982) 'The M-Form: Industrial Groups, American Style', *European Economic Review*, 19, 3–23.
—— (1990) *Scale and Scope: the Dynamics of Industrial Capitalism*, Cambridge, Mass.: Harvard University Press.
—— (1992 [1984]) 'The emergence of managerial capitalism', in M. Granovetter and R. Swedberg (eds) *The Sociology of Economic Life*, Boulder, Colo.: Westview Press.
Channon, D. (1973) *The Strategy and Structure of British Enterprise*, Cambridge, Mass.: Harvard University Press.
Clark, P. A. and Mueller, F. (1994) 'Organisations and Nations: From Universalism to Institutionalism?', Research Paper Series 9404, University of Aston Business School.
Couret, A. and Martin, D. (1991) *Les Sociétés Holdings*, Paris: Presses Universitaires de France.
Daems, H. (1978) *The Holding Company and Corporate Control*, Leiden: Martinus Nijhof.
Demsetz, H and Lehm, K. (1988) 'The structure of corporate ownership: causes and consequences', in H. Demsetz (ed.) *Ownership, Control and the Firm*, Oxford: Blackwell.
Dyas, G. P. (1972) 'The strategy and structure of French enterprise', unpublished dissertation, Harvard Business School.
—— and Thanheiser, H. (1976) *The Emerging European Enterprise*, London: Macmillan.
Ezzamel, M. and Watson, R. (1993) 'Organizational form, ownership structure and corporate performance: a contextual analysis of UK companies', *British Journal of Management* 4: 161–76.
Fligstein, N. (1990) *The Transformation of Corporate Control*, Cambridge, Mass.: Harvard University Press.
—— and Brantley, P. (1992) 'Bank control, owner control or organizational dynamics: who controls the large corporation', *American Journal of Sociology* 98(2): 280–307.
Geroski, P. and Gregg, P. (1994) 'Corporate restructuring in the UK during the recession', *Business Strategy Review*, 5(2): 1–19.

Granovetter, M. (1992) 'Economic institutions as social constructions: a framework for analysis, *Acta Sociologica* 35: 3–11.

—— (1994) 'Business groups ' in N. Smelser and R. Swedberg (eds) *Handbook of Economic Sociology*, New York: Sage.

Hickson, D., Hinings, C., MacMillan, C. and Schwitter, J. (1974) 'The culture-free context of organizational structure: a tri-national comparison', *Sociology* 8: 59–80.

Hill, C. (1988) 'Corporate control type, size and financial performance', *Journal of Management Studies* 25(5): 403–17.

—— and Pickering, J. (1986) 'Divisionalisation, decentralisation and performance in large UK companies', *Journal of Management Studies* 23(1): 26–49.

Hollingsworth, J. R. (1991) 'The logic of coordinating American manufacturing sectors', in J. L. Campbell, J. R. Holingsworth and L. N. Lindberg (eds) *The Governance of the American Economy*, Cambridge: Cambridge University Press.

—— and Streek, W. (1994) 'Concluding remarks on performance, competitiveness and convergence', in J. R. Hollingsworth, P. Schmitter and W. Streek (eds) *Governing Capitalist Economies*, Oxford: Oxford University Press.

Jensen, M. C. and Ruback, R. (1983) 'The market for corporate control: the scientific evidence', *Journal of Financial Economics* 11: 5–50.

Kerdellant, C. (1992) *Les Nouveaux Condottières*, Paris: Calman-Levy.

Kerr, C., Dunlop, J. T., Harbison, F. and Myers, C. E. (1960) *Industrialism and Industrial Man*, Cambridge, Mass.: Harvard University Press.

Lane, K. (1992) 'European Business Systems: Britain and Germany compared', in R. Whitley (ed.) *European Business Systems*, London: Sage.

Leser, E. and Vidalie, A. (1991) 'Le capital des 200 premières entreprises francaises', *Science et Vie Economique* 76 (October): 46–57.

Lévy-Leboyer, M. (1980) 'The large corporation in France', in A. D. Chandler and H. Daems (eds) *Managerial Hierarchies*, Cambridge, Mass.: Harvard University Press.

Liedtke, R. (1994) *Wem Gehört die Republike?*, Frankfurt-am-Main: Eichborn.

Morin, F. and Dupuy, C. (1993) *Le Coeur Financier Européen*, Paris: Economica.

Palmer, D., Friedland, R., Devereux Jennings, P. and Powers, M. E. (1987) 'The economics and politics of structure: the multidivisional form and the large US corporation', *Administrative Science Quarterly* 32: 25–48.

Pavan, R. J. (1976) 'Strategy and structure: the Italian experience', *Journal of Economics and Business* 28: 254–60.

Pugh, D., Clark, T. and Mallory, G. (1993) 'Organization structure and structural change in European manufacturing organizations: a preliminary report on a comparative study', Seventh British Academy of Management Conference, Milton Keynes, September.

Rumelt, R. (1974) *Strategy, Structure and Economic Performance*, Cambridge, Mass.: Harvard Business School Press.

Schmitz, R. (1989) 'Zur Erfolgsrelevance der internen Organisation börsennotierter Industrieaktiengesellschaften', in Albach, H. (ed.) *Organisation*, Wiesbaden: Gubler.

Scott, B. (1973) 'The new industrial state: old myths and new realities', *Harvard Business Review* March–April: 133–48.

Scott, J. (1991) 'Networks of corporate power: a comparative assessment', *Annual Review of Sociology* 17: 181–203.

Servan-Schreiber, P. (1990) 'Bernard Arnault: le prince de l'avenue Montaigne', in J.-L. Schreiber (ed.) *Le Métier de Patron*, Paris: Livre de Poche.

Sorge, A. (1991) 'Strategic fit and the societal effect: interpreting cross-national comparisons of technology, organization and human resources', *Organization Studies* 12(2): 161–90.

Sorge, A. and Warner, M. (1986) *Comparative Factory Organization: An Anglo-German Comparison of Management and Manpower in Manufacturing*, Aldershot: Gower.

Thanheiser, G. (1972) 'The strategy and structure of German enterprise', unpublished doctoral dissertation, Harvard Business School.

van Iterson, A. (1994) 'Holding companies, family-owned SMEs and the anchorage debate', paper presented to the EMOT workshop, Berlin, April.

Whitley, R. (1991) 'The Social construction of business systems in East Asia', *Organization Studies* 12(1): 47–54.

—— (1992) 'The comparative study of business systems in Europe: issues and choices', in R. Whitley (ed.) *European Business Systems: Firms and Markets in their National Contexts*, London: Sage.

—— (1994) 'Dominant forms of economic organization in market economies', *Organization Studies* 15(2): 153–82.

Whittington, R. (1992) 'Putting Giddens into action: social systems and managerial agency', *Journal of Management Studies* 29(6): 693–712.

—— (1993) *What is Strategy – And Does it Matter?*, London: Routledge.

Williamson, O. E. (1975) *Markets and Hierarchies: Analysis and Anti-Trust Implications*, New York: Free Press.

—— (1985) *The Economic Institutions of Capitalism*, New York: Free Press.

Ziegler, R. (1984) 'Das Netz der Personen- und Kapitalverflechtungen deutscher und Österreichischer Unternehmen', *Kölner Zeitschrift für Soziologie und Sozialpsychologie* 36: 585–614.

Part II

The institutional specificity of firms in Europe

5 Comparing typical firms in Denmark and Finland

The basis of the Danish and Finnish case-studies

Peer Hull Kristensen, Kari Lilja and Risto Tainio

After the Second World War, the social sciences developed a standard method of comparative analysis. Usually it was considered imperative to establish a universal theory and then investigate comparatively to what extent different nations complied with the universally valid concepts of rational social structures. Nations that proved statistically close to the rational structures were considered to be more highly developed, while other nations defined their developmental problems in terms of the gaps which became apparent in this way. Thus some nations discovered that they were not developing mass-production, M-form firm structures, hi-tech sectors or R&D-intensive products to the same extent as other, more fortunate nations.

This comparative approach implicitly assumed that the more advanced nations would show the less fortunate nations which path they must follow, and that the secrets of growth and development could be revealed by universal economic theorizing. Thus each nation was graded by a growing number of international organizations and financial institutions. This type of comparative enquiry still dominates debates, in particular over national industrial policies.

However, a new type of comparative research was established with the work of Maurice *et al.* (1979). In their comparative analysis of similar firms (in terms of sector, size, technology) they found that work organization, managerial role, occupational structure, etc. differed significantly between two nations, France and Germany, which were seen to occupy similar positions on the scales of national economic development. Since then, this type of comparative analysis has become more widespread, as more and more research compares identical firms (in terms of market, number of employees, technology used) across countries, contributing in this way to our awareness of the fact that the social structures underlying the economic institutions of Western countries are highly dissimilar and that the social significance of similar organizational phenomena differs strongly from nation to nation.

The following two essays on Denmark and Finland were written from the convictions provided by the latter type of comparative analysis; however, they also attempt to provide a framework for understanding this type of distinctive pattern of national economic development and in so doing challenge the former type of comparative analysis.

The purpose of the two national analyses is to reveal the distinct logics of economic development inherent in each country. Our purpose is to contribute to a situation in which, instead of talking about developmental problems as they may be defined by theories said to be universally valid, we can begin to understand the specific totality of a nation and within that framework understand the dynamics of evolution and devolution. We find such an approach very promising but are aware of the difficulties involved in carrying out such a project, which will require the attention of scholars for several decades to come. For this reason both essays are seen as hypothetical in their nature, though they both attempt to embrace our best abstracted knowledge of the two countries at this moment.

Whereas the criteria guiding the comparative analyses of the two above-mentioned types of research are very clear, it is not at all clear what we should look for when we want to understand the immanent logics of economic development and organization within a single national economy.

Our approach has been pragmatic, rather than based on eternal scientific principles. Guided by Whitley's (1992a: 9, 1992b) characteristics of business systems, we have discussed Denmark on each dimension on the basis of what the Finnish team knew from Finland, and vice versa. These discussions were both very extensive and very intensive, enabling us to draw up a schematic pattern pairing the two national business systems dimension for dimension. Each of the two teams then worked with these schematic comparisons to establish a coherent modelling of the logic within each of the two systems. This effort makes up the core content of the following two essays.

The basic focus of the research is a 'typical firm' in each of the countries. The theoretical reasons for selecting the 'typical firm' have not yet been fully explicated. Choosing the typical firm as the focal concern, however, is a radical break away from the comparative analysis through matched pairs as chosen by Maurice and his group. This becomes very clear from comparing the Finnish study against the Danish. Here the Finnish vertically integrated, relatedly diversified firm, based on raw materials, is contrasted with the Danish SMEs organized in a fragile, highly interactive and modernized form of a putting-out system.

It is quite clear that a typical firm in our case is not an average firm in a statistical sense. A typical firm in our terminology is rather exceptional. Its typicality is based on the priorities found in the national economy and in the society as a whole. A typical firm has profound multiple effects on the whole economy, and the organizing dynamics of the entire national economic system are highly influenced by this firm-type.

The conceptual image of a typical firm, towards which we are aiming, comes close to the concept of 'real type' formulated by Spiethoff (1953). It differs from the Weberian ideal type in the process by which it is constructed or arrived at. An ideal type is based on abstract dimensions and their interrelated configurations. It is used as a tool for discovering to what extent reality conforms to the ideal type which is based on one-sided exaggerations of certain aspects of the concrete reality. In a real type 'the object of research is a particular aspect or a part of a total situation' (Spiethoff 1953: 459). The conceptual form of the object of research reflects 'the sum total of actually existing uniformities, everything that is essential in relation to a given phenomenon' (ibid.: 447). 'Essential are those phenomena which appear to be causes and conditions of the one under investigation or indicative of those causes and consequences' (ibid.: 446).

The two essays are structured in a similar way. The first section offers an analytical abstraction, i.e. a grounded theory of the nature of the firm, and explores how this firm-type will act strategically towards other firms, how its external and internal ability to control and coordinate resources is established. Our aim in these sections was to achieve a type of modelling by which we could understand the actors involved in the life of the firms from an internal spectator's view: what types of social relations help the actors to perceive the world in such a way that they act so as to reproduce the firms in the typical way?

In the second section of the two essays, we take an external observer's view and specify the social space of the typical firm in its historical, societal and institutional context. The constitutive mechanisms provided by institutions, élite formations, and social groups provide social space to the typical firm, but this social space is only present to the extent that the firm is able to take 'strategic action' to exploit the constitutive forces. In this way the firm fills the social space and reproduces it. This is the way institutions reinforce the specific nature of the typical firm we are talking about, and in this way the firms make the institutions institutions. Many of the constitutive forces in the Danish and Finnish cases derive from the geography and institutions of the pre-industrial society. For instance, in Denmark the formation of capitalist firms is a direct continuation of the guild system, whilst in Finland the 'forest industrialization' had no connection to the guild system but was certainly linked to the country's geography.

In identifying the typical firm in Denmark and Finland we have tried to be as sensitive as possible to the specific national reality. In the Finnish case the choice was not difficult, because the chemical forest industry firms have been the economic motor of the country since the 1930s; furthermore, since the seventeenth century the forests have in various ways been the main natural resource on which the Finnish economy has been based. In the Danish case the choice was based on the earlier findings of Kristensen, which scrutinized the 'official' view of the development of firms and management in Denmark and situated the SMEs at the core of its dynamic, rather than as archaic forms of economic organization heading towards extinction. This approach by necessity leads to over-simplification. Both teams are aware of the fact that in Finland it is possible to identify clusters of firms which can be understood from the perspectives offered within the Danish analysis and, vice versa, it is possible to identify Danish corporations working within a logic that is close to the Finnish pattern. These cases, however, will be exceptions, which we think should be investigated with the suggested 'real types' in mind. How could they have become established within the framework of the two 'real types'? What are the terms of their exceptional existence? How do they function in relation to the more widespread pattern, which we try to model in the two essays?

From both essays there emerges a model, in the sense that it is possible to evaluate what happens when the 'model' is confronted with challenges of a new type. This is documented as both essays end up evaluating in which ways international challenges, among them the Single European Market, will affect the modelled patterns of behaviour. Whilst in the Danish case the persistent division of economic roles between 'skill containers' and 'project-coordinators' becomes increasingly formally institutionalized, the Finnish vertically integrated firms and their associated power blocs seem to become disintegrated by this development.

At the end of the essay on Finland we attempt to draw up some comparative differences between the Danish and Finnish models and sketch further possible improvements in understanding the national 'real types' by continuing this comparative research.

REFERENCES

Maurice, M., Sellier, F. and Silvestre, J.-J. (1986) *The Social Foundations of Industrial Power: A Comparison of France and Germany*, Cambridge, Mass.: MIT Press.

Spiethoff, A. (1953) 'Pure theory and economic Gestalt theory; ideal types and real types', in F. C. Lane and J. C. Riemersma (eds) *Enterprise and Secular Change*, Homewood, Ill.: Richard D. Irwin.

Whitley, R. (ed.) (1992a) *European Business Systems*, London: Sage.

—— (1992b) *Business Systems in East Asia*, London: Sage.

6 On the constitution of economic actors in Denmark

Interacting skill containers and project coordinators

Peer Hull Kristensen

THE NATURE OF DANISH FIRMS

Until recently the dominant theoretical picture of the firm has been the mass-producing giant. Its core activity was a specific product brought to mass markets by marketing and sales outlets. Integrating supplies reduced transaction costs and stabilized flows. Aiming at continuous growth and protecting their financial flows, such firms would gradually turn into multi-product firms. Williamson (1975) and Chandler (1977) have claimed this evolution of firm-organization to be 'ideal-typical'.

In Denmark the business system never followed this American evolutionary process. As demonstrated elsewhere (Kristensen, 1988, 1989a, 1989b, 1992a, 1992b; Kristensen and Sabel, forthcoming), powerful economic agents, reinforced by crédit mobilière-type institutions, tried through cartels and trusts to impose on Denmark an industrial organization similar to those of Germany or France during the last decades of the nineteenth century. These agents had little success, however, as craftsmen and farmers joined forces in village communities in the countryside during the same decades. Fighting for social space, these two groups formed cooperative institutions as 'immediate producers' to protect themselves from becoming dominated by an élite of large corporations. Protecting themselves in this way farmers and craftsmen established institutional formations, which reproduced these two groups as communities of peers, distributing land and industrial knowledge as direct possessions of the members of the two communities. From 1880 to 1918 the farmers dominated economic dynamics in Denmark, creating one of the most elaborate peer group organizations ever seen (Kristensen and Sabel, forthcoming). From 1920 to 1945, the dominant role shifted to craftsmen, but then from 1945 to 1970 it appeared that international trade liberalization had given large Copenhagen-based corporations a chance. This change, however, has proved limited. The development of the volatile economy since 1975 has confirmed that the dynamic core still rests with the craft-industrial sectors of the Danish economy (Kristensen, 1992a and 1992b).

Thus, although Denmark is inhabited by a great variety of economic types of organizations within manufacturing industry, its core consists of craft-based producers, predominantly appearing in industrial statistics as small- and medium-sized firms (SMEs). These SMEs constitute a persistently dominant fraction of industry, and they seem increasingly to dominate the organizing dynamics of other firm-types within the Danish context. The core of these firms are within manufacturing industries such as metal-working (primarily engineering and machine shops), furniture and woodworking, and garments – quite traditional industries, which have shown comparatively high growth performance compared with other OECD countries. However, they also play a role in sectors such as electronics and even some process industries.

Our aim is to investigate the pattern within this segment of Danish industry, which we think makes up the core of Danish industry's dynamics, while we neglect the more capital-intensive large firms, which are usually the focus of analysis in other countries.

Whereas Williamson (1975), as mentioned in the introductory chapter to this volume, sees peer groups as a transaction-cost-inefficient form of organization, Denmark may be said to have established this very form of organization based on a simple governance system consisting of reputational linking.

In the Danish case the social division of economic roles may be observed in the coexistence of two distinct phenotypes of firm: the skill container and the project coordinator.[1]

Skill containers

Skill containers have their origin in the craft shop. Their organizing principle is that a *Meister* recruits a number of skilled workers and equips them with the necessary machines and tools and a place to work from. This operating core is what makes up the identity of the firm, and other social groups within the firm are considered to be 'helping hands' to this core. Two different types of 'helping hands' are typical. On the one hand a group of unskilled/specialized workers assist skilled workers, enabling them to concentrate their work on tasks in which their skills are useful and needed. The second type of 'helping hands' are an administrative staff that keep the books, pick up the phone, contact customers, pay wages, etc. The 'entrepreneur' is often an active member of the operating core, and sees the evolution of this core as the major aim of his 'firm', rather than growth of the firm as such. Consequently, within the firm, managers in the traditional sense of the word (see, e.g., Penrose, 1959; Galbraith, 1958, 1972) play a largely insignificant role. In the Penrosian firm, growth originates from an established managerial team capable of developing and institutionalizing new operational routines within the lower hierarchy of the firm, whereas the shifting operational contingencies of a skill container set the agenda for managerial workers. Some of the mechanisms that are crucial to growth are therefore absent, and the firm seems much more dependent on external contingencies for its evolution than the typical Anglo-Saxon enterprise. Forward and backward integration is a strategy that is alien to the nature of such firms; when it happens, it serves to stabilize the shop against the fluctuations of the economy.

But the skill container firm's dependence on the economy at large is of a different sort. While the typical mass producer is highly dependent on the general level of activity, the skill container is contingent on the functioning of a narrow number of linkages. Customers ask the firm for its services, and as past services are the basis of the firm's reputation, this reputation may lead to new demands as its reputation spreads. Being dependent on this mechanism for growth and survival, the critical growth variable is the firm's capacity to recruit new skilled workers who can meet or improve the reputational standards. Thus, the major problem of stabilization is to be able to keep these skilled workers attached to the firm in spite of fluctuating demands. Such firms seldom start by producing a specific product, but they may sometimes gain a particularly significant reputation within a specialized field and consequently become specialized suppliers of a certain range of products.

The firm as a skill container is observable at many levels within the Danish industrial structure. Its purest form is a team of workers, who, as a group, secure employment on a large building and construction project. Such a team is often hired out collectively to work in another firm than their formal employer, for example a shipyard or one of the large engineering firms in Denmark. Second, factories have often been divided into workshops along craft- or processing specialities, rather than on the basis of a specific flow in logistics, for the reason that these workshops could be combined differently for different products over time. A third illustrative case is the craft or industrial organization of railway towns in agricultural districts. Here, all sorts of craft shops were established side by side, making it easy for customers from the region to have produced a complex good or service by having the various shops combine skills and equipment according to specific, individual needs.

Historically, Rådvad was the archetype of such an organization. Rådvad produced a whole range of products for the Copenhagen hardware dealers. In this case, the hardware dealers' guild owned the factory building, but the individual *Meister* was formally independent, paying rent for his workshop, recruiting his own workers, paying their wages and running the shop; the hardware dealers supplied raw materials and bought the finished goods. At the turn of the century, many trades within the Copenhagen industry were made up of such workshops, coordinated externally by different buyers (of furniture, musical and other instruments, machines, etc.) who brought products to the market without engaging themselves in production as such.

Project coordinators

The second type of firm we call project coordinators. These are typical entrepreneurs who have a specific product idea which they want to bring to the market. As they are operating within an industrial structure of the type just mentioned, they are able to realize their project without investing large resources in fixed assets. Their task is to identify and coordinate two networks: combinations of suppliers that can produce the product which they want to sell, and channels for bringing the product to the final market.

Project coordinators are often able to make an income by exploiting personal networks. However, they typically have no resources for aggressive marketing and, if they do, their supplier network may soon impose limits on their growth, as suppliers will typically be hesitant to allocate more than one-third of their capacity to an individual customer. Furthermore, suppliers are unable to increase capacity quickly since their recruiting practice, as mentioned above, is highly dependent on the maintenance of reputation. Consequently, if the project coordinator starts out on a small scale, the growth process tends to be limited and much of the work concerns keeping the network in place and gradually expanding it. Most of the project coordinator's assets are intangible and therefore very difficult to finance through the Danish financial system. Also, it is very difficult to hand over to employees the task of keeping in touch with such networks, either forwards or backwards in the value chain. The solution to growth is to ask personal contacts, whom the project coordinator trusts, to do some of the networking, i.e. to let a customer sell some products for other markets and to let a supplier organize subcontracting from other suppliers. Consequently, profits are increasingly dissipated to many agents in the network rather than being accumulated at one point, and this leads to gradual growth of the entire 'system', rather than to exceptional growth of particularly successful project-coordinating firms.

Combined skill containers and project coordinators resemble a modernized form of the historical 'putting-out system' – but only resemble. In Denmark, the union movement was one of the most active forces in modifying the putting-out system. They tried hard to have workers employed in workshops, rather than being self-employed at home. Whereas in some places it was the entrepreneurs' wish to impose discipline on the workers that led to factory production (Marglin, 1974), in Denmark it was the unions' fight to reduce sweated labour and undue competition that worked in favour of workshop organization. This union strategy, though often resulting in conflict with individual employers, also played an important part in maintaining an enduring social space for the craft *Meister*. Unintentionally, the strategy restricted the normal development pattern of putting-out systems, in which power, market relations and capital gradually become concentrated in the hands of a merchant, while the immediate producers gradually became dependent on the merchant for supplies as well as for orders. In the present Danish system it is difficult to identify large-scale merchant houses, as in Japan, which dominate a large amount of subcontractors; nor is it possible to see a large producer, as in the German *Bosch* system, capable of dominating customers. Power and influence seem pretty equally balanced, and the system is so generalized that project coordinators can choose from among many alternative suppliers, and suppliers provide several rather than only a few customers with their services.

The principle of combining skill containers and project coordinator can be applied to an endless number of areas and can be organized in an infinite number of hierarchies and non-hierarchies. The classical example could be the building engineer who tenders with a number of different *Meisters* for the construction of a building. In Denmark, development engineers often work in extremely small R. & D. teams and make only very rough sketches of a new machine, then contact different specialist machine-makers to take part in different parts of the construction. In Danish shipyards this system is applied internally in the 'firm', involving an endless number of varying external subcontractors, depending on the particular needs of the end-customer.

Another example is the design company producing a fashion collection and then driving down a road in Ikast to combine knitters, wage-sewing shops, weavers, etc. to make different parts of the collection. But the system is also applied in 'hi-tech' areas. Many of the new electronics instrument producers, who set up small firms in Copenhagen in the late 1970s, concentrated on designing new instruments and outsourced the actual production to subcontractors (Kjeldgaard and Nielsen, 1988). The same can be observed within biotechnology (Norus, 1993). In these cases, the project coordinator becomes a container of specialized engineering skills, basically employing a group of R. & D. engineers who operate, as much as possible, as if they were still working in university labs. Many of the major Danish consulting firms, selling huge constructions for waste disposal, harbours, and turn-key factories to foreign countries, are in fact project coordinators that have grown large enough to undertake huge projects involving the coordination of a large number of skill containers of many sorts, as well as financial, political and diplomatic channels. Through these mechanisms, the different professions, though not immediately cooperating within the single firms, are mutually dependent for their operations, though they are often allocated to different firms, which can then concentrate on organizing cooperation among colleagues.

The division of labour between skill containers and project coordinators is never a settled game; on the contrary, it is often shifting. To be able to even out demand, skill containers will often take advantage of projects they have learned about through certain customers and then try to sell something similar to other customers. The knitting factory which gets involved in special fabrics for one customer may know that these fabrics can be sold on a market in which the initial customer is not operating. Balancing between what may be termed 'cheating', and good well-established honourable conduct becomes a matter that is continuously subject to test. But the regulating principle is, of course, that the individual skill container does not harm his general reputation, so destroying the basic means for staying in business as a skill container. Most firms will probably act with alternating intensity in both roles, as is the normal pattern in, for example, the construction industry, where *Meisters* sometimes act as main contractors and sometimes as subcontractors.

Acting in these networks in shifting roles is something which has to be learned by experience, and it requires a developed reputation as insurance to prevent customers or subcontractors from misinterpreting your acts. For this reason, it is in no way simple for a *Meister* to hand over his firm to a professional manager, to run the company along formal rules and contracts. We know of several examples where such a change has destroyed the firm – whether it was predominantly playing the role of project coordinator or skill container (an illustrative example is given in Andersen and Christensen, 1993). This is one of the reasons why the system seems unable to develop rapidly into a more structured system of subcontracting, as in the case of the Japanese or the *Bosch* systems. Trust seems to be non-transferable from the personal to the institutional level. The same applies when the initial entrepreneur retires and hands over his firm to a son or a daughter. Networks and coalitions are built, but they never become long-lasting power blocs.

This pattern, however, is not caused by the *Meister*-entrepreneur monopolizing the firm's external relations. Rather the reason is that he, like the rest of the operating core, operates through an informal system of relations, while managers recruited from outside this web of ties tend to formalize and therefore destroy the pattern involved in making and enacting market relations.

Market relations

As project coordinators choose subcontractors according to their reputation, the best strategy for the subcontracting skill containers to confirm these reputational linkages is to relate with the customer through people who possess the most relevant combinations of skills. As the task often shifts from one customer to another, it is highly varying combinations of employees with whom firms discuss a potential transaction. Many levels of skill containers may be involved in transactional negotiations in various situations. During the initial phase of the 'negotiations', representatives of a project coordinator will often meet a whole group of people from the skill container to discuss how a job can be done technically. At this stage the subcontractor tries to meet the project coordinator's needs by redefining the task according to his immediate capabilities. The principle of 'available resources' governs discussions in order to determine the need for additional investments or complementary subcontractors. Such negotiations solve many of the problems usually associated with product-maturing during the R. & D. phase of a large integrated firm. The people directly involved in this initial process are people who possess (the skilled workers) or who represent (the *Meister*) the skills involved in doing a job. Only later, when the technicalities have been solved, are the administrative staff called in to make calculations and write up tenders or estimates. They then connect to other groups in the project coordinating firm so that, by the end, the firms involved are connected on many layers before a contract is finally decided and confirmed between two formal representatives, often the owners themselves.

This process of enacting market relations confirms that it is not managerial levels that take actions, but rather the operative core. 'Managerial' levels act in assistance of this acting core. And it is exactly through this logic of market relating, i.e. engaging reputational skills in solving technical problems before the potential economic benefits and costs are evaluated, that it becomes possible to engage in a close cooperative project between two or more parties. Trust does not rest with the institutional structure of the system, it arises through the order of steps involved in the process. The system, however, is very efficient in reducing 'opportunistic' or over-optimistic promises as this reversal of the process, compared to the textbook forms of transactional logics, makes it possible for project coordinators to have the reputation of skill containers confirmed before any party has to decide on asset-specific investments. Economic calculation and managerial activities do not lead to the definition of projects, rather economics and managerial skills are employed to evaluate whether a technically defined project is feasible between two actors, who may then become partners.

It is fair to say that building business relations this way, though it only involves investments in tangible assets to a limited extent, implies large transaction costs in terms of how much time individuals representing the two actors have to spend on making a project possible. For these reasons there will be strong personal feelings involved in breaking a relation, as it means that individuals in both the involved firms will have to go through a new, long and painful process with individuals in other firms. Self-interest, thus, in a very simple way, works to create factions in each firm which act in favour of confirming and evoking the new 'contract', which therefore may often be extremely informal, a verbal promise. During the process, the two firms may even create a cross-firm coalition of technicians combining their technical creativity in order to convince calculators and decision-makers that the new engagement is economically sound.

Many projects between the two phenotype firms arise from the day-to-day contact between the two. Visiting fitters from a skill container doing a job at a project coordinator's plant may point out new opportunities and then engage the two parties in a larger project. Staying in contact through the bonds of their crafts, workers may find out how one firm can get some problems solved by another firm. Strategies evolve from daily operations, rather than vice versa.

Authority relations

It would be erroneous to say that in Denmark authority has been delegated to the operating core of skilled workers or technical specialists. In numerous articles we have tried to show that the opposite is true. The operating core has never accepted the delegation of many tasks to an increasingly autonomous managerial level. The separation of planning from execution, which was Taylor's core idea, was not in general accepted in Denmark. Danish firms, therefore, seem to operate with much less formal planning than firms in other countries (Ackelsberg and Harris, 1989).

The lack of formal planning is due not only to internal managerial weaknesses. Rather, as it will become clear below, 'managers' are much less dependent on convincing principals, whether financial institutions or state bodies, about their deeds. In many countries formal plans are used to legitimize strategies to external stakeholders, and having accomplished this these plans must be implemented in order to prove a firm trustworthy to its environment. Plans acquire an authority of their own, which employees have to accept as part of 'deals' of a higher order than they may influence. Such abstract and distant mechanisms of power and authority have been difficult to adopt within the Danish system. Consequently, in Danish enterprises managers have been unable to develop their own discourse and thereby to achieve a specific reflexivity, which reflects, on the one hand, the Danish practice and, on the other hand, a common concern for enlarging the social space for managerial action. This leaves the discourse on industrial strategy in the hands of the state and the interest associations' technocrats, who have very limited knowledge about the actual operation of Danish firms.

Consequently, Danish managers seem to operate in an extremely egalitarian way:

> An eloquent point can be made in this connection, namely that
> Danes generally resent the word 'power', which has all the nega-

tive connotations of superiority, force, domination, and coercion. No Danish manager would refer to the power he (she) has, but he (she) would willingly speak of his (her) responsibilities, a word which has positive connotations of work, competence, and obligations towards others. In consequence, what is important in a Danish setting is less who has authority over whom as who is responsible for what.

When many people have decision-making authority, each within their domain, managers have to work in constant cooperation with lower layers of the hierarchy, making all parties inter-dependent. In such a context, decision-making becomes a mixture of top-down and bottom-up decisions. This is what Hofstede (1984) would call a short power distance, and his findings on this dimension seem most convincing (Denmark is extremely low, number 37 out of 40 countries).

(Fivelsdal and Schramm-Nielsen, 1993)

However, we do not think that this pattern can be explained simply by attributing egalitarian values to Danish managers. Rather, another principle of authority, we argue, has such a predominant position in Danish society that it enforces on managers this egalitarian behaviour in order to survive as a group within firms.

Discipline is constituted through horizontal codes of work ethics. These codes are established during vocational training – at school and in the workshop during apprenticeship – and they are enforced by a tacit set of professional standards which skilled workers and other professionals expect each other to obey. Finally, these codes are policed by unions. To accomplish a job calls for the ingenuity and skill of each of the individuals involved. Therefore, the primary test of the individual worker is towards his mates, who will have to compensate if he fails to do a good job. It is acceptable to fail for specific reasons sometimes, but it is indeed not acceptable to fail many times without trying to compensate in other situations. A group of skilled workers must protect their collective reputation. Therefore, the individual worker has to protect his own reputation within the group, otherwise the group will exclude him after some time. The standards defining honourable work conduct are not easy to detect but, since they have been established through vocational training and job practice, they have reached a certain degree of isomorphism in different regions of Denmark.

Following Chester Barnard's argument (1938: 163) that 'the decision as to whether an order has authority or not lies with the persons to whom it is addressed, and does not reside in "persons authority" or those who issues these orders', the manager has to work through these horizontal codes of work ethics, rather than against them. This can only be done if the manager himself knows how they function. This implies that managers working in close cooperation with lower-level workers, or even originating from the very same system, are best able to work with these horizontal codes, and to exploit the opportunities to issue orders in situations when they know that such orders are not against collective principles.

For these reasons, we think, most managers have to be able to manage by demonstrating a positive contribution to a group's performance in such a way that they improve their collective reputation. There are several ways of doing so. One particularly effective way is to contribute, through instruction, to the improvement of individual skills or the entire group's skills. They must be able to hire new workers, who fit into the group's standards of work, and to fire those who do not fit in.

To manage in order to retain and improve a group's performance is a very difficult task. Each individual in such a group operates very independently, also in external relations, and it is in the nature of the whole thing that each worker tries to improve the group's external reputation by doing a good job in direct contact with customers or suppliers. Consequently, each worker engages in a reputational network with people in other firms, and it is therefore easy for him to evoke offers of a new job in another firm, if he feels he is being treated poorly. Even merely conducting his usual business, he will often receive such offers unprovoked. For these reasons also the reputations of various managers spread fast, to the effect that egalitarian 'values' spread amongst managers.

The combination of these dynamics of authority works to establish a hierarchy amongst groups of workers and certain managers. It imposes competition on firms to attract and to keep a group of workers of high reputation. Firms following the logic of skill containers are subject to endless efforts to position their workshop technically and, in terms of quality, at the high end of the scale. This monitoring principle then lies in the system as such, rather than in the authority of managers, but it certainly helps select the kind of authority by which a manager may operate.

It follows from what we have said so far, that the managerial task of formulating a purpose for the organization is needed less than in most cooperative systems (see Barnard, 1938). This purpose is generally established through the business system: the common purpose of establishing and improving the skills and reputation of the firm by improving exactly the same properties at the levels of individuals and groups within the informal organization.

Modes of growth in Danish firms

The growth of Finnish firms, as we shall see in Lilja and Tainio's contribution to this volume, follows some very simple rules as growth represents a means of protecting initial large-scale investments. One initial step, so to speak, necessitates the next. In Penrose's (1959) general theory, however, totally different mechanisms are used to explain the growth of a firm. This theory emphasizes the ability of a group of managers to establish routines of cooperation and routines for doing the jobs in which the firm specializes, thus enabling managers to devote themselves to new tasks and in so doing gradually to expand their field of operation. Managers' motivation for expanding their firm's space is less clear in Penrose's works, but it is easy to combine with Galbraith's theory of career patterns and motivation for the technocracy within large American firms.

Compared to these two examples, the reasons for and mechanisms of growth are much less clear in the Danish case, which is puzzling not only to the observer. Most firms stay rather small and often die if they try to grow fast. However, the Danish industrial structure contains a comparatively high number of medium-sized firms, which seem to be one of the groups in most other countries that have the greatest difficulties in surviving. Growth is possible for some and they seem to be able to create a place for themselves and play a role within the Danish industrial structure.

We think that the process of metamorphosis of the two phenotypes discussed above is that, first, skill containers grow gradually into multi-product contractors; while, second, project coordinators gradually transform into assemblers. One of the major reasons for growth among skill containers is a specific way of managing a specific type of risk. The worst that can happen to a skill container is facing a decline in orders and thus being forced to fire skilled workers on whom the firm's reputation rests. We shall show that in Denmark, firms have very few external institutions with which to share their risks. Project coordinators formulate their strategy on this basis and reduce their own risks by outsourcing to subcontractors. Subcontracting skill containers thus accumulate risk and their strategy in turn decides whether the system as such may be able to stabilize.

The normal stabilization pattern among skill containers is always to be looking for alternative employment of their skills and resources. For two reasons, subcontractors in Denmark do not just passively await growing orders from one customer. The first reason is that they would be investing in increasingly specialized machinery, which often requires financial and technical resources to manage. Second, such firms will know that they risk losing their most able and skilled workers if they simply follow a strategy that leads to an increase in the size of batches. On the other hand, the *Meister* knows that he always risks losing a customer and he is always trying to balance demand among several rather than a few customers, never trying deliberately to let one customer take up more than about 30 per cent of his total capacity. In order to be able to act in this way he will often be prepared to make additional, complementary but marginal investments in general-purpose machinery in order to be able to add a new customer to his existing group of customers.

Compared to their size, skill containers will often possess machine capacity in excess of what is needed, compared with the demands they meet and the number of workers they employ. In terms of profitability they often do a bad job, but these are the costs involved in protecting themselves against loss of core workers while, on the other hand, at short notice being able to increase temporarily just-in-time deliveries for a customer.

In periods of increasing demand, skill containers try to recruit new workers, whereby the *Meister* discovers that among them are a few persons with complementary skills and ability who fit into the core group and to combine these with the rest of the group in such a way that the group improves its level of self-management. This approach increases the responsibility of the *Meister* to look for additional customers and to purchase complementary general-purpose machinery.

Having started with a certain group of workers with specialized skills, and a certain group of specialized machines, though of a general-purpose nature, the firm gradually develops into a very complex machine-shop with many different processing skills. In many cases it is now able to perform the entire processing and assembly of a large number of different products. In this situation it has transformed itself into a factory that produces products for a whole mass of industrial customers who just bring the products to the end-user. Often this position involves the complicated administration of a whole group of subcontracting skill containers at lower levels of the value chain to do the final completion of products to many different customers. In order to be able to manage such a set of complicated tasks, these multi-product contractors have to specialize. Therefore, they gradually select those areas in which they have the highest reputation, enabling them continuously to attract skilled workers and customers by applying the same strategy.

Project coordinators dealing with skill containers in order to grow in their main field, i.e. bringing a product to a market, will have to develop strategies for dealing with the strategies of skill containers. They will often be forced to meet increasing demands by increasing the number of suppliers. To do this without risking high variations in product quality they will have to expand their technical skills in organizing supplies, quality testing, etc. But the real core problem is that of finding a firm that will take responsibility for all the final assembly work. Often they will have to invest in facilities and workers to do this themselves.

On the surface this implies that project coordinators and skill containers develop towards a similar type of medium-sized firm. This happens only occasionally, however, because the two logics are very different indeed. Skill containers develop this form of organization in order to buffer their core skills from cyclical, seasonal or structural fluctuations; consequently, skill container firms often only assemble such semi-finished product groups that have very critical measures for performance; the project coordinators, on the other hand, take on assembly tasks only to be able to combine many semi-finished products into a finished product, the assembly of which is quite unsophisticated.

The organization of the medium-sized skill container is continuously run from below, whereas the project coordinator often develops some of the more usual traits of a Fordist mass producer: a larger group of managers relate to customers and suppliers in the network through which the firm operates and it employs a basically low-skilled core of (usually female) assemblers organized in a very autocratically run factory, often located far from the city where its headquarters is based.

It follows that growth within skill containers and project coordinators happens as a consequence of the basic structure of the system in which an abundance of small skill containers and small project coordinators are evolving their strategies. They have to grow because of the strategies that others develop to escape from becoming dependent on firms like themselves. Therefore it rather adds growth to the system than alters the system and the relations among firms.

Another reason why relations do not change with growth is that project coordinators that reach a high turnover of similar types of products seldom use this position to dominate their Danish subcontractors. As soon as the quantity which they demand from subcontractors reaches a level that can be more efficiently negotiated with large foreign component or subsystem producers, imported components will substitute for Danish subcontractors. This, in turn, reinforces the latter's determination never to become dependent on one large customer.

In other words, firms which grow to such proportions that they would tend to have the capability and power to change the prevailing pattern of peer-group relations, tend to choose to develop relations with the international system rather than to establish a domestic hierarchy of the normal type, either in terms of a Fordist vertically integrated firm, or an external Japanese-type hierarchical system among subcontractors. In any case, these strategies make it possible even for firms with a high turnover to remain rather small in terms of numbers of employees, and to avoid establishing the kind of authority system which is associated with industrial activity in most other countries.

The managerial tasks which arise in such firms are less a matter of being able to coordinate and control; rather, their tasks are associated with negotiations and 'horse-trading'. Growth thus makes it possible for managers to establish a place for themselves within the project coordinator type of firm in Denmark but, rather than the managerial tasks and functions associated with running factories, these roles rest on traditions developed in large trading-houses and among merchants.

Summary of the business system characteristics of the typical firm: a comparative classification of Danish SMEs

The social division of economic roles between skill containers and project coordinators may look very similar to the division of roles found elsewhere, where SMEs play a major part in the formation of firms. Are there any differences between the Danish pattern, as modelled above, and the Japanese *kaisha*, which group subcontractors around a dominating manufacturing concern? Are the division of roles and the interactions among skill containers and project coordinators not similar to the division found in some Third Italy industrial districts between the middlemen, *impannatore*, whose contacts with foreign buyers make it possible for the small subcontractors of the districts to have their goods sold on the international market? Finally, is Denmark's persistent SME structure not very much the same as that found among overseas Chinese family firms?

In our view the decentralized production systems of both the Japanese *kaisha* and the Third Italy represent closed associations in the sense that many SMEs participate in an integrated and closed value chain. Japan has become notorious for being able to keep foreign firms out and imports low (van Wolferen, 1989). Beccattini (1979) originally used the *filiére*, i.e. the vertically integrated sector, instead of the industrial sector statistically defined to characterize industrial districts in Italy. The dynamics of the system are determined by the organizing abilities of the dominating manufacturing concern in Japan, which has succeeded in creating a hierarchy of 'careers' among their subcontractors, monitored in much the same way as the internal labour force (Sabel, 1993). The organization of the system of subcontracting firms by the *impannatore* of the Third Italy seems, at first sight, more occasional and of a broader scope for alterations in roles among peers. The evolution of Benetton's network into a hierarchy seems to indicate that it is possible to change Italian districts into Japanese *kaishas* (Harrison, 1994).

In the Danish case 'the sector' cannot be anticipated as being vertically integrated. On the contrary, since at least the mid-1960s production of most standardized components and intermediary products has been lost to foreign suppliers. Denmark had neither the strong business groups, like the Japanese *keiretsu*, nor the artisanal associations such as the CNA, to develop strategies by which it could organize modernization of such types of production. Apart from their strategic importance, the production of standardized components and intermediary products offers rich opportunities for developing interactions and networks among enterprises and helps establish innovative user–producer relations throughout the economy. But it is also often along these networks that power and dominance most often are established.

For these reasons, Danish skill containers cannot simply identify themselves or have project coordinators define their place and role in the vertical division of labour. Rather, they have to play rapidly changing roles in many, rather than a few, 'value chains', if they want to survive. Typically, they improve their ability to do that by helping their customers buy cheap components and intermediary products from the world market by being agents for foreign mass-producers of the same type of items they themselves supply in customized form. Second, they expand their own capabilities by being able to organize occasionally a short-term value chain with other national skill containers. And this pattern helps explain why Danish project coordinators are unlikely to become as crucial in organizing skill containers as the *impannatore* of Third Italy or Toyota of Japan.

The key source of the difference between Denmark and Italy and Japan, we think, is the skilled workers in the three countries. Whereas economic pressures in Italy may force firms into 'sweating' and dependence on a few customers, and thus establish a lasting reconfiguration of the system, it is very difficult for a Danish SME to survive through such a strategy. The team of skilled workers, constituting skill containers in Denmark, will soon leave such firms and reinforce from within the destruction imposed on it from the outside. The difference between Denmark and most other SME-intensive countries is simply that 'the firm' plays a less significant role in the institutional construction of Denmark than it does in most other countries, where firms *are* the way to organize a team of workers. We admit these differences to be more hypothetical than conclusive, not least because many of the studies on workers and work organization in the districts of the Third Italy have been rather superficial.

According to Redding (1990) and Redding and Whitley (1990) overseas Chinese capitalism is consistently characterized this way:

1 small scale, and relatively simple organizational structuring;
2 normally focused on one product or market with growth by opportunistic diversification;
3 centralized decision making with heavy reliance in one dominant executive;
4 a close overlap of ownership, control and family;
5 a paternalistic organizational climate;
6 linked to the environment through personalistic networks;
7 normally very sensitive to matters of cost and financial efficiency;
8 commonly linked strongly but informally with related but legally independent organizations handling key functions such as parts supply or marketing;
9 relatively weak in terms of creating large-scale market recognition for brands;
10 a high degree of strategic adaptability.

(Redding and Whitley, 1990: 86)

Against this framework, we would characterize Danish SME organization in the following way, referring to similar dimensions as Redding and Whitley:

1 small scale and relatively simple organizational structuring of the individual firm, due to the complex separation of operational and market-related activities between different types of firms;

2 normally focused within skill containers on a small number of processes, which can be adapted to an endless number of different activities, while project coordinators either present a distinct product-palette in many variants, or customized turnkey equipment for many different markets;

3 decentralized decision-making by operating teams, often represented by middle managers or shop stewards, while the top executives do the final formal checking;

4 ownership by a former craftsman in the case of skill containers is important for keeping the organization balanced in favour of the teams of skilled workers, and the owner often takes action to prevent both his/her family members and managerial groups from taking control of the firm;

5 as long as an entrepreneur craftsman runs his own skill container a paternalistic atmosphere prevails, but it is rooted in his reputation as a craftsman, rather than in his ability to create clientist relations to his workers;

6 linked to the environment through personalistic networks, but whereas these linkages are centralized to the dominant executive in the Chinese case, in Denmark they get established at many levels of the organization mutually between Danish skill containers and project coordinators. The dominating language is by craft specialization and the linkages reinforce the sense of craft community between independent firms;

7 normally very slow to recognize poor profitability, because it is difficult to calculate the costs of individual projects; financially very conservative, as it would typically rather choose to reduce financial costs than to optimize financial gearing;

8 commonly linked informally and weakly to a number of independent organizations, which recognize the reputation of the firm from having experienced its services in times of troubles;

9 project coordinators are often able to take advantage of the underlying system of reputational linking, establishing themselves as representatives of 'Danish design' and achieving large- scale market recognition among distinct market seg-

ments, which are able to evaluate high quality. This may both
be observed in industrial markets for reliable equipment, and
in consumer markets for connoisseurs;

10 a low degree of strategic adaptability; instead of being decided
among top executives, strategies emerge as an evolutionary
pattern from intended and unintended consequences of
actions taken among a multiplicity of teams of skilled workers.

THE HISTORICAL AND SOCIETAL CONSTITUTION OF THE TYPICAL FIRM IN DENMARK: THE SOCIETAL PLACE OF THE FIRM

We have elsewhere tried to explain why the immediate producers
(primarily farmers and craftsmen) were able to establish an industrial regime under their direct control (Kristensen and Sabel,
forthcoming) and have argued why strategies from agents that want
to impose on Danish firms a centralized structure have failed
(Kristensen, 1992a, 1994a). In the following section we shall try to
investigate this matter in depth, focusing on the behaviour of potential principals. Why did neither the state, the financial élites, the
engineers nor the managerial professions succeed in making firms
agents of their own projects in Denmark? We will conclude this
section by interpreting the societal place of the firm in the Danish
context.

The state, élites and business associations in Denmark

In many business systems, the state plays a crucial role in economic
development. Thus Johnson (1982) has characterized the Japanese
state as developmental, against the more regulatory states of the
Anglo-Saxon world, while Wade (1990) distinguishes between regulating and governing the market. The Danish state, though among
the oldest in Europe, can neither be characterized as developmental
nor as governing the market. Compared to such strong states as
France, which are able to concert action between state bodies, banks
and business groups, the Danish state looks very weak indeed. More
important, however, it seems to have been unable to develop a role
as mediator, common to both Sweden and Finland, where the state
may monitor negotiations among different business groups.

One reason for this weakness is probably the state's inability to
act as an integrated body; it seems to be lacking an integrating or
centralizing principle, be it a military purpose or belief in the divine

nature of the state. The reasons are to be found in the organization of the Danish state and the way in which the Danish welfare state emerged.

First, municipalities and counties are constitutionally independent authorities in Denmark, with legal rights and obligations for independent taxation and public spending. Thus, it is impossible to implement a developmental strategy without first consulting and negotiating with major representatives at these decentralized levels, and it would be difficult to reach consensus on favouring some regions and not others.

Second, many so-called public institutions, though funded primarily by the state, are 'self-owned'. The reason is historical, as most social groups had created their own institutions for social welfare, health insurance, education, etc. before the emergence of the Danish welfare state during the 1930s. While the creation of the welfare state in many countries rested on a central design, the Danish welfare state was established through the state's 'inclusion' of institutions created during the self-help movement around the turn of the century. It thus became an odd assembly of privately founded 'bodies'. The result of this process of state 'formation' is a complex segmentalism. Very different rules are applied in various sectors and areas, making any unifying principle for state action short-lived and dubious, as the constituent parties, who have captured the right to negotiate, vary significantly among various 'segments'. For example the 'folk-high-school movement' works through a complicated private and 'public' network by which it is self-administering, though receiving large funds from the state. Similarly, the unions and the employers' associations, together with representatives of the schools within the vocational training system, dominate all levels of this system. There is a large number of such segments, as the Danish welfare state was created as a compromise, guaranteeing some groups benefits in exchange for helping other groups. Consequently, the state is weak in rejecting demands from new grass-roots movements and has to include new segments as they arise, because it can claim no legitimate principle for exclusion (Fonsmark, 1990). For these reasons we characterize the state as decentralized, segmentalist but inclusive.

Whether this role of the state is an effect or a cause of the very fragmented situation of the Danish élite can be a subject of infinite discussion, as in the case of the chicken and the egg. The typical pattern is that the various fragments of the state are governed by representatives, who have been selected from the decentralized bodies of the civil society. Consequently, the career pattern, determining who will achieve a high position at state level, is decided by the circumstances governing that area of civil society in which people act. Consequently, the folk high schools, the vocational training system, the universities, etc. tend to staff the corporatist bodies governing their own segments. The same phenomenon applies to bodies that more directly affect industrial development, for example export subsidies or subsidies for technological innovation. Inclusion into these many fragmented parts of the élite is governed by no universal selection criteria, and in Denmark there is no specific group, such as the *grandes écoles* in France, from whom to select the élite. There is no élite university as, for example, in Japan (van Wolferen, 1989) that ensures access to core positions. For these reasons neither a certain style of governance, nor a dominant form of discourse, that may help select developmental strategy, has established itself to legitimate resource-allocation. The strong pressure on government spending, however, has made budgetary discourse particularly strong, but always underlining the dangers of disequilibrium between the public and private economy, rather than pointing towards a coherent developmental strategy.

This does not, of course, mean that there is no élite in Denmark. Rather, the implications are that the actual élite is short-lived, dependent on personal relations and often the result of actions at the lower part of a segment. As ties to these lower parts tend to weaken while being in a power position, membership of an élite tends to destroy rather than to reinforce the position of power. Academic titles are, in general, less important to this recruiting process than in any comparable country. In Finland, for example, the title of doctor seems to be important to both political and administrative appointments.

To explain how the Danish élite arrived at its present situation, characterized by competing factions applying ambiguous recruitment criteria for being appointed to corporatist positions, would require an analysis of the transitional period from the absolutist monarchy to the present day. Østergård (1992) gives impressionistic sketches for such an analysis, emphasizing the power which the peasants gradually gained in Danish society. However, this growing role of the peasants, rather than being a cause, ought to be explained as an effect of the élite's weakness: for what internal reasons did the Danish élite disintegrate?

We think that a study of the provisional governments[2] from 1875 to 1894 would reveal some of the reasons for the disintegration of the Danish élite. First, during that period estate owners and the old administrative élite became associated with the old Conservative party (Højre) which was seen as seizing power against both the constitution and the popular will, which at that time was represented by the Liberals (Venstre). The Liberals, broadly speaking, turned their back on the state during these crucial decades of modern Danish economic history and channelled much of their energy into the development of the locally based farmers' cooperative movement. Thus the Danish state was left in the position of a passive spectator during a period in which a much more Saint-Simonian state-building took place in Germany and France. This weak role of the Danish state was self-reinforcing. Instead of inducing coopera-tion among its élite, the state became a victim of rivalries among the emerging élite factions.

This rivalry was particularly strong amongst the circle of people connected to the three newly established Copenhagen banks, lasting from 1870 to the turn of the century. Tietgen, the Danish counterpart to Morgan in the USA (Kristensen and Sabel, forthcoming), and Adler of Privatbanken were in open rivalry with Gedalia and Glück-stadt of Landmandsbanken, while Fonnesbech, belonging to the latter group, was in conflict with Estrup, chairman of The Copen-hagen Bank of Commerce (Handelsbanken). To complicate this picture, Adler later joined the Bank of Commerce group in oppo-sition to his old coalition partner, Tietgen (Gejl, 1989). Had this rivalry only concerned the fight for a dominating role of the banks *vis-à-vis* the economy, it would probably not have differed much from the struggles going on in most European countries at that time. However, these factions were directly and very deeply involved in rivalries for state power. In 1875, Fonnesbech had to leave his post as head of the government to Estrup, who simply assigned all the former members of the board of the Copenhagen Bank of Commerce (Handelsbanken) as cabinet ministers (Fink, 1986). We have limited knowledge of how this group around Estrup used its state power, but it is rather revealing that Tietgen added no new 'gründer-activity' to his former long list after 1876, and until 1894 he was often in open opposition to the many governments under Estrup's leadership. These rivalries among the élite made it impos-sible for the state to act as a coordinating agent for industrialization and destroyed the large banking groups' chances of gaining a coordi-nating power similar to that of other economic agents in many other European societies.

Probably it is also during this period that the state bureaucracy learnt to behave obediently, whereas it formerly had tended to be a much more significant power within the élite. During these years of rivalry between various factions of capital and political parties, the bureaucracy institutionalized a behaviour of being loyal to the party in power, whatever its colour was, and did not develop economic dependence on any particular power-constituencies. Danish bureaucrats thus seemed to be neither easy to corrupt nor to become strong advocates of a lasting developmental logic involving a certain faction of a current business élite.

This situation left the yeoman communities with time to act and create institutions supportive of small-scale capitalism based on local circumstances, thus institutionalizing the potential for rival factions on an enlarged scale, so to speak. In addition, the state permanently lost its ability to hegemonize the discourse in such a way that the population would interpret anything that came from those sources as supporting superior national interest. Rather, in Denmark the state represented an arena where private interests could fight for public financial support. Consequently, we argue, the state has been unable to ask business enterprises to perform certain tasks or to be seen as an agent of national development. Rather, the causality worked the other way round. Public policy looked more like private appropriation of public money and the state became a means rather than an end.

The state being a weak agency, civil society was created by a very intensive process of forming associations from the 1870s to 1914. The farmers' cooperative movement, the labour movement, the craft movement and so on, all created associations able to act, where state initiatives were found deficient. Private associations came to regulate, quite autonomously, their own social spaces and even to create – as in the case of the employers' associations and the unions – their own laws and rules for negotiating conflicts between social groups and spaces. One effect was that Danish society, for a longer period than any comparable Western society, lacked laws defining the rights and obligations of limited liability companies (Just, 1986; Michelsen, 1991), making principal–agent relations dependent on social relations and thus very informal. Agreements often had to be negotiated directly by the parties involved, who lacked rules defining when an association was a firm, a cooperative or a simple partnership between private persons. The background for this method of approaching and building a capitalist economy was that the farmers' cooperatives benefited from tax laws by not being too well-defined *vis-à-vis* limited liability companies. The lack of definition, thus, reflected the sharing of power in the early phase equally between yeoman producers and large corporations.

The strength of private associations and the weakness of the state combined later to develop a society in which the business community lost its basic tools for mediating cooperation and a cooperative search for strategy. Being unable autonomously to regulate the flow of goods and raw materials during bilateral trade in the 1930s, the state had to ask business associations to take on this regulating role. As a consequence, these business associations became extremely centralized and had to coordinate the Danish business world top-down, cooperating very tightly with a number of business-oriented ministries. For natural reasons, many of the costs associated with running the new bureaucracies of the business associations were paid by the state. As in various social welfare provisions, the associations prospered by state inclusion, and the bodies of ministries and associations became very tightly interlocked. While leaders of business associations often functioned as decision-makers on corporatist bodies within the state, the administrative functions of the private and the public organizations involved also became tightly inter-locked, as administrators would often climb the career ladders by zig-zagging between the two – a pattern which still exists (Fivelsdal *et al.*, 1979).

These very direct mechanisms for state inclusion integrated state and business associations very tightly into one social field. The state helped associations finance their activities, making it possible for them to offer to their constituent business firms services at very low costs. For this reason it has been very easy for these associations to maintain a large constituency and formally to look very representative. However, it has also created a cleavage between the constituencies and their associations. Member firms no longer see them as mediators in interest conflicts, neither do they regard them as important bodies for formulating a strategy towards the state and for their industry's development. Rather it has become increasingly obvious that these associations are undertaking the task of turning private interests into public policy.

Business associations are important arenas in which particular factions of the business community create coalitions that enable them to dominate these associations and to be represented in the bodies that allocate public funds. From such positions they can create alliances which can direct several institutions into some kind of concerted action that may assist particular firms in a major way. Such forms of concerted action, however, can never be legitimized by talking very concretely about the projects involved. But the administrative bodies of both associations and public institutions are, in general terms, able to legitimize these deeds by referring to universal theories or attractive lessons from other countries. In effect, the Danish business associations act as discursive bodies in which the universal or global discourse on industrial development is repeated to legitimize the concealed public financial support of private interests. Consequently, discourses that explicitly recognize past experience of the Danish business community and identify its particular needs are excluded. Such discursive practices, however, are not very resistant to criticism, and other factions refrain from such criticism only as long as their particular projects receive public finance.

Because of these mechanisms it seems as if consensus prevails, though it is not very clear to an external observer what the parties agree about. What has been destroyed during the process is an industrial public, which could have pointed out the tasks of the state and furnished the parties involved with an aggregated understanding of their common project.

Business associations in some countries, especially for small firms in Italy, are able to formulate their interests against the state and other associations, for instance associations of large firms in Italy, enabling them to enact their development projects bottom-up. However, in other countries such processes lead directly to the choice of top-down strategies, as in France. In Denmark this process has led only to short-lived, rather unconscious cooperation between different groups of firms, public financed 'self-owned' institutions and corporatist bodies assisted by administrators in associations and ministries. It enables particularistic projects to be carried through, without violating the dignity of the civil service. History is filled with examples of such coalitions. However, due to their nature they do not take on organizational form or become a well-defined strategic recipe to be imitated over and over again, and both the state and the élite become very volatile.

Financial institutions in Denmark

Though the three dominating banks were rivals, they probably imitated their German counterparts until the end of the First World War. Like Tietgen, they tried to mediate collaboration within groups of enterprises belonging to their sphere of interest. By 1905 they were represented on the boards of one-third of the 90 joint stock companies in Denmark. This third, however, accounted for 56% of the total assets of the publicly held corporations. Consequently, they were able to coordinate a major share of the largest enterprises at the turn of the century. But this potential collaborative and coordinated economy had ended in scandals by the beginning of the 1920s. Intrigues between the two tycoons of that time, the founder of the East-Asiatic Company, H. N. Andersen, and Glückstadt from Landmandsbanken, by then the largest bank in Scandinavia, led to the Landmandsbanken being revealed as a club of speculators. This club included a large group of people in the highest circles in Copenhagen and had used the savings of private depositors in an unhealthy – and criminal – way for self-enrichment, but had failed (Mørch, 1986). The state hastened to limit the scandal, bailing out the troubled ship with taxpayers' money. However, the large banks had lost their position. This started a process through which they lost their ability to act like their German colleagues as coordinators and mediators of cooperation. They were no longer allowed to possess stocks and to be represented on the boards of industrial enterprises. Therefore only through great efforts could they establish the ties that make it possible for banks to act as principals towards agent enterprises.

The effect of this disruption of a credit-based system quite similar to that of Germany has not, however, been a transition to a typical Anglo-Saxon capital market-based system. In Denmark the stock-market has developed much more slowly than in these countries (Michelsen, 1991). Two institutions, in part, help explain this paradox. First, the building societies play a much stronger role in Denmark than in any other comparable society, allowing the building and equipment of private housing, farms and enterprises largely to be financed by these credit associations, which have deliberately been designed to prevent the borrower from becoming dependent on the lender. By issuing bonds in large series to finance their lendings, building societies rule out the possibility of establishing a principal–agent relationship between a specific borrower and a specific lender. Risks become socialized and statistical, rather than specific. The second institutional mechanism is the traditionally strong position of local banks and savings banks, which were created by the farmers to prevent themselves from becoming dependent on merchants and banks of larger towns. Though these savings banks could only engage themselves in loans to private customers, who could provide security in real estate, they have been able to play an important role, given the existence of basic financial means for fixed assets from the building societies. Both these financial institutions benefited small producers whose major assets were farms or craft-shops and dominion.

By establishing cooperative facilities among themselves, savings banks have gradually been able to engage in an increasing number of sophisticated banking services. In order to serve local customers they developed a sophisticated technique for assembling complicated portfolios of financial sources when communitarian ties either induced such or forced them to do so. Such communitarian relations have continued to be effective even after many of these local banks and savings banks have merged with the large Copenhagen banks, as they had already developed the capacity to act on their own within a larger context before becoming subsidiary branches.

The social effects of banks and the state on the firm

If we are right in our characterization of the state, élites, business associations and financial institutions, the consequences are important. In many countries such contextual elements condition the behaviour of firms. In the Danish case the business system lacks this very conditioning. If it exists at all, our argument leads to the conclusion that such conditioning acts at a local, rather than national, level. Proximate institutions of the sort analysed so far give no indications of a certain type of isomorphism being imposed on firms.

In both France and Germany the institutional levels mentioned combine to create strong societal mechanisms which the firm has to address either by passive conformism or by intelligent strategizing. Even in the more institutionally pluralist Anglo-Saxon models, the strong impact of the capital market system makes the business firm engage actively in financial auditing, portfolio management, etc. which combine to pull managers into an earnings growth strategy. Being neither directed by the logic of the capital market, nor offering principals in a credit-based system channel of influence, the firm in Denmark, at this stage of the analysis, seems much less defined in its social role, as the external stakeholders are unable to ask for formalization and conforming behaviour.

Some would probably argue that this situation of the firm resembles the classical concept of 'free enterprise' which only has to adapt to the logics of the free market. Our argument is rather that the nature of the firm becomes radically different from our normal concepts. As we shall see in the coming section on other proximate institutions (vocational training system, unions and professions) the lack of these conditioning factors creates less social space for managers and entrepreneurs to exercise their capabilities.

In our view, it is by combining often ambiguous demands, by coupling different partly conflicting rationalities or, in Barnard's (1938) terms, by reconciling ethical conflicts, that managers/entrepreneurs take on a social 'function' and thereby create a social space for themselves. In the Danish case, conflicting demands make it less possible to argue with some stakeholders against others, and vice versa. Consequently, it becomes quite difficult to import rationalities from a major part of the social fabric in order to legitimize authority. Management strategies become less self-evident and legitimate when they cannot be prescribed by a greater social context or be legitimized through a general discourse penetrating also institutions outside the firm. The naked state in a way leaves managers naked, too. When the agent can no longer refer to a principal, his ability to enact the role of a principal is rather weakened than strengthened. In a 'free enterprise', institutionally speaking, managers and entrepreneurs enjoy little autonomy, especially when this combines with proximate institutions which help employees achieve a high degree of autonomy in their jobs.

Vocational training in Denmark

At a very general level of analysis, Denmark's system of vocational training resembles the German dual system. Skills and testing are constituted by triparite commissions involving employers' associations, unions and public authorities at local levels for schools, at the national levels for specific trades and finally at a commission, which tries to create uniform modules among different trades. Compared to the German system, Denmark's has been modernized with the introduction of the EFG reform. As a rule, apprentices start with one year of basic training before entering their apprenticeship and selecting a narrower field of specialization. As in the German system, the Danish apprenticeship opens up a multitude of educational careers, for example to become a foreman/*Meister* or a *teknikum*-engineer. Such career paths have traditionally been very strong in manufacturing industry and crafts, making it possible for skilled workers gradually to approach managerial levels or to establish their own firms within their trade.

In recent years this career pattern has increasingly been contested by academic engineers or business-school graduates, and the enrolment rate of skilled workers to these traditional, advanced educations has declined. Instead, a new pattern is emerging (Kristensen and Petersen, 1993) in which, having concluded their apprenticeship, skilled workers embark with increasing intensity on modules of further training at the publicly financed technical schools. Local schools of different orientations have started to collaborate on new curricula, enabling quite advanced courses to be shaped entirely at the local level. In some localities workers can shift between still more advanced courses by combining the knowledge of different schools and holding different job positions, gradually learning the theoretical foundations of their speciality, and gradually expanding their ability to integrate the skills connected to their job. At the same time, they often move from one work space to another, thus achieving the skills necessary for integrating a number of job roles within a factory. This pattern makes them particularly qualified for the managerial or technical tasks which involve swift communication between the firm's higher managerial, R. & D. or sales-oriented activities. Consequently, a complex web of managerial tasks at the lower level becomes intensively populated by former skilled workers who have personally experienced conditions on the shop floor.

During the last forty years unskilled workers have also been very successful in establishing their own training system, the AMU centres, enabling them continuously to contest the skills of the skilled workers by initiating similar courses at their schools. Consequently, within many Danish firms unskilled and skilled workers are competing incessantly to operate specific work-places and machines. On the other hand, the skilled workers continuously compete with technicians about the demarcation between these two groups, which consequently are involved in continuous competition over the technical and managerial tasks involved in running the factory, if not the entire firm.

Since these dynamics are rooted in the vocational training system which, due to state inclusion, is primarily publicly financed and hence a general national system, firms are only in part able to regulate such dynamics within their own domain. Achieving these skills at schools and through publicly regulated apprenticeships, employees at all levels are very mobile horizontally. Consequently, firms are forced to apply generalized criteria for job design, autonomy, etc. if they want to be able to recruit workers with good skills. Taking advantage of this system, firms have had no need for business services like those discussed in recent debates on the continual renewal of the Third Italy small business system (Brusco, 1992). The reason is simple. By sending their workers on further training courses, Danish firms achieve at little cost what their Italian colleagues have to pay for through cooperative business services.

In short, the vocational training system is an offer which only fools refuse. However, the effect of not refusing it is that the skills to operate, staff and plan the jobs at the shop floor are introduced to the firm through the workers, rather than through managerial and technical staff. New routines, thus, do not originate from an established team of managers within the firm, as in Penrose's (1959) theory, but often arise from workers' participation in vocational training.

As the intensity and the quantity of different further training courses are much higher in Denmark than in any other European country (Höcker, 1992; Auer, 1992), each individual worker acquires an almost unique combination of skills. Unlike the dominant picture of the German system, it will evoke tension and poor utilization of these skill combinations if a workshop is managed according to a set of standard skills, as in the case of the traditional craft-dominated factory said to prevail in Germany (Maurice *et al.*, 1986). Rather, these skill combinations can best be utilized if they combine directly among the workers at the shop-floor level. Therefore, managers have to know these strange combinations from having worked within a number of various projects over the years. They have in part to share biographies with those whom they are supposed to manage. In such a system, recruitment is not a simple task. While neither tasks nor skills are managed according to predefined standards, the simplistic rules of meritocracy are inapplicable. What a system like this requires is, on the one hand, workers and other employees with a certain combination of skills, and, on the other hand, a collective ability to exercise different combinations of skills in different situations within changing group compositions.

Craft-dominated unions in Denmark

As indicated above and also elsewhere (Kristensen, 1989b, 1992a, 1992b), one of the major reasons for the dynamics and hence the importance of the Danish vocational training system is that the unions compete for the right to organize different jobs by pushing their members to undertake further training, providing them with the skills to legitimize the unions' claims.

The origin of this pattern is to be found in the core role played by craft unions during Danish industrialization. This core role again was the outcome of several interacting dynamics. One cardinal point was the discovery within the Social Democratic labour movement that it was much easier to organize unions if they followed the demarcations of the old crafts rather than those of general or industrial unions. This principle of organizing made the Social Democratic union movement in Denmark the strongest in Europe from 1880 to 1920. Simultaneously, the craft unions' role was reinforced by the wider craft movement. While gradually becoming enemies over the wage issue, the employers' trade associations, following basically the old guild divisions, collaborated intensively with their journeymen's unions to protect their trades against becoming proletarianized and/or destroyed by industrialization. They joined forces in setting-up and improving a system for vocational training by which both parties hoped to be able to regulate their numbers, improve and modernize skills and hence protect their trade from cut-throat competition and sweating.

In many industries this strategy proved successful and as the growing skill level amongst skilled workers helped them develop professional identities and continuously, despite industrialization, to strengthen their sense of belonging to a craft community, which would gradually spread from the old guild towns to include the craftsmen of agricultural areas. In effect, the remaining workers had to organize accordingly: males in the unskilled workers' union and females in their own union.

Compared with Germany this unionization pattern evokes very different dynamics among the different groups of workers. Conflicting interests cannot hide within the internal fight over hegemony of one union. Rather, these interest conflicts are fought out in the open and within individual firms employing different groups of workers. In central negotiations these different groups are able to develop different strategies in which their mutual rivalry plays an important part.

One important aspect of these strategies is that while the unskilled workers' and the females' unions have been in favour of centralized wage negotiations, most craft unions have maintained the right to negotiate wages locally after and between central negotiations. This gives the craft unions a very far-reaching range of adaptability and it is remarkable that in times of employment reduction, craft-workers are able to protect themselves from unemployment by being less demanding in local negotiations, while during booms they can change strategy rapidly.

However, by using this tool to protect their social space in the factories during the 1930s and the 1940s, they forced the unskilled workers to contest the skilled workers on the basis of their skills. By first setting up evening courses and later on schools for specialized workers, the unskilled workers tried to compete over skills and consequently turned themselves into a consortium of specialized workers, contesting continuously, now as an institutionalized pattern, the skilled workers on many fronts. In short, the craft workers have imposed their own strategy on the unskilled and turned the unskilled union into a craft union. That this dynamic is very different from the German pattern is shown by the fact that in Denmark the intensity of further training among the so-called unskilled is the highest in Europe, while Germany shows one of the lowest intensities (Auer, 1992).

Another remarkable difference between the German and the Danish systems is the fact that a Danish worker who becomes a foreman or a *Meister* has to leave the union and become a member of another union. This difference in associative practice is due to the fact that in Denmark many of the first strikes broke out because foremen/*Meisters* tried to impose rules which were in conflict with the rights and obligations of the old guilds. These new 'factory regulations' became a core issue during the intensive strikes and lock-outs around 1900. The employers won the right to organize their factories in exchange for recognizing the unions as legitimate negotiators. The effect, however, is strange. Foremen and *Meisters* are in the middle, belonging neither to the workers' nor to the managerial side, while the shop steward or 'trust man' is the true negotiator and mediator elected by the workers and to be approved by the managers.

However, the election of the shop steward is no straightforward matter. Each branch of workers, belonging to a certain union, has the right to elect their own shop steward. The 'local' shop stewards are then represented by a convenor who negotiates on their behalf with the managers.

Being excluded from this game, the Danish *Meister*, compared to his German colleague, loses a major part of the authority by which he could speak with his superiors, while he also knows that many of his superiors' decisions have to be negotiated directly with the convenor and 'his' shop stewards. Consequently, formal authority is reduced in the lower end of the managerial ladders and much autonomy is in the hands of the workers, who possess the skills to integrate planning and operations. At the same time, the workers' collective, by electing most often very experienced workers as convenors and shop stewards, monopolizes the knowledge about which skill-combinations are truly capable of being integrated. Consequently, employers have the formal right to manage the factory but seldom possess the knowledge that makes this possible independently of the convenors.

In playing this game, the group that possesses the largest and broadest scope of skills tends to win the game of how to run the factory most adequately. For these reasons the game is, in most cases, easy to dominate for craft workers, and therefore union politics, also within firms, tend to be craft-dominated, even in cases where craft workers play the minority role.

Professions in Denmark

In many countries, primarily Saint-Simonian France but also in the USA (Noble, 1977) and in Norway, as shown by Halvorsen *et al.* in this volume, the engineering profession has played a remarkable role in designing the industrial firm as a social space within which the importance of its own role is confirmed by the whole set-up of the organization. The professional hegemony of accountants within firms in the UK is another well-known example of professional influence on the social construction of the firm.

In Denmark such influence seems to be limited, as most new managerial or industrial professions have lost to the craft-oriented complex. The case of the civil engineers in particular is enlightening. The educational reforms initiated in the beginning of the nineteenth century, which led to the establishment of the engineering profession, was seen by Ørsted as contesting the old guilds' influence on production. Before the turn of the century, however, the civil engineers had decided to contest the military engineers in their struggle for social space. They aimed, in particular, for dominance in the construction of public facilities and infrastructure (Kristensen, 1942). Then, from the First World War and until the end of the 1960s, the *teknikum* engineers, by building their education on top of the apprenticeship system, ousted the civil engineers both in numbers and importance in most industries. At the same time a complex web of further training schemes made it possible for skilled workers to compete for the positions arising with the imitation of American scientific management.

Today this means that the engineering profession is separated into three different formal types, each with a very different profile (civil, academic and *teknikum* engineers), where the *teknikum* engineers are particularly strong in areas of managing and monitoring production, sales, etc., i.e. typical managerial tasks of manufacturing industry, while civil engineers in particular dominate R. & D., construction, external negotiations, etc. (Jensen and Jørgensen, 1984). Unlike in Norway (see Halvorsen, Sakslind and Korsnes' contribution in this volume) this separation of tasks has made it difficult for engineers to form a coalition against other interest groups within firms. The *teknikum* engineers will often share interests with workers, while civil engineers may often be much more prone to get involved in projects with other firms' R. & D. departments, public-financed bodies and R. & D. institutes and thus become quite marginalized in terms of internal interest formation. However, during the last couple of decades, civil engineers seem increasingly to have created their own social space in terms of large, engineering consulting firms populated with people of marginalized relations to the firm now acting formally, as they have often done informally, as external consultants. Probably a similar pattern applies to business graduates with an academic degree.

This pattern has important consequences. Most academically educated managers within manufacturing firms are recruited to formal high-level positions, where they thus become socially isolated. Therefore, they often consider such positions within firms as temporary. The limited number of steps to climb of the career ladder within a Danish firm simply makes it impossible to imitate the universal career patterns of these groups, if they are not continuously looking for jobs in other firms. Danish top executives thus become a very mobile group. For that reason top executives are often considered unimportant in coalition formation, which then takes place at lower levels of the hierarchy. Rather than becoming top managers who possess the capacity to solve ethical and politically complicated issues within the informal organization, which is said to be the function of the executive (Barnard, 1938), top managers as a collective are nomadic, travelling from one firm to another with some universal theoretical schemes about how firms may reorganize and be changed. Again academically trained managers appear in the social role of the consultant, rather than that of the executive manager.

The social role of the firm

It follows from what we have said so far, that the firm in Denmark is unable to attire itself in some sort of divine or superhuman dress. Compared with Finland, for example, where the state sees firms as means of national development, the difference is great. For no group or institution is the firm as such a means for larger than human interests. Like the Danish state, the firm is naked. It is simply a means by which men (and women) express their industriousness and through which they may aim to change their local positioning. While in many countries the state anticipates the supply of goods in general and hi-tech sectors of strategic interest in particular (Sweden some years ago even declared shoes to be one such sector) and of military importance, Danish firms have never been able to claim military importance.

Few, if any, firms in the industrial sector, would be able to mobilize more than a small gang of external stakeholders to act in their favour, politically or financially. No groups, organizations, or institutions are involved in the destiny of a firm to such an extent that they see their own survival as being dependent upon the survival of that firm. One may say that the core interest holders, apart from an entrepreneurial owner, are the skilled workers, but their relation to the firm is institutionally defined through their horizontal mobility on a labour market, where the state compensates their wages, should they lose employment.

Consequently, the core motivations for setting up and running a firm must be explained at the community level and, in particular, in terms of the individual's relations to this community, the extent to which this community celebrates, blames or counteracts the existence of firms and entrepreneurial activity (Kristensen, 1994b). It is at the communitarian level, rather than the institutional or the societal level, that it is decided whether the firm, as an institution, will be able to mobilize larger societal reserves and capabilities, should they be needed.

Our argument is that the firm as an isolated institution is not an agency in Denmark from the perspective that its strategies in themselves can create and restructure the context. Rather it is through the involvement of communitarian groups within and around the firm that are able to combine in such types of strategies that the firm as an institution will be helped to survive, to grow, or will be rejected and doomed to decline.

However, in retrospect, if we consider the totality of what has been said so far, it all adds up to a very peculiar way of developing an economy. Whereas in many countries the state shares risks with firms as a means of development, the Danish state rather seems to share the risks with the population in which it invests large resources to enable the citizens to act upon shifting circumstances. If they fail in this endeavour the state again socializes the costs. The firm in this setting becomes merely a social space for the temporary exercise of human capabilities enabling individuals to express and position themselves within their community. The logic is no less holistic than in most economies within so-called development states, but it is indeed a very different logic.

A COMPARATIVE CHARACTERIZATION OF THE ENTIRE DANISH BUSINESS SYSTEM

As is generally the case of Anglo-Saxon countries, the Danish economy could be said to be partitioned, as major actors maintain arm's-length relations to each other (Whitley, 1994). In the Danish case, however, the partitioned nature rather expresses itself in fragmentation (Kristensen, 1992a). What is related are not major oligopolistic competitors, as in the case of the USA and the UK, but rather a mass of highly specialized SMEs. Another difference is that Danish society offers a rich variety of ways to mediate informal cooperation along different communitarian relations. Among such communitarian linkages we have emphasized in particular the tight social bonds in small railway towns, and collegiate relations among craftsmen (Kristensen, 1992a, 1992b). However, we wish to emphasize the opportunities that such ties also offer business associations and the state. Contrary to Germany and France, for instance, where such ties allow firms to establish more lasting forms of cooperation, the nature of these ties seems more fragile in Denmark. Here, they enable the formation of short-term project-oriented coalitions but do not lead to the institutionalization of a lasting bloc of dominant actors. Though the business system thus is partitioned among major players forming coalitions in order to compete for the control over associations, and through this control over public finance, the communitarian ties among SMEs make such mutual relations possible in that they are both protected from being controlled by fragile dominant agents and avoid the evolution of the centrifugal type of economy, which is said to characterize Chinese business systems, for example (Whitley, 1992a, 1992b).

THE CHANGING NATURE OF THE TYPICAL DANISH FIRM

In the first section of this essay we suggested the governance system among skill containers and project coordinators and within skill containers among various teams of workers to be rooted in reputational linking. Unfortunately, at this moment, we have been unable to investigate whether this principle of governance is aided by nationally instituted mechanisms. It is obvious that standard-setting, technological measurement and public testing facilities, all of which Denmark has a great deal of help establish such a governance system and make possible the evolution among these two typical firm-types in Denmark.

However, we think that the major mechanism by which this governance system has hitherto worked in Denmark is close personal relations, though these personal relations, rather than being established through kinship, have become rooted in the craft educational complex. Whereas a conservative craft-educational complex may help establish very clear and enduring criteria for good and bad reputation, it is obvious that a craft-educational complex as dynamic, in technological terms, as the Danish will experience great troubles in retaining such criteria. Instead firms, both skill containers and project coordinators, are continuously infused with new methods of work, which have to be institutionalized as routines through interaction in a process that accepts no margin of time to separate execution from planning. It is precisely the ability to reduce planning time that enables Danish firms to gain a place in the international division of labour. Therefore, in general there is no time available to have a complex set of publicly financed institutions to define standards for reputation.

For these reasons, so runs our hypothesis, it is necessary for firms and teams of workers to establish their own reputations and test the reputations of others through a direct process of shifting collaboration. We think that Denmark, so far, has been unable to do this in other ways than by communitarian mediation. Since the craft districts in Copenhagen, in which certain crafts were clustered around a certain place or along a specific road, started to break up around 1930, the city has gradually lost the type of agglomerated economies in which skill containers and project coordinators interact. Simultaneously, it is obvious that the small village communities of Western Jutland have gradually increased their share in the total industrial development in Denmark. In these smaller communities extra-economic ties help establish such intensity of interactions that they can help sustain often only occasional business exchanges.

The ability to tie together a number of complementary skill containers on a short notice is, we think, what makes up Denmark's comparative advantage in the international market. This ability enables firms which are acquired by large multinationals to play a distinct role within such new corporate settings (see Kristensen, 1994a). As far as we know, such relations may rather reinforce than weaken these nationally specific traits. However, this strategy is more often a defensive reaction than an offensive determination of their own endogenous nature.

A more offensive response, which has been known about for a long time but more systematically explored only during the last decade, is to establish skill-container consortia. This strategy was adopted in Copenhagen at the turn of the century when, for example local cabinet-makers would join together and set up a cooperative store and showroom, which could sell to customers a whole range of different furniture. The same concept has often been employed, when Danish furniture-makers have joined together and appeared as full-range providers of all sorts of furniture at international trade-fairs. Today, this pattern among Danish furniture makers has been further elaborated, as they have set up a federative organization selling and exporting a whole group of furniture-makers' products internationally (Henriksen, 1994).

What happens in such cases is that a group of skill containers set up a cooperatively owned project coordinator that can act independently in given markets. Among machine-shops this approach has lately found widespread attention as it enables a consortium of firms to market an integrated set of abilities and offer sophisticated services to foreign firms in industrial markets. What is marketed is not a distinct product or specific subcontracting, but rather an ability to solve complex technological problems.

The evolutionary processes of growth and the problems of monitoring such federative types of firms in which peer-group relations are constituent of the organization is less than clear at this moment. In our view it seems as if, again, it will enable Danish firms to develop international strategies in a way that reinforces their basic identities, rather than changing them towards universal 'ideal types'.

NOTES

1 These two phenotypes are often integrated, as we shall see, in individual firms and for that reason it has been difficult to identify clearly such distinct roles being played out in the Danish case. The investigation of a network of firms focused on a lamp producer, by Poul Andersen and Paul Rind Christensen (1993), suddenly made the systemic pattern more clear to me. I owe much to them for this clarification, though the typification of the two phenotypes and the theorizing about them in what follows is my own responsibility.

2 The period when the Danish administration was carried out under provisional Finance Acts, not voted by the Lower House.

REFERENCES

Ackelsberg, R. and Harris, W. C. (1989) 'How Danish companies plan', *Long Range Planning* 22(6): 111–16.

Andersen, P. and Christensen, P. R. (1993) 'Internationalization in loosely coupled business systems', paper presented at workshop on 'The Danish Business System', in Århus, 6–8 October (typescript).

Andersen, S. (1992) *Dramaet i Hafnia – historien om Villums verden*, Copenhagen: Børsen Bøger.

Auer, P. (1992) 'Further education and training for the employed (FETE): European diversity', discussion paper, FS I 92-3, WZB, Berlin.

Barnard, C. (1938) *The Functions of the Executive*, Cambridge, Mass.: Harvard University Press.

Becattini, G. (1979) 'Dal settore industriale al distretto industriale: Alcune considerazioni sull'unita di indagine deell'economia industriale', *Revista di Economia e Politica Industriale* 5: 7–21.

Boissevain, J. (1974) *Friends of Friends*, Oxford: Basil Blackwell.

Brusco, S. (1992) 'Small firms and the provision of real services', in F. Pyke and W. Sengenberger (eds): *Industrial Districts and Local Economic Regeneration*, Geneva: IILS.

Chandler, A. D. (1977) *The Visible Hand. The Managerial Revolution in American Business*, Cambridge, Mass.: Harvard University Press.

Clegg, S. R. and Redding, S. G. (eds) (1990) *Capitalism in Contrasting Cultures*, Berlin: Walter de Gruyter.

Fink, T. (1986) *Estruptidens Politiske Historie*, Vols I and II, Odense: Odense Universitetsforlag.

Fivelsdal, E. and Schramm-Nielsen, J. (1993) 'Denmark', in D. J. Hickson (ed.) *Management in Western Culture. Society, Culture and Organization in Twelve Nations*, Berlin: Walter de Gruyter.

Fivelsdal, E., Jørgensen, T. B. and Jensen, P.-E. D. (1979) *Interesseorganisationer og centraladministration*, Copenhagen: Nyt Fra Samfundsvidenskaberne.

Fonsmark, H. (1990) *Historien om den danske utopi*, Copenhagen: Gyldendal.

Galbraith, J. K. (1958 and 1969) *The Affluent Society*, London: Penguin Books.

—— (1972) *The New Industrial State*, London: Penguin Books.

Gejl, I. (1989) *Indenfor Snorene. Fondsbørsvekselerernes historie – især til 1945* Århus: Erhvervsarkivet.

Gerschenkron, A. (1992) 'Economic backwardness in historical perspective', in M. Granovetter and R. Swedberg (eds *op. cit*).

Granovetter, M. and Swedberg, R. (eds) (1992) *The Sociology of Economic Life*, Boulder, Colo.: Westview Press.

Harrison, B. (1994) 'The Italian industrial districts and the crisis of the cooperative form: part II', *European Planning Studies* 2(2): 159–74.

Henriksen, L. B. (1994) 'The Danish furniture industry: a case of tradition and change', mimeograph, Institute of Production, University of Ålborg.

Höcker, H. (1992) 'Berufliche Weiterbildung für Beschäftigung in Dänemark', Discussion Paper FSI 92-8, WZB, Berlin (typescript).

Hyldtoft, O. (1984) *Københavns Industrialisering 1840–1914*, Herning: Systime.

Jensen, P. A. and Jørgensen, U. (1984) *Udviklingstendenser i ingeniørarbejdet 3: Typer af Ingeniørarbejde*, Copenhagen: teknisk Forlag A/S.

Just, F. (1986) *Banen fri for fremtiden – eller kampen om andelsloven 1909–1917*, Esbjerg: Sydjysk Universitetsforlag.

Johnson, C. (1982) *MITI and the Japanese Miracle*. Stanford, Calif.: Stanford University Press.

Kjeldgaard, M. B. and Nielsen, P. (1988) 'Industrielle distrikter, specialerapport, ISP, RUC, Roskilde.

Kristensen, J. (1942) *Dansk Ingeniørforening gennem 50 år, 1892–1942*, Copenhagen: Dansk Ingeniørforening.

Kristensen, P. H. (1986) *Teknologiske Projekter og Organisatoriske Processer*, Roskilde: Forlaget Samfundsøkonomi og Planlægning.

—— (1988) 'Virksomhedsperspektiver på industripolitikken: Industrimodernister og industriens husmænd', *Politica* 20(3): 282–97.

—— (1989a) 'Denmark: An experimental laboratory for new industrial models', *Entrepreneurship and Regional Development* 1(3): 245–56.

—— (1989b) 'Denmark's concealed production culture, its socio-historical construction and dynamics at work', in F. Borum and P. H. Kristensen (eds) *Technological Innovation and Organizational Change – Danish Patterns of Knowledge, Networks and Culture*, Copenhagen: New Social Science Monographs.

—— (1990) 'Technical projects and organizational changes: flexible specialization in Denmark', in M. Warner *et al.* (eds) *New Technology and Manufacturing Management*, London: John Wiley & Sons Ltd.

—— (1992a) 'Strategies against structure: institutions and economic organization in Denmark', in R. Whitley (ed.) *European Business Systems. Firms and Markets in their National Context*, London: Sage.

—— (1992b) 'Industrial districts in West Jutland, Denmark', in F. Pyke and W. Sengenberger (eds) *Industrial Districts and Local Economic Regeneration*, Geneva: IILS.

—— (1994a) 'Strategies in a volatile world', *Economy and Society* 23(3): 305–34.

—— (1994b) 'Spectator communities and entrepreneurial districts', *Journal of Entrepreneurship and Regional Development* 6(2): 177–98.

—— and Petersen, J. H. (1993) *Actors Adjusting to a Volatile Economy. Firms, Employees and Institutions in Denmark*, report prepared for CEDEFOP, Berlin.

—— and Sabel, C. F. (forthcoming): 'The small-holder economy in Denmark: the exception as variation', in C. F. Sabel and J. Zeitlin (eds) *Worlds of Possibility: Flexibility and Mass Production in Western Industrialization*, Paris: Maison des Sciences de l'Homme.

Marglin, S. S. (1974) 'What do bosses do?', *Review of Radical Political Economy* 6(2): 60–92.

Maurice, M. F., Sellier, F. and Silvestre, J.-J. (1986) *The Social Foundations of Industrial Power: A Comparison of France and Germany*, Cambridge Mass.: MIT Press.

Michelsen, J. (1991) *Pengene eller livet. Privat Ejendomsret, aktieselskaber og politik*, Esbjerg: Sydjysk Universitetsforlag.

Mørch, S. (1986) *Det Store Bankkrak. Landmandsbankens sammenbrud, 1922–1923*. Copenhagen: Gyldendal.

Noble, D. F. (1977) *America by Design. Science, Technology and the Rise of Corporate Capitalism*, New York: Alfred A. Knopf.

Norus, J. (1993) Bioteknologi i små og mellemstore virksomheder, Tietgenprisopgave', IOA, CBS, Copenhagen (typescript).

Østergård, U. (1992) 'Peasants and Danes: the Danish national identity and political culture', *Comparative Studies in Society and History* 34(1): 3–7.

Penrose, E. T. (1959) *The Theory of the Growth of the Firm*, Oxford: Basil Blackwell.

Pyke, F. and Sengenberger, W. (1992) *Industrial Districts and Local Economic regeneration*, Geneva: IILS.

Räsänen, K. and Whipp, R. (1992) 'National business recipes: a sectoral perspective', in R. Whitley (ed.) *op. cit.*

Redding, S. G. (1990) *The Spirit of Chinese Capitalism*, Berlin: Walter de Gruyter.

—— and Whitley, R. (1990) 'Beyond bureaucracy: towards a comparative analysis of forms of economic resource co-ordination and control', in S. R. Clegg and S. G. Redding (eds) *op. cit.*

Sabel, C. F. (1993) 'Learning by monitoring: the institutions of economic development', mimeographed paper, Massachusetts Institute of Technology.

—— and Zeitlin, J. (forthcoming): 'Stories, strategies, structures: rethinking historical alternatives to mass production', in C. F. Sabel and J. Zeitlin (eds) *Worlds of Possibility: Flexibility and Mass Production in Western Industrialization*, Paris: Maison des Sciences de l'Homme.

van Wolferen, K. (1989) *The Enigma of Japanese Power*, London: Macmillan.

Wade, R. (1990) *Governing the Market*. Princeton, N. J.: Princeton University Press.

Whitley, R. (ed.) (1992a) *European Business Systems. Firms and Markets in their National Context*, London: Sage.

—— (1992b) *Business Systems in East Asia*, London: Sage.

—— (1994) 'Dominant forms of economic organisation in market economies', *Organization Studies* 15: 153–82.

Williamson, O. E. (1975) *Markets and Hierarchies: Analysis and Antitrust Implications*, New York: The Free Press.

7 The nature of the typical Finnish firm

Kari Lilja and Risto Tainio

INTRODUCTION

It is a bold abstraction to talk about a typical economic actor in any society. The array of firms is wide in all developed societies. However, in the Finnish case as well as in the Danish case we believe that it is possible to detect a specific type of firm which sets the tone and pace for the economy, and even for the wider society. The purpose of this chapter is to take a look at how the interplay of the typical firm and the wider institutional setting has occurred in Finland from an implicit comparative perspective and to draw explicitly contrasts with the Danish case (Kristensen, in this volume). Due to the dramatic institutional changes in Europe and the internationalization of the typical Finnish firm, we also analyse the changing nature of the typical Finnish firm and the development of new managerial capabilities.

In Finland, this typical firm is a capital-intensive raw materials processor which builds its competitive position on privileged access to raw materials and an aggressive pattern of investment for economies of scale and upgrading of the system of production for intermediate industrial products. In more concrete terms, we are referring to Finnish forest product firms, which nowadays are large, vertically integrated corporations. They have gone through several waves of mergers and acquisitions, become diversified, multi-divisional and international corporations since the 1970s (Lilja *et al.*, 1991, 1992; Räsänen, 1993). Due to their small number, the 'typical' firm in fact constitutes an exception among the whole population of firms in Finland. To sharpen this statement further we could say that at the present stage of development we are describing a real type based on four leading forest product corporations (Enso, Kymmene, Metsäliitto Yhtymä and Repola, the owner of United Paper Mills). But the phenotype model of the typical firm applies equally well to some large mining, construction materials, energy and basic chemical corporations.

Following Whitley's (1994) model of the components of business systems, we shall first analyse the nature of the typical Finnish firm in terms of the components of its business system. Then we shall relate the Finnish case to Whitley's (1994: 170–5) typology of business systems to specify the relationships of the typical firm to the wider institutional system and elaborate specific mechanisms of the ways in which typical firms internalize societal resources and set standards for general societal evolution.

From the description and analysis there emerges a substantive model of the typical Finnish firm. Due to the internal transformation of such firms into Europe-wide players, and within the radically changed institutional environment of the European Union, we indicate also that the typical Finnish firm is currently experiencing a major qualitative change, especially in terms of its operating context. The paper is written in a way which makes it possible to distinguish the major differences between typical Danish and Finnish firms and concludes by drawing up some of these differences.

ACTORS AND OPERATIONS OF THE TYPICAL FIRM

The nature of typical firms as economic actors

Even at the very beginning of the process of industrialization, the typical Finnish firm was large and beyond the control of single individuals. By that we mean that the essential factors of production and business were not readily at hand in the immediate context of the people amidst whom the firm became established. Considerable economic, cultural and cognitive barriers had to be overcome when starting up a business. For instance, the amount of capital needed for the establishment of pulp and paper mills during the latter part of the nineteenth century – as today – exceeded the resources of a single entrepreneur. Thus the joint stock form was important in facilitating the pooling of capital for the huge construction projects and to buffer the risks inherent in the long payback periods of such investments. The histories of single firms exhibit long periods of losses, periodic takeovers by banks and bankruptcies. Decade after decade, the distribution of good years and bad years was very much skewed to the latter (Standertskjöld, 1973).

It is essential to recognize that Finland has been a thinly populated area and a frontier economy. In order to get the production and logistics to function, firms have had to establish whole communities and facilitate their functioning. From this mill-community tradition it is understandable that forest product firms eventually diversified to various unrelated businesses like engineering, construction, printing, publishing, agriculture, leisure activities, community services, etc. Thus the scope of the business activities has been very wide among the major forest products corporations, to the extent that they were at the same time leading machinery makers for the pulp and paper industry (as in the cases of Ahlstrom, Kymi-Strömberg, Rauma-Repola, Tampella and United Paper Mills; see, e.g., Räsänen, 1993; Kosonen, 1994; Laurila, 1995). This trend towards (seemingly) unrelated diversification continued until the middle of the 1980s, when there was a clear change in strategy. After that turning-point the forest products corporations started to rationalize their business portfolios, and have developed more specialized and international product-based divisions. Here are some of the internal seeds of the qualitative change of the typical firm.

For explicating the societal space within which the autarky of the firm existed, it is necessary to make reference to the concepts of company town or mill village. In several cases, mill communities were able to separate themselves from the surrounding municipalities and establish themselves as independent municipalities, having local taxation rights, considerable autonomy in local administration and democratic institutions. The personalized power structure derived from ownership and positions of top management was, however, very visible (see Koskinen, 1987a, 1987b).

But there is an interesting paradox in the way the self-sufficiency of the firms must be conceptualized. Within the existing sphere of operations, the typical firm was very autarkic. On the other hand, however, when strategic moves had to be made the firm was very dependent on other sources of economic power and the nature, timing and the inter-organizational composition involved in the strategic move had to be negotiated.

Modes of organic growth at the mill sites

The basic consideration and competence in continuous process production systems is to keep the production going close to the limits of the system's capacity and to avoid breakdowns. However, in order to be able to carry out maintenance, the whole production system has to be shut down periodically. The main implication of this duality is that there are two very different logics of action and sets of hierarchically organized practitioners: one for the continuous process and the other for planned shut-downs and emergency break-downs (Penn *et al.*, 1992). During the continuous process considerable autonomy is granted to both sets of practitioners, to different organizational levels and occupational specializations. This leeway is disciplined by the impersonal technological rationality. The danger of breakdowns is always present and they are disliked by everybody due to the social inconveniences related to firefighting activities, close direct control, time pressures and huge economic losses.

Learning to orchestrate the complementary codes of the two logics of action within the reproductive mode is the first source of organic growth. By gradual experimentation it becomes possible to spot the contingencies which are related to breakdowns and to find the bottlenecks in the continuous production process. This experi-mentation goes on from the initial start-up and over the years can improve the yield from the initial capital investment by up to one-third (Lilja, 1989). In a multi-machine corporation it can during a year equal the value of a new paper machine. For this reason a special concept – the ghost machine – has been introduced to describe the emergence of new capacity arising from the trimming efforts of a corporation.

The second mode of organic growth is to enter into a huge development project, the purpose of which is to create a new-generation machine or mill design. The development project is a mobilization of the sector level technological community (cf. Tush-man and Rosenkopf, 1992) involving a wide range of firms and research institutes. The final phase lasts from two to five years until the new production capacity is in use. The bringing on stream of completely new capacity is the most dynamic form of growth. An interim mode of growth is to make an upgrade in the production process by a machine rebuild.

The choice of the operating modes and their combinations occurs in capital intensive industries under the dynamics of competition and the decision to enter the developmental mode is typically trig-gered by a forecast gap in the demand and supply of an intermediate product. But because this choice is dependent on what competitors do, there is much uncertainty as to the right timing of the invest-ment. This is complicated by two other external contingencies: tech-nological advances in the downstream industries and in the upstream supplier industries. New technological opportunities and customer needs set the scene for an investment race (cf. Ghemawat, 1991).

Authority relations within firms

Authority relations within the typical firm at the mill level are conditioned by the needs of the two operative modes. The work contexts of both the reproductive and the developmental modes are characterized by teamwork, where hierarchical differences are played down. The reputation of individual engineers is built upon the quality of their contribution to the daily problem-solving activities conducted in teams, in wider meetings and in workshops. In this professional context peer evaluations are a major source of personal pride and reward. However, there is a huge difference in the complexity of social relations and knowledge bases involved in the reproductive and developmental operating modes. In the reproductive operating mode there is a need to create direction for practitioners of internal technological disciplines, whilst in the developmental mode the assignment deals with coordinating the work with external technological communities, i.e. linked with machine suppliers, R. & D. institutions, technological consultants and the technological trajectories of customer firms. The difference between the reproductive and developmental operating mode is also built into the career paths of engineers.

The reproductive context of work is important for finding technological talent among professionals and the work force. For university-educated engineers the research assignments related to the various phases of the production process are the critical initiation tests for analytical skills as well as for social skills because some of the information has to be collected from individual workers and work crews. They have their own norms for revealing and concealing relevant work-related information. These shifting codes are both person- and work-place-climate related. Having the skills to manage the person-related contingency is a good omen for a career in production management. Besides the analytical dimension of compiling results from on-going observations and small-scale experiments, a successful experience curve effect is built from a collective evaluation of the presented evidence and a synthesis which consists of the modelling of the process variables, the technological solutions or the improvements, their cost calculations and implementation plans which take into account not only the improvements but also the lost production during the shut-down.

The process of collective evaluation goes on simultaneously with the more operative tasks of keeping the process at the limits of capacity. Every morning the working day starts with a session where all the professionals collectively share their views on the most important aspects of the on-going development work. The developmental operating mode is organized around projects and there are different degrees to which these project organizations have experts assigned to them on a part-time or full-time basis. In the case of a new mill development project, there is an autonomous project organization which has a core of experts who are in charge of the planning assignment and who can draw on both internal and external resources for special tasks (Alajoutsijärvi, 1993). Participation in the developmental mode of work, from a career point of view, is more attractive than the reproductive mode because it prepares an engineer either to take responsibilities in the next reproductive phase of the project or to enter a similar type of large-scale developmental project. Recruitment processes receive wide attention in the sectoral technological community and are subject to internal politics within the firms. The timing of large-scale investments occurs in anticipation of the growth phase in the business cycle. For this reason they have a national character, they are followed up in the media step by step, and the final go-ahead decisions can change the whole economic climate from recession to boom.

There is strong social pressure for recognition, in the form of official status and a designated organizational empire defined by formal organizational structure and title. This concern has a long historical heritage in the traditions of the forest product firms, because formal positions were linked with a variety of privileges and visibility both in local and regional contexts. In order to make a career progression from the sphere of production management and engineering to the ranks of general management it is typical that the person will have been in charge of several successful development projects.

Work-place industrial relations

The mill community and company town tradition had as its social core a strong paternalistic employment and industrial relations model which relied on personalized social relationships of the employer and the employees and the exclusion of the trade union movement. Social activities in the village were as important as interactions at work for creating a high commitment to work and to socialization into skilled identities, generation after generation

(Koskinen, 1987a). In many cases the social standards and practices developed in the mill communities were highly advanced compared with those in the surrounding society (Haapala, 1986). This created an identity of the mill community which bridged hierarchical and economic differences between the employer and the various groups of employees and paved the way for a deferential stance towards the employer. Thus it was quite evident until the end of the Second World War that the social relations of the typical firms differed from the dominant pattern of social and industrial relations in Finland, which was mostly adversarial (Lilja, 1992).

Since the Second World War, paternalism has been replaced by a pluralistic system of work-place industrial relations and a collectively regulated system of internal labour markets. How has this influenced the classic dilemma in interest representation: that of either dividing or expanding the cake? In the typical firm, long-term considerations for growth have received most attention. The basic reason for that is rather simple: workers themselves have made many types of mill site specific investments. These are related to their careers in the internal labour markets, covering often several members of an extended family and often two generations. Housing and summer cottage investments are not liquid in small communities, etc. This contingency has made it possible to integrate the workers' work-place organization and especially its leadership into both operating modes of the mill sites.

The learning curve effect is supported by clauses on productivity bargaining in the industry level collective bargaining agreement (Koistinen and Lilja, 1988). Additionally, the senior shop steward has an astonishingly strong position, working full-time in the negotiation and participatory organization of the mill site and for the reproduction of the informal workers' work-place organization (Lilja, 1987). Typically, they have had a long career in the work organization as well as in the shop steward committees and the government of the local union before they become elected to the highly prestigious position of the senior shop steward. In that position their visibility extends far beyond the work place and the local community. They have a strong incentive to listen to their constituency because their position is subject to election every third year. With the current technocratic openness of the present generation of managers, the representatives of the workers are fully aware of the general strategic perspectives of the mill sites and can read the terse messages of the corporate management for those aspects of strategic moves which are not publicized.

Thus in the contemporary work organization of the typical firm there is a mixture of organizational principles in use which regulate and switch the locus of authority. The system of work-place industrial relations is only one example of this. It complements the occupation-based hierarchical division of work and has diminished the status of the foremen and changed their encompassing role to that of a technician or an administrator. Another example is the team- and project-based organization of the developmental mode which draws human resources from all hierarchic levels, across functions, across mill sites and across company boundaries. This script for managing is based on the awareness of the need for multiple types of expertise, covering both theoretical and tacit forms of knowledge.

From the above description it can be concluded that the typical Finnish corporation is a complicated technological system designed for large-scale cost efficient production and to the constant upgrading of the technological system by making both incremental improvements and quantum enlargements in capacity with qualitatively new technological features in the processes and products. This expansionist and aggressive approach to competition, compared with Canadian, Swedish and US firms (Jörgensen and Lilja, 1994), would not have been possible without a set of inter-organizational and intersectoral connections which link the typical firm to the wider contexts of the Finnish economy.

Market relations

Technological innovations have been important in sensitizing entrepreneurs for the location-specific opportunity in Finland to exploit wood chips. But without a market pull they would not have entered into such very risky investments. However, with few exceptions, the established firms lacked strong customer connections. This problem was solved by forming joint sales associations for various products. These associations were so efficient that very few firms attempted to organize their sales independently. Price competition was cut off in export markets and the Finnish sales associations have maintained high visibility and market leadership in many European countries due to their large size and the completeness of the product assortment.

Due to the stability of the relationships between the production-oriented firms and their joint sales associations, there is only a formal similarity with the duality of skill containers and project coordinators, described by Kristensen in the previous chapter. The sales associations paid the producing firms upon shipment of their products irrespective of the time when the final customer paid. Thus the sales associations took care of financing the on-going production operations. In the case of new customers, they were also in a powerful position because they had a chance to influence to which company the initial contact and order was directed. The operating arms of the sales association have always been near to the customer, stationed in the various geographic market areas of Europe and elsewhere. Thus the sales personnel have been expatriates who have had great incentives to adopt the values and lifestyles of their customers in order to be able to integrate into local business communities and to structure deals which served the interests of both customers and suppliers. This integration extended to heroic attempts to meet tight time-tables or other special requirements. Such deeds are still recollected often decades after they have been achieved. They become the symbols of the reciprocal obligations and commitments tying seller and the buyer into a long-lasting relationship (cf. Klint, 1985).

It has to be added that the use of joint sales organizations was by no means restricted to the forest industry. It was a common practice also in the textile and engineering industries. Finnish market relations have also been mediated by several large general trading companies for supplying manufacturing customers in Finland and operating as export companies for manufacturers, especially in distant markets (see Inkiläinen, 1994). This tradition is very similar to arrangements institutionalized in Germany and Japan (Orrù, 1993: 187–8). In the retail sector the channels have been organized and to a large extent owned by strong wholesale firms which do not give much space for independent shopkeepers. All these features have important implications for the class structure: role models of independent entrepreneurs have been rare and the small relative size of the petit bourgeoisie in Finland is conspicuous.

A summary of the business-system characteristics of the typical firm in Finland

The descriptive characteristics of the model of the typical firm can be condensed into a characterization of a collective survival recipe. Its core is to extend the life cycle of a mill. Technologically it consists of the right balance of the reproductive and developmental operating modes. In terms of managerial growth strategies it has meant increased vertical and horizontal integration. These shorthand expressions hide the social side of the typical firm. The major internal actor groups consist of:

- the variety of engineering professionals linked horizontally to external technological communities of the engineers;
- the core process and maintenance workers tied to the internal labour markets and to the local community by their mill site-specific personal investments and;
- the sales professionals servicing customers in various market areas.

Enlargement investments have been seen by the engineers as a solution not only to technological problems but also as a way of attracting top-quality recruits from other firms and from the technological universities, as well as for keeping up with technological progress and career advancement. For the core workers their meaning is related to continuity of employment and the survival of the local community. Increased volumes have allowed the growth of the sales office network, and the differentiation of product grades the opportunity to move away from commodity types of transactions to more specific and stable customer niches. Because of the linking of these social stakes to the technological trajectory of a mill site, political processes within and around the typical firm can easily be analysed using a social movement perspective (Laurila, 1995). But there are many more contingencies for the survival of the typical firm. By looking at the historical and societal constitution of the model it becomes possible to give an historically specific explanation of how to secure the economic, human and political resources for the waves of expansion and how to stabilize the system?

THE HISTORICAL AND SOCIETAL CONSTITUTION OF THE TYPICAL FIRM

In this section we elaborate the characteristics of the typical firm by locating it in the wider societal and geopolitical structures. We will start the analysis of the simultaneous constitution of the typical firms and their structural contexts by describing the emergence and maintenance of nationally significant economic power blocs.

Economic power blocs and financial institutions

During the six hundred years to 1809, Finland was part of Sweden. After that it became a Grand Duchy as part of the Russian empire. In the newly formed autonomous Grand Duchy the language of the educated élite was Swedish. In the 1880s the number of Finnish speaking population was 85 per cent.

It was this Swedish-speaking élite which was most active in taking advantage of the new business opportunities which were created by technological development, the industrial revolution and increasing free trade in international markets. Those families which were significant owners of the new businesses were often relatives and part of the same inner circle. This social homogeneity of the upper class became an obstacle to the development of Finland as an independent nation-state, and so part of the ruling élite decided to integrate themselves with the Finnish-speaking majority by adopting the Finnish language and supporting its use as a source of identity for the emerging nation. This faction of the national élite was called the fennomanic movement. Its programme towards nation-building escalated from cultural, social and political arenas to the economic field during the 1880s (Kuisma, 1993: 403 10). At the end of the 1880s, members of the fennomanic movement started to campaign for the establishment of firms in the financial sector dominated by the Swedish-speaking business élite. Thus the business community became divided by a linguistic cleavage between Swedish- and Finnish-speaking industrialists and businessmen. Two economic power blocs started to emerge.

The Finnish-speaking élite established a commercial bank (KOP) first, in 1889, and two insurance companies (Suomi, in 1890 and Pohjola, in 1891). These firms started to build their own financial group with a sphere of influence in manufacturing and distribution. The flagship corporation of this financial centre has been what is now called Repola Oy and it was created by several waves of mergers and acquisitions between corporations belonging to the same financial group. Currently, part of Repola's corporate empire is also United Paper Mills, the forest products corporation of the flagship.

The emergence and growth of firms owned by this Finnish-speaking business élite led to rivalry at the bloc level, which strengthened the ties of the Swedish-speaking business élite. However, the integration of the Swedish-speaking firms into a bloc happened much more slowly than on the Finnish side, because individual firms were much stronger, having accumulated capital over many decades. Two commercial banks, which later merged to form what is now called the Union Bank of Finland, became the core financial firms of a set of manufacturing firms with Swedish-speaking owners. In the field of the forest industry, the flagship corporation of the Swedish-speaking economic power bloc has been Kymmene Oy, similarly the result of a long chain of mergers and acquisitions starting in 1904 when Kymmene became one of the largest paper product firms in Europe.

The significance of bloc formation was soon recognized by the farmers and the working-class élites. They launched similar collective projects in various other fields of economic life. For both of these social classes the cooperative movement was the major economic form for mobilizing the masses and controlling their assets. The farmers' cooperative movement has been able to create one of the major forest products firm in Finland, today called Metsäliitto Yhtymä, as well as a bank group with its sphere of influence especially in the food industry. The workers' economic power bloc has not, however, tried to establish firms in the forest products industry. It has been most influential in retailing, food manufacturing, financial services and construction. The major structural change during the last few years has been the withering away of the workers' economic power bloc.

When entering into the developmental mode, the typical firms needed a strong bank connection. The capital intensity as well as the long payback periods of the investments have necessitated access to bank loans (cf. Zysman, 1983). Equity capital has always been scarce in the Finnish financial markets. On the other hand, the typical firms were good customers for the banks and in most cases the banks and typical firms were tied to each other by cross-ownership and cross-representation at supervisory board level or even on the boards of directors. These double positions gave access to inside information and coached both parties in the specific business logics of both manufacturing and financing. In the forest products firms the main substantive issue is the necessity to understand the importance of the long-term which means at least seven to ten years, the whole business cycle and the even more longer-term, twenty to thirty years which is the technical usability time of major capital investments. There are numerous cases in which top managers have during their managerial career held top positions both in the banks and in the typical firms. This sharing and circulation of managerial cadres within the bank spheres of influence is typical also in Japan (Orrù, 1993: 190). In the Finnish case the engineering background of the top management of the typical firms and their synchronization with the banks has led to a growth mode in which all kinds of strategic and internal management problems are solved by investing in the technological base.

There are few cases in which the bank spheres of influence have been broken through acquisitions, and hostile takeover bids have been rare and, if tried, not successful. This constitutes a striking contrast to the Anglo-American market for corporate control and attempts to make money by selling acquired assets to new hosts. The banks have taken care of the competitiveness of their flagship corporations by restructuring manoeuvres.

The role of the state in the economy

The role of the state in the economy has to be looked at from four angles. First, how did Finland's position as a Grand Duchy within the Russian empire give the initial demand pull for the typical firm? Second, how did the economic power blocs use the independent Finnish state after its emergence in 1917 to further their collective projects? Third, how did the state copy the model of the typical firm and implement it in its own sphere of economic influence? Fourth, how did the state expand its own sphere of influence through trade relationships with the Soviet Union?

Since the beginning of the Russian era, Finnish firms were able to export goods to Russia without paying customs duty, or at least paying lower duties than firms in central and western Europe. This advantage gave the initial impetus for investments in the pulp and paper industry in the eastern parts of Finland after the beginning of the 1870s. From this corner of Finland, there was a good railway connection to the heartlands of Russia and its empire. The growing demand, good quality and cost-efficient production gave the Finnish firms a competitive edge over the Russian pulp and paper firms and led to the construction of capacity which greatly exceeded the national demand in Finland. The Russian revolution changed these commercial relations completely. Finland became independent in 1917 and bolshevik Russia adopted a mercantilistic trade policy. The forest industry was, however, able to find new markets in western Europe where it established a viable position. Trade with Russia dropped from a very high level in 1913 to zero in 1918, and stayed low until the 1950s when it started to grow as a natural continuation of the war indemnity which was demanded by Soviet Union after the Finno-Soviet war of 1941–4.

After independence in 1917 it became possible to launch a nationalist industrial policy. A paradigmatic case of this active and interventionist economic policy was the acquisition of a forest products corporation, Enso-Gutzeit Oy, which had been under the ownership of Norwegian entrepreneurs (Kuisma, 1993: 509–31). Thus the state was used to bring one of the core forest products firms into Finnish ownership. It is also important to note that the acquisition of Enso-Gutzeit was a continuation of the strategy of the fennomanic élite. In general, it has been characteristic of élites in Finland to operate through and with the state.

The state-owned manufacturing sector expanded from forest products to mining, engineering, energy, chemicals and even to oil-refining based on imported crude oil. If private firms were not willing to take the huge initial risk in making the investment and financing the project while no cash flow was available, the state would do so. In the late 1940s and the 1950s, the establishment of state-owned firms supported regional development which was especially important for farmers and the agrarian/centre party. The expansion of the state-owned manufacturing sector was as eagerly promoted by the social democrats and the communists, who had an increasing base of support at the large industrial work places. State-owned firms have strengthened the Finnish-speaking business élite and stabilized its self-esteem to the point where the language cleavage no longer figures.

Having established firms in many industries, the state became responsible for their future. One key to this problem was trade politics. After the Second World War, trade with the Soviet Union started to grow. The institutional peculiarity of this trade was that it was based on agreements made between the states, and was monitored by bilateral commissions controlled by the states, causing an exceptional centralization in the trade relationships with clearly identifiable figures, such as the state presidents and the chairmen of the commissions who were influential top politicians. The major actor on the Finnish side was the state-owned oil-refining corporation, Neste, which had the right to import oil from the Soviet Union. In exchange for this oil the other Finnish corporations could sell products to the Soviet Union at prices fixed in bilateral negotiations. These trade arrangements boosted the establishment and growth of state-owned manufacturing corporations in Finland, and an unusual degree of state intervention in the economy, compared with other west European countries. This policy supported the diversification of the manufacturing base in Finland and provided business opportunities for other firms operating as suppliers or in the service sector. Additionally, the technological community of engineers has provided the complex applied engineering knowledge needed in the processing of the varied raw materials.

Economic interest organizations

The need for specialized economic interest organizations of the economic élite emerged with the radical parliamentary reform which occurred in Finland in 1906. In the earlier estate-based parliament, economic and political representation were unified and the nobility, clergy and bourgeoisie could easily shape the legislation according to their economic interests. Thus the development of class-based organizations experienced a major shift after the parliamentary elections of 1906, in which women also had voting rights, for the first time in Europe.

The distinct position and interests of the typical firm in the total population of manufacturing firms can easily be detected by looking at the history of the economic interest organizations of firms. The typical firms – being forest products firms – were strongly oriented towards exports and contributed until the late 1950s about 80 per cent of export revenues (Seppälä *et al.*, 1980). Thus it is very clear that the interests of the typical firms and those of the home market firms differed as to the economic policies of the state. Consequently, these lines of manufacturing industry had a separate peak interest organization until 1976. By that time firms in other industries than the forest product industries had gained market shares in international trade and the views on state economic policies, especially on currency policies, had become more homogenized to allow the creation of a joint peak organization.

Besides influencing the economic policies of the state, the economic interest organizations of the forest industries have had important functions for fostering cooperation between the member firms. A good example of the latter role of the Central Association of the Finnish Forest Industries is a commission which regulated and controlled the investments for new capacity of the chemical forest industry companies. The commission was established in response to the competitive over-investments of the corporations in the early 1960s, which resulted during the recession of 1966–7 in a huge overcapacity. The commission was in operation from the end of the 1960s until the middle of the 1980s. Such an exceptional mechanism between major competitors and members of different power blocs was possible because the Bank of Finland was informally involved in its operation. Foreign currency exchange was regulated by the central bank until 1986. Because major investments often required loans from abroad, the consent of the Bank of Finland was important for the final investment decision. Another concern was the sufficiency of wood raw materials in the forests. These issues drew the firms into joint negotiations.

Because of the large number of state-owned corporations, leading politicians and civil servants have been on the boards and supervisory boards of the firms owned by the state. They have been as well-informed of the industry logics of the typical firms as the directors of the financial groups. That is why it has not been difficult to communicate the needs of the typical firms to those arms of the state machinery which formulate the economic policies of the state (Tainio *et al.*, 1989).

The density of membership in the various interest organizations is high. The main motivation for that has been the great importance of centralized representation in policy-making committees of the state concerning economic policies and negotiating collective bargaining contracts. The interest organizations of the business community constitute the fourth pillar in the corporatist negotiating system operating between them and the state, the farmers' interest organization and the labour movement. Due to the class coalition of the business community and the farmers, the labour movement has not had such a central position in the system of political power as has been typical in Sweden or in Denmark. Another peculiar feature has been the powerlessness of the representatives of the small business sector. The main explanation for this is the narrow social base of small business in Finland, implied by the dominance of large firms both in manufacturing and distribution, with a heritage of being self-sufficient in a wide range of operational tasks.

The system of collective bargaining

The chemical paper industry has set the tone for the development of the Finnish industrial relations system in three different phases. First, after the civil war in 1918, the united employers' front refused to enter into collective bargaining agreements with the unions. This stance was led by the employers' association of the forest industries. Thus Finland was cut off from the development of the Scandinavian model of industrial relations (Lilja, 1992). Employers' associations in Sweden, however, were eager to persuade their Finnish colleagues to adopt industry-level collective bargaining because they estimated that cheap labour in Finland was a major advantage for the Finnish firms in the international markets where they competed (Kalela, 1981).

Second, after the ending of the Finno-Soviet war in 1944, it was the employers' association of the forest industries which made the first industry-level collective bargaining contract and opened the gates to normalization according to western European standards. This move, and the subsequent approach of the employers' association, paved the way towards a very exceptional track in industry-level collective bargaining: whilst Finland is known for its high propensity to strike in manufacturing, and there have been several waves of worker mobilization, the Paper Workers' Union has not called full-scale industry-level strikes because of disagreements after the negotiations (Lilja, 1983, 1992).

Third, at the end of the 1970s when attempts to introduce a law for regulating employees' participation in firms was about to be passed, the chairmen of both the employers' association and the Paper Workers' Union intervened and were able to shape the law to reflect the basic features of the system of workers' participation in the pulp and paper industry. This intervention prevented the system of shop stewards being overridden by a heavy compulsory mechanism of works councils, and there is less separation in the systems of collective bargaining and employees' participation. Similarly, the negotiating mechanism stipulated by the law in the event of essential changes at the work-place imitated the clauses of the collective bargaining contract in the paper industry. In this way the typical firms were able to continue their established pattern of work-place industrial relations by making minor adjustments, whilst small and medium-sized firms experienced the regulatory change as a problem which required top management attention. This ability to build on internally created institutions is a major strength of typical firms.

Based on the decision made in the convention of the central organization of the workers' unions in the early 1920s, the union structure was designed according to the principle of industrial unionism. This reflects the relative weakness of the craft unions at that time. Their relative weakness was mainly due to the fact that craft unions were not direct inheritors of the traditions of the guild system. Thus the Paper Workers' Union has had a long tradition of being an industrial union. However, in maintenance departments there have been pockets of electricians who have belonged to the Electrical Workers' Union, due to their education and past employment history. Similarly, workers in mechanical maintenance have belonged to the Metal Workers' Union, which has been the strongest industrial union in manufacturing. Little by little, however, the growing prestige of the Paper Workers' Union and the improved wages of the core process workers have drawn other blue-collar workers at the mill sites to the Paper Workers' Union. Thus, in practical terms, the employers at mill sites are facing a single local union for the blue-collar workers and its shop steward committees. The foremen and clerical staff have their separate local units of representation.

The 'labour aristocracy' character of the paper workers is very visible in the union structure: workers in mechanical woodworking or in forestry do not belong to the Paper Workers' Union – the former belong to the Mechanical Wood Workers' Union and the latter to the Union for Rural Workers. This separation represents the technological and locational core–periphery segmentation of the workers in the typical firm. It is the more significant because on the employers' side the corporations typically have all these related industries under the same authority structure. Very often the mechanical forest products factories are on the same integrated mill site, but even so paper workers have insisted on the separate union structure due to the greater heterogeneity of the other related industries. Thus at the industry level the representation of the employers' interests is unified in one association, but workers are in three separate unions. This separateness has, however, not weakened the bargaining power of the paper workers.

The associational strategy of the Paper Workers' Union can be understood better if we look at the operating procedures inside the union. The striking feature in the union government is the strong position of the rank-and-file representation. There is no other union in Finland where the distribution of power in a union is balanced between the union officials in the central office and the work-place representatives. In the case of the Paper Workers' Union it is possible to talk about dialogical union democracy in a very exceptional sense (cf. Lipset *et al.*, 1956; Offe and Wiesenthal, 1980). The reasons for this exceptionality are interesting, not only for understanding the classical theme of the iron law of oligarchy (Michels, 1949) but also how the union leadership conditions the typical firm.

There are about fifty large mill sites in Finland, which account for about 80 per cent of the workers in the paper industry. The senior shop stewards of these work-places have an annual conference at which they, together with the central office, plan the collective bargaining strategy. Because they know the economic situation of each of their firms, they are in a good position to put effective pressure on the employers. Both sides are intimately aware of the situation-specific bargaining power of the other party. There is a very rare link with talk and action, not only in the off-the-record informal negotiations but also in the publicized views of the parties. Thus it has become possible to create a tradition where neither side pushes short-term power advantages too far in the industry-level collective bargaining, on the basis of shifts in the business cycle. That would lead to an escalating spiral in the use of open power. However, the employers' association has had to strike a balance between resisting inflationary wage pressures and running the risk of lost production and reliability in servicing the customer. So far preferences have been skewed to the latter.

The educational system

The typical firms were among the first to establish private primary schools in the late ninteenth-century Finland and later on, especially in the inter-war years, private vocational schools, as part of their community-building efforts. Similarly, the typical firms, along with other large firms, have been instrumental in setting up and supporting higher education at technical universities and business schools. However, when analysing the interrelationship of the typical firm and the Finnish educational system over the long term, the dominant trend has been the externalization of the basic education of the labour force, as well as the higher levels of specialist and professional education, from the typical firm to the state and local authorities, keeping only highly specific tailor-made schemes for further training in the joint domain of the typical firms.

These externalization efforts have also been favoured by the Finnish state, which adopted a universalistic approach to the structures of sectoral administration. The Finnish-speaking élite has supported this strategy because it was part of the emancipation strategy for opening all levels of education to the whole population. Though this administrative universality seemingly has no linkage to the internal functioning and social codes of the typical firm, there are many informal practices which bring the special interests of the typical firms into the educational agenda. The most conspicuous example is the sectoral specialization of the technological universities in research and teaching of the technologies linked to the forest sector. Thus, for instance, the Helsinki University of Technology has the largest and most diversified department by staff, research and teaching in the whole world which specializes in the process technologies of chemical forest products. Moreover, in other departments and laboratories of the university a complementary specialization is well known. Similar forest sector-specific approaches to education and research are typical also in other technological universities and faculties, as well as in ordinary universities and business schools.

The socialization of the university-educated engineers to the technological problems and organizational cultures of forest product firms has in most cases started much earlier than in the university. Very often their parents have worked in forest products firms. Thus some of the social skills related to forest products operations are learned at home. Partly they are acquired during the informally dualistic educational system of the university-educated engineers, who work as trainees during their summer holidays. During their studies they take assignments as foremen and technicians and finally, at the end of their studies, they produce a master's thesis on a problem suggested (and also paid for) by the employer. This gives a socialization period of ten years during which the interaction of both practical duties, social relationships at work and theoretical studies prepares the university-educated engineer both for a specialist or more managerial phase of his/her career.

The emphasis on training of the core process and maintenance workers was part of the paternalistic employer policies from the early days of the forest product firms. Since the 1970s, this tradition has been backed up by considerable training budgets and several mills have adopted a policy whereby workers are not laid off during recessions, when the mills are shut-down, but instead participate in in-house or external training courses. The Paper Workers' Union has demanded the introduction of a sixth shift to the prevailing five-shift manning scheme to formalize the training logic as the newest layer in the multiplicity of organizational principles of the mills.

The professions: interpersonal social networks

In Finland, the role of civil society is restricted. Personal life projects and local grass-roots initiatives are squeezed either by the universalistic and bureaucratic principles of the state administration and its sectoral policies, or by the well-elaborated societal programmes of the economic power blocs enhanced by corporatist negotiations. For this reason, professional communities do not have a societal significance beyond the established structures of the power blocs and their typical firms. Moreover, the centralization of societal decision-making can extend even beyond the power blocs, due to the existence of cross-sectoral and inter-bloc social networks. Such top-level network connections make those based on professional logics less significant. But at a more humble level of the routines of typical firms, the professions have significant effects.

Though the loyalties of the professionals are divided, with several powerful spheres of influence among the engineering professions, there is a long-established tradition for sharing experiences on the working of specific machines, technologies and work routines (cf. von Hippel, 1987). This sharing occurs across corporate boundaries at the individual level due to various kinds of cohort effects (e.g. joint education or work history) and at a more formalized collective level through the activities of the professional associations and their educational centres. Thus, for instance, the educational centre of the engineers arranges workshops in which highly focused problems of leading-edge technologies are reviewed and where examples are presented from firms which have had relevant experience. These workshops allow suppliers, users, researchers and technological consultants to confront each others competences. They are part of the technological innovation networks through which the technological trajectories of the whole sector are explored. This sharing of insights upgrades the technological competence of the whole profession, irrespective of specific roles and corporate connections (cf. Tushman and Rosenkopf, 1992).

Central characteristics of the Finnish business system: deep and wide mobilization and centralized risk-sharing

This analysis of the Finnish case corroborates Whitley's suggestion that the elements of business systems have strong interrelationships and that distinct national patterns can be discerned. In the Finnish case we can talk about a collaborative or a coordinated type of business system (Whitley, 1994: 170–5). The nationally specific features of the typical firm consist of an inner and outer layer of actors and two linking mechanisms between these layers.

The first linking mechanism consists of the deep and wide mobilization of actors for ambitious technological leaps expanding the capacity or conquering new upgraded product segments for the typical firm. We have shown that in the Finnish case the vertical synchronization of actors for large-scale investments in the typical firms is extremely deep. Not only banks and the bank-linked power blocs have been involved, but also the state, through its top civil servants and politicians and through its ownership of typical firms and by multiplying the forest products firm-based model in other raw-material processing industries. At the other extreme, the vertical synchronization of stakeholders extends to the shop floor, at least as to the style the leadership of each mill site's workers' work-place organization chooses for interest representation. The width of the mobilization is related to parallel intentions of the typical firms and power blocs: they compete with each other in most of the product groups. Because there are short leads and lags in the diffusion of strategic knowledge for new investment opportunities, all of the typical firms and their power blocs have attempted to adopt similar strategic moves. This contingency has resulted in periodic over-investments, overstretching of resources and overheating of the economy. The demands of the typical firms for supplies which are basically internal to the nation-state trigger huge multiplier effects in the whole economy. Thus the parallel vertical mobilizations add a further degree of ferment to the inherent instability of the Finnish economy which has been based on the export of very cyclical inter-mediate industrial products. For this reason there has been a strong need for risk-sharing and multi-level associative mechanisms.

Due to periodic economic crises, the power blocs and the state have been forced to take over the risk-sharing function, adding another dimension to the very centralized system of national decision-making. To moderate the competitive races over new investment opportunities, informal and formal practices for inter-bloc coordination have emerged. Neutral meeting places, provided by annual meetings of some jointly owned firms, state committees, sports and cultural organizations have been important. They have allowed focused communication, informal exchanges of ideas, oppor-tunities to initiate conciliatory processes and mutual adjustments. Periodically these neutral meeting places have been turned into influential 'quasi-boards' where inter-bloc and inter-sectoral policy making occurs (Korhonen, 1990).

THE CHANGING NATURE OF THE TYPICAL FIRM

While there are some routines and managerial competences of the typical firm which can be maintained despite the changing insti-tutional environment, or which can even be transferred to different institutional environments, it is not difficult to point out wider con-textual changes which create considerable pressure for the repro-duction of the typical Finnish firm. We first highlight these erosive trends in the institutional embeddedness of the typical firm. Second, we specify the rational core and the learning gaps of the manage-ment of the typical firm in the new context. Third, because the success path of the typical Finnish firm has been very much a product of a collective project, the question must also be asked: in what ways is there still the basis for a collective project?

Contextual pressures for change

The factors tending to erode the institutional security of the typical firm can be quite extensive. Some of the key issues are:

1 withering away of power blocs and bank control;
2 decreasing relevance of national level institutional support;
3 competing sectoral logic.

Withering away of the power blocs and bank control of the typical firm

During the long recession of the early 1990s it has become obvious that risk-sharing within the economic power blocs is no longer possible. It led to the collapse of the economic power blocs of the working class and the collapse of the savings bank group. The whole banking sector was maintained only by massive state support. The whole concept of the banks' sphere of influence has come under scrutiny, for five reasons:

1 The EU directives and Finnish banking laws set strict limits on the risk concentrations of the commercial banks, as well as requirements for the minimum proportion of own capital within the total balance sheet. These regulations set limits to lending for the flagship corporations and put pressure on their liquidity and solidity.
2 Due to the deregulation of the financial markets most large firms have set up their own intra-firm financial units, which are often located abroad. These units are capable of operating in financial markets with international merchant banks in a way which make these services of the Finnish banks redundant or at least subject to competitive bids.
3 The size of the typical firm is now such that during booms their cash flow allows them to make large-scale investments without borrowing money.
4 Foreign investors revived their interest in Finnish corporations at the bottom of the recession in 1993, when the Finnish mark was weak and the stocks were undervalued. As the restrictions on foreign ownership have been abolished, the level of foreign ownership has jumped in many core Finnish corporations. The attractiveness of the stocks of the Finnish-based corporations has also revitalized the privatization of the state-owned corporations. Most of the investors are pension funds which do not intend to

exert voting power in the corporations. However, the existence of loose, short-term placements looking for profits in the markets indicates that foreign firms may try to get decisive control of the typical Finnish firms. There have also been negotiations in which mergers across the banks' spheres of influence have been tried out (e.g. between Kymmene and United Paper Mills). Thus the sacred status of the ownership connection to a bank is diminishing and the propensity of the typical firms to search also for cross-border mergers has increased in line with other industries (e.g. construction materials, electrical engineering, shipbuilding, etc.).

5 The rationalization needs of the Finnish banking system are widely acknowledged. Rumours of the merger of the main two commercial banks have been strong. Such a move would completely undermine the concept of economic power blocs.[1]

All these developments lead to the conclusion that the flagship tradition of the major commercial banks is becoming outdated because large corporations will no longer commit themselves to one bank in exchange for an open-ended risk-sharing contract. Nor is the bank control of the typical firm through ownership possible any longer because of the wide diffusion of ownership of the typical firms and the danger of law suits from other owners in cases where particular owner interests are violated.

The decreasing relevance of national level institutional support

Finnish management has been characterized as strong in operational and institutional management. The success path of the typical firm can be explained in terms of these managerial competencies. It has not, though, demonstrated a high level of excellence in business management and/or strategic management. In the new European and global context the old competence in institutional management is less relevant. There are no Europe-wide power blocs on whose support in risk-sharing the typical firm can rely. Nor are there sympathetic state authorities to lobby for a stabilization of the institutional environment. Even the most primitive aspects of organizational intelligence have to be reorganized in order to be able to make sense of the on-going European-wide transformation in each relevant industry network. The new managerial agenda is filled with European-wide R. & D. consortia of various sorts of technologies which directly influence the shape of the offerings of the typical Finnish firm. New regulatory pressures for preserving the natural environment are also causing radical rethinking on raw material inputs, in processing technologies, product choice and mill locations.

Competing sectoral logics

The sector-based competitive advantage of the forest firms has been considered an impediment for the diversification of the Finnish economy because the economic policies of the state have, especially during crises, aligned with the needs of the forest sector firms (Lilja *et al.*, 1992: 144–5). By becoming international firms through foreign direct investments and becoming partly owned by foreign owners, the Finnishness of the typical firm has dramatically diminished. At the same time some dominant firms in the economy have cut their roots to the forest products industry (e.g. Nokia) or the wider forest sector industries (e.g. Kone). The success of some of the smaller research based corporations has given new momentum to the hi-tech lobby in Finland. It is clear that the notion espoused by the forest industry of being the leading national industry is now easier to challenge. The technological policies and venture capital funding of the state are being geared increasingly to the new, product innovation-based industries than to the well-established typical firm.

The hard core and learning gaps of the typical firm

It is obvious that the professional and craft-based competencies linked to the two operating modes of the typical firm constitute its hard core. These competencies contain deep and wide sectoral link-ages and the sector-wide upgrading dynamics. The abundance of management skills of both the operative and the developmental mode is a partial explanation for the fact that Finnish firms have been able to increase their number of production units at a quicker pace than their competitors, allowing them to be first movers in upgraded products with technologies based on economies of scale. However, depending on the complexity of the technological package and the intended operating mode, there are clear interrelated infra-structural, social and geographic constraints.

An obvious issue is the inclusion of the marketing profession and sales organizations into the structure of the typical firm and its various divisions and profit centres. The abandonment of the joint sales associations has developed to the point where practically all major pulp and paper corporations have their own sales organization. However, it does not mean that cross-functional managerial capabilities have emerged. The marketing function is still a very underdeveloped activity (Rohweder, 1993).

Through the disintegration of the sales associations the independent sales office network at local market areas has become thinner and perhaps less visible. It also means that the new sales offices cannot offer a full range of products or their technical properties. It also takes a long time for new offices and their personnel to establish social relationships with the customers and a sense of belonging to the local business community. Though in some cases Finnish firms have been able, through acquisitions, to buy themselves into local business communities by retaining the earlier owners and key managers as part of the new management team, the amount of investment needed in communicating commitment to a market area is underestimated. This is basically due to the fact that the production end of the chain is not sufficiently well aware of the activities carried out at the sales end. Also the shift to more customer-specific products is a rather recent phenomenon which means that the 'bulk product, anonymous market' mode is still the actual script for calibrating the relevance of marketing investments.

The internally generated growth path has led to the establishment of European-wide divisions. A third of the capacity of the Finnish-owned paper production industry is already abroad. This has increased the variety of both cross-national organizational cultures and work-place industrial relations. Attempts to lever increased economies of scale by rationalization of the types of production runs are very vulnerable to the defence mechanisms of local mills and sales offices. It is easy to get the support of established customers against switching production from one country to another within the division. Brand naming of products, which is the newest development in printing and writing papers, locks customers even further into existing locations of production. Though the Swedish and Finnish organizational cultures and institutional traditions are not so far apart in European-wide terms (e.g. Hofstede, 1980), Finnish managers have already encountered in Sweden an organizational culture which they are not so well equipped to deal with. Basic criticisms of the Swedes are related to weaknesses of the new owners in communicating strategic intentions in case of acquisitions, intolerance of lengthy discussions and negotiations, etc. (Vaara, 1992).

The managements of the new European-wide divisions are facing radically different regulations on industrial democracy, consultation and collective bargaining. Subsidiarity means that this heterogeneity is going to persist. It is clear that when traditional cleavages between management and workers are complemented by national and mill-specific cleavages between the management and employees of a European-wide division, it also makes the handling of division-wide organizational politics extremely difficult. It means that perceived synergies are difficult to realize within the divisions.

The old raw material-based identity of large process-oriented corporations has proved to be inert in the face of new market niches and end-uses of pulp and paper-based products. These industries are becoming more and more segmented as to the nature of raw materials, production processes, product grades, delivery modes and value constellation in which many firms jointly produce the offering (Normann and Ramiréz, 1993). A good example is the printing and writing papers, where the rapid diffusion of home printers, copiers and telefaxes has made office papers a consumer product (Rosenbröijer, 1994). This market demands a completely different distribution and logistical chain than that required by the graphic industry and large corporate and public sector customers. In paper converting, the segmentation of separate businesses becomes a hundred times more complex than in the paper business, due to the delicate differences in the end-uses of converted paper. In this changing context the typical Finnish firm has adopted a rather monolithic stance, emphasizing quick implementation of European-wide domination strategies in advanced printing and writing paper grades but relying on scale economies. For instance, US forest product corporations have adopted a completely different strategy in Europe, being able to conquer the most consumer-oriented market: the production and distribution of tissue papers. The complexity of the whole chain, from fibre cultivation to consumption, is open for different types of business concepts and there will be considerable variety in the future configuration of types of business logics. For Finnish-based corporations this potential variety is an opportunity space where they clearly have new inter-organizational roles to learn.

The disappearance of the collective project?

In the agenda of the typical firm, one of the top priorities is to become more focused in business operations and to reach a higher position in the European or even global league in the industries and product groups in which the firm chooses to operate. A necessary condition for such a development path is that managerial comet-

ences for both business and strategic management become institutionalized within the typical firms. This implies a higher degree
of self-sufficiency at the level of extended competition, i.e. in the
competition for future business opportunities. If this agenda is
implemented, is there still something to be achieved by the collective
project approach which for so long has dominated the Finnish
economy? Recent history offers some clues to the future.

There are two stepping stones for business operations on a European and global scale for Finnish firms. The first is the existence of
world-class knowledge of the whole range of forest sector technologies. The second is the captive market of Finnish-owned forest
industry business units already existing, or planned to be established,
abroad. This 'international' demand has formed the basis of internationalizing business operations of Finnish firms beyond the forest
industry. These two conditions have helped to develop international
business operations for the following types of businesses: forestry,
pulp and paper and mechanical woodworking machinery, industrial
textiles, filler minerals and coating chemicals, finance and investment
banking, insurances against breakdowns, consulting for forestry, technological and management issues, auditing, EDP-based communication network services, software products for mill-wide operations
control, etc. Thus it appears that there is a special Finnish way of
internationalizing business operations based on the tight coupling
of inter-firm relations in connection to a sectoral knowledge base.

COMPARATIVE CONCLUSIONS

Though, in international comparisons of nation-states, Denmark and
Finland share many similar features such as size, prosperity and overt
institutional framework of the Scandinavian tradition, the descriptive
account of the models of the typical firms (see Table 7.1) and their
institutional embeddedness has revealed striking differences. By not
choosing a matched pair design for the coordinated research, the
differences in the models of the typical firms is not the message. The
point is to illustrate how the types of relevant social actors, typical
firms and institutions systematically differ between two small
developed countries. Differences in raw material base, pre-industrial
heritage and geopolitical position are important initial conditions but
in a period of over one hundred years there is considerable space
for social actors to shape their values, world-views and interrelations.

Table 7.1 The nature of the firm

	Denmark	*Finland*
Phenotype	(1) skill container; (2) project coordinator.	Vertically integrated mill sites in multi-business corporations.
Market relations	Many-layered relations connecting skills across firms.	Oligopolistic buying operations; joint sales associations with institutionalized customer relations.
Authority relations	Technical superiority of managers; horizontal codes of work honour.	Efficiency through technically rationalized obligations; innovations by respecting the plurality of knowledge bases.
Mode of development	Reducing market dependency by expanding to: (1) multi-product contractor; (2) assembler.	Experience curve effect; new generation design for technological leaps; adding new business units.

The main coordinates along which the Danish and Finnish business systems differ are the centralization–decentralization of the system and the relevant time horizon. Centralization is accentuated in the Finnish case due to the large size of the typical firm, its power bloc connection, the collective nature of the establishment and expansion of the typical firm (involving also the employees and local communities), and the importance of state mediation in copying and multiplying the typical firm model and in its being involved in risk-sharing. In the Danish case the skill containers and project coordinators are built bottom-up through the accumulated skills of clearly identifiable individuals and primary groups, with locally known reputations. The system is kept together through social ties and shared history of joint project-type business operations with infrastructural support only of the institutional system of the wider society (cf. Kristensen in this volume). The major constitutive mechanisms underlying these differences are summarized in Table 7.2.

Differences are similarly dramatic on the temporal dimension. In the Finnish case the relevant timescale for major changes in the question of being or not being in business is the interval of the whole

Table 7.2 The societal place of the firm

Constitutive mechanisms	Denmark	Finland
	Partitioned economy with communitarian cooperation.	Collaborative economy with state meditation.
State	Decentralized segmentalist but inclusive.	Centralized unified.
Élites	Competing fractions with unclear recruitment criteria.	Overlapping interest structures.
		Enforced consensus due to external threat.
Associations of the business community	Independent of their constituency; state inclusion; mechanisms for imposing particularized private agendas on the state.	Forums for intersectoral and inter-élite negotiations of the agenda.
Financial memberships	Variety of institutions, e.g. building societies, as a source of independent finance; lack of bank representation in manufacturing.	Influential bank groups; inter-board memberships; shareholdings between banks and manufacturing.
Vocational training	Dual craft system; vertical and horizontal mobility.	School-based state-regulated occupational layers; horizontal mobility of professionals.
Unions	Craft-dominated.	Industrial.
Professions	Weak associations; weak ties to industry.	Weak associations; strong ties to industry.
Social role of the firm	Means for human expression and communitarian positioning.	Symbol of power bloc capabilities.

business cycle or the time-span of the technological viability of a machine or mill investment. From a social point of view, the latter time horizon is relevant because in most cases of failure, firms or their production units have found new parents, whilst the old owners have suffered the losses. This does not mean that the timing of the huge capital intensive investments is not important. Its evaluation is possible only on a longer term. In the Danish case the critical time period is months rather than years because the customized project assignments do not last long. Orders cannot be stockpiled because the inputs are essential for the work processes of other skill containers or project coordinators. Relationships between firms are as strong as the last delivery. At the extreme, it could be said that the reputation of a social actor is created by being able on a daily basis to improvise and adjust to the unexpected contingencies of the inter-firm and customer-mediated production processes. The difference in the relevant time horizon of the typical Danish and Finnish firms is strongly correlated with the structural shape of the business systems and is reflected in many of the individual institutional dimensions.

ACKNOWLEDGEMENTS

We are indebted to Peer Hull Kristensen for the many years of fruitful discussions which have helped us to discover important aspects of the Finnish peculiarities. Tables 7.1 and 7.2 have been compiled together with Peer Hull Kristensen. We are also thankful for the comments of Markku Kuisma and Richard Whitley. We gratefully acknowledge the economic support of the Finnish Academy, which has financed our sabbatical leaves.

NOTE

1 In February 1995, the two major commercial banks in Finland made an announcement of their merger, ending the era of separate 'Swedish-speaking' and 'Finnish-speaking' financial power blocs. This agreement is going to have deep-rooted consequences to the ownership structures of firms in all sectors of the economy.

REFERENCES

Alajoutsijärvi, K. (1993) Asiakas-myyjä -suhteen muutoksista ja niiden syistä: tulkintaa Kymmenen ja Valmetin suhteen kehityksestä vuosina 1948–1990. Jyväskylä. Jyväskylän yliopisto. Julkaisuja N:o 90/93.
Ghemawat, P. (1991) *Commitment. The Dynamic of Strategy*, New York: Free Press.
Haapala, P. (1986) *Tehtaan valossa. Teollistuminen ja työväestön muodostu-*

minen Tampereella 1820–1920. Historiallisia Tutkimuksia 133, Helsinki-Tampere: SHS.

Hofstede, G. (1980) *Culture's Consequences*, Beverly Hills, Calif.: Sage.

Inkiläinen, R. (1994) *Transformation Beyond Skill. A Process of New Capabilities Development in a Trading Company*, Helsinki: Helsinki School of Economics.

Jörgensen, J. and Lilja, K. (1994) *Explaining Business Level Differences in Canadian and Finnish Forest Product Firms*, Helsinki School of Economics. Working Papers.

Kalela, J. (1981) *Taistojen taipaleelta. Paperityöläiset ja heidän liittonsa 1906–1981*, Tampere.

Klint, M. B. (1985) *Mot en konjunkturanpassad kundstrategi – om den sociala relationens roll vid marknadsföring av massa och papper*, Uppsala: Uppsala University.

Koistinen, P. and Lilja, K. (1988) 'Consensual adaptation to new technology: observations from the Finnish case', in R. Hyman and W. Streeck (eds) *New Technology and Industrial Relations*, Oxford: Basil Blackwell.

Korhonen, M. (1990) *Metsätalouden Institutionaalinen Johtaminen*, Helsinki: Helsinki School of Economics.

Koskinen, T. (1987a) *Tehdasyhteisö*, Vaasa: University of Vaasa.

——— (1987b) 'Herruutta, hallintaa vai vuorovaikutusta?', *Hallinnon Tutkimus* 6(2): 101–5.

Kosonen, P. (1994) *Corporate Transformation and Management*, Helsinki: Helsinki School of Economics.

Kuisma, M. (1993) *Metsäteollisuuden maa*, Jyväskylä: Suomen historiallinen sensa.

Laurila, J. (1995) *Social Movements in Management: Making a Technological Leap in the Case of the Anjala Paper Mill*, Helsinki: Helsinki School of Economics.

Lilja, K. (1983) *Workers' Workplace Organisations*, Helsinki: Helsinki School of Economics.

——— (1987) 'Workers' collectivity at the workplace as an independent organizational mechanism', *Scandinavian Journal of Management Studies* 3(3–4): 197–211.

——— (1989) *Epics and Epochs: Organisational Learning and the Kaskinen Pulp Mill*, Helsinki: Helsinki School of Economics.

——— (1992) 'Finland: no longer a Nordic exception', in A. Ferner and R. Hyman (eds) *Industrial Relations in the New Europe*, Oxford: Basil Blackwell.

———, Räsänen, K. and Tainio, R. (1991) 'Development of Finnish corporations: paths and recipes', in J. Näsi (ed.) *Arenas of Strategic Thinking*, Helsinki: Foundation for Economic Education.

———, ——— and ——— (1992) 'A dominant business recipe: the forest sector in Finland', in R. Whitley (ed.) *European Business Systems*, London: Sage Publications.

Lipset, S. M., Trow, M. A. and Coleman, J. A. (1956) *Union Democracy*, Glencoe, Ill.: Free Press.

Michels, R. (1949) *Political Parties. A Sociological Study of the Oligarchical Tendencies of Modern Democracy*, Glencoe, Ill.: Free Press, reprinted edn. (orig. 1915).

Normann, R. and Ramírez, R. (1993) 'From value chain to value constellation: designing interactive strategy', *Harvard Business Review*, July–August.

Offe, C. and Wiesenthal, H. (1980) 'Two logics of collective action: theoretical notes on social class and organizational form', *Political Power and Social Theory* 1: 67–115.

Orrù, M. (1993) 'Institutional cooperation in Japanese and German capitalism', in S.-E. Sjöstrand (ed.) *Institutional Change*, Armonk, N.Y.: M. E. Sharpe.

Penn, R., Lilja, K. and Scattergood, H. (1992) 'Flexibility and employment patterns in the contemporary paper industry', *Industrial Relations Journal*, 23(3): 214–23.

Räsänen, K. (1993) 'Paths of corporate change and the metaphor of "sectoral roots": the case of Finnish corporations 1973–1985', *World Futures* 37: 111–42.

Rohweder, T. (1993) *Product Reorientation in the Finnish Paper Industry*, Helsinki: Helsinki School of Economics.

Rosenbröijer, C.-J. (1994) *The Changing Relationships and Strategic Identities of Actors in Industrial Distribution Channels*, Helsingfors: Swedish School of Economics.

Seppälä, H., Kuuluvainen, J. and Seppälä, R. (1980) *Suomen metsäsektori tienhaarassa. Folia Forestalia 434*, Helsinki: Metsäntutkimuslaitos.

Standertskjöld, J. (1973) *Kaukas*. Lappeenranta.

Tainio, R., Ollonqvist, P. and Korhonen, M. (1989) 'In search of institutional management, The Finnish forest sector case', *International Journal of Sociology and Social Policy* 9(5/6): 88–119.

Tainio, R., Lilja, K. and Santalainen, T. (1994) 'Changing managerial competitive practices in the context of growth and decline in the Finnish banking sector.' Paper prepared for the EMOT workshop on Financial Services in Europe, Paris, 30 Sept.–1 Oct.

Teulings, A. (1986) 'Managerial labour processes in organised capitalism: the power of corporate management and the powerlessness of the manager', in D. Knights and H. Willmott (eds) *Managing the Labour Process*, Cambridge: Cambridge University Press.

Tushman, M. L. and Rosenkopf, L. (1992) 'Organizational determinants of technological change', in B. M. Staw and L. L. Cummings (eds) *Research in Organizational Behavior*, Greenwich, Conn.: JAI Press.

Vaara, E. (1992) *Mergers and acquisitions between Finland and Sweden 1981–1991*. Helsinki: Helsinki School of Economics.

von Hippel, E. (1987) 'Cooperation between rivals: information knowhow trading', *Research Policy* 16: 291–302.

Whitley, R. (1994) 'Dominant forms of economic organization in market economies', *Organization Studies* 15(2): 153–82.

Zysman, J. (1983) *Governments, Markets and Growth*, Ithaca, N.Y.: Cornell University Press.

8 Institutions and types of firms in Belgium

Regional and sectoral variations

Ad van Iterson

INTRODUCTION

Belgium is a newcomer to nationhood. Independence from the King-dom of the Netherlands was gained in 1831, when the Belgian Revolt broke out.[1] Before the 'Dutch rule', which had commenced in 1815 after the Treaty of Vienna had incorporated the 'Belgian' provinces in the new Kingdom of the Netherlands, Flanders and Wallonia had been annexed by the French (in 1795); before that, for centuries Belgium had been a distant province of, successively, the Spanish and Austrian empires.

> La Belgique n'a jamais été dans sa conception initiale, qu'un glacis jeté entre quelques puissances d'Europe occidentale. Rien d'étonnant dans ces conditions à ce que la région ait dans ce pays un contenu émotionnel, linguistique et politique comme on n'en rencontre que dans les 'terres d'entre-deux'.
>
> (Romus, 1979: 73)

A mere 160 years later, Belgium is perhaps again on its way to collapse. Anyhow, it is safe to assume that the state of Belgium is heading towards a federalist constitution. Since 1970 on, when the first constitutional reform was agreed upon, Dutch-speaking Flanders, French-speaking Wallonia[2] and the bilingual capital, Brussels,[3] have become to a considerable extent 'regionalized'. At present, the three regions have their own governments with power of decision in fields such as education and industrial policy.[4] When, in autumn 1995, separate elections are called, Belgium may be considered a federation of two or three semi-autonomous states. The hottest political issue, in this process, is the social security system. Payment of social benefits is still coordinated by the central government, as are most taxes, such as corporation tax. Federalization of the former would prove very unfavourable for Wallonia, which has been in decline for some three decades, socially and economically.

Many see the disintegration of the Belgian nation-state as an inevitable outcome of a 'false', illogical start. 'The Belgian state began its life as an uneasy alliance of French and Flemish against the domination of the North, and ever since then its two halves have been drifting towards a polarization' (Shetter, 1987: 299). The alliance is believed to be uneasy as both halves differ not only linguistically, but also in social and economic respects.

It has been argued that the French-speaking industrial élites were the moving spirit behind the Belgian Revolt and Secession. As the 'Walloon steel barons' sought protection of their young industrial enterprises, the interests of their trading counterparts from the Northern Netherlands, who still had the most influential voice and defended the economic doctrine of free trade, were felt to be incompatible. Be that as it may, from the outset the Belgian state showed a strong commitment to the Walloon large-scale industries, to the neglect of the more 'traditional' Flemish economy. However, the craft-based pattern of production in Flanders survived in a considerable number of consumer goods industries, as a sort of organizational and sectoral undercurrent, and has become more successful in recent decades, among other things because the region profited from the foreign direct investments which gained momentum in the 1960s and concentrated on the Dutch-speaking part of the country. Thus, we see that not only do the dominant types of firms differ between both principal regions, but also that these economic actors are active and more or less successful in different sectors.

The broad purpose of this contribution, then, is to highlight the role of regional and sectoral variations in the social construction of economic actors. First, the development of distinctive types of firms in both parts of Belgium will be discussed. In providing explanations, which is the next step, the analysis will focus on the influence of the state, the financial and the labour system (See Whitley, this volume). Finally, the question will be raised as to whether Flanders can be considered another Italian-style industrial district.

DISTINCTIVE TYPES OF FIRM IN WALLONIA AND FLANDERS

Wallonia is the cradle of industrialization on the European continent. As early as 1789, the British industrial consultant, William

Cockerill, had introduced mechanical carding and spinning to the woollen industry of Verviers, in the Ardennes. In 1807, Cockerill moved to Liège, where he opened a workshop for the manufacture of textile machinery. Cockerill's son John became the leading figure in the Belgian – and indeed European – machine industry (Henderson, 1965). The centre of his activities was Seraing, a boom town outside Liège, which is therefore considered as the birthplaces of continental industrialization (e.g. Lebrun *et al.*, 1981). Together with textiles and machinery, the Walloon area witnessed the emergence of a modern coal mining, iron, steel, non-ferrous minerals and glass industry. Mining of coal, iron, zinc and tin was a centuries-old tradition in the Walloon provinces of Liège, Namur and Hainault. This led to the establishment of well-developed craft industries such as the manufacture of armaments and nails in Liège. The existence of this proto-industry was one of the reasons why the modern industries 'took off' so early and so fast in the valleys of the Meuse and Sambre, and in the Borinage (e.g. Mokyr, 1976).

As early as the 1830s, the limited liability company form had started to diffuse in Wallonia. Cockerill's enterprise, for instance, became a joint-stock company ('Société Cockerill') in 1842. It would, however, be wrong to state simply that the managerial enterprise was the distinctive type of firm in nineteenth-century Wallonia. First, the majority of the industrial enterprises were still family firms – not untypical in the initial phase of western industrialization (e.g. Kocka, 1979). Second, and more importantly, control of financial resources of both familial and managerial enterprises was increasingly acquired by holding companies – particularly the Société Générale.

Industrial entrepreneurs in the post-Napoleonic Low Countries were hindered by limited availability of finance for investments,[5] so in 1822 the King of the Netherlands, supplying three-fifths of the founding capital, set up the Société Générale, the world's first mixed bank, to provide investment credits for, as it happened, mainly Walloon entrepreneurs. In the 1830s, the Société Générale (by now in the hands of the provisional Belgian government) started serving as a vehicle for establishing firms and merging small family enterprises.[6] All these new firms were limited liability companies – as was the Société Générale itself. Shortly after the winning of official independence in 1839, a large number of shares owned by the Dutch king were purchased by private investors, particularly the Brussels' banking families (Bolle, 1972), who had already contributed to the Société's founding capital.

This financial hegemony over industry not only determined the course of Walloon industrialization in the nineteenth century, but also remained dominant in the twentieth century. Control of the largely basic Walloon industries by the Société Générale, and its bank, the Générale de Banque, paved the way for the (large, industrial) holding company system which remains a characteristic of the Walloon business system today. 'Roughly 150 years ago the institution was doing what it does today, issuing publicly financial claims to hold claims in companies with the objective of monitoring these companies financially and otherwise, if necessary' (Daems, 1978: 36). Daems qualifies the holding company system in Belgium as 'remarkably stable' – the more so, since in the United States the holding company was only a transitory economic agent (roughly between 1880 and 1914), a predecessor of the fully owned diversified firm, the Chandlerian giant (cf. Mayer and Whittington, this volume, who argue that the holding company is not necessarily an intermediate type).

One can indeed recognize today the nineteenth-century pattern of ownership and control of industrial enterprises by holding companies, usually labelled as 'financial capitalism'. Most of the contemporary Belgian holding companies are incorporated, and their shares are often actively traded on the Brussels Stock Exchange. The dispersion of these shares shows an interesting dual pattern. Private households are important investors in holding-company stocks, owning about 30 per cent. However, '[m]ost of the controlling interests in the holding companies are held either by financial interest groups (Société Générale and Almany) or by wealthy families (Electrorail and Bruxelles-Lambert)' (Daems, 1978: 22). This simply means that the majority of the shares of the Belgian holding companies have been acquired by other Belgian holding companies.[7]

The companies in which the holding companies hold claims are among the largest industrial and financial enterprises in Belgium. As to the former enterprises (which are also active on the stockmarket), nearly all holding companies operate in basic and other traditional capital-intensive industries – the newer industrial sectors (e.g. chemicals and mass-produced consumer durables) being left to foreign groups or to joint ventures with other financial groups. Finally, most of the Belgian holding companies hold diversified portfolios, as did the Société Générale. A minority, however, specialized in specific industries such as glass, petrol, electricity and tobacco.

The intriguing part of the first Daems quote is the phrase: 'to hold claims in companies with the objective of monitoring these companies *financially and otherwise, if necessary*. It is this 'struggle for control' which distinguishes the holding company from other financial institutions, such as mutual funds, and is, according to Daems, the holding company's very *raison d'être* (ibid.: 64). Control is first and foremost sought via large shares of equity capital. Since the shares of both the holding companies and the companies in which they hold a share of equity are publicly traded, the financial monitoring activities of the former are quite visible.[8] Less visible is the control exerted via reliance on family ties or other trusted persons to influence the decision-making process in the 'subsidiaries', to use Daems' term and, most important, via their representatives on the board of directors. Control via trust relations and board membership enables holding companies also to influence corporate strategic (and maybe even operational) decision-making: the 'otherwise' which is sometimes deemed 'necessary'.[9]

Clearly, control over strategic issues is but an additional instrument. The holding companies only seek *some* influence on companies' policies to prevent or correct unwished-for managerial decisions. In explaining the continued existence of holding companies, Daems refers solely to the willingness of small savers to pay a higher price in exchange for risk reduction. However, the limited involvement of holding companies in the management of their subsidiaries might also have its roots in the traditional preferences of the French-speaking, mainly Brussels' *haute finance*, which after all is in control of the holding companies. To exert *some* influence might be sufficient to secure the financial interests of this group, which sees no accumulation of status capital in managerial activities. This is not surprising, given the social and cultural gap which has characterized relations between the Brussels' financial élites and the Walloon industrial élites right from the beginnings of Belgian industrialization in the early nineteenth century (e.g. Belder, 1977; Lebrun *et al.*, 1981). However much both groups have needed each other in pursuing their 'economic' objectives, the world of money and the world of machines have always remained quite separate in French-speaking Belgium. This identity-related institutional feature differs remarkably from the German pattern, where banks and (heavy) industry feel mutually committed, but it fits with the aloof attitude of the French financial institutions.[10] Other evidence supporting the assumption that holding companies seek to keep involvement in management of their subsidiaries as limited as possible might be found when looking at growth patterns of the holding companies. The prevalence of share price growth over market share growth of a holding company's 'subsidiaries' would be indicative of these preferences for financial management. For sure, holding companies are traded very actively on the Brussels stock-market: together with banking and energy they represent the top three sectors. But the very closeness of Belgian financial élites hampers a better insight into this subject matter. 'Pas de chiffres' (no numbers) is a notorious response in the Belgian business world.

So, the stability of the Belgian holding company system might not be that 'remarkable', as long as this *haute finance* succeeds in retaining its financial and network power to choose a mix of governance structure which is optimal from its own point of view: financial control and, if inevitable, as limited control as possible over strategy and operations via trust relations and board membership.

Flemish industrialization did not gain momentum until the last quarter of the nineteenth century, along with Dutch and German industrialization. The spin-off from Walloon industrialization has always been modest. Apart from 'rational' considerations related to the lack of infrastructure and natural resources,[11] ethnocentric feelings played an important role as well: before the 1950s, Flanders hardly seems to have existed in the eyes of the French-speaking élites.[12] It is argued (somewhat exaggeratedly, maybe) that the most important reason for establishing manufacturing firms in Flanders was if one considered the production process too dangerous or polluting for the densely populated urban areas of Wallonia (Vandewalle, 1977). Most such firms, owned by the Société Générale, are active in metal processing.

The belated diffusion of the limited liability company in Flanders, compared to Wallonia, is in accordance with the region's retarded industrialization. But the reason for the limited diffusion of this judicial form ever since must be sought in the very absence of state-supported finance through the holding company system. This, and the unavailability of other credit suppliers, gave the family a pre-dominant role in Flemish economic organization. It was a group of locally oriented industrial entrepreneurs, using their savings as capital and their large families as labour (Mok, 1993: 13), who in fact initiated the process of industrialization in Flemish-speaking Belgium. This resulted in a structure where the family firm was the dominant type until the 1950s.

Many Flemish family-established and family-owned firms originated in the rural areas around smaller towns such as Aalst, Bruges, Courtrai and Malines. These KMOs ('Kleine en Middelgrote Ondernemingen', or SMEs) show a strong dynastic tradition. Most of them have succeeded to this day in keeping ownership and control in the family. Family capital accumulated chiefly through non-payment of dividends. Attracting outside capital was avoided as much as possible.[13]

The Flemish familial enterprise was, and still is, particularly active in the consumer goods sector[14] – more specifically, 'traditional' consumer goods such as textiles, clothing, food, carpets (Vanhaverbeke, 1992), furniture (Boone, 1992), etc., albeit that these craft-based firms thoroughly modernized their manufacturing processes as well as their products. Many Flemish SMEs in these fragmented industries are market-nichers. Another feature of Flemish SMEs in recent decades has been their strong international orientation. Exports rose at a high pace.[15] And production followed products: more and more parts of the transformation process are sourced out to lower-wage countries (e.g. the Santens group, which relocated a large part of their textiles production activities to Ireland). Undoubtedly, for these traditionally local-oriented firms, this strategy involves unprecedented issues of coordination and control.

Some of these late-nineteenth-century family-established firms evolved into large family-owned managerial enterprises. The most famous examples are Bekaert, manufacturer of steel wire, near Courtrai, and Gevaert, outside Antwerp, which produces photographic chemicals. By now, both enterprises have been taken over by foreign investors, which brings us to the next dominant type of firm in Flanders, and indeed all of Belgium: the foreign multinationals' subsidiaries.

In the 1950s, when Belgium, and especially Flanders, faced alarming unemployment rates due to a too-slow post-war recovery, the state framed so-called 'expansion laws' aimed at attracting foreign investment. Multinational companies turned out to be particularly interested in the strategic position of the port of Antwerp, in the heart of Western Europe, and the low wages in the Flemish-speaking provinces at that time, so the Flemish economy profited most from this foreign influx. Those Flemish SMEs which were active in machine-building and speciality chemicals found new outlets as suppliers to multinationals such as Ford and Volvo.

However, in the last few years a widespread anxiety about 'economic colonization' (Crooijmans, 1991) has arisen. That this so-called 'anchorage debate' only broke out some two decades after foreign firms had started to invest on a large scale can be explained by the fact that these multinationals changed their expansion policy around 1985 from opening greenfield production facilities (which

were greeted enthusiastically by the governments, the unions as well
as the Flemish employers) to outright takeovers (Daems and van
de Weyer, 1993). Provoked by the fear of losing control,[16] once more
the emotional split between the French-speaking and the Flemish-
speaking communities is felt. The takeover of the Société Générale
by the French Suez group, to mention the most spectacular
example,[17] was fiercely rejected in Flanders, where France is seen as
the natural ally of Wallonia. Whether, in the ongoing process of
federalization, the Flemish and Walloon cultural identities – and
with those, preferences for different types of firms – will gain force
or not, is difficult to predict. Much will depend on the outcome of
the power struggle between the federal and the regional governments. In the case of a dissolving Belgian state structure, the likelihood that subsidiaries of foreign multinationals will become the
prevalent type of firm will strongly increase, unless powerful regional
state structures resist such a 'selling-off'. This brief discussion of the
major differences between typical firms in Wallonia and Flanders is
summarized in Table 8.1.

INSTITUTIONAL FEATURES AFFECTING REGIONAL
AND SECTORAL VARIATIONS

In this section I examine the extent to which these differences, and
changes in them, can be explained by the institutional features
distinguished by Whitley in his first paper in this volume. With
respect to state structures and policies, it seems accurate to catego-
rize Belgium – at least until recently – as a 'strong' state, to which
claim has to be added immediately the rider that this state support
and *dirigisme* was directed almost exclusively at the French-speaking
region. The state's relative newness (1831, see above) might help to
explain the large extent to which it dominated the economic system,
and the high level of risk-sharing and other support it offered. This
pattern can be discerned in other countries where state formation
more or less coincided with industrialization: 'where the modern
nation state became established after the first industrial revolution
and was linked to national economic development, as in many
nineteenth-century European states, political and bureaucratic élites
are much more likely to identify their interests with industrial
growth and commit state resources to it' (Whitley, 1992: 29).[18] The
case of Belgium, again, calls attention to the fact that regions can
profit unequally from such identification.

From the start, the Belgian government pursued the same policy

Table 8.1 Major differences in characteristics of dominant types of firms in Wallonia and Flanders

Differences in characteristics of economic actors	Wallonia	Flanders
Dominant type of firm	The large limited liability firm: managerial enterprise and holding company.	The small- and medium-sized family firm; foreign multinationals' subsidiaries.
Sectoral emphasis	Basic industries: coal mining, iron, steel, non-ferrous minerals, machine-building some 'lighter' industries: textiles, glass, ceramics, etc.	(Family firms): 'traditional' consumer goods industries: textiles, clothing, foods, furniture, carpets, etc.
Diversity of activities and capabilities coordinated through authoritative communication	(Managerial enterprises): medium. (Holding companies): ambiguous.	(Family firms): rather low. (Multinationals' subsidiaries): high, respecting the taking-over of local firms since 1985.
Extent of radical discontinuities in activities and capabilities over time	Low.	(Family firms); low or, when internationalizing, medium. (Multinationals' subsidiaries); high, respecting the taking-over of local firms since 1985.
Ownership	(Holding companies): shares owned by: (1) (other) holding companies; (2) domestic savers.	(Family firms): family-owned; but increasingly foreign ownership, e.g. Bekaert and Gevaert. (Multinationals' subsidiaries): foreign-owned.
Control	Financial control by holding companies; sometimes additional control over strategic issues via trust relations and board membership.	Mostly family-control; in some cases professional management.

as its former head of state, the King of the Netherlands, whose Société Générale was certainly not the only indication that he was a true believer in industrialization (Demoulin, 1938). The first action of the provisional Belgian government was the setting of high protective tariffs in 1834. A year later, the Banque de Belgique was established to grant credits to industry (in imitation of the Société Générale) and to subsidize the railway and waterway building programme.[19] The success of Walloon firms in the basic (and also some 'lighter') industries, discussed above, cannot be explained only with reference to the availability of natural resources and a proto-industry. Much more important was the state support by way of protection, infrastructural improvements and granting credits via the Société Générale and the Banque de Belgique.

As these mixed banks were the main providers of investment capital, they can be classified under the institutional feature of financial system as well. Since the Société Générale soon became a limited liability company, it could be argued that this holding company operated in a capital-based context. Indeed, Société Générale shares, too, have always been widely dispersed amongst small domestic savers. On the other hand, it should be remembered that large portions of equity remained concentrated in the hands of the Brussels' banking families, as well as the Belgian royal family; and this again argues in favour of a credit-based context, the more so considering the control over strategic issues which these families exerted.[20] The subsequent holding company system, described above, is also a credit-based rather than a capital-based system,[21] particularly if the control over strategic issues which the Belgian holding companies not infrequently pursue is considered. The interlocking fates of the holding companies and their subsidiaries explains why these latter Walloon industrial enterprises rarely have diversified into unrelated areas: after all, the subsidiaries' risks are borne by the holding companies (which pursue a portfolio investment strategy) and, thus, can be considered as 'externalized'. This absence of the necessity to diversify, in turn, might contribute to the explanation why Walloon firms, which are after all concentrated on the basic and other declining industries, have performed so poorly in recent decades.[22] In a sense, the stability of the holding company system, once it was established by the young Belgian state, is a major cause of change and helps to explain the decline of Wallonia.

As to the labour system in Belgium, it is worth mentioning that the unions, as in France, are first of all organized along religious and ideological lines. Theoretically, this should limit their ability to influence firms' decision-making. Unlike their French counterparts, however, the Belgian unions have given up an adversarial strategy (cf. Poole, 1986) for a more consensus-oriented strategy, comparable to those of the Dutch and German labour movements. With a membership density of over 70 per cent,[23] Belgian unions have acquired considerable bargaining power (Spineux, 1990: 43), especially in highly centralized negotiations. So, next to the state and the financial institutions, the labour system, too, hinders radical discontinuities in business policies – and this contributes to the marked invariability of the activities and resources coordinated and controlled by the larger industrial firms. But, in this domain as well, there is a regional dimension. In Wallonia, the socialist union is dominant, in Flanders, the Catholic one.[24] Given its rather militant history, the socialist union's opposition to business change is strongest. It is also important to note that trade unions have never had much hold over the small and medium-sized Flemish family firms. This is due not only to aversion to outside interference,[25] but also to the fact that the Flemish SMEs rely almost entirely on the local labour market for workers, who show – or have to show – a high level of firm loyalty. Therefore, outsourcing production, or other strategic decisions aimed at increasing flexibility, do not provoke such loud objections from organized labour. Furthermore the state (to return once more to this major institution) has always remained at arm's length from Flemish family firms, reluctant as it was to regulate small-scale production and retail trade. These differences between major institutions in Wallonia and Flanders are summarized in Table 8.2.

In a federalizing Belgium it is far from unreasonable to suppose that the willingness of the regional government of Flanders to share risks with Flemish SMEs and support intermediate associations and inter-firm cooperation will increase. At present, however, the regional governments have neither sufficient legal autonomy, financial resources nor fiscal powers to carry into effect far-reaching plans. Therefore, the modest activity of Flemish intermediate associations, such as the Flemish Employers' Association, and the merely informal character of inter-firm cooperation in that region, will remain a reality in the near future.

According to Donckels, a specialist on KMOs, the Flemish entrepreneurs form a 'very heterogeneous' group of economic actors; accordingly, everyone 'behaves individualistically'. They operate in isolation. This makes it difficult to organize promotion of interests *vis-à-vis* the government and other stakeholding parties (Donckels

Table 8.2 Major differences in institutional features affecting characteristics of Walloon and Flemish firms

Differences in institutional features affecting characteristics of economic actors	*Wallonia*	*Flanders*
Extent to which state dominates the economic system	Traditionally high.	Traditionally low.
Level of state support and commitment to business	Traditionally high (notably through the Société Générale).	Traditionally low (until the 1950s: measures aimed at attracting foreign investors).
Financial system	More credit-based than capital-based: holding companies (including the Société Générale) operating as investment banks, which are the other credit suppliers; a proportion of the managerial enterprises, however, operates directly on the stock-market.	(Family firms): capital accumulation through reinvestments and (additionally) bank credits (e.g. Kredietbank). (Multinationals' subsidiaries): dependent on financial system in home country.
Involvement of financial élites with enterprise management	As low as possible.	Not applicable.
Significance of labour movement in strategic decision-making	Rather high in managerial enterprises.	Rather low in familial SMEs.
Strategy of labour movement toward business management	Rather oppositional towards business change.	Cooperative.

et al., 1988: 43). Although Donckels seems to underestimate informal cooperation, which often results from contacts via local politics and upper-class social events, it seems appropriate to doubt whether, in such a fragmented situation, powerful institutionalized inter-firm cooperation has a chance to develop without the guidance and support of the government and government-initiated intermediate associations.

The question, then, whether there is another 'Third Italy'[26] to be found in Flanders' fields, must be answered in the negative. The recent success of the Flemish family enterprise is therefore all the more remarkable. The shift of the past decades in economic power from Wallonia (and Brussels) to Flanders can only be partly explained by the crisis of the western basic industries, which, of course, did not pass Belgium by. There must be more to it than that. A crisis elsewhere (read: Wallonia) does not bring you (read: Flanders) success of itself. Now, it has been argued that the foreign direct investments from roughly 1950 to 1985 had an extremely important impetus on Flemish SMEs. But grasping the new possibilities presupposes the organizational capability of creative adaptation. This has been achieved, so to speak, without much institutional help: state support so far has been mainly indirect,[27] banks and other financial institutions little appealed to and trade unions kept out.

Such a conclusion does not, of course, deny the importance of regional and sectoral variations in the social construction of economic actors. Above, it has been maintained that the Walloon decline was to a certain extent the consequence of the rigidity of institutional arrangements and resultant attitudes, established in the formative years of the Belgian state and aimed at a rapid development of large-scale industrial production in the French-speaking region. Where these institutional influences were much less active, as in Flanders, it was easier for economic actors to reap the fruits of new business opportunities, particularly those offered by the post-war foreign investments.[28] Opportunities were seized in a direct way, by entering a supplier relationship with the multinationals' subsidiaries, but also in an indirect way, by taking advantage of the boom and the open climate which the multinationals brought about – taking advantage, that is: modernizing their production as well as products and becoming internationally oriented themselves.

Instead of seeking strength in inter-firm cooperation and via intermediate associations within a region, which is part of the 'magic' of the Italian industrial districts, the Flemish craft-based family firms rather demonstrate flexibility in responding individually to the internationalization of their region. However, as the 'economic colonization' by foreign enterprises continues, it would not be surprising if the atomistic community of Flemish familial SMEs were to be subjected to severe pressures, and even to disappear before too long. Again, only the government – federal or regional, that is to be seen – can prevent such a change in dominant types of firms.

ACKNOWLEDGEMENTS

The author would like to thank Dr Christophe Boone, Professor Dr Paul van der Grinten, Dr Wim Vanhaverbeke, Dr René Olie and Professor Dr Arjen van Witteloostuijn for their comments.

NOTES

1 *De jure* independence was gained in 1839, when the Treaty of London sealed the separation of the Low Countries in two kingdoms. The Grand Duchy of Luxemburg belonged to the Dutch Crown until 1890.
2 Near the German border, Wallonia contains a small rural area of about 100,000 German-speaking inhabitants, the 'Ost Kantons'.
3 A few demographic facts: Flanders has a population of 5.5 million (56 per cent of the total population on 44 per cent of the total land area); Wallonia: 3.2 million (33 per cent of the population on 55 per cent of the land area); Brussels: 1.1 million (11 per cent of the population on 1 per cent of the land area). After the Second World War, the decades-old migration movement from Flanders to Wallonia and Brussels reversed.
4 Besides the three regions, there are also two (purely linguistic) communities in the Belgian political landscape: the Dutch-speaking and the French-speaking communities. Where the former is politically represented by the Flemish regional government, the latter has its own regional government. The situation of the German-speaking Ost Kantons is simple: they are represented by the Walloon regional government, but not, of course, by the French-speaking community. The situation in Brussels is both complicated and delicate. While the capital is a region in its own right, at the same time it is part of both the Dutch-speaking and French-speaking communities, depending on the language spoken in the school, sporting club or arts centre concerned.
5 In Belgium, industrial pioneers were largely dependent on family wealth produced by ownership of land and/or estate or by non-industrial activities. The importance of making 'a good marriage' should not be underestimated.
6 A forceful example of the concentration activities of this powerful holding company *cum* bank is offered by the glass industry. In 1836, the Société Nationale pour Entreprises Industrielles et Commerciales, a daughter company of the Société Générale, established the Société Anonyme des Manufacture de Glaces, Verres à Vitres, Cristaux et Gob-

eleteries, merging two famous glassworks: the Val St Lambert near Seraing and the Mariemont in the province of Namur. In a period of only a few years, most other Belgian (family-owned) glassworks were also absorbed. By 1850, Belgium was the leading glass producer on the Continent (Chambon, 1955).

7 Note that institutional investors (pension funds, insurance companies) are only very modestly active on the Belgian capital market, in strong contrast to their counterparts in the Netherlands.

8 According to Daems, holding companies play a crucial and strategic role in organizing, coordinating and controlling the accummulation, allocation and flow of capital within the Belgian market setting.

9 To be sure, holding companies do not seek control to achieve more efficient coordination of production and market policies *between* the different companies of a portfolio. Otherwise, states Daems (ibid.: 106), this coordination would almost 'automatically' lead to full mergers, given the fact that Belgian anti-trust legislation has been very permissive.

10 The aloofness of the Belgian financial institutions is perhaps even greater, if one considers that in France at least individual careers break through these barriers between finance and manufacturing. Not infrequently, French managers shift from financial to managerial functions. The old-boy network, which typically originates at the grande école, facilitates this career merry-go-round (e.g. Barsoux and Lawrence, 1990: chap. 4). Such cross-sector mobility is almost unthinkable in Belgium. A Brussels' banker will never enter a Liège or Charleroi boardroom.

11 Coal mining in Flanders only became feasible in the early twentieth century.

12 To state it bluntly, the Congo – Belgium's large African colony; now Zaïre – was a more interesting territory for exploitation.

13 But if these entrepreneurs did or could not avoid attracting outside capital, they turned to Flemish banks, such as the Kredietbank, which collects mainly small savings of Flemish families.

14 'In Belgium the family-controlled company held out longer in the consumer goods sector than in the basic industries. The reason might be that in those industries family wealth could provide the necessary initial funds and internal funds were sufficient to finance the modest expansion' (Daems, 1978: 31).

15 In the tufted carpet industry, for instance, the annual growth rate of exports was 10.36 per cent between 1972 and 1989, in which year a trade balance of 60,848 million BEF was achieved (Vanhaverbeke, 1992: 23).

16 Note that the market for corporate control in Belgium, as in the Netherlands, has always been very limited. Takeover bids were mostly aimed at achieving geographical diversification or a rationalization of production. Between 1964 and 1972, there were only fifty-two takeover bids. Beyond that, in forty cases a bidder offered to buy shares in a company where he already held a controlling interest.

17 It was the largest cross-border takeover in Europe to date.

18 This has also found expression at 'superstructure' level: 'The sudden independence of Belgium for the first time in history coincided with

the peak of the Romantic movement in Europe, which required all the idealism and outward trappings of "national identity". Belgian statehood was steeped from the start in the Romantic nationalism that is so conspicuously missing in the North' (Shetter, 1987: 289). (By 'the North', here, is meant the Netherlands.)

19 Between 1834 and 1859, 861.4 km of railway were built.

20 The firms established and merged by the Société Générale did, of course, unquestionably face a credit-based financial system.

21 This is not to suggest that the holding companies (including the Société Générale) are the *only* providers of capital. A proportion of the Walloon managerial enterprises rely on investment banks or capital from the Brussels stock-market.

22 One might wonder, then, why the holding companies did not shift their assets out of the declining basic industries. Again, a part of the explanation for the existence of these 'psychological' exit barriers can be found in the strength of the ethnocentric sentiments of the French-speaking élites. In their perception, the rise of Belgium as a stable nation and a prosperous economy is unthinkable without the Walloon heavy industry, which their ancestors and predecessors in their Brussels' offices have financed. Applied to the domain of financial management, one could label the effects of these exit barriers (cf. Porter's argument on managerial exit barriers, 1976) as 'portfolio inertia'.

23 Visser (1991) states that if one excludes unemployed or retired union members, the density is only 53 per cent. But that is still an impressive figure.

24 In 1990, the regional membership distribution of the two main Belgian unions was as follows (Vilrokx and Van Leemput, 1992: 368):

	Flanders	*Wallonia*
Socialist union	454,397	418,204
Catholic union	984,719	290,638

25 It is a widespread practice amongst Flemish enterprises to split up their firms into separate legal entities in order to avoid having to install a works council, which is compulsory if the number of employees exceeds fifty.

26 Some have compared the group of family firms in the Courtrai area, in the province of West Flanders, to the industrial districts of central and north-east Italy (Charter 99, 1989). Although one can indeed find a number of Courtrai firms applying the system of flexible specialization, a politically constructed industrial community (cf. Piore and Sabel, 1984: chap. 8) seems to be absent, since the existing local intermediary associations (a regional development bureau, *Leiedal*, and a training centre for KMO entrepreneurs) do not in my view really justify such a description. It is rather the case that 'le Courtraisis [the Courtrai area] c'est traditionellement caracterisé par ... une adaptabilitié impressionante a l'environment changeant et une motivation de la part des individus a conquérir une autonomie a un niveau personnel et familial, tout en

208   *Institutional specificity*

defendant simultanément et collectivement l'autonomie locale par rapport au monde extérieur' (Musyck, 1994: 26–7).
27 Think again of the 'expansion laws' which aimed at attracting foreign investors.
28 Who were, ironically, a result of an exception to the Walloon bias: the aforementioned 'expansion laws' which were aimed at attracting foreign investors in all regions.

REFERENCES

Barsoux, J.-L. and Lawrence, P. (1990) *Management in France*, London: Cassell.
Belder, J. de (1977) 'Het sociale leven in België. Adel en burgerij 1844–1914', in D. P. Blok *et al.* (eds) *Algemene Geschiedenis der Nederlanden* (vol. 12), Haarlem: Fibula-Van Dishoeck.
Bolle, J. (ed.) (1972) *Société Générale de Belgique, 1822–1972*, Brussels: Société Générale de Belgique.
Boone, C. A. J. J. (1992) 'Onderzoek naar het verband tussen de perceptie van controle van bedrijfsleiders en de strategie en de resultaten van ondernemingen in de meubelindustrie', Antwerp: RUCA (unpublished dissertation).
Chambon, R. (1955) *L'Histoire de la Verrerie en Belgique du IIe Siècle à nos Jours*, Brussels: Editions de la Librairie Encyclopédique, SPRL.
Charter 99 (1989) *Charter 99: 'Een streekstrategie voor Zuid-West Vlaaneren', delen I en II, Kortrijk*, Kortrijk.
Crooijmans, H. (1991) 'Economische kolonisatie. Belgisch bedrijfsleven valt in handen van buitenlanders', *Elsevier* 47(45): 64–8.
Daems, H. (1978) *The Holding Company and Corporate Control*, Leiden/Boston: Martinus Nijhoff.
——. and van de Weyer, P. (1993) *Buitenlandse invloed in België. De gevolgen voor strategische beslissingsmacht*, Brussels: Koning Boudewijnstichting.
Demoulin, R. (1938) *Guillaume Ier et la Transformation Economique des Provinces Belges*, Luik: Bibliotheek van de filosofische en letterkundige faculteit.
Donckels, R., Degadt, J. and Dupont, B. (1988) *KMO's in België. Sociaaleconomische betekenis*, Leuven/Amersfoort: Acco.
Henderson, W. O. (1965 (1954)) *Britain and Industrial Europe 1750–1870*, Leicester: Leicester University Press.
Kocka, J. (1979) 'Familie, Unternehmer und Kapitalismus', *Zeitschrift für Unternehmengeschichte*, 24.
Lebrun, P., Brunier, M., Dhont, J. and Hansotte, G. (1981) *Essai sur la révolution industrielle en Belgique 1770–1847*, Brussels: Palais des Académies.
Mok, A. L. (1993) 'Belgium: management and culture in a pillared society', in D. J. Hickson (ed.) *Management in Western Europe. Society, Culture and Organization in Twelve Nations*, Berlin/New York: de Gruyter.
Mokyr, J. (1976) *Industrialization in the Low Countries, 1795–1850*, New Haven, Conn.: Yale University Press.

Musyck, B. (1994) 'Les caracteristiques de l'industrialisation autonome dans le sud de la Flandre Occidentale', *Bulletin de l'IRES*, 172.

Piore, M. J. and Sabel, C. F. (1984) *The Second Industrial Divide. Possibilities for Prosperity*, New York: Basic Books.

Poole, M. (1986) *Industrial Relations: Origins and Patterns of National Diversity*, London: Routledge & Kegan Paul.

Porter, M. E. (1976) 'Please note location of nearest exit: exit barriers and planning', *California Management Review* 19: 21–33.

Romus, P. (1979) *L'Europe et les régions*, Brussels: Editions Labor.

Shetter, W. Z. (1987) *The Netherlands in Perspective: The Organization of Society and Environment*, Leiden: Martinus Nijhoff.

Spineux, A. (1987) 'Trade unionism in Belgium: the difficulties of a major renovation', in G. Baglioni and C. Crouch (eds) *European Industrial Relations: The Challenge of Flexibility*, London: Sage.

Vandewalle, G. (1977) 'De economische ontwikkeling in België 1945–1980', in D. P. Blok, *et al.* (eds) *Algemene Geschiedenis der Nederlanden* (vol. 15), Haarlem: Fibula-Van Dishoeck.

Vanhaverbeke, W. (1992) 'The tufted carpets industry in Belgium', Barcelona: IESE (unpublished paper).

Vilrokx, J. and Van Leemput, J. (1992) 'Belgium: A new stability in industrial relations?', in A. Ferner and R. Hyman, *Industrial Relations in the New Europe*, Oxford: Blackwell.

Visser, J. (1991) 'Tendances de la syndicalisation', in OECD, *Perspectives de l'emploi*, Paris: OECD.

Whitley, R. D. (ed.) (1992) *European Business Systems. Firms and Markets in their National Contexts*, London: Sage.

9 Continuity and change in an emergent market economy

The limited transformation of large enterprises in Hungary*

R. Whitley, J. Henderson, L. Czaban and
G. Lengyel

INTRODUCTION

The political and economic transformations taking place in Eastern Europe since 1988 have often been characterized as radical transformations of monolithic command economies into decentralized market economies. The former coordinated economic activities centrally through the state plan, while the latter rely on privately owned firms coordinating their inputs and outputs through market contracting. Thus, a crucial component of the transformation process is the replacement of state ministries and planners as key economic decision-makers, by owners and managers of separate and autonomous firms. This obviously requires the development of such firms as discrete economic actors, either through the growth of small businesses or through the restructuring and privatization of state-owned enterprises (SOEs) (Estrin, 1994a). In these European countries, then, a major political and economic concern has been the establishment of economic actors as distinct and independent agents which can organize and control economic activities in a competitive market economy.

Given the very limited, not to say minuscule, role of the private sector in most state socialist societies, and hence the considerable time and effort needed to develop significant privately owned enterprises from existing or newly founded small firms, most attention has focused on the corporatization and privatization of SOEs, and there has been a plethora of publications about how this could be achieved (e.g. Baldassarri *et al.*, 1993; Estrin, 1994a; Frydman and

* The research reported in this paper is being funded by the British Economic and Social Research Council under grant number R234422.

Rapaczynski, 1993; Frydman *et al.*, 1993). Much of this literature has concentrated on questions of ownership and assumed that once the appropriate transfers to private interests had taken place, fully fledged capitalist firms – typically seen as Anglo-Saxon corporations – would magically emerge.

However, it is becoming increasingly clear that, just as the general transformation process is proving much more gradual, varied and indeterminate than once thought likely (not least because of significant differences between state socialist regimes and their political economies: Grabher, 1995; Stark, 1992; Tatur, 1995), so too the establishment of capitalist firms in Eastern Europe is proving a long-term process which is occurring in different ways under different circumstances. Furthermore, although the nature of such firms remains unclear, it seems unlikely that they will closely resemble Anglo-Saxon ones, given the different kinds of institutions governing the availability of labour power and capital in most of these societies and those characteristic of most Anglo-Saxon societies. Additionally, the varied success of large-scale privatization processes so far have shown that changes in ownership *per se* are not as simple and easy to achieve as some commentators have assumed, and that restructuring is neither dependent upon such ownership transfers, nor follows directly from them (Carlin *et al.*, 1994; Estrin, 1994b; Konecki and Kulpinska, 1995). Top management changes, the influence and policies of key interest groups, the structure and policies of state agencies and the availability of capital and new technologies are all critical factors in the reorganization of SOEs, which may or may not be tied to changes in ownership. In accounting for the sorts of economic actors that are emerging in the new market economies of Eastern Europe, these – and other – factors are often more significant than simple transfers of property rights.

The limited extent of enterprise transformation in these economies, even in those organizations which have been privatized, and the incremental ways in which many top managers are pursuing strategic changes, can be seen in the actions of many large organizations in Hungary during the initial transition period from 1990 to 1994. In so far as independent, decision-making capitalist firms co-ordinating economic activities have developed in any of the former state socialist countries in the 1990s, they are most likely to be found in Hungary because of its lengthy period of reform since 1968 and the varied forms of subcontracting and cooperative work units that were established in the 1980s (Laky, 1988; Neumann, 1993; Radice, 1981). As part of a longer-term study of emerging firms and markets in Hungary, we interviewed the top managers of ten large former SOEs (or their successor organizations) to see how they were adapting to the large-scale changes in their environments and whether they were becoming autonomous economic actors of a distinctive kind.

These former SOEs had been major components of vertically integrated combines dominating particular industrial sectors, but were now (late 1993 and early 1994) established as separate corporate entities owned either by state agencies or varying mixtures of state and private, bank, employees and foreign shareholders. In this variety of ownership patterns they were typical of the complex and wide-ranging forms of ownership found in Hungary and other former state socialist economies during the early 1990s (Stark, 1992, 1993). Seven remained in some form of state ownership, one was owned by a leading commercial bank in combination with private entrepreneurs who now ran it and constituted the largest component of an SOE that had been liquidated, one was owned through an employee share ownership plan (ESOP) and the last was jointly owned by the state and a foreign manufacturer. Three were in the non-electrical machinery sector, including transportation equipment, five in the chemical and allied industries – broadly defined – one in metallurgy and one in electrical and electronic machinery. In all we interviewed forty-six top managers between October 1993 and February 1994 about ownership and control issues, strategic priorities and preferred ways of achieving these, major product line and technology changes, organization structures and internal coordination and control procedures. Here we report on their relations with owners, both state and private, their strategic preferences, changes in their outputs and markets and in their overall structures and decision-making processes.

On the whole, they appeared to have altered less than might have been expected, given the massive changes that had occurred in the political system and the need to compete for customers in traditional markets. This was partly because the state recentralized control over state enterprises in 1990 as a result of widespread concern about the mushrooming of 'spontaneous privatization' of SOEs by top managers after the 1988 Company Law provided for the formation of limited liability and joint stock companies, which had effectively enabled managers to transfer major assets to subsidiaries leaving the accumulated debts of the enterprise in the holding company (Canning and Hare, 1994; Frydman *et al.*, 1993: 107–45; Stark, 1990, 1992; Voszka, 1992). The establishment of the State Property Agency

(SPA) to take control of all state firms prior to privatizing them, and, in 1992, of the State Asset Management Company (SAMC), or 'state holding', to manage the state's long-term holdings in 'strategic' enterprises, meant that earlier patterns of vertical dependence on state agencies were reproduced, albeit in different ways, especially as the state pursued fluctuating and, on occasion, rapidly shifting privatization policies which increased the uncertainties faced by top managers (Henderson *et al.*, 1995).

OWNERSHIP AND CONTROL

Considering first issues of ownership and control, it can readily be seen from Table 9.1 that the ownership structures of the ten large enterprises we report on here are quite diverse, even among those still in state hands. The seven state-owned firms are divided into two groups, those making large losses and those breaking even or making an operating profit in 1992 and/or 1993. All of the latter were wholly or partly owned by the SAMC and were not considered likely to be completely divested by the state as they were thought to be of strategic significance. The major loss-makers were expected either to be privatized or to be substantially restructured in the near future, depending on the policies of the new government. As we will see, they tended to be more closely supervised by the SPA or SAMC than did the other SOEs. The majority bank-owned firm had acquired many of the assets of a liquidated former SOE and was staffed almost entirely by its former employees – albeit in much smaller numbers. Although this bank was itself owned by the state, in practice it seemed to have developed considerable autonomy and was able to pursue its distinctive interests. The owner-managers came from a private firm which had grown rapidly from a cooperative in the 1980s and clearly dominated the day-to-day management of this firm. In the case of the employee-owned firm, the employee share ownership plan – in which 1,200 of the 1,400 employees participated – held a majority of the shares, and the firm itself held a further 27 per cent which it was required to dispose of within a year. The joint venture enterprise is now majority-owned by the foreign partner and is effectively becoming managed as one of its subsidiaries.

In view of the concern over spontaneous privatization, it is worth briefly considering the growth of limited company subsidiaries of these organizations, and further varieties of ownership of them. While three enterprises, A, D and E, had over thirty subsidiaries

Table 1 Ownership, employment and financial performance of ten large Hungarian enterprises

Enterprise	Ownership		Employees at 1.9.93	1993 turnover (in HUF million)
State-owned (major loss-makers)				
A	SPA	100%	3,932	12,000
B	SAMC	99.8%		
	Municipalities	0.2%	5,253	32,000
C	SPA	94%		
	Municipalities	6%	2,250	1,800
Other state-owned				
D	SAMC	100%	21,000	345,000
E	SAMC	83%	11,500	70,000
	State Development Institute[a]	12%		
	Municipalities	5%		
F	SAMC	40.8%	7,094	19,600
	State Development Bank[b]	51%		
	Municipalities	8.2%		
G	SAMC	61%	6,286	22,900
	Customer	30.5%		
	Commercial bank	4.5%		
	Trading firm	3%		
	Foreign investors	1%		
Private and bank-owned				
H	Commercial bank	66%	5,236	11,000
	Top managers	29%		
	Foreign investors	5%		
Employee-owned (ESOP)				
I	ESOP	56.6%	1,400	2,400
	Limited	27.2%		
	Retained shares	10.0%		
	Municipalities	6.2%		
Joint venture with foreign firm				
J	SAMC	43.4%	3,056	15,800
	Foreign firm	51.0%	(at 1.1.94)	
	Employees	5.6%		

[a] Established in the late 1960s as a state long-term loan agency.
[b] Owned by the SAMC and effectively run by it up to early 1994.

each, five had fewer than ten and most were fairly small in size. There were only seventeen subsidiaries whose capital amounted to over a tenth of that of the whole enterprise, and twelve of these were wholly-owned. In no cases were these larger subsidiaries minority-owned and in only five did they have foreign shareholders. On the whole, then, most subsidiaries were small, typically established for trading purposes, and clearly controlled by the parent company. With the exception of enterprise G, whose largest customer had taken a considerable shareholding, trading partners were not significant owners.

Ownership and control are not, of course, synonymous, and the extent to which state and bank ownership resulted in strong day-to-day control over decisions varied in these enterprises. In general terms, the involvement of owners in the management of companies depends considerably on the degree of mutual commitment between property rights holders and managers, which, in turn, is strongly affected by the nature of the financial system and, *inter alia*, dominant institutions governing trust relations in a society. Credit-based financial systems (Zysman, 1983) tend to encourage greater degrees of mutual dependence between owners and managers of large enterprises than do capital market-based ones, because markets in financial assets are relatively illiquid, and so owners, trustees and investment managers tend to become locked into particular firms. This then encourages the development of specialist knowledge of those firms and their businesses so that banks etc. become more committed to them and also focus on providing additional specialized services to these particular customers (Whitley in this volume). As a result, information flows and consultations between owners and/or leading creditors and managers are likely to be larger and more frequent in these kinds of financial systems than where large, liquid capital markets play the major role in allocating financial resources.

Similarly, societies where institutions governing the commitment and sanctioning of contractual, competence and goodwill trust (Sako, 1992) are weak and/or highly informal and personal are unlikely to generate remote and intermediated connections between owners and managers. Instead, owners will seek to maintain close involvement with firms' activities and will probably not be willing to rely on purely formal, standardized financial accounting information in monitoring their investments. In the case of Hungary, and most economies undergoing large-scale transformation, the nature of the financial system is not yet firmly established, but the high level of indebtedness of enterprises, and the small size of the capital markets that have developed, suggest that owners, especially the state, banks and firms, are all locked into each other's destinies, except where foreign buyers can be found, and the management of outstanding debt, as well as any new investment or working capital that might become available, is a political/administrative matter rather than being decided by market processes. Similarly, the relative lack of formal rules and procedures for controlling exchange relationships between strangers which have been institutionalized for some time, coupled with the strong reliance on personal contacts and networks to deal with the previous 'shortage' economy, are likely to limit owners' reliance on purely formal means of monitoring performance and to increase their involvement in decision-making processes.

Overall, the involvement of the state agencies, banks and others who held shares in the ten large enterprises discussed here was considerable, and certainly greater than is typical for investment fund managers and owners in capital market financial systems, although its degree did vary between firms. Considering owner representation on the board of directors first, it can be seen from Table 9.2 that the SAMC and/or the SPA and the leading banks dominated these, as they also did the supervisory committees. It should be noted here that under Hungarian law the board of directors has equal standing with the supervisory committee and is directly responsible to the general meeting of shareholders for the conduct of the enterprise. The firms where top managers were significantly (i.e. $\geq 50\%$) represented on the Board were those where they owned some shares in the business. This is partly because directors are elected by the general meeting of shareholders for five years specifically to represent the owners, in a role which it is felt may conflict with that of a salaried manager. The one exception to this generalization is enterprise C, where the CEO was appointed by the SPA as bankruptcy commissioner and acted as the representative of the SPA rather than as a salaried manager initially. Since the interviews were carried out he resigned because of a dispute with the SPA.

In these enterprises, then, the boards of directors were overwhelmingly constituted by representatives of the shareholders and so owners received regular reports on the activities of their firms. In addition to being formally involved in strategic decision-making, or at least required to give or withhold approval, through board meetings, owners were also reported to be extensively involved in many important decisions on a continuing, informal basis. This was especially the case for the three enterprises which had made continuing losses. In these firms, the state agencies had to approve virtually all new investment decisions, all new product or service introductions, all top management appointments and decisions to close down or sell off departments and subsidiaries, as summarized in Table 9.3.

Table 9.2 Membership of boards of directors of ten large enterprises

Owner	Enterprise									
	State-owned							Private	ESOP	J.V.
	Large loss-makers			Others						
	A	B	C	D	E	F	G	H	I	J
SAMC		3		6	4	1	3			2
SPA	3		1							
State Development Institute					1	4				
Development Bank										
Commercial Bank							1	1		
Ministry of Industry and Trade					1	1				
Major supplier		1								
Major customer							5			
ESOP									4	
Foreign firm										2
Owner managers							3			
Non-owning managers	2	1	2	3	1	2	2	0	2	1
Total board membership	5	5	3	9	7	8	11	4	6	5

The four state-owned firms that were not making large losses in 1992 or in 1993 appeared to have slightly more autonomy with regard to main product changes and small capital investments, but still had to consult frequently with staff in the SAMC about any significant changes that were being proposed. As one CEO put it: 'they demand information continuously', and another claimed that the SAMC behaved in a similar manner to ministries under the old regime, in that they frequently asked for information without saying why or providing any feedback. In other words, even when state owners did not directly intervene in the day-to-day management of these former SOEs, they were in frequent contact and managers felt that the SAMC could issue instructions at any moment without warning.

Table 9.3 Owners' veto powers over strategic decisions in ten large
Hungarian enterprises

Enterprise	Capital expenditure (HUF million)	Strategic decisions		
		New product introduction	Top mgt appointments	Creating or closing depts
State-owned major loss-makers				
A	Any amount	yes	yes	yes
B	Any involving new units	yes	yes	yes
C	Any amount	N.A. (no new products)	yes	yes
Other state-owned				
D	500	no	yes	Not normally
E	500	Only if new investment involved	yes	yes
F	500	no	yes	yes
G	Any amount	yes	yes	yes
Private and bank-owned				
H	Policy, not individual decisions	no	yes	yes
ESOP				
I	200	no	yes	yes
J.V.				
J	100	yes	yes	yes

The three privately-managed enterprises also had a little more
autonomy from their owners than the large loss-makers, but still
were quite limited in their ability to make investment decisions and
restructure departments or business units. It is particularly interesting to note how low the investment expenditure ceiling is in the
joint-venture, and the need to gain the parent companies' approval
for introducing new products. As we will see later, this centralization
of owner control was reflected in a high level of centralized decision-
making within this enterprise.

As well as exercising strong veto rights over many decisions, the
owners of these enterprises also frequently initiated contacts with
top managers, especially with requests for information, and required

frequent CEO visits to report on progress. This was particularly the case for the loss-making state firms, as is shown in Table 9.4, but it is clear that nearly all the owners of these enterprises were involved in strategic decision-making and expected to be consulted frequently on major issues.

The influence of other groups and organizations, such as lenders, suppliers and customers, appeared less significant than that of owners. Where the banks had large outstanding loans, but were not shareholders, they typically received reports on the balance sheet, cash flow and sales turnover on a monthly or quarterly basis, although the more profitable enterprise only reported formally every six months. On the other hand, the banks usually initiated contacts for specific information much more frequently, in two cases daily and never less than monthly, so that information flow was high and frequent, particularly in the loss-making enterprises. However, it was clear that the top managers involved saw their relationships with the owners as more critical to decision-making processes and, in at least one case, were attempting to distance themselves from their main bank by developing links with other banks and by issuing bonds at a lower interest rate than applied to bank loans. Such efforts to increase managerial autonomy are, of course, easier and more realistic when at least an operating profit is being made and the enterprise is very large.

Suppliers and customers were only rarely considered influential organizations. In one case, it was the set of multinational firms who subcontracted component production to the enterprise which was important, in another it was one of the major raw material suppliers which was invited to assume part of the firm's outstanding debts in exchange for an agreement to buy a key input from them. The only other important agency mentioned was the Ministry of Industry and Trade, referred to by five firms, which substantially influenced most large SOEs before 1989. Because of their extensive knowledge of personnel in these enterprises, officials in this ministry were often asked for their views when making managerial appointments. It is worth pointing out that many ministries are represented on the Board of the SPA and so can indirectly influence enterprise behaviour.

On the whole, then, owners, whether state agencies, banks, other organizations or managers, were the dominant force in strategic decision-making and were often involved in operational, day-to-day matters as well. Owner control was thus high in these enterprises and the degree of salaried managerial autonomy correspondingly

Table 9.4 Ownership and control in ten large Hungarian enterprises

| Enterprise | Role of Owners and Banks | | | | | |
	Involvement in day-to-day mgt	Involvement in strategy	Frequency of owner contact	Frequency of CEO visists	Frequency of bank contact
State-owned major loss-makers					
A	Limited	Crucial	> Weekly	> Weekly	Monthly
B	Significant	Crucial	Weekly	Weekly	> Weekly
C	Negotiations with creditors	Crucial	> Weekly	> Weekly	> Weekly
Other state-owned					
D	Information requests	Significant	> Weekly	2 × a month	Monthly
E	Information requests	Significant	> Weekly	2 × a month	Monthly
F	Information requests	Significant	> Weekly	2 × a month	Weekly with HIDB
G	Information requests	Crucial	> Monthly	2 × a month	> Weekly
Private and bank-owned					
H	Limited except for owner/managers	Crucial	> Weekly	2 × a month	> Weekly with owning bank
ESOP					
I	None	Significant	Monthly	Monthly	Weekly
J.V.					
J	Limited	Crucial	< Monthly	Quarterly	Monthly

limited, indeed probably rather less than in the late 1980s when they were formally part of the MIT. It is worth pointing out, in addition, that in the three firms which were not directly owned and controlled by state agencies, the level of control exerted by owners who were not managers was quite considerable, so it cannot be assumed that this high degree of owner control in Hungarian large firms is simply a residue from the command economy. Indeed, there seems no good reason to expect owners to distance themselves greatly from managerial decision-making, as long as political and economic uncertainty remains high.

STRATEGIC PRIORITIES AND CHANGES IN ACTIVITIES

Strong owner control is compatible with a variety of strategic preferences and does not, of course, automatically lead to an emphasis on short-term profit maximization, especially where the state remains the dominant force in economic decision-making and firms are highly dependent on political *cum* bureaucratic decisions, such as those concerning enterprise debts. Furthermore, the interests and objectives of state agencies as owners are not likely to coincide with those of private owners or investment fund managers in capital market-based financial systems. While most of the enterprises we studied were primarily concerned with survival in the face of the loss of former markets and intense competition for western European markets, there were some interesting variations in how their major objectives, current strategies and sources of competitive advantage were perceived.

Considering first firms' dominant objectives, it is worth noting that nearly all the top managers considered both increasing sales growth and increasing market share to be very important objectives, as shown in Table 9.5. The major exception, enterprise C, could not obtain the financial resources to expand sales, despite having potential customers, because of its losses and debts. On the other hand, only three firms' managers regarded shareholder wealth maximization to be a very important goal. Two of these had substantial private shareholdings and, in one case, the managers themselves owned some shares. However, the liquidated firm with substantial top manager shareholdings also considered sales growth and increasing market share to be key objectives, and in general did not seem to be espousing goals that were greatly at variance with those claimed by the SPA- and SAMC-owned enterprises. Overall, then, the ten large former SOEs wished to pursue growth goals and were

Table 9.5 Dominant objectives of top managers of ten large Hungarian enterprises

Owner	Enterprise							Private	ESOP	J.V.
	State-owned									
	Large loss-makers			Others						
	A	B	C	D	E	F	G	H	I	J
Increasing output	4	2	1	2	4	2	1	2	3	2
Increasing earnings per share	3	2	1	1	2	3	3	3	2	1
Increasing sales growth	1	1	4	1	1	1	1	1	1	2
Increasing market share	1	1	3	1	1	1	1	1	1	1
Maximizing shareholder wealth	3	2	3	1	2	3	4	1	3	1
Increasing rate of new product introduction	1	2	1	3	2	1	1	1	1	1
Improving quality of products	1	1	1	1	1	1	1	1	1	1
Improving employee skills	3	3	2	1	3	2	3	3	1	1
Increasing employee productivity	3	2	1	1	3	2	2	1	1	1
Producing production costs	2	1	1	2	1	3	3	2	2	2
Reducing direct labour costs	4	3	1	1	4	3	4	1	3	1

Note: 1 = very important, 5 = unimportant.

not especially concerned with increasing short-term profits at the expense of growth.

Preferred strategies for achieving survival and growth combined a focus on new product introduction – usually under licence rather than developed internally – and improving product quality with cost reductions. However, many firms did not consider a reduction in direct labour costs to be important, and only three thought that production costs as a whole had to be reduced as a priority, or that low-cost production was crucial to survival and growth. In

contrast, nine claimed that increasing the rate of new product introduction was either an important or very important objective and all
ten also said that improving the quality and performance of outputs
was a very important objective. This suggests that the top managers
of most state or bank-owned enterprises gave product improvement
and change a higher priority than cost reduction, possibly because
many of them had already undergone substantial staff reductions,
but even the three enterprises that had not substantially reduced
employment since 1989 also shared these priorities. When asked
about their sources of competitive advantage, though, all ten enterprises said that low prices were either important or very important,
together with an ability to meet customer requirements. Less advantage was attached to high-quality design and performance or after-
sales service.

In developing new products and services, the necessary skills and
resources can either be acquired through market transactions or
developed internally. Only one of the enterprises studied (the bank
majority-owned firm with substantial managerial shareholdings)
unequivocally said they would rely on external acquisition of such
capabilities. None of the directly state-owned enterprises or the
other two privately owned firms said they would prefer to acquire
rather than develop internally new resources. Similarly, when asked
about diversification policies, managers of all seven SPA- and
SAMC-owned firms stated that diversification was closely linked to
current technologies and markets, as did the CEOs of the ESOP
and the J.V. firms. However, the CEO of the bank-owned, previously
liquidated, firm asserted the contrary, but in practice intended to
remain in the same industrial sector.

In other words, the dominant pattern in these large enterprises
was to concentrate on developing internal resources and remain in
current areas of expertise rather than considering buying new assets
and skills or moving into radically different markets. Strategic
change was seen by nearly all these top managers as an incremental
rather than discontinuous process. This was partly due to political
pressure from the SPA and the SAMC to limit redundancies,
especially in the crisis regions of Hungary, and it should be noted
that the owners' approval had to be sought to close down or sell
off subsidiaries. Another important factor is the traditionally high
degree of vertical integration of most SOEs in state socialist societies
and their corresponding monopolization of industry-specific skills.
Given the highly sector-focused nature of most managers' knowledge and experience in these firms, it is not surprising that they

would find it difficult to diversify into radically new areas of business. Equally, integrating new organizations and people from other sectors into their enterprises would be seen as difficult, given the lack of experience of an inter-firm managerial labour market and limited familiarity with financial techniques for managing diversified firms, in much the same way as in post-war Japan (Clark, 1979; Kagono *et al.*, 1985; Whitley, 1992).

This preference for incremental change can also be seen in the limited extent of product and output changes since 1990. In six enterprises the major product lines, broadly conceived, had not changed at all over this period. Moreover, the proportion of total sales contributed by each product line had not altered by more than 10 per cent over the last three years. Two firms had stopped producing one set of products but still manufactured the same two most important outputs in 1993 as they had in 1990. Although one firm had introduced some new products under licence from foreign firms, these did not individually contribute a substantial amount (i.e. 10 per cent or more) to total turnover. Another enterprise had dropped two product lines which together had contributed around 10 per cent of sales in 1990, and had boosted the output of the fourth most important product line from 5 per cent in 1990 to 19 per cent in 1993. However, it had not introduced any new products on a significant scale. Only four of these ten firms had introduced new products, as distinct from modifications of existing ones, in 1993, and in only three firms did products introduced since 1989 contribute more than 15 per cent of turnover in 1993. These were the bank-owned firm, the ESOP and J.V. firms. Overall, then, considerable product upgrading had taken place, but these large enterprises remained in substantially the same lines of business and, in many cases, were producing the same sorts of outputs in much the same proportions as in 1990. While individual outputs had changed over this period – more in some enterprises than in others – the dominant patterns of activities and products clearly did not change greatly in these firms.

ORGANIZATIONAL CHANGE AND DECISION-MAKING

This broad impression of limited transformation and incremental changes to these ten large enterprises is echoed by the considerable degree of continuity of managerial personnel, including top management, and the restricted extent of organizational restructuring that had taken place since 1988. As mentioned earlier, the so-called 'spontaneous privatization' movement in 1989 and 1990 had resulted in the widespread establishment of subsidiary companies by managerial élites wishing to escape from state control and to separate the major assets of SOEs from their debts, which typically remained the responsibility of the holding companies. In some cases, these latter entities became 'shell enterprises' that owned little except enormous debts (Canning and Hare, 1994; Frydman *et al.*, 1993; Stark, 1993). After the establishment of the State Property Agency in 1990 in response to public anxiety about this effective denationalization of public assets on the cheap, central control over SOEs was reasserted and this in turn encouraged a recentralization of control within the enterprises, as we shall see. Although, then, there has been considerable corporatization of the former SOEs, and most have set up a large number of formally distinct subsidiaries as separate limited companies, they remain quite similar forms of organization, with the legal changes masking much continuity.

Considering, first, overall changes in employment, while some of the former SOEs discussed here had severely reduced the total numbers of employees, between 1990 and 1993, for instance from 9,360 to 3,932 and from 12,523 to 7,138, others had made remarkably little change to their payroll over the previous four years, considering the major changes in their markets and financial positions. Indeed, one had actually increased its staff as the result of the state transferring another production unit to it. One of the striking characteristics of the composition of the workforce in 1989 was the high proportion of skilled manual workers. As many as 75 per cent of the total manual workforce were certified skilled workers at one enterprise, which ran the industry training school, while two others had 64 per cent and 62 per cent in the same category. By September 1993, this proportion had dropped to 51 per cent in the first case, but the other two firms maintained high levels of skilled manual employment – i.e. over 60 per cent – into the autumn of 1993.

It is interesting to note here that the firm which had gone bankrupt and been bought by a bank and managers from another firm had deliberately increased the number of unskilled manual workers, to the extent that they now numbered 1,742 as compared to 1,640 skilled ones. This was a direct response to the widening of differentials between skill levels in Hungary, and may possibly also reflect the growing ease of obtaining standardized supplies, and the associated reduced need to rely extensively on skilled workers to cope with the frequent unpredictable interruptions characteristic of the shortage economy. It is also worth pointing out that most skilled workers in Hungarian industry are male, whereas female workers are disproportionately represented among semi-skilled workers. In the enterprise which has undergone the most radical transformations of manual workforce composition, then, the overall reduction in skill levels has been accompanied by a shift in gender composition. It is not clear at the moment whether the other former SOEs will follow this path, or will retain large numbers of skilled male manual workers as they adapt further to changed market conditions. Given the desire of many enterprises to close their substantial training schools, which produced large numbers of skilled workers and technicians, their supply may well reduce considerably over the next decade in any case.

Much of this reduction in employment was achieved by closing or selling off subsidiaries, workers' hostels, schools and other enterprise-provided welfare facilities. Many of the firms discussed here had also severely reduced, or closed completely, their R. & D. units and had attempted to dispose of their non-production-related facilities. However, the recently resurgent trade unions and their political allies have restricted the ability of firms to drop all their welfare and training functions, just as local politicians appear to have been successful in severely limiting the extent of restructuring in one large enterprise in a poor part of the country, despite its considerable losses. Most of these firms' largest production units were still operating and performing similar activities to those carried out in 1990, albeit with somewhat reduced workforces and now constituting distinct limited companies. Indeed, in one case no departments or subsidiary units had been sold or closed since 1989.

Continuity was also evident in the composition of the top management teams of these enterprises. In only three cases were over half the current top management from outside the enterprise. Taking all fifty-five top managers from these ten firms together, thirty-six had worked in the same enterprise for most, if not all, of their working lives. Even in the now privately controlled firms, seven out of the fifteen top managers had been internally promoted, so that major changes in ownership and control did not appear to result in wholesale external recruitment to top posts. Greater change had occurred, though, among the chief executives. Over the past four years, all ten enterprises had changed their CEOs at least twice, and half of the current general directors had not worked in these firms before.

A similar pattern of continuity was evident among middle managers and employees as a whole. Although their numbers had declined substantially in some, but not all, of these enterprises, and restructuring had meant that many were now doing new jobs, and combinations of old ones, the vast majority of employees had worked in the same firm since leaving full-time education. As this implies, nearly all appointments to supervisory and managerial posts were internal, and recruitment from other organizations was quite rare. Essentially, then, the bulk of managerial, technical, clerical and manual workers in these enterprises had no experience of working in other firms or industries – even in the liquidated enterprise, 70 per cent of the workforce had worked in it since leaving school or university. This is not so surprising, given the high degree of sector monopolization and vertical integration in the post-war Hungarian economy, and the consequent lack of an external labour market among different employers in the same or related industries.

There had, though, been considerable movement between operating units and functions, especially for the engineers, who might start out in the production or technical departments but then move into personnel and, sometimes, general administration. On the whole, economics graduates were less mobile across functions, specializing mostly in accounting and commercial activities, although they were more mobile between firms. In terms of the skills that were acquired externally, there was no clear area of functional expertise that these firms felt had to be met by external recruitment. Despite much external trade being carried out by separate foreign trade organizations in the past, most marketing and sales posts were filled internally, perhaps because of the relatively low salaries available.

The restructuring of these enterprises during and after the period of spontaneous privatization had, though, increased the autonomy of the operating units, according to the top managers we interviewed. Many were now limited companies operating as distinct profit centres. Factory managers were beginning to deal with suppliers and/or customers directly and had more scope to make operating decisions, within agreed targets and budgets. In some cases these subsidiaries now had functional specialists who could manage relations with the business environment without consulting the central staff units and they also could buy most of their inputs from other companies and sell outside the parent enterprise.

In practice, however, this apparent decentralization and devolution of managerial authority to operating units was quite limited. Since the state had reasserted its control over the large enterprises, even though it was committed to privatizing most of them, the activities of the limited companies had become more centrally controlled, and operating autonomy fell far short of the usual Anglo-Saxon profit centre concept. Partly because of their typically poor financial position, the top managers of most of these enterprises centralized cash management and insisted that all payments should be made to the centre initially, not to the subsidiaries. Similarly, they often reserved the right to deal with important customers and suppliers themselves and the revamped personnel departments were currently engaged in standardizing job descriptions and grades, reward systems, recruitment and promotion procedures and training programmes across all the subsidiaries. In one case, the accounting and management control functions for each factory were carried out by groups under the finance director at head office. Also, because most still had to deal with state agencies on a daily basis, they could not decentralize many decisions to the operating units, given the general uncertainty about state policies and privatization procedures.

The overall structure of these enterprises had changed quite considerably in formal terms, although this seemed less significant in decision-making and control.terms. In most cases, individual plants and work-sites now had functional specialists in finance and personnel attached to them, and sometimes marketing and sales as well, and were regarded as separate business units reporting directly to the CEO. The two largest enterprises had, however, established a small number of major divisions which coordinated a variety of smaller units and most of the critical staff functions. Even here, though there were large and significant central functional departments headed by directors or vice-presidents reporting to the CEO and, in general, these directors were more likely to be regarded as members of the top management team than the managers of the production facilities.

Certainly, in most cases, the status and authority of the subsidiary managers were lower than those of the functional directors, unless they also had responsibilities for major staff functions. They typically reported weekly to the CEO and had limited or no control over decisions about new product introduction, pricing and many personnel matters. The major divisional directors of the two largest enterprises did have more control of activities in their divisions but were still subject to central coordination, and the business units were less independent than appeared from the organization chart. Overall, then, the structural changes that had occurred since 1989 in these large enterprises were less important in practice than they seemed, and subsidiaries were closely controlled by central departments in most companies.

In examining the degree of centralization of decision-making within these large enterprises, we followed the Aston studies' practice of asking respondents to identify the major levels of authority and to provide examples for each. In nine of them, the same six distinct levels were differentiated. At the top was the supervisory committee and general shareholders' meeting, i.e. the group(s) to whom the general director was responsible. Level five was represented by the general director, sometimes with the executive board. Level four consisted of the top functional directors. Level three referred to the factory and limited company managers, while level two was represented by factory sub-unit managers and level one by first-line supervisors. The ESOP firm had only five authority levels, since the production teams were managed by supervisors who in turn reported to the sub-factory managers who were responsible to the business unit directors. Given the considerable size of these nine enterprises, (i.e. $\geqslant$ 2,250 employees in 1993), it is not surprising that six distinct authority levels were identified, although in other studies only five were distinguished (e.g. Child and Kieser, 1979). The important point to bear in mind here is that level 5 constituted the top manager of the entire enterprise, not of sub-units within it, whereas in other research this referred to the main board or corporate parent level of authority.

Following the example of Lincoln and Kalleberg (1990), we asked top managers both which authority levels were formally responsible for making a range of decisions on personnel, administrative and operational matters, and which in practice usually did so. However, while in their study of Japanese and US factories, the actual decision-making level was normally lower than the formal one, in the ten Hungarian former SOEs considered here it was often higher, so that, for instance, while factory managers were supposed to decide the prices of outputs in three enterprises, in practice this was usually done by the director of economic affairs or the commercial director.

Overall, in seventy-six out of 220 decisions across all ten enterprises the actual decision-making level differed from the formal one. Of these, thirty-nine were decided at a higher level while thirty-seven were made at a lower level. This reluctance to delegate decision-making power in practice to subsidiary managers, even when it has been formally agreed may, of course, simply be a residue of the highly centralized cultures of the command economy (cf. Radice, 1981), although it is worth noting that the firms which had undergone the most radical changes in ownership were no different in this respect. It may also, though, reflect the current crises that most of these enterprises are undergoing and the strong pressures from their owners to reduce losses and debts. Even those which were breaking even or making operating profits, though, seemed reluctant to delegate authority in practice. Indeed, the most profitable enterprise, the foreign-controlled joint venture, was the most centralized one in respect of nearly all the decisions discussed.

Turning to consider the management levels at which different kinds of decisions were formally taken, those involving top managers most often were major administrative and organizational matters, and financial procedures, as shown in Table 6. Three questions dealt with changes to the responsibilities and/or work of staff functions, line management departments and opening or closing down major organizational units. The average level at which these decisions were formally taken in these six enterprises was 4.375, i.e. between the chief executive and functional directors. In practice, this occurred at level 4, i.e. the level of functional directors and, as might be expected, decisions about closing down departments were nearly always matters for the CEO to deal with. Even deciding about creating a new job was the concern of factory managers and limited company

Table 9.6 Average levels of decision-making authority in ten large enterprises

a) *Decisions about major organizational and administrative matters*	
Level of formal decision-making authority	:4.375
Level of decision-making in practice	:4.0
b) *Financial management procedures*	
Level of formal decision-making authority	:4.2
Level of decision-making in practice	:4.1
c) *Decisions about personnel management procedures and policies*	
Level of formal decision-making authority	:4.3
Level of decision-making in practice	:4.2
d) *Decisions about personnel appointments and promotions*	
Level of formal decision-making authority	:2.95
Level of decision-making in practice	:2.97
e) *Decisions about purchasing and marketing*	
Level of formal decision-making authority	:3.9
Level of decision-making in practice	:3.77
f) *Production management decisions*	
Level of formal decision-making authority	:2.1
Level of decision-making in practice	:2.3

Level 5 = CEO, level 4 = functional director, level 3 = factory manager, level 2 = factory sub-unit manager, level 1 = first-line supervisor directors, who were often responsible for the work of over a thousand people. The allocation of unbudgeted funds, selection of costing methods and decisions about what was to be costed were usually matters for the economic director to decide and in practice it was this level which did control those decisions.

At the other end of the hierarchy, production decisions were mostly the province of first- and second-line supervisors, as Table 9.6 shows, but even here the factory managers were often involved. The four decisions considered here dealt with the allocation of work, the selection of equipment and work methods and when overtime was to be worked. Formally the average decision-making level in these six enterprises was 2.1, i.e. just above the factory sub-unit manager level. In practice, the average level rose to 2.3, i.e. between the overall factory managers and sub-unit managers. This difference was especially noticeable for the question about working overtime, which seemed to require top factory management approval. Decisions about personnel procedures and policies were naturally taken at higher levels than those about actual appointments and promotions. Typically, the CEO or the personnel directors were formally responsible for the former, while the latter fell within the province of factory directors. Even in practice the personnel director was mostly responsible for deciding labour force needs, selection methods and training programmes and in some cases was also involved in decisions about the appointment and promotion of supervisors.

It is clear from these results that the autonomy of factory directors in personnel matters was severely restricted as personnel directors standardized procedures and insisted on being consulted over decisions regarding any employee above the operating level. Similarly, the functional directors at head office were able to play a significant role in product pricing, supplier selection and order priority decisions.

Although these were often – though by no means always – supposed to be the province of factory directors, in practice they were often taken by the economic or commercial directors, and the operating independence of the limited companies was quite limited. New product introduction was likewise most often decided at the functional director level so that the overall picture of decision-making in these ten large enterprises, both formally and in practice, is one of considerable centralization despite the frequent claim that, compared with 1989, managerial authority had been decentralized to the limited company subsidiaries. While this might be so when contrasted with the heyday of the command economy, the operating subsidiaries of these enterprises had remarkably limited autonomy in comparison with many of their Western counterparts. Given the strong degree of owner control discussed earlier, and the high level of market and political uncertainty, this is not too surprising, nor is it necessarily counter-productive.

This high level of central control over many decisions appeared to be equally strong across the ten enterprises considered here. Certainly, private ownership did not result in greater decentralization, either formally or in practice. The one firm that did decentralize most decisions to the greatest extent was the bank and privately owned enterprise H, but the ESOP-controlled firm and the joint venture were mostly more centralized than the seven state-controlled enterprises. While the latter's highly centralized decision-making practices may be due to the uncertainties of assuming control by the foreign parent, and in time the formalization of control procedures may enable greater decentralization, it is clear that strong central control in large Hungarian enterprises is not just a result of state control but is widespread across a variety of ownership types. Whether this will change as formal procedures and controls become more institutionalized, central cash control becomes less critical and owners develop greater trust in managers, remains to be seen, but at the moment it seems to be a general feature of large firms in Hungary.

CONCLUSIONS

The dominant conclusion to be drawn from this brief discussion of the ownership, control and decision-making processes in ten large enterprises in Hungary is that the considerable changes in forms of property and increase in competition since 1988 have had only a limited impact on the structure and activities of leading economic actors there. Even where there have been radical reductions in the number of employees (which, as we have seen, is by no means universal) and considerable restructuring of operating units into ostensibly separate 'profit centres', the bulk of the management and workforce in these enterprises has had no experience of any other firm or industry, and continues to produce much the same sorts of goods and services as they did in 1990. Given the continuity of personnel and the lack of a managerial labour market this should not be too surprising. Furthermore, most top managers of these large enterprises saw their future as being predominantly in the same sector, with only related diversification taking place, and that more through internal development than by acquisition. Large-scale disposals of assets and activities were not envisaged, and radical discontinuities in dominant strategies and organizational competences not expected.

Exceptions to some of these views were expressed by some of the top managements of the non-state-owned enterprises and it may be tempting to infer from these examples that, as more SOEs are allowed to become bankrupt and their component parts are broken up through liquidation, a greater extent of change and discontinuity may become more widespread in Hungary. However, it is important to note that the actual changes in the nature of products made by these companies since 1989 were rather limited, and the new product lines which had been introduced were in the same industrial sectors as existing products. Additionally, any anticipated changes in resources and activities were unlikely to lead to radical diversification into new fields. Even the bank-owned firm, which expressed a wish to acquire new capabilities rather than develop them internally, intended to continue to exploit its leading position in consumer markets in Eastern Europe and the former Soviet Union, while developing new technological expertise through subcontracting and acquiring small companies with complementary capabilities. In this case, although substantial restructuring had taken place, and the labour force composition had shifted considerably, the enterprise remained in the same industry, making substantially similar products for 73 per cent of its turnover and expected to continue to produce related product lines.

This prevalent continuity in the personnel, product lines and strategies of these former SOEs, despite formal changes in ownership and legal structures, reflects, we suggest, both the incremental changes that had already taken place in the Hungarian economy since 1968 and the continuing dominance of the state since 1989. As Stark (1990, 1992, 1993), amongst others (e.g. Radice, 1981), has emphasized, the loosening of direct state control of enterprises which began in 1968 but became more marked in the 1980s, permitted a variety of corporate forms to develop, albeit perhaps less than the official rhetoric suggested (Laky, 1988), and enabled managers to develop some autonomy and gain experience of a more decentralized economy. Thus, the legal and political changes in 1988 and 1989 were less of a 'big bang' in Hungary than elsewhere and had a less radical effect on enterprise structures and activities.

Perhaps more significant has been the continued importance of the state in dealing with economic restructuring – especially in deciding how to manage the debts of enterprises and the banks – and in mitigating the social consequences of radical economic change, especially after the taxi and lorry drivers' strike in 1990. Despite the public commitment to radical transformation of the Hungarian economy, in part designed to satisfy the IMF and Western governments, it is clear that, so far, neither politicians nor élite bureaucrats wish to break up the former SOEs and force them into liquidation and/or fundamental restructuring. However, the large amount of enterprise debt, together with that of the major banks, has forced the government to organize various credit-consolidation programmes which reflect both bureaucratic and political rivalries and interests. Similarly, privatization strategies and tactics have fluctuated over the past four years, as have the main personalities involved, so that the ownership, control and direction of many former SOEs have been quite uncertain and dependent upon both political and bureaucratic battles (Henderson *et al.*, 1995). Given the continued high levels of enterprise dependence on the state in Hungary – particularly with regard to debt management, investment funds, foreign trade rules and organizational restructuring – it is not surprising that top managers spend much of their time and energies negotiating with politicians, state secretaries in the ministries and SPA/SAMC staff, as well as with their main banks. The primary way of dealing with the greatest source of risk and uncertainty during this period of transformation is to focus on relations with the state, in a manner comparable to the pre-1988 situation, albeit with different actors and interest groups.

This focus, in turn, limits the degree of radical change in enterprise activities because the primary assets of top managers in these negotiations stem from their continued provision of employment, particularly in the poorer parts of Hungary, from continuing economic activities which generate some cash flow and tax income for the state, and from the sheer size of the enterprises, which renders their dissolution politically very risky. To break up and change radically these former SOEs voluntarily – i.e. without state support and risk-sharing – would be to risk losing influence and diminishing the assets under one's control so that top managers have little interest in pursuing discontinuous, radical strategies. Similarly, state agents have only limited interest in reducing the value of the enterprises under their current control, for an unknown and risky future pay-off, particularly if there is no obvious source of funds to pay off the accumulated debts.

Overall, then, the development of new economic actors pursuing distinctive strategies with restructured organizations has been less dramatic and less far-reaching in the first four years of the post-state socialist period in Hungary than might have been expected. Even where a foreign firm has taken effective control, radical changes have not been evident, at least so far, and other forms of private ownership have also led to incremental developments, rather than discontinuities in enterprises' activities and competences. While the new government in Hungary is intending to pursue privatization more vigorously, particularly through foreign ownership, and may be more effective than its predecessor because many of its key personnel have had prior political and bureaucratic experience, the continuity of many, if not most, managerial staff, lack of capital for major technological improvements, and continued critical role of the state in steering economic development, suggest that Hungarian firms will evolve gradually, rather than through qualitative shifts in personnel, products and skills.

REFERENCES

Baldassarri, M., Paganetto, L. and Phelps, E. S. (eds) (1993) *Privatization Processes in Eastern Europe*, London: Macmillan.

Barta, G. (1993) 'The role of foreign investors in the restructuring of the Hungarian economy', paper presented to a conference on 'The Social Embeddedness of the Economic Transformation in Central and Eastern Europe' held at the WZB, Berlin, 24–5 September.

Canning, A. and Hare, P. (1994) 'The privatization process – economic and political aspects of the Hungarian approach' in Estrin, S. (ed.) *op. cit.*

Carlin, W., Reenen, J. V. and Wolfe, T. (1994) 'Enterprise restructuring in the transition: an analytical survey of the case study evidence from central and eastern Europe,' Working Paper No. 14, London: EBRD.

Carroll, G. R., Goodstein, J. and Gyenes, A. (1988) 'Organisations and the State: effects of the institutional environment on agricultural cooperatives in Hungary', *Administrative Science Quarterly* 33: 233–56.

Child, J. and Kieser, A. (1979) 'Organisation and managerial roles in British and West German companies', in C. Lammers and D. Hickson (eds) *Organizations Alike and Unlike*, London: Routledge & Kegan Paul.

Clark, R. (1979) *The Japanese Company*, New Haven, Conn.: Yale University Press.

Estrin, S. (ed.) (1994a) *Privatization in Central and Eastern Europe*, London: Longman.

—— (1994b) 'Economic transition and privatization: the issues,' in Estrin, S. (ed.) *op. cit.*

Frydman, R. and Rapaczynski, A. (1993) 'Evolution and design in the East European transition', in Baldassarri *et al.* (eds) *op. cit.*

Frydman, R., Rapaczynski, A., Earle, J. S. *et al.* (1993) *The Privatization Process in Central Europe*, London: Central European University Press.

Grabher, G. (1995) 'The elegance of incoherence: institutional legacies in the economic transformation in East Germany and Hungary', in E. Dittrich *et al.* (eds) *Industrial Transformation in Europe*, London: Sage.

Henderson, J., Whitley, R., Czaban, L. and Lengyel, G. (1995) 'Dilemmas of state economic management: contention and confusion in the Hungarian route to industrial capitalism', in E. Dittrich *et al.* (eds) *Industrial Transformation in Europe*, London: Sage.

Kagono, T., Nonaka, I., Sakakibara, K. and Okumara, A. (1985) *Strategic vs. Evolutionary Management*, Amsterdam: North Holland.

Konecki, K. and Kulpinska, J. (1995) 'Enterprise transformation and the redefinition of organizational values in Poland', in E. Dittrich *et al.* (eds) *Industrial Transformation in Europe*, London: Sage.

Laky, T. (1988) 'Half-hearted organisational decentralisation: the small state enterprise', *Acta Oeconomica* 39: 247–70.

—— (1992) 'Special traits of Hungarian privatisation and some of its social effects', in G. Lengyel *et al.* (eds) *Economic Institutions, Actors and Attitudes: East-Central Europe in Transition*, Budapest: University of Economic Sciences Sociological Working Papers, Volume 8.

Lincoln, J. R. and Kalleberg, A. L. (1990) *Culture, Control and Commitment*, Cambridge: Cambridge University Press.

Neumann, L. (1993) 'Decentralization and privatization in Hungary: towards supplier networks?' in G. Grabher (ed.) *The Embedded Firm: on the socioeconomics of industrial networks*, London: Routledge.

Radice, H. (1981) 'The state enterprise in Hungary: economic reform and socialist entrepreneurship' in I. Jeffries (ed.) *The Industrial Enterprise in Eastern Europe*, New York: Praeger.

Sako, M. (1992) *Prices, Quality and Trust*, Cambridge: Cambridge University Press.

Stark, D. (1989) 'Bending the bars of the iron cage: bureaucratization and informalisation in capitalism and socialism', *Sociological Forum* 4: 637–64.

—— (1990) 'Privatization in Hungary: from plan to market or from plan to clan?', *East European Politics and Societies* 4: 351–92.

—— (1992) 'Path dependence and privatisation strategies in East-Central Europe', *East European Politics and Societies* 6: 17–51.

—— (1993) 'Recombinant property in East European capitalism. Organizational innovation in Hungary', paper presented to a conference on 'The Social Embeddedness of the Economic Transformation in Central and Eastern Europe', held at the WZB, Berlin, 24–25 September.

Tatur, M. (1995) 'Towards corporatism? The transformation of interest policy and interest regulation in Eastern Europe', in E. Dittrich *et al.* (eds) *Industrial Transformation in Europe*, London: Sage.

Torok, A. (1993) 'Trends and motives of organizational change in Hungarian industry – a synchronic view', *Journal of Comparative Economics* 17: 366–84.

Voszka, E. (1992) 'Spontaneous privatization in Hungary: preconditions and real issues', in G. Lengyel *et al.* (eds) *Economic Institutions, Actors and Attitudes: East-Central Europe in Transition*, Budapest: University of Economic Sciences Sociological Working Papers, volume 8.

Whitley, R. (1992) *Business Systems in East Asia: Firms, Markets and Societies*, London: Sage.

Zysman, J. (1983) *Governments, Markets and Growth: Financial Systems and the Politics of Industrial Change*, Ithaca, N.Y.: Cornell University Press.

Part III

The role of social groups in the structuring of firms and sectors in Europe

10 Contracting systems in the European construction industry

A sectoral approach to the dynamics of business systems

Graham Winch

INTRODUCTION

An important conceptual thread running through the contributions to this book is the relationship between firms, understood as economic actors, on the one hand, and the national institutional context in which they operate, on the other. These two are seen as mutually constituted through time to produce nationally distinctive configurations of relationships between the actors in the system. The aim of this chapter is to explore this dynamic in the context of a specific industrial sector – construction – in two different countries, France and Great Britain. In so doing, it will be contended that a full understanding of the dynamics of business systems can only be achieved by locating the analysis in the context of a specific set of production processes, for it is through the production of goods and services that firms create value and thereby generate returns for their stakeholders in forms such as salaries, dividends and tax payments; it is production which gives the firm its rationale.[1]

The industrial *sector* is thus an important level of analysis for comparing the dynamics of different business systems, and may be defined as the grouping of firms which participate both competitively and collaboratively in a common set of production processes, from material inputs to the final customer. Both conceptually and empirically, the sector is the link between the organization of the individual firm, and the organization of the national business system. A comparison between industrial sectors across different countries might be expected to show both a *national* effect, deriving from the national business system, and a *sectoral* effect, deriving from the nature of the associated production processes. Individual firms will vary in their responses to these two effects, whilst displaying strong commonalities in comparison to other sectors and other nations.

Construction is a particularly good choice for comparing business systems at the sectoral level. First, it is very large (7–10 per cent of GDP in most developed countries) and hence of considerable importance to the overall economy. Second, it is widely advocated by writers such as Michael Piore and Charles Sabel, and Paul Lawrence, as a model for the future development of the mass production sectors (Winch, 1994b). Third, construction services are not often traded internationally at present, but, under the auspices of the European Commission (EC) and the latest GATT round, national markets are being opened up to international competition. As the process of internationalization can therefore be studied from its earliest stages, this allows better testing of hypotheses regarding the derivation of competitive advantage from national business systems. Finally, the EC has been particularly active in developing directives specifically aimed at the sector.

The chapter will first introduce the main features of the organization of production in construction, so that the reader can understand the specific problems that actors in the sector are trying to solve. In this respect there are two distinctive features which need to be explored, before moving on to the comparative analysis of specific organizations – the organization of production around projects; and the collaborative nature of transactions within the production process. The relationships between these two features will then be summarized in the notion of the contracting system as a sectoral level business system. The chapter will then go on to explore the dynamics of relations between actors in the contracting systems of Britain and France, presenting the data, analysis and conclusions from the empirical investigation of the two construction projects chosen for comparative study. In conclusion, the paper will refer back to the more general set of issues posed in this book and specifically address the question of how economic actors are constituted in the construction sector of Britain and France, and the implications that this has for the competitive advantage actors derive from these systems in the nascent single European market.

THE PROJECT-ORIENTATED ORGANIZATION OF PRODUCTION

A production process consists of flows of information and materials within and between firms (Winch, 1994a: chap. 4). Within a single firm, the organization of the resources required for these information and materials flows can take a number of forms, the most common of which are the *functional* form and the *product* form (Mintzberg, 1979). In the functional form, the resources required for production are organized into discipline-based departments, and the flow of information and materials in the production process passes sequentially from one to another as required. These functionally organized resources may be shared between a number of production processes. In the product organization, all the resources required for the production of a particular product are organized into a single organization, often called a product division. The advantage of functional organization is that it facilitates the efficient use of resources, while the latter favours responsiveness to market needs. Inversely, product organization can be inefficient, while functional organization can be inflexible.

Where a combination of market responsiveness and efficient resource utilization is required, the matrix form of organization is sometimes chosen where both functional and product-orientated managers collaborate. Such organizational forms tend to be unstable, because of conflicts between the functional and product-orientated managers, and are not widely used at the firm level. However, a version of the matrix form – project organization – is well established in a number of industries, and the evidence is that its use is becoming more widespread. Its main distinction from matrix organization is that it is temporary in character (Bryman *et al.*, 1987), and usually operates as an overlay on the functional form (Winch, 1994a). While the life of a matrix organization is normally indeterminate, that of a project organization is clearly determinate, with a delivery date identified as part of its declared objectives. The aim of a project organization is to mobilize the required resources from their functional bases towards the market demand; it can be considered to be a 'création collective, organisée dans le temps et l'espace, en vue d'une demande' (Giard and Midler, 1993: 18).

Thus, as discussed by Kristensen in Chapter 6 in the context of the organization of Danish industry, project organization can be seen as consisting of two types of actor – skill containers and project coordinators. Skill containers provide the resources required for the effective flow of information and materials in the production process. In construction these are of varying types – architectural practices, trade contractors and the like. Project coordinators ensure their effective deployment to meet clients' needs for a particular product – these include project managers, construction managers and main contractors in construction, and programme managers, project divisions and the like elsewhere. These interact in what Miles and Snow

(1986) have called 'dynamic networks', where project coordinators act as brokers of the services of skill containers. The trend during and since the 1980s in Britain has been for the increasingly clear separation of these two roles both within and between firms – see Masterman (1992) for construction, and Winch (1994a) for engineering.

The time component of project organization lends a particular characteristic. Projects are only mounted when some aspect of the product is customer-specific and the product cannot be purchased from the output of a mass production facility. Projects are, therefore, inherently innovating and so the project information flow consists of a process of uncertainty reduction through time (Usmani and Winch, 1993). Where this process of uncertainty reduction is shared between firms, collaboration is required. Thus in industries such as electronics, construction and power engineering, the engineering and manufacture of components and subsystems require interactive information processing – transactions in the production process are inherently *relational*, rather than *junctural*. That is to say, the procurement of a good or service is not a spot transaction, but can take place over a period of many months, or even years. The classical distinction between make or buy is blurred, because transaction-specific commitments must be made by both parties to ensure effective information processing. The following sections will explore what is meant by collaborative transaction governance, and then indicate how construction fits into the broader pattern.

THE DEVELOPMENT OF COLLABORATIVE TRANSACTION GOVERNANCE[2]

The work of Williamson has been seminal in developing our understanding of the constitution of economic action. His early work (1975) emphasized a sharp polarity between market and hierarchical forms of transaction governance, with the economizing choice depending upon the degree of uncertainty and asset specificity (small numbers) inherent in the transaction. The inadequacies of this early conception have been widely recognized, not least by Williamson himself. His later work (1985) developed a number of more mixed intermediary forms depending on the degree of transaction frequency and the asset specificity of the investment. In particular, he identified trilateral transaction governance which includes provision for arbitration between the parties, and bilateral transaction governance where transaction-specific governance structures are developed.

For a given level of uncertainty, both forms are favoured where asset specificities are mixed, while trilateral governance is favoured where low transaction frequency prevails. Powell (1990) has gone on to argue that rather than being merely intermediate, what he dubs 'network' forms of transaction governance are of an equal status with the poles advocated by Williamson. This argument is persuasive, but the literature on network forms of transaction governance encompasses a diverse set of organizational forms, with little attempt to systematically differentiate types. Further development of the concept is required.

A different exploration of the issues is provided by Stinchcombe in his analysis of the North Sea oil industry where he argues that when contracts are made under uncertainty regarding the performance of the parties, market transaction governance takes on hierarchical forms. Specifically (1985; see also 1990), the problems arise from:

- difficulties in prediction of the client's desire for contractor performance;
- uncertainty about the costs of performance, resulting in the client retaining the right to alter performances throughout the project life cycle;
- inability of the client to clearly measure the relative performance of the separate parties.

Due to these problems, market contracts are written in such a way that they achieve hierarchical effects by:

- specifying authority systems to facilitate change;
- providing incentive systems to motivate the project actors;
- using administered pricing systems to handle uncertainties such as bills of quantity;
- providing conflict resolution procedures;
- providing standardized operating procedures.

These features are clearly related to Williamson's concept of trilateral transaction governance, but the case illustrates that intermediate contractual relationships can be much more complex than those captured in his discussion of the neoclassical contracting which underlies trilateral transaction governance.

In order to help clarify these issues, the literature on strategic alliances provides some useful frameworks. A spectrum of collaborative forms can be identified. The first dimension by which such forms vary is degree of interdependence[3] – collaborative arrangements can be either project-based – and therefore temporary, with a clean separation of resources allocated to the project and the returns generated from them at the termination of the project – or indeterminate in duration, with much greater difficulty in separating returns and the development of relationship-specific investments. The second dimension is power balance – the relationship may be one between equals; alternatively, power within the network may clearly favour one member.[4] From these two dimensions, four basic types emerge:

- The *consortium* is formed when firms collaborate on an equal basis to achieve a particular end, and then separate once it has been achieved.
- The *joint venture* is formed between parties who intend a continuing relationship, which is usually symbolized by the investment of equity in the joint venture and the right of the joint venture itself to keep at least some of the returns from that investment.[5]
- The *coalition* is formed when firms come together on a project basis, but in a clear principal contractor and junior contractor relationship between the parties; its dynamics will be explored in the following sections.
- *Quasi-firms* are formed where a powerful lead firm with a node position in the production process – often a final assembler – mobilizes a network of suppliers and distributors. There is again a clear hierarchical relationship between principal and junior contractor, but the relationship is continuous. This may be because the relationship continues from project to project, or because production is on a continuous basis. Apart from the human capital resources which are built up in such continuing relationships, both buyers and suppliers may make fixed capital investments which are dedicated to the transaction series, and so the cessation of the relationship may be very traumatic, particularly for the junior member of the quasi-firm. Quasi-firms reach their strongest form in franchise networks. Atmosphere considerations may favour equality of power and longer-term relationships.

Firms may move from one governance form to another in the process of adaptation to the changing institutional environment. Merger and acquisition are the conventional paths from market to hierarchy through vertical integration. Firms can also move towards collaboration, while retaining many of the features of hierarchy through joint ventures and consortia. Likewise, they may move towards collaboration while retaining many of the features of market governance through coalitions and quasi-firms. Following Powell, collaboration is presented as a third generic type, rather than an intermediary form between poles in the manner of Stinchcombe and Williamson, because, in practice, firms rarely move through collaboration on the way between market and hierarchy, but consistently choose to transact in this manner rather than one of the polar types. The next section will explore the distinctive character of transaction governance in construction, using this framework.

TRANSACTION GOVERNANCE IN CONSTRUCTION

How then does the organization of production in construction fit into the overall picture of collaborative production organization analysed above? First, construction is inherently project-orientated – buildings and infrastructure facilities are built to order, with only rare exceptions. This has led to some debate amongst specialists on construction as to whether it is the firm or the project which should be considered as the primary unit of analysis. However, it is clear from reading Williamson that the most helpful perspective is to take that of the firm (Winch, 1989); in particular, analysis should start with the client, and then move backwards down the production process. In terms of the transaction cost analysis reviewed above, construction can be considered to be characterized by low asset specificity, low transaction frequency and high uncertainty. The market for the vast majority of construction services is highly competitive; indeed, it is considered by some to be too competitive, and clients may deliberately limit tender lists to ensure that poor competitors do not drive out good ones. Clients, even 'experienced' ones, procure relatively few buildings each year, and even when they do procure more, this burst of activity is unlikely to be sustained year on year.[6]

Construction projects can be considered to suffer from high levels of uncertainty (Winch, 1989). In terms of *dynamism*, they usually suffer from a lack of task information. The site-specific nature of construction means that each project has a high number of unique features which need to be resolved through the project life cycle. At the early stages, factors such as the interaction of the project with existing facilities, regulated through urban planning procedures, and the dynamic nature of the client's requirements, can generate considerable levels of uncertainty which can only be reduced by negotiation, reworking and abortive work. For larger infrastructure projects, political considerations, particularly budgetary ones, can generate considerable dynamism. This high level of dynamism at the early stages means that it is difficult to smooth programmes of projects so that productive resources can be easily transferred from one to another. Once on site, dynamism generated by the uncertainties of natural conditions – both geological and climatological – generates further difficulties. These are reinforced by the temporary nature of the project organization – many of the actors will not have worked together before, and this creates an organizational dynamism which can easily generate conflict rather than cooperation within the project coalition. As the organization is temporary, the returns to building long-term relationships are inherently limited, and so atmosphere considerations are muted in their effects.

This dynamism is compounded by complexity. At the upper end, construction projects are amongst the most complex of all production undertakings. While it remains true that construction is largely an assembly industry, that assembly work has to be undertaken on sites which, for the reasons described above, are inherently dynamic. The components to be assembled vary considerably in character and in the skills that they require for their assembly. These components range from low-tolerance simple components such as bricks, to high-tolerance complex components such as advanced engineering services installations. Particular problems derive from the interactions between such components or, more correctly, component systems. There is also a trend through time for this complexity to increase, due to technological change and more demanding client requirements. The combination of high dynamism with medium to high complexity on most construction projects generates high levels of uncertainty.

These high levels of uncertainty would be enough to drive construction procurement towards hierarchy, were it not for the low asset specificity and, especially, very low transaction frequency. The overwhelming preference by clients is for market governance of construction procurement. This preference is shared by the principal actors within the project organization. The coalition form, as defined above, tends to be favoured. The relational character of transactions pervades the entire production process. Its most important result for our purposes here is that once contracts have been exchanged, considerable asset specificities are generated – the transformation is truly fundamental (Williamson, 1985: 61). The costs of replacing a project actor part-way through their service delivery are normally punitive. It is for this reason that elaborations of the trilateral-type governance of transactions both between project coalition members themselves, and between the client and the project coalition, are favoured. This point is illustrated by the prevalence of complex contract forms such as the Joint Contracts Tribunal (JCT) in the UK, the Code des Marchés Publics (CMP) in France and the Verdingungsordnung für Bauleistungen (VOB) in Germany.

Lorange and Roos (1992) assert that no firm will enter a strategic alliance when it can operate alone, due to the greater costs associated with working collaboratively. These costs are a combination of loss of autonomy, and hence power, and the increased transaction costs inherent in inter-organizational relations. Only where the gains outweigh the costs will collaborative forms be preferred. By extension it may be argued that unbalanced power relations will be preferred by powerful project actors in such collaborations. In other words, coalitions and quasi-firms will be favoured over consortia and joint ventures by those actors who are nodal in the project information flows. These nodal actors in construction are normally the principal designer (architect or civil engineer) and the principal contractor (main contractor or construction manager).[7]

THE CONTRACTING SYSTEM IN CONSTRUCTION

A contracting system (Bowley, 1966) is the institutional structure of a construction industry which defines the relationships between the various members of the project coalition. It therefore provides the context for the organization of construction projects, and is a sector-specific 'business system' in the sense that it specifies the 'distinctive configurations of hierarchy–market relations in which firms function as actors' (Whitley, 1992: 18). Within each contracting system various procurement options are available, but they all tend to share a common basis rooted in the relative power and competence of the actors within the system. The various reviews which are available – for instance Hillebrandt (1984) and Carassus (1987) – indicate how remarkably different the French and British systems are. It is the state which is the prime mover in establishing the institutional structure of a country's contracting system. It does this in two ways – as a client and as a regulator.

In most European Union countries, the state and its agencies account for up to 50% of construction demand. Thus, as a client, the state, by its sheer dominance in the market-place, sets an example of how to procure the built product – it establishes procedures for tendering, the responsibilities of each of the actors and the methods of payment. Such procedures can vary from the relatively transparent, where cost is the prime criterion for selection, to the relatively opaque, where negotiation predominates. Such practices, codified in the standard forms of contract identified above, tend to be borrowed by all except the most experienced clients in the private sector. The importance of such procedures for the character of the industry, and indeed the whole economy and polity, is illustrated by the case of Italy, where, at the time of writing, the political crisis was largely related to the construction industry (Cascio, 1993).[8]

Thus, the way in which the state acts as a client, rather than a regulator, has a profound influence both directly and through a demonstration effect. Bowley (1966: chap. 14) shows the way in which local authorities adopted the traditional British system for the procurement of social housing during its first great expansion after 1918. More recently, the changes in social housing procurement in both countries have been driven by changes in its method of financing (Campagnac and Winch, 1993). The contracting system and its regulatory context in turn operate within the broader context of the national business system.

It is clear from the argument above that a comparison of inter-relationships within systems, rather than the roles and responsibilities of particular actors in isolation, is vital for gaining an understanding of the dynamics of the different construction contracting systems in Europe, and indeed elsewhere (cf. Maurice *et al.*, 1982). The main features of national contracting systems can be summarized in terms of their three principal nodes: conception, construction and control:

- Conception, as will be shown in later sections, includes all the activities associated with design, and is normally shared between the professionals appointed by the client, such as the architect and the consulting engineer, and the principal and trade contractors for the site works. The typical balance between these two is a major differentiator between systems.
- Construction includes the planning of site activities and the execution of the works on site. The main differentiator here is whether the principal contractor adopts a strategy of internalizing or externalizing risk by subcontracting. This, in turn, is a function of both the contractor's responsibility for conception, and the broader context of the national business system favouring industrial or financial strategies.
- Control includes all those activities which ensure that the client's interests are served by the members of the project coalition. It is

usually carried out by professionals acting in third-party relationships to the main contracts between the parties. In terms of the typology developed by Winch and Schneider (1993), it is carried out by actors trading in *probity*, rather than creativity or technology. The main example of this type of actor is the quantity surveyor in the British system, and the BdC in the French system.

All three of these activities are carried out within every system – the questions of comparison revolve around how they are shared between the different types of actor within the project coalition, the effectiveness with which they are carried out and the extent to which those activities are determined by the regulatory context created by the state.

The regulatory context has four main features. The most important is the range of procurement routes offered within the contracting system, the rigidity with which they are enforced, and the underlying law of contract. The various missions under the CMP and the standard forms of contract offered by the JCT both provide a variety of procurement routes, each strongly influenced by the historical development of the national contracting system. For instance, the role of the BdC was given a big boost by the Spinetta amendment to the CMP in 1978. British clients are freer to adapt the standard forms to meet the needs of a particular project than their French counterparts. In particular, the ways in which liabilities for building failure are allocated will have a profound effect on the behaviour of actors in the system.

The second is the arrangements for the enforcement of building norms and standards. This is usually done by the local authority, although self-certification is becoming more common in Britain. Where norms and standards are performance-related, as in France (Bazin, 1993) it is likely to encourage the growth of specialists in interpreting them. The third is the policy for urban planning – an interventionist planning policy will tend to mean that more design is done pre-tender, as a contractor is unlikely to take the risk of problems with local urban planners. Finally, the mode of regulation (Boyer, 1986) of the labour market can have a profound effect upon the options available to management. It is clear that the remarkable growth of self-employment in the UK construction industry would not have been possible under German labour regulation, where self-employment levels have been stable over the last twenty years (Bögenhold *et al.*, 1993).

THE COMPARATIVE ANALYSIS OF CONTRACTING SYSTEMS

The only sustained attempt to provide a typology of the organization of the construction sector within the EU is that of Campinos-Dubernet (1988). She argues, on the basis of comparative case-studies in France, Britain, Italy and (west) Germany that two types of principal contractor strategy can be identified. There is the Franco-German type, where firms display an *industrial strategy* which places the emphasis upon the effectiveness of the process, and the Anglo-Italian type where a *financial strategy* predominates in which greater emphasis is placed upon the circulation of capital. The implementation of the industrial strategy is characterized by an internalization of variability in the production process which allows investment in plant and the training of the continuously employed workforce. The implementation of the financial strategy, on the other hand, is implemented through an externalization of variability characterized by the disengagement from the production process through subcontracting, the hiring of plant, the use of a casually employed workforce and low investment in training.

Focusing more specifically on the organization of projects in Britain and France, Campinos-Dubernet makes a number of observations which will be explored in this chapter:

- the importance of the independent professional in the British system;
- the separation of responsibility for the control of cost on the project from control of quality, due to the role of the quantity surveyor;
- the very detailed approach to specification practice in Great Britain;
- the fragmented character of the project coalition in Britain due to subcontracting.

Campinos-Dubernet's work is an impressive attempt to analyse in a rigorous comparative manner the behaviour of actors in the construction sectors of Europe's four largest economies. However, it has some limitations which warrant further investigation. First, there is a strong tendency to present each country's contracting system as homogeneous, and no sense of the range of procurement options available within each system is conveyed. Second, the British system is characterized as ossified (1988: 159), yet the last decade has been one of remarkable innovation (Masterman, 1992); it is clear that her comments apply mainly to the traditional British system as embodied in JCT 80. Third, she misses important features of the French system associated with quality control. Finally, despite being based on six case-studies from each country, Campinos-Dubernet provides only an overview, and no detail which would allow a deeper understanding of the dynamics of the contracting system studied. Her account lacks the richness that a presentation of case-studies allows and it is difficult, therefore, to identify how the relationships between the principal actors in each system actually differ. The following sections will empirically investigate these issues.[9]

RESEARCH METHODS

The research presented here is informed by the belief that a valuable way to gain a satisfactory understanding of the dynamics of business systems is through the comparison of matched case-studies. The comparative method has been central to sociological enquiry since at least the work of Max Weber, although its application in cross-national comparisons of socio-economic phenomena is remarkably rare. The research methodology selected had two central elements. First, it aimed to maximize the benefits of the comparative method, while ensuring the fully interactive interpretation of the findings through the methodology *croisée* in which the British researcher conducts the fieldwork in France, and the French researcher conducts the fieldwork in Britain. Second, it took a longitudinal approach in which data were collected over the project life cycle, rather than cross-sectionally. For these methodological reasons, the main research effort was devoted to two cases which were matched as closely as possible for size and building type.

Conceptually, the research took the 'tectonic approach' to the analysis of organizations (Winch, 1994a) which emphasizes the dynamic interplay between structure and process in organizational change. The emphasis is upon comparing organizational configurations in terms of both their structure, and the flows of information and material that those structures allow. The following discussion examines first project structure, and then project process, before examining in more detail the control of project objectives. These data are then brought together in an appraisal of how risks are allocated on the two projects. The projects selected for study were held by the informants to be typical of social housing procurement in the two countries at the time of fieldwork. While the depth and nature of the research meant that only one type of procurement route could be investigated in each country, social housing is, we believe, a good example of the general run of publicly financed building projects in both countries.

Project coalition structure

The structure of the French project is shown in a simplified form in Figure 10.1. It is a distinctive type of project coalition, which may be called co-contracting (*groupement conjoint*), which has become an increasingly popular procurement route in recent years (Armand 1991). Under this route, the principal contractor (*entreprise de gros œuvre*) is responsible directly for the structural works, which it carries out mainly with its own directly employed workforce. However, while the principal contractor has agreed a lump sum price with the client (*maître d'ouvrage*) for all the works, the finishing trades (*second œuvre*) contractors are placed in direct contract with the client, and the principal contractor is paid a fee for their management. They are, therefore, called co-contractors (*co-traitants*) to distinguish them from sub-contractors (*sous-traitants*) who are in direct contract with the principal contractor. From the principal contractor's point of view, the arrangement carries less risk. Only those in

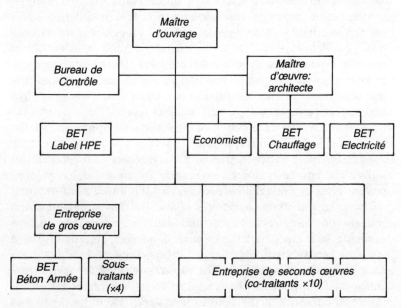

Figure 10.1 French project organization

direct contract with the client are subject to decennial liability (*garantie décennale*) under the CMP. This means that the principal contractor carries the liability if works performed by subcontractors fail during the ten-year period. By adopting the co-contracting form of organization the principal contractor loses turnover and, therefore, profit opportunities, but also minimizes the risk of exposure under decennial liability. Subcontracting is restricted to specialist services integral to the structural works, such as earthworks, piling and concrete finishing.

A second distinctive feature of the project is the organization of the design process. Only the architect (*maître d'œuvre*) has a contract with the client; all the other independent consultants associated with the design – the mechanical and electrical services engineers (*bureau d'études technique*) and the building economist (*economiste*) – are subcontractors to the architect. However, the most notable feature is the responsibility of the principal contractor for structural design. In this case, these tasks were subcontracted to an independent structural engineering consultancy (*bureau d'études béton armée*), but in larger companies, such work may be carried out in-house. The critical point is that the choice of structural technology is made largely by the principal contractor, and not mainly by the architect as is the case in Britain.

The design process is regulated by the control office (*bureau de contrôle*) (BdC). A minimum level of control by this body is obligatory under the CMP. The main task of the BdC is to ensure the integrity of the structure and to ensure that various building regulations are followed with respect to public health, energy and fire. The mission includes both approval of the designs and quality control of the works on site. Control offices are selected by the client on the basis of price, and quality of service offered. A high quality of service from the control office can ease the acceptance of the building by the public authorities (*Commission de Sécurité*) and reduce the risk of building failure thereby ensuring that rates for project insurance (*dommage ouvrage*) are kept to a minimum.

The organization of the project coalition described above can be sharply contrasted from the structure of the British project, shown in Figure 10.2. Here the client's professionals are each in direct and separate contract with the client. In contrast, the site works are let on a lump sum basis and are the full responsibility of the principal contractor. Detail design work is subcontracted to professional practices, while the site works are then subcontracted to specialist trade contractors, with the exception of the structural trades of carpentry

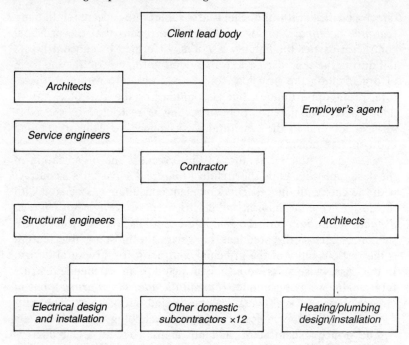

Figure 10.2   British project organization

and brickwork, which are let on a labour-only subcontract basis. The reason for this is that subcontractors in these trades are normally too small to finance the purchase of the weekly volume of materials required to keep the project on programme. The principal contractor directly employs neither design professionals nor operatives.

The main attraction for the client of the procurement route chosen is that it offers cost certainty once the tender has been accepted, which is very important under the present funding regime for social housing. Effectively, the contractor takes the risk of any unforeseen problems, such as with the terrain. The client retains an architect to develop the overall scope of the project and obtain planning permission, while the contractor retains an architect and other designers as appropriate to carry out detailed design work. Such work may also be carried out by trade subcontractors. The more experienced client may choose not to appoint a project manager, but in this particular case an employer's agent had been appointed. This was the same quantity surveying practice that had provided cost advice prior to tender.

Responsibilities for the project information flow

The analysis of structural relationships establishes roles, but it does not give much insight into how the different actors interact on the project. This section will present a processual analysis in an attempt to clarify how members of the project coalition interact over the project life cycle. Figure 10.3 presents a generic model of the project as a flow of information which generates and controls a flow of materials on site. The model is intended to summarize the stages through which any project must pass. It is deliberately abstracted from existing process models – the CMP and the British RIBA Plan of Work. This is to allow an analysis which is not biased by the framework of either the French or the British systems, and hence

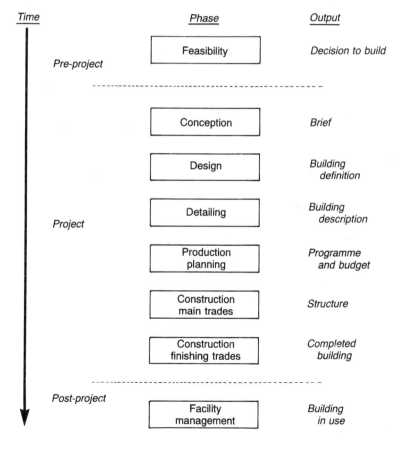

Figure 10.3 The construction process: a generic model

an ethnocentric way of looking at the project process. The project stage is divided into six main phases, each with its distinctive output. Essentially, the process is a flow through time of information and materials which increasingly define and realize the finished building. Using this model, Figure 10.4 indicates responsibilities for the two projects – its aim is to visually represent the balance of responsibilities, rather than to define precise contractual roles. Responsibilities are indicated in terms of those actors in a direct contractual relationship with the client, and exclude the supervisory duties of the employer's agent, control office or architects during the construction phases of the project.

There were also important differences in the volume of information flowing within the two project coalitions. While the amount

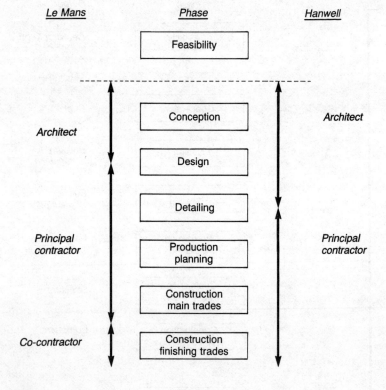

NOTE:
Defined by contractual relationship to client
Excludes supervisory duties

Figure 10.4   Main actors: Britain/France

of written information contained in specifications was about the same, the British architects produced on behalf of the client five times as many drawings as their French counterparts, most of which contained additional specification information. The principal contractors tendered against this information. Post-contract, the British principal contractor's architects and engineers produced roughly the same number of detail drawings again, while the French produced merely a number of shop drawings. It is clear that French contractors build from a much less detailed description of the building than British contractors, and have much more scope after tender for influencing the detailed specification than a British contractor.

Project objectives and their control

One major difference between the two project coalitions is in the responsibility for the control of cost and quality, and this difference reflects major differences in the organization of the French and British contracting systems. The difference revolves around the performance criteria which are externalized from the main actors in the project coalition and given by the client to an independent party. In the British system, the control of cost against the budget is usually the responsibility of an independent quantity surveyor who is answerable to the client. The quantity surveyor has a role during the design stage advising the client on the likely cost of the building and during the construction stages controlling the progress of the project against the budget, and valuing any variations to the contract. Post-tender, these functions are performed by the employer's agent. The control of the quality of specification in terms of building and planning regulations is the professional responsibility of the designers. During the construction phases, the control of quality in terms of conformance to specification is the responsibility of the principal contractor, although the client did appoint a clerk of works to perform supervisory duties.

In France, by strong contrast, at both the design stages and construction stages, quality is controlled by an independent party, the BdC. At the design stage, the drawings and specifications are checked to ensure conformance with the building regulations. The BdC, rather than the designers or the contractor, is responsible for ensuring that the design and construction meet the approval of the building control officers. During the construction stages, the elements of the structural works in progress are inspected and tested, and the final performance of the building on parameters such as acoustic isolation is also checked to ensure conformance to specification. The representatives of the BdC have a right of access to the site at any time, and can inspect any aspect of the works within their jurisdiction. The difference in the importance given to third-party control of quality in France compared to Britain is indicated by the fact that all the employees of the BdC were graduate engineers backed by a central building research capability, while the clerk of works was an ex-tradesman.

Control over costs within the French system is much more the responsibility of the contractor. The building economist's task, as a subcontractor to the architect, is to provide a cost envelope prior to tender, and to ensure that it is within the reference price for social housing. The architect and economist are then liable for this estimate, and can be fined by the client if the final cost of the project exceeds the envelope by more than a specified amount. Post-tender, the economist's role is limited to approving monthly progress payments to the contractors, and approving variations, rather than taking an active role in negotiations. Cost information is largely the preserve of the principal contractor, and the contractor may use these data to propose variations (*variantes*) in order to reduce costs to the client either at tender stage, or post-tender if the overall budget is being exceeded. The client is protected against degeneration of the specification through this process by the oversight of the BdC. The difference between the role of the French building economist and the British quantity surveyor is indicated by the fact that the latter chaired site meetings on the British project, while the former took a passive role in site meetings, which were chaired by the contract manager.

The differences between the emphasis placed on the control of costs against budget, in the British system, and the emphasis placed on the control of quality in terms of both the level of specification and conformance to that specification, in the French system, is remarkable. A considerable effort under the British system is placed on controlling the shape of the project cash flow S-curve; in the absence of major variations, the activities of the quantity surveyor after tender can make virtually no difference to total project cost, which is determined through the market by the price agreed with the contractor. In the French system, on the other hand, greater effort is put into ensuring a high level of specification and consummate conformance to that specification throughout the project.

The allocation of risk between coalition members

Perhaps the feature with the most significant behavioural implications is the way in which risk is allocated within the two project coalitions. On the evidence of these cases, the French coalition is characterized by a greater horizontal sharing of risk, while the British is characterized more by a vertical shedding of risk. In the French risk-sharing process, the provisions of the CMP and the role of the BdC are crucial. Liability under the CMP only exists for those in contract with the client. Unlike under English law through provisions of back-to-back contracts, the contractor cannot pass liability on to a subcontractor, therefore it often prefers to place other contractors responsible for specialist trades in direct contract with the client, through co-contracting, whilst retaining overall project management responsibility. The BdC acts to protect the client's interests by ensuring that the architect's work meets national standards, and preventing the contractor from compromising the specification to cut costs. However, the inverse of this role is that the risks of innovation are shared – if an actor proposes an innovation and it is approved by the BDc, with its vast technical resources, then liability is shared by the innovator should the BdC approve it. It may be suggested that such an arrangement is likely to inhibit innovation (Meikle and Hillebrandt, 1989: 50); in particular, because the BdC has no incentive to take risks. However, one key informant argued that the BdC facilitated innovation through this risk-sharing. Observation of the level of technology deployed on the case-study site supports this contention. This means that contractors in the French system can propose *variantes* to the specification which adapts it more closely to their technical capabilities and they are, therefore, more ready to internalize variability in the manner suggested by Campinos-Dubernet.

In Britain, on the other hand, the contract is used by the client to pass risk on to the principal contractor. This a major feature of the procurement route chosen (Pain and Bennett, 1988), and is the main reason behind its widespread adoption by housing associations (Hutchinson and Putt, 1992). At the same time the housing association's architects specified the design so completely that the principal contractor could not innovate and thereby absorb the risk. Indeed, the employer's agent informed us that attempts to innovate by proposing alternative methods were actively discouraged as a point of principle in the name of fair competition. The only option open to the principal contractor is to pass this risk on again to trade, specialist and labour-only subcontractors. Here lies the motivation to externalize variability noted by Campinos-Dubernet. The problem with this approach is that the risks end up by being carried by organizations that are ill-equipped for that burden – under-capitalized trade contractors and labour-only gangs.

THE CONTRACTING SYSTEM IN BRITAIN AND FRANCE

Turning back to the points of difference identified by Campinos-Dubernet between British and French project coalition organization, the data from these two detailed cases partially support her con-clusions. First, the relative power of the British professionals is remarkable in comparison to their French colleagues. Child and his colleagues (1983) have noted how the strength of professionalism in British manufacturing industry compared to that of (west) Ger-many has led to a relatively high level of occupational specialization defined in terms of professional competence, and a devaluation of the role of production management in favour of staff professionals.

The evidence from these cases certainly supports the contention that the British system is professionally orientated. The way in which the client's architects leave the principal contractor responsible for production, with almost no room for innovation, makes the case well. The point is most telling with reference to the employer's agent, or quantity surveyor. Although this actor is responsible for appraising tenders on behalf of the client, the quantity surveyor has no technical competence and is not, therefore, prepared to consider variations from the contractor which would save the client money. On the other hand, the BdC has very strong technical capabilities, and can make a thorough appraisal of variations proposed by con-tractors to give the client better value for money. Campinos-Duber-net's third point was clearly supported. Compared to their French counterparts, British principal contractors receive vast amounts of information at tender stage, and then generate even more them-selves in order to actually build. On the one hand this would appear to be a result of the professionalism of the British architects; on the other, it suggests a lack of technical competence on the part of the principal contractor itself.

However, her other observations were not supported. The French project coalition was more fragmented than that of the British, and even at site level the number of actors was about the same in each case, despite that fact that the French principal contractor deploys its own workforce for much of the structural works. Second, the separation of the control of quality from the control of cost is not supported at the level of the project coalition as a whole. Here, quality control in the French system, and cost control in the British system, are both separated out into the professional roles of the control office and the quantity surveyor respectively. Spencer Chapman and Grandjean (1991: chap. 3) argue that the British system is characterized by poor quality control, while the French system is characterized by poor cost control. They offer no evidence for these assertions, but it is certainly clear that the institutional emphasis within the contracting systems favours cost control in Britain and quality control in France.

From this evidence, a number of important points of difference can be noted between the British and French projects studied. First, the responsibility of the professionals appointed by the client for *conception* is much larger in Britain than in France. The ability of the architect to specify what actually happens on site is much weaker on the French project than the British. Conversely, the responsibility of the principal contractor for conception is much greater. While responsibilities for *construction* are broadly the same, they are organized in very different ways. The French contractor internalizes variability by retaining a large direct labour force which can be deployed on every project undertaken, and refusing responsibility for trades which are not within its competence, and are more variable between projects, by co-contracting. The British contractor externalizes variability by subcontracting all trades.

So far as *control* is concerned, the British professionals have much greater autonomy with respect to quality, while their French counterparts are subject to the oversight of the BdC. Similarly, on site, the contractors are subject to the overview of the powerful BdC and the architect, while the British client's interests are protected only by the clerk of works. Turning to control over cost, the British system has the quantity surveyor who both provides cost information pre-tender, and exercises a strong overview as employer's agent post-tender. The French building economist has a relatively weak role in providing a cost envelope, and approving interim payments post-tender. The major source of cost information is the contractor, and this information is deployed in the context of relatively high rigidity in the social housing funding formula. Features of the design which increase costs have to be paid for by savings elsewhere in the budget. This creates a situation in which all the members of the project coalition have an interest in finding savings to ensure that the project goes ahead, a motivation reinforced on the part of the *maître d'œuvre* by the fines levied for cost overruns. This is done by the contractor proposing variations, subject to the approval of the architect and BdC. The fact that the reference price is not routinely increased to allow for inflation reinforces this dynamic. The more flexible British funding system does not enforce the same dynamic – none of the members of the British project coalition have an interest in reducing costs in the same way. This is clearly shown by the way that the contractor is actively discouraged from proposing variations which would allow savings for the client. In this way, the management of costs on the French project can be considered to be a cost *reduction* process, while that on the British project can be considered as a cost *control* process.

CONCLUSIONS: CONTRACTING SYSTEMS AS BUSINESS SYSTEMS

This chapter has woven a substantive and a methodological theme together. The methodological theme is a comparison of construction project coalition organization in Britain and France within the societal tradition identified by Sorge in the concluding chapter. This type of analysis in terms of the mutual constitution of organization structures, and flows of information and materials within and between those structures has been christened elsewhere (Winch, 1994a) the 'tectonic approach' to organizational analysis. Campinos-Dubernet (1988) completes her own analysis by drawing on the same societal approach to conclude that societal factors outweigh sectoral factors in constituting the organization of the construction sector. Like this study, her work did not compare organizations *between* sectors, and so her evidence can neither support nor gainsay such an assertion. The point about sectors and societies that follows is slightly different – societal analysis can *only* become fully meaningful in combination with sectoral analysis, for it is at the level of the sector that firms as actors find their rationale.

The actions of the firms who collaborate in the project coalitions analysed here can only be meaningfully interpreted in the context of the contracting system in which they operate. These actors create value by providing buildings and similar facilities for clients in the public and private sectors through the collaborative organization of transaction governance due to their inherently relational nature. The contracting system has evolved into a distinctive configuration of market-hierarchy relations through negotiation between the actors in order to provide a stable framework for such collaboration. In turn, the system turns back upon the actors to constrain their activities as actors through the process of structuration. The same fundamental problems of transaction governance face both French and British construction firms, yet the ways in which they have solved these problems is quite distinct. While these distinctions may well largely derive from a societal effect, the problems in the first place derive from a sectoral effect. The contracting system in construction is the outcome of the interaction between the societal and sectoral effects.

A few brief examples will illustrate the point. While relative roles of architectural firms in the two countries can be partially explained by the greater professionalization of British firms in general, as argued by Child and his colleagues, it is also the case that both contracting systems share identifiably similar groups of firms, called architectural practices, which are virtually unique to the sector. While the industrial strategy of French principal contractors and the financial strategy of the British identified by Campinos-Dubernet lead to differences in behaviour towards the rest of the project coalition, both project coalitions displayed remarkably clear distinctions between the skill container and project coordinator roles which, as Kristensen argues, are often combined within a single firm in other sectors. Major elements of national business systems are often adapted to suit particular sectors. For instance, construction escaped the reform of the UK training system which led to the abolition of all statutory industry training boards except for the two for construction. The EC, in its reform of the system for health and safety has singled out construction EU-wide for special attention under the Temporary or Mobile Sites Directive.

The substantive theme is a development of the conceptual framework of transaction cost analysis and its application to a particular sector characterized by the project organization of the production process where transactions are inherently relational rather than junctural. The market governance of transactions is therefore impossible due to the fundamental transformation, yet hierarchy is also discouraged due to low transaction frequency, despite high uncertainty.

This conceptual work was necessary to clear up some of the confusion surrounding non-polar transaction governance modes, and thereby to locate for the reader the distinctive configuration of transaction governance in the construction sector within the generic triad of possible modes. The dynamics of transaction governance on a British and French social housing project were explored and characterized as being governed by coalitions of actors operating within distinctive contracting systems. The British coalition was shown to be a risk-shedding one, driven by a cost-control dynamic, while the French one was demonstrated to be a risk-sharing one characterized by a cost-reduction dynamic. As a result, the French system was argued to be more innovative than the British.

While it is the similarities between sectors cross-nationally that configures the dynamic of actor and system in construction, it is the differences between them that present the opportunities to develop sustainable competitive advantage. Tsoukalis (1993: chap. 4) argues that, increasingly, theories of international trade are stressing the advantages deriving from the institutional context of national systems. The most obvious manifestation of this trend is the work of Porter (1990). He starts with the observation that those countries which have a world-class competitor tend to have more than one, and to have clusters of world-class competitors in related industries. He argues from this that such firm-based competitive advantages are derived to an important extent from features of the national business system for that sector. He identifies four main features of national business systems – factor conditions, demand conditions, related and supporting services, and firm strategy, structure and rivalry. A full application of this model must await another paper, but developments in the European construction industry show how important national demand conditions are in the emergence of a European construction industry.

Observation of these indicates that it is the more powerful actors within each contracting system that have competitive advantage in the single market. British architects and engineers have been remarkably successful abroad, particularly in France and Germany, while entry to the British market remains difficult for architects and engineers from anywhere except the United States. Similarly, it is the French contractors which have been most active at a European level, and have also successfully defended their home market. British contractors, on the other hand, are increasingly obliged to enter into joint ventures with contractors from either the USA or the other main European countries in order to secure the larger contracts in the UK. Where national systems have developed distinctive competencies, these can also become the basis of competitive advantage internationally. This appears to happen mostly around the control function. The French BdC have been successful in exporting their services to other European countries. For instance, SOCOTEC, the largest BdC, is well established in Germany, Italy and Spain. Similarly, British quantity surveyors have been able to export the project management aspects of their service to a number of other countries, particularly on behalf of international clients.

Of course, it may be argued that another reason for this pattern of competitive advantage is that different systems have greater levels of openness to foreign firms. For instance, the French system of architectural competitions (concours) makes entry very easy compared to the predominance of appointment in Britain. Similarly, the relative transparency of British construction procurement and the more thorough implementation of EC directives makes it easier for foreign contractors to enter the UK market. These arguments certainly have weight, but it is also the case that the most open parts of each system are those where the domestic actors are weakest. Competitive advantage and market opportunity are interdependent, deriving from the dynamics of the national contracting system, and the balance of power between the actors in the project coalition responsible for conception, construction and control.

NOTES

1 The firm is here distinguished from the corporation, which consists of a portfolio of firms and may have a purely financial rationale.
2 The arguments in this section are developed in more detail in Winch (1995).
3 This dimension is taken from the work of Lorange and Roos (1992). Their work is very much focused on questions associated with corporate strategy, while the focus here is on the organization of production by business units. However, any arrangement made on behalf of a business which involves equity would need the authorization of the corporate centre, and so corporate and business strategy are not clearly distinguishable here. The issue is more one of perspective – whether the collaborative arrangement is made to improve the competitiveness of a particular business activity, or to develop an aspect of corporate strategy such as the portfolio.
4 Lorange and Roos (1992) discuss 'dominant' and 'shared' strategic alliances, but restrict their analysis to the global companies. Even here, the fundamental issue would appear to be that of the balance of power between the strategic alliance ·members. The introduction of power relations into the analysis of transaction governance is one Williamson would resist (1985: chap. 9, 1993), but I concur that with the critique of Francis (1983), Perrow (1986) and others that not all forms of transaction cost governance can be explained by economizing. The cases presented later will indicate the ways in which power imbalances arise after the fundamental transformation.

5 This distinction is in line with the traditional economic definition of a joint venture (Clark and Ball, 1991).
6 The main exception to this is maintenance work, which is beyond the scope of this paper.
7 Where actors do move towards consortia for uncertainty coping, atmosphere, or asset specificity reasons (Clark and Ball, 1991), then this normally only involves the nodal actors, leaving the rest of the project organization as a coalition. Where transaction frequency rises, such as in housebuilding, elements of the quasi-firm may also emerge (Eccles, 1981). However, the vast majority of construction projects are of the pure coalition type.
8 Recent political turmoil in Japan is also significantly linked to corruption scandals in construction procurement (Kurosaki, 1993).
9 These findings are more fully reported in Winch and Campagnac (1995). The research was financed by the Economic and Social Research Council (award No. R000232937), and the Eurorex programme of Plan Construction et Architecture.

REFERENCES

Armand, J. (1991) *La Coordination de Travaux*, Paris: Editions du Moniteur.
Bazin, M. (1993) 'Analyse stratégique en science et technologie', *Cahiers du CSTB* No. 2643.
Bögenhold, D., Staber, U. and Winch, G. (1993) 'History and uncertainty: a dynamic perspective on human resource management', *Zeitschrift für Personalforschung* 7.
Bowley, M. (1966) *The British Building Industry*, London: Cambridge University Press.
Boyer, R. (1986) *La Flexibilité du Travail en Europe*, Paris: Editions La Découverte. Translated as (1988) *The Search for Labour Market Flexibility*, Oxford: Clarendon Press.
Campagnac, E. and Winch, G. (1993) 'Approche comparée du système de production du logement social en France et au Royaume-Uni', *Actes de Colloque: Les Entretiens de L'Habitat*, Nancy: ADUAN.
Campinos-Dubernet, M. (1988) 'Diversité des formes de gestion de la variabilité des processus du bâtiment: effet sectoriel ou effet national?', *Actes de Colloque Europe et Chantiers*, Paris: Plan Construction et Architecture.
Carassus, J. (1987) *Economie de la Filière Construction*, Paris: Presses Ponts et Chaussées.
Cascio, F. (1993) 'Privatisation in Italy: Impact on the Construction Industry', MSc Architecture Report, University College London.
Child, J., Fores, M., Glover, I. and Lawrence P. (1983) 'A price to pay? Professionalism and work organization in Britain and West Germany', *Sociology* 17.
Clark, I. and Ball, D. (1991) 'Transaction cost economics applied? Consortia within process plant contracting', *International Review of Applied Economics* 5.
Eccles, R. G. (1981) 'The quasifirm in the construction industry', *Journal of Economic Behavior and Organization* 2.

Francis, A. (1983) 'Markets and hierarchies: efficiency or domination?', in A. Francis, J. Turk and P. Willman (eds) *Power, Efficiency and Institutions*, London: Heinemann.

Giard, V. and Midler, C. (1993) *Pilotages de Projet et Entreprises*, Paris: Economica.

Hillebrandt, P. (1984) *Analysis of the British Construction Industry*, Basingstoke: Macmillan.

Hutchinson, K. and Putt, T. (1992) *The Use of Design/Build Procurement Methods by Housing Associations*, London: RICS.

Kurosaki, F. (1993) 'Investigation into Japanese procurement procedures and case study about privatization of the Japanese National Railways', MSc Architecture Report, University College London.

Lorange, P. and Roos, J. (1992) *Strategic Alliances*, Oxford: Blackwell.

Masterman, J. W. E. (1992) *An Introduction to Building Procurement Systems*, London: E. & F. N. Spon.

Maurice, M., Sellier, F. and Silvestre, J.-J. (1982) *Politiques d'Education et Organisation Industrielle en France et en Allemagne*, Paris: Presses Universitaires de France. Translated as (1986) *The Social Foundations of Industrial Power*, Cambridge, Mass.: MIT Press.

Meikle, J. L. and Hillebrandt, P. M. (1989) *The French Construction Industry*, London: CIRIA.

Miles, R. E. and Snow, C. C. (1986) 'Organizations: new concepts for new forms', *California Management Review* 29.

Pain, J. and Bennett, J. (1988) 'JCT with contractor's design form of contract: a study in use', *Construction Management and Economics* 6.

Perrow, C. (1986) 'Economic theories of organization', *Theory and Society* 15.

Porter, M. E. (1990) *The Competitive Advantage of Nations*, New York: Free Press.

Powell, W. W. (1990) 'Neither market nor hierarchy: network forms of organisation', *Research in Organizational Behavior* 12.

Spencer Chapman, N. F. and Grandjean, C. (1991) *The Construction Industry and the European Community*, Oxford: BSP Professional Books.

Stinchcombe, A. L. (1985) 'Contracts as hierarchical documents', in A. L. Stinchcombe and C. A. Heimer *Organizational Theory and Project Management*, Oslo: Norwegian University Press.

—— (1990) *Information and Organizations*, Berkeley, Calif.: University of California Press.

Tsoukalis, L. (1993) *The New European Economy* (2nd edn.), Oxford: Oxford University Press.

Usmani, A. and Winch, G. (1993) *Management of Design: the Case of Architectural and Urban Projects*, London: Bartlett Research Paper 1.

Whitley, R. (1992) *Business Systems in East Asia*, London: Sage.

Williamson, O. E. (1975) *Markets and Hierarchies*, New York: Free Press.

—— (1985) *The Economic Institutions of Capitalism*, New York: Free Press.

—— (1993) 'Transaction cost economics and organization theory', *Industrial and Corporate Change* 2.

Winch, G. (1989) 'The construction firm and the construction project: a transaction cost approach', *Construction Economics and Management* 7.

—— (1994a) *Managing Production: Engineering Change and Stability*, Oxford: Clarendon Press.

—— (1994b) 'The search for flexibility: the case of construction', *Work Employment and Society* 8.

—— (1995) 'Project management in construction: towards a transaction cost approach', London: Le Groupe Bagnolet Working Paper 1.

—— and Campagnac, E. (1995) 'The organisation of building projects: an Anglo-French comparison', *Construction Management and Economics* 13.

—— and Schneider, E. (1993) 'Managing the knowledge-based organisation: the case of architectural practice', *Journal of Management Studies* 30.

11 The social constitution of supplier relations in Britain and Germany

An institutionalist analysis

Christel Lane

Recent theoretical analyses of changes in industrial organization (Piore and Sabel, 1984; Sabel, 1989, 1990; Sengenberger and Pyke, 1990; Atkinson and Meager, 1986), as well as theoretical and practitioner discussions of Japanization, have asserted that outsourcing of production tasks, due to the new strategic importance of this inter-film relation (Semlinger, 1991), has undergone a fundamental change of character. The buyer demands quality assurance, cost reduction through improved efficiency, technological know-how and just-in-time (JIT) delivery. In return, the supplier gains longer-term contracts and may be designated a 'preferred supplier', as well as receiving various kinds of technical assistance. More generally, inter-firm relations are said to have become closer and more diffuse and trusting. Supplier relations have been variously reconceptualized as 'collaborative manufacturing' (Sabel, 1990), 'obligational contracting' (Sako, 1992), or as partnership subcontracting (DTI, 1991). Such conceptualizations imply convergence towards one uniform type of supplier relations, described by the shorthand term 'Japanization'.

This paper will show, through comparative analysis of the contractual environment in which supplier relations are situated, that there remain distinctive national patterns in which firms and inter-firm relations are organized. Firms are viewed in terms of roles and role identities, and differing national understandings of these roles also lead to distinctive patterns of interaction between firms. Relations within and between firms will be analysed by reference to the notions of trust and power, and ideal-typical specifications of national patterns of supplier relations will be developed.

Although there is considerable stability in roles and role relations, these are not conceptualized as invariant. In the second part of the paper, an examination of empirical evidence from a range of industries will assess both the degree of variation in the organization of supplier relations within countries, and the extent and nature of emergent change. Such changes are being set in train by various developments in the contractual environment, and the label of Japanization is only very partially adequate to describe and explain them.

THE THEORETICAL FRAMEWORK

The nature of relations between buyer and supplier firms (supplier relations) is influenced by a number of environmental factors, situated at various levels

The first environmental influence is that of the firms involved in supplier relations: their size and mode of ownership, corporate strategy (products, technology and markets); second, supplier relations are shaped by the industry environment (degree and nature of competition, technology intensity and product cycle); a third important influence flows from the national social-institutional environment (for details, see below); last, the nature of supplier relations is shaped by the international environment (intensity of competition, degree of uncertainty and instability in international markets and the example of the economically dominant nation). Factors at each level influence those at the other levels, and their combined effect structures roles and role sets within firms and, consequently, inter-firm relations. Of these various environments, only the national institutional environment will be given systematic consideration here.

The second part of the paper will systematically show how national institutional environments constitute supplier relations and exert a strong homogenizing influence on industries and firms within national boundaries. The third part of the paper considers variation within countries, due to different responses by individual actors to factors, connected with industry and global environments. It is held that, despite growing economic globalization, the national level remains important in as far as it determines the competitive positioning of national economies within the world economic order (Porter, 1990).

Supplier relations have often been conceptualized by reference to the notion of trust (e.g. Lorenz, 1988; Sabel, 1989; Sako, 1992). Sako's influential theoretical specification of supplier relations further elaborates the notion of trust. She distinguishes between contractual, competence and goodwill trust and links these to dichotomous ideal types of supplier relations – arm's-length contractual relations (ACR) and obligational contractual relations (OCR) (ibid.: 11, Table 1.1). (Sako's definitions of trust are given in the appendix to this chapter.) Whereas the notions of competence and contractual trust are very useful for the analysis of supplier relations in Britain and Germany, the notion of goodwill trust and that of obligational contractual relations built on it appear to be culture-specific to the Japanese context. The Japanese predilection for particularist roles and diffuse relations between role holders, in which mutual obligation receives strong emphasis, finds no equivalent in Western firms. A less normatively charged notion of trust, defined simply as reliance on the predictability of mutual behaviour, will, therefore, be adopted in this paper. Sako's notions of contractual and competence trust fit well with such an expectations-based notion of trust and will be interpreted as signalling behavioural expectations in specific areas of business relations. A low-trust relation is then equated to arm's-length contracting, whereas a high-trust relation is referred to as relational contracting. Different national patterns of interfirm relations can then be situated on a continuum between these types.

Furthermore, it will be argued that it is insufficient to characterize supplier relations only by reference to the notion of trust, and that they must additionally be conceptualized as power relations. Trust and power are constantly in tension with each other and appear in complex mixes in different contractual environments. As supplier relations are frequently between large buyer firms and small and medium-sized suppliers, it is important to examine how differences in the balance of power between large firms and small and medium-sized enterprises (SMEs) will influence the degree of trust which is developed. Whereas Sako tacitly deems extreme power inequality in supplier relations compatible with the development of trust relations, this paper is sceptical on this point.

The degree of power is not simply a function of the size and market share of a firm but, in the context of supplier relations, is also related to the extent and scarcity of supplier technical expertise and/or design capacity. This, in turn, is crucially influenced by the conditions under which SMEs gain access to sources of long-term capital, skill and R. & D. knowledge. Degree and conditions of access will determine the size of the gap between large and small enterprises in terms of capital and labour productivity and R. & D. capacity (Vitols, 1994) and hence shape power relations. Lastly, the establishment of both trust and power relations is not solely a matter of managerial choice in individual firms but is profoundly affected by environmental factors, and particularly by the national institutional framework in which firms are embedded.

Following an institutionalist theoretical approach, supplier relations in Britain and Germany will be typified by elaborating how they are constituted by their national social-institutional frameworks. The systematic reciprocal influence between firms and their market organization, on the one side, and their social institutional environment, on the other, is conceptualized as industrial order.

The institutionalist analysis of such processes of interpenetration builds on the work of theorists who posit the embeddedness of organizations in their social-institutional environment (e.g. Granovetter, 1985; Hall, 1984, 1986; Thelen, 1991; Powell and DiMaggio, 1991). While the latter work theorizes the constitution and reproduction of organizations, Hall and Thelen provide insights into how organizational actors adapt structures and bring about organizational change.

Institutions are seen as patterns of action and complexes of both formally fixed rules and of informally generated cultural understandings which have acquired stability over time. These patterns assume a 'taken for granted' quality and thus provide shared cognitions to organizational actors. Their influence over industrial organizations stems from the fact that they channel and constrain the actions of members of organizations. Institutional rules define how roles are understood and whether power relations are seen as legitimate. Institutional factors thus influence what goals are adopted and the manner in which they are pursued. Role sets, in turn, shape the identity of firms and the nature of their interaction with their environment.

The 'taken-for-granted' quality of modes of thinking prevents individuals from perceiving alternatives and thus results in structures which are, to some extent, self-sustaining. Many institutionalists thus are forced into a position of structural determinism of actors and roles and become unable to explain change. But theorists who view relations within or between organizations in terms of interests and power, i.e. from a perspective of political economy, are more likely to consider actors as initiators of change, particularly if external shocks have changed the balance of power.

Institutions that are seen to be particularly influential in constituting business organizations are those which shape the conditions under which factors of production are created, deployed and coordinated, both within and between firms. In the area of supplier relations the following are deemed to exert important influences:

the state; the financial system; industry associations; the system of industrial relations and 'human resources' development and the legal system. The reciprocal relations between this complex of institutions and firms and markets is viewed in systemic terms as constituting a society's industrial order. Industrial orders assume their distinctive character during the process of industrialization and develop gradually over time in response to external stimuli and as the result of internal struggles between key actors.

The following section will examine the impact of British and German industrial orders on supplier relations. This examination will consider how far different institutional arrangements create or destroy the preconditions for the development of trust, on the one hand, and how they influence the distribution and exercise of power, on the other.

THE IMPACT OF INDUSTRIAL ORDER ON SUPPLIER RELATIONS: BRITAIN AND GERMANY COMPARED

The state

Britain

The British notion of the state is closely bound up with a long tradition of political and economic liberty (Macfarlane, 1978; Fox, 1985). This has manifested itself in pronounced individualism and a reluctance to recognize any central power which claims a transcendent reality and purpose. The emphasis on voluntarism resulting from this is maintained by state functionaries and representatives of industrial capital alike. It has resulted in an arm's-length relationship, inimical to state promotion of 'grand strategy' in the industrial field, to detailed legal regulation of industrial activity and to risk-sharing with industrial firms. The low degree of legal regulation, in turn, leaves more scope to how individual actors define their roles and thus preserves a high degree of heterogeneity between regions, industries and firms.

Traditionally, the British state has adopted only a limited role in industry, and both state institutions and personnel have adapted very late and inadequately to informed and sustained intervention. On those occasions when industrial crisis has called forth more extensive state intervention, these structural and cultural limitations have usually resulted in sub-optimal policy outcomes. The loose ties between state and industry are also expressed in the provision of a social infrastructure which is only poorly attuned to the needs of industry, particularly in the fields of financial risk-sharing, research, education and training. A last notable feature of state structure in this context is the relatively high degree of centralization of state power, impeding the decentralization of economic resources and economic policy-making to the regions and municipalities, as well as making policy implementation more problematic.

The effects of these institutional and cultural peculiarities of the British state on supplier relations have been manifold. They have dispersed individualism and aversion to dependency right through the industrial system, as well as leaving enterprises socially isolated. On the one side, it has fostered the development of entrepreneurialism where role understanding is not rigidly bound by conventions. On the other side, however, lack of state support for favourable access to capital, skill and R. & D. has left firms socially isolated and has reinforced the risk-aversion and short-termism fostered by the financial system.

This has consequences for investment and innovation behaviour and has borne down particularly heavily on small and medium-sized supplier firms (SMEs). The latter have been particularly severely affected by the lack of a socialized system to provide expertise and skill and by inadequate access to long-term finance, due to lack of government risk-sharing with banks. SMEs, furthermore, have also been adversely affected by economic centralization which, it is commonly held, makes states less well attuned to the particular needs of SMEs – the bulk of supplier firms. For these and other reasons, British SME suppliers are generally not of the 'innovative problem-solver' type which is now actively sought by larger buyer firms, and power inequality between large firms and SMEs is high in many British industries. The remoteness of the state from industry also renders it incapable of acting as an 'orchestrator of consensus' (Hirst and Thompson, 1992) and prevents it from resolving conflicts between large buyer and smaller supplier firms. Lastly, the underdeveloped regulatory activity of the British state has resulted in the absence of general, widely accepted norms of inter-firm relations, regulating competition and cooperation.

Germany

The ideological underpinnings and structure of the German state are a complex amalgam of pre- and post-war features. Structural features, such as federalism and a penchant towards industrial self-administration by the organizations of industrial capital and the banks, date from before the Second World War, as do attitudes of greater recognition and acceptance of state authority on the part of the industrial community than is the case in Britain. But, at the same time, new structures and philosophies were adopted in order to avoid the prewar pattern of dominance of the German state over the economy, without, however, enfeebling the state. The philosophy of ordo-liberalism, the foundation of the social market economy, is of particular note in this respect. On the one hand, it extols the idea of a free market but, on the other, it counsels state intervention to counteract market imperfections and to compensate the victims of this free market. The impact of market liberalism is tempered by the fact that the state is supportive of industrial self-organization. It often provides the material means to be allocated to firms through trade associations, chambers of craft and industry and banks, resulting in a climate of risk-sharing and of long-termism in investment behaviour.

The central state is also very influential in providing a strong regulatory framework and, together with local states, in providing a social infrastructure that is highly supportive towards industry. Regional and municipal governments play a much larger role in all aspects of industrial policy (*Strukturpolitik*), as well as in education, training and research, and they are much more attuned to the needs of SMEs. In some industries, this has degenerated into protectionism. Small-firm policy has long been informed by the realization that, as suppliers, they make a strong indirect contribution to the efficiency of large firms (Bannock and Albach, 1991: 14). The overall result of these various institutional and cultural influences is an ideology of limited communitarianism and a culture of networking, pervading the industrial order. This differs significantly from British individualism but is also far removed from the Japanese industrial philosophy of mutual dependence.

These institutional and cultural features of the German state have a bearing on the way in which roles are constructed and supplier relations are established and maintained. Most notable is the fact that enterprises are much more embedded in regional and national associational networks which collaborate with regional and national state agencies. Local states' support for education and training and research and the provision of long-term, fixed-rate investment capital are of particularly strong benefit to small and medium enterprises (SMEs). Hence small and medium-sized supplier firms in Germany are much more likely to have the design capacity and

278 Social groups and structuring

technological know-how which make them valuable partners in the new subcontracting relationship, and which lessens power distance between them.

The financial system

Britain

The British financial system is market-based, and, although bank lending to industry has assumed growing importance, the stock-market is still the centre of the system (Prowse, 1994: 31). Relations of firms with both banks and shareholders are of an arm's-length nature, and sharing of risks is not on the agenda. The constraints for short-term high returns on share capital, exerted by the discipline of the stock-market, are said to have fostered management attitudes of short-termism and risk-averseness in investment activity. A powerful constraint towards short-termism flows from the fact of the much greater danger of takeover in the British as compared with the German financial system, and the ensuing lack of stability for managerial career planning within a given firm. According to Franks and Mayer (1990), the danger of takeovers discourages managers and other employees from making long-term firm-specific investments, as changes in ownership may deprive them of returns on such investment.

Another effect, connected with the greater ease of takeover and the inadequate provision by banks of growth financing for smaller firms, is that small promising firms have a much smaller chance of growing into medium-sized firms – a claim borne out by the much smaller proportion of medium-sized manufacturing firms in Britain than in Germany (Hughes, 1990).

Access to finance is particularly problematic for SMEs. The high degree of concentration in the British banking system and the lack of access by banks to long-term, fixed rate (LTFR) capital constrains them to give mainly short-term loans with variable interest rates which are well above those of capital available on the money market for large corporations, and significantly higher than those paid by German SMEs (Vitols, 1994: 5).

These structural constraints have important implications for the nature of supplier relations. First, constraints on long-term investment in people and technology incline firms to adopt a market strategy which emphasizes low price, rather than technologically complex, high-value products and customer service. This applies to large firms and even more to smaller firms, albeit for different reasons. Such firms are less inclined to establish relational contracting. Furthermore, these same financial constraints constitute an impediment to the development of supplier firms of the 'innovative problem-solver' type – valuable in the new partnership relations, and takeover of successful smaller firms works in the same direction. Large firms are also less concerned to establish partnership relations with smaller innovative firms, if they can acquire their know-how through takeover (Saxenian, 1989; Walsh, 1991).

Second, pressures towards short-time horizons from managers' own employment durations within a given firm are inimical to the establishment of the new longer-term supplier relations; the disruption of established supplier relations following a merger are also well documented (Hughes, 1992: 27). Risk aversion, born of short-termism and social isolation, militates against relational contracting and perhaps even single-sourcing. SME supplier firms, in their turn, are also loath to give up their independence and tie their fortunes to only one or two firms. Other inter-firm financial ties, such as cross-shareholding, which incline firms towards relational contracting, are rare in the British financial system. Last, the exceptionally high degree of industrial concentration in British industry, and the under-capitalization and lack of development funds for smaller firms, fostered by the financial system, serve to create very unequal power relations between large and giant firms with strong market control, and predominantly small, under-capitalized and technologically weak firms with relatively few foreign customers.

In sum, the financial system has a profound impact on managerial role understandings and hence also on inter-firm relations. Short-term financial preoccupations and orientations towards the external labour market for career advancement structure managerial identities and pose obstacles to the establishment of relational contracting.

Germany

The German financial system is bank-centred and credit-based and has a weakly developed stock-market. Long-established close ties between the large, joint-stock banks and large firms in many sectors are based on a plurality of factors: cross-holdings of shares; inter-locking directorships; proxy voting rights of banks on behalf of small shareholders; and the provision of long-term credit, backed up by consultancy services. Banks are not only involved in individual firms but may intervene to restructure whole sectors. In addition to cross-holdings of shares between banks and industrial firms, there is also extensive cross-shareholdings between industrial firms.

In addition to the Big Three, there exist two other more decentralized banking sectors which are oriented specifically to the lending to SMEs. The large number of publicly owned savings banks and of cooperative banks have a legally defined and institutionally secured obligation to their local communities' economic welfare and SMEs – both local politicians and businessmen sit on their boards. The links of these community-embedded banks to their own higher-tier banks and to publicly owned credit institutes[1] enable them to both provide LTFR credit on comparatively favourable terms, and a number of valuable services (Skidelsky, 1993; Vitols, 1994). Thus, 60 per cent of German FTR loans are made for a period of longer than a year (mostly for four years), and the rates are only 1–2 per cent above those for long-term corporate bonds for large companies (Vitols, 1994: 6). The existence of these banking sectors does much to compensate SMEs for the diseconomies of small scale. Finally, due to high ownership concentration, the underdevelopment of the stock-market and legal protection, hostile takeovers are extremely rare in the German system (Prowse, 1994).

This easier access to long-term finance and the greater stability in large and smaller firms alike finds one expression in a large proportion of technologically advanced firms, trading on quality and service, and another in relatively long managerial service and internal promotion, further reinforcing stability. A third important consequence is the much smaller capital constraint gap than in Britain between large and smaller firms and hence in investment behaviour and also in export orientation (Vitols, 1994). This translates itself into a much-reduced dependence by SMEs and a lesser power differential. A last significant consequence of the financial system's greater support for small firm growth and the absence of hostile takeover is the higher proportion of medium-sized firms in the German economy – another factor to reduce power distance.

All these factors have shaped managerial identities and structured interaction between firms in definite ways. They have encouraged managers to adopt longer investment horizons, concerning both people and technology, as well as being open to technological updating and process innovation. This has made a market strategy, stressing quality and innovation – conducive to the development of relational contracting – very prevalent among German firms. It has also led to a more balanced composition of firms in terms of size and provides large buyer firms with a wealth of indigenous supplier firms, suited to the new partnership relation. Although SMEs are by no means equals in terms of market power possessed, most have at least sufficient power to deter excessive large firm opportunism. Multiple support for long-termism and for technological updating provides further favourable preconditions for allowing managers to create long-term, stable and close relations with supplier firms which provide fertile soil for the mutual adaptation of expectations and hence the development of trust. Lastly, cross-holdings of shares between customer and supplier firms, as well as interlocking directorships, create broader and deeper inter-firm relations than in Britain, where the commercial tie is frequently the only one.

Industry associations and chambers

Britain

Trade associations have a long history and have developed in a voluntarist manner without state regulation. As a consequence there are often several associations within an industry, competing for membership and income. The services they offer to their members are mostly concerned with providing individual rather than collective goods, and they also represent the interests of their members *vis-à-vis* the government. Due to their fragmented character, their only moderately high membership and material and organizational resources, and to their voluntarist ethos, they tend to find it hard to command their members' loyalty and to influence their membership collectively.

Chambers of commerce have a more local focus and act on behalf of businesses across sectoral boundaries. They, too, lack statutory rights, obligations and powers, and depend on voluntary membership and hence relatively low incomes from fees. Like trade associations, they provide mainly individual goods. Membership ties are of an instrumental kind, and chambers lack the support and influence to mobilize their diverse membership around collective interests.

How do these associations impact on supplier relations? Due to their deeply ingrained voluntarism and weak influence over their membership, neither type of association can provide the regulatory or organizing capacity to set and enforce standards for inter-firm relations which contain harmful competition and foster cooperation. Individual member firms will not forfeit short-term gains for the longer-term collective good, and associations, in this value context, cannot become the arbitrators of reputation. Nor have they been able to give the necessary support to SMEs which would enable them to fulfil the growing quality, design and prompt delivery demands of large buyer firms. Trade associations thus enhance the role understandings of managers as relatively autonomous actors, or, in difficult times, as being isolated and unsupported.

Germany

German trade associations are fully inclusive organizations within an industry and region and thus are able to exert strong influence both over their members and over the government. They are quasi-political organs of self-administration within their industry and exercise an important role in setting and monitoring standards for inter-firm relations, as well as providing many collective goods.

Chambers of commerce and industry and of craft (*Handwerk*) are statutory bodies with compulsory membership for firms within their spheres of influence. They have quasi-political functions, such as monitoring standards in vocational training, issuing licences and settling disputes, as well as providing collective support for smaller firms, such as organizing trade fairs in foreign countries or providing further training (Streeck, 1992). They frequently organize working groups of industrialists, conducive to the dissemination of information and the building up of contacts and relationships (interview notes, 1993).

The combined effect of German associational ties on trading relations is that both large firms and SMEs can rely on support networks, are used to organize collectively and to moderate competition in some areas with collaboration in others. Inter-firm relations are not simply the concern of the two firms involved but are in the semi-public domain. Being part of this associational network reduces uncertainty and risk and encourages conformity to collective norms. The more public nature of norms and reputations, together with the role of associations as brokers, serves to build relationships and to reduce opportunism among powerful firms. This expectation of reduced opportunism, in turn, provides a fertile soil for developing trust, particularly competence trust and contractual trust, but also more person-based trust. Managers see themselves as tied into resultant networks and more bound by collective norms and standards. While this is viewed as generally supportive of relational contracting it is, at the same time, a restraint on more individualistic managerial role understanding and behaviour, conducive to innovation.

System of industrial relations and employment relations

Britain and Germany

The systems of industrial relations and of vocational education and training (VET) are of slightly less relevance than the other institutional complexes reviewed, and Britain and Germany will be discussed together. The first influence is that the larger incidence of industrial action in Britain than in Germany, due to structural features of the system (Lane, 1989: chap. 8), renders a switch to single-sourcing in supplier relations a more risky business in Britain. However, even in the less conflictual German system the technique of pinpoint striking, which seeks to cause the maximum degree of disruption to production networks, could make German managers wary of entering into single-sourcing arrangements. In this respect, both British and German managements face greater risks than their Japanese counterparts.

A second feature associated with the system of industrial relations, but also with the system of VET, is the degree of employment security possessed by employees. Whereas in Germany the existence of co-determination at board level in companies with more than 500 employees has served to create relatively strong employment rights, in Britain there exist no such institutional safeguards and only weak legal protection. Unions have traditionally had only marginal influence over hiring and firing practices, and employment security is lower than in Germany. This applies both to employees in general (Lane, 1989: 286) and to managerial employees in particular (Franks and Mayer, 1990). Greater German employment security is also connected with the higher investment in skill development by German firms and the necessity to profit from it in the longer term. The consequences in terms of stability of staff engaged in maintaining inter-firm relations must be an important ingredient in maintaining long-term supplier relations in Germany and constitutes a difficulty in this respect in Britain (Sako, 1992: 204). The impact on employee loyalty to the firm and the degree of involvement generated by it should also be considered important for overall market strategy.

Last, the differences in training practices between the two countries have multiple effects on supplier relations. The British deficiencies in the area of skill training and the ensuing widespread practice of poaching skilled staff fosters suspicion and fear by smaller supplier companies that customer companies may poach their skilled technical staff. The negative implications for technical cooperation and trust are obvious. In Germany, where all firms engage in extensive skill training at all levels, such mistrust of poachers finds less fertile soil.

Differences in human resources development exist also at the managerial level, counterposing British generalists – often with a relatively low level of formal education – to German functional specialists (Lane, 1989; Stewart *et al.*, 1994). This has a bearing on career paths. British managers move much more frequently for promotion between firms, as well as changing far more between functional specialisms within firms than German managers (ibid.). Consequently, continuity of tenure in purchasing and sales functions – one acknowledged precondition for the development of trust relations – is much less likely to be found in the British than in the German context. Highly developed functional specialization among German managers particularly aids the development of competence trust. Thus, to conclude this section, the systems of industrial relations, employment and promotion practices and managerial education impact very differently on role definitions of managers and hence on inter-firm relations. Whereas in Britain interaction is channelled in the direction of shorter-term, commercially oriented supplier relations, in Germany longer-term technology-focused relations are more likely to evolve.

The legal system

Hofstede's (1980) study of national organizational cultures posits uncertainty avoidance, i.e. 'the extent to which people ... become nervous in unstructured, ambiguous situations and try to avoid such situations by strict rules of behaviour' (Hofstede, 1993: 3) as one of four basic value constellations. The much higher tolerance of uncertainty in Britain than Germany found by Hofstede (1980) is also confirmed by Stewart *et al.* (1994). Hofstede (1993: 5), following a long sociological tradition of linking legal rules with social facts, plausibly traces back different national patterns in this respect to countries' legal systems. Whereas Germany's system of civil law, heavily influenced by Roman law, is distinguished by abstract, systematic and detailed codification, British common law is based on legal precedent and avoids such systematizing (Zweigert and Koetz, 1987) although differences are less pronounced in commercial law. The German system is also more professionalized, employing a much higher number of professional lawyers and judges (ibid.; Markesinis, 1990), and engaging in litigation is considerably cheaper in

Germany than Britain, providing greater equality of access to the courts (ibid.: 253). Recourse to litigation by buyer or supplier companies is, however, very rare in Germany (interview notes, 1993).

This German propensity for formal and detailed codification, and the British more empirical approach and tolerance for a higher degree of uncertainty, are well reflected in national patterns of industrial organization. The best documented and most discussed manifestation of this German–British contrast is the system of industrial relations, where a highly juridified German system is contrasted with a British system in which a pronounced voluntarism and a disdain for legal regulation has been partially changed only through recent legislation under Conservative governments of the 1980s and 1990s. There is evidence that a similar contrast applies to the way in which supplier relations are regulated. Thus German fieldwork has established that firms nearly always have a written contract – usually only the standard general business conditions issued by the trade associations – whereas contractual regulation in Britain, according to Sako (1992), is more haphazard. This raises the interesting empirical problem of how the more-pronounced German resort to a formal legal regulation of supplier relations relates to the hypothesized greater importance of trust in the German context. Whereas Sako's typology implies that contractualism and trust are mutually exclusive, other commentators see contracts as generating a climate of goodwill in which trust may grow (Gambetta, 1988; Deakin *et al.*, 1993). This latter view will be adopted in this paper, and the notion of contractual trust is regarded as an important component of trust in more general terms.

Clues on how a more or less juridified supplier relation might work for or against the cultivation of trust are given by the legal regulation of payment periods for supplied goods. In Britain, delayed payment by large firms has always been problematic and has become a major problem for smaller firms in the recession of the 1990s (CBI, 1991). The National Federation of the Self-Employed and Small Businesses has campaigned for a tightening up of legal procedures to enforce prompt payment, but the government insists on voluntarism (Sako, 1992: 174). 'In Britain, the legal framework is abstentionist. It therefore gives more scope for the powerful party to a relationship to go unchecked if it intends to delay payment' (ibid.: 175). Reputation damage does not arise if a large number of firms engage in this practice (ibid.: 176). In Germany, in contrast, the general business conditions stipulate a thirty-day payment period, and a discount for prompt payment, so that non-payment is very rarely an issue in German supplier relations (interview notes, 1993).

Both adversarialism and short-termism are said to be enshrined in English commercial contract law itself. The latter lacks a notion of good faith (Brownsword, 1994). Short-termism is indicated by the fact that, in the case of unforeseen difficulties in a longer-term contractual relation, English law envisages termination of contract, whereas continental law is more likely to opt for renegotiation (McKendrick, 1994: 12–13).

Another important sociological aspect of comparative commercial law emerges from an exploration of property law. In Britain there is prime emphasis on shareholder rights, whereas in Germany employees are also considered important stakeholders and have many legally defined rights (Franks and Mayer, 1990; Charkham, 1994). This different interpretation of the rights of various stakeholders will influence the degree of employee loyalty to the firm and the viability of the notion of a works community; both will, in turn, either favour or impede the cultivation of long-term supplier relations.

To conclude this section, polar opposites in British and German institutional environments affect role conceptions within firms and the nature of interaction between firms in highly divergent ways. British managers see themselves as both less constrained and less supported by institutional rules. While managers in large firms would be more apt to stress the low degree of constraint, those in SMEs are more likely to focus on the weak institutional support. This two-edged influence of institutions leads one to expect more heterogeneity in both types of firms, and in inter-firm relations. In Germany, in contrast, where firms are more deeply embedded and power differentials between them less pronounced, managers may also experience less scope for individualistic and innovative role definitions and, consequently, inter-firm relations are likely to show greater conformity to a given type, as well as being less responsive to organizational learning from industrially hegemonic countries. In both countries, however, supplier firms are apt to avoid dependence on powerful buyer firms, albeit for different reasons and with different degrees of success. The typification of British and German supplier relations emerging from this institutionalist analysis is summarized in Table 11.1.

The above analysis shows that the British pattern of supplier relations is likely to be situated at the pole of the continuum characterized as adversarial contracting, while the German pattern tends

Table 11.1 Salient features of British and German supplier relations

Britain	Germany
Short-termism	Long-termism
Risk-averseness	Risk-sharing
Informal	Formal
Low level of information diffusion	High level of information diffusion
Low degree of predictability	High degree of predictability
High-power asymmetry	Low-power asymmetry
High degree of dependence avoidance	

towards the type of relational contracting. Although most features can be specified in dichotomous terms, the last feature – dependence avoidance – is shared by both sets of firms. The analysis also indicates that greater power inequality in the British context serves to reinforce the ACR pattern, whereas in Germany reduced power incquality inclines towards relational contracting. Differences between British and German firms in terms of power resources are depicted in diagrammatic form in Figure 11.1.

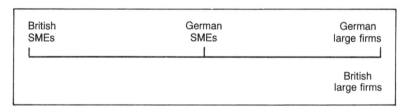

Figure 11.1 British and German firms: power inequalities compared

THE CHANGING NATURE OF SUPPLIER RELATIONS: THE EMPIRICAL EVIDENCE

Having established the predisposition of British and German firms towards different types of supplier relations in theoretical terms, it is now in order to survey the available empirical evidence on what actual patterns exist. This investigation will establish how both global and industry environments intervene and refract the homogenizing influence of national institutions. Here it is particularly interesting to explore whether institutional constraints severely restrict managerial choice in the face of new challenges posed by international competition, or whether one can detect transformations in supplier relations which go against the institutional logic of the industrial order.

The empirical evidence considered for this purpose comes mainly from secondary data, but will be supplemented by first results from the author's fieldwork. The latter was conducted in 1993 and consisted of two-hour interviews with either top managers (in smaller firms) or purchasing and sales managers (in larger firms). The six buyer and sixteen supplier firms were evenly divided between the industries of mining machinery and kitchen furniture.[2]

The empirical evidence does indeed show that relational contracting is more typical in Germany, whereas adversarial contracting is more likely to characterize British supplier relations. It is also notable, however, that patterns in both countries are variable between industries and, to a lesser degree, between firms within industries, and that uniformity between industries and firms is more pronounced in Germany than in Britain. It is also evident that, due to influences flowing from the international environment, patterns of supplier relations in both countries have been undergoing change in recent years. Let us first review the evidence which gives support to the conclusion reached earlier that supplier relations in Britain and Germany are polar opposites in most respects.

Many small-scale investigations of subcontracting in Britain have asserted that the ACR pattern is the norm and that it is difficult in the British institutional environment to establish relational contracting (Hirst and Zeitlin, 1989; Dellbridge *et al.*, 1992; Turnbull, 1989; Penn, 1992; Rainnie, 1993). Sako (1992) draws a more differentiated and changing picture, but still places strong emphasis on the ACR type. Features militating against the widespread and thoroughgoing introduction of relational contracting are many: first, there are still too few large British firms with a market strategy which consistently puts high quality and technological innovation above considerations of price (Porter, 1990: 499) and which possess matching investment patterns (O'Mahoney and Wagner, 1994) and production performance (New and Myers, 1986). Even where commitment to quality is now stronger, institutional constraints still impede consistent implementation of this commitment. Thus, for example, purchasing personnel in electronics firms identify more with the financial than with the engineering concerns of the firm (Sako, 1992: 89) and thus remain beholden to the old notion of price-cutting. Thus widely proclaimed shifts in managerial strategy often conflict with persistent managerial role understandings and identities.

Second, there is a great shortage of SMEs of the 'innovative problem-solver' type (Doran, 1984; Hirst and Zeitlin, 1989; Penn, 1992), due to the institutional constraints outlined earlier. Many

British supplier firms have been unable to comply with the much-increased demands by customer firms in terms of quality, design, prompt delivery, etc. They have simply gone out of business, leaving the market to their more-skilled European or Japanese competitors. This has been the case in a range of modern and traditional industries: in the car industry, where some sophisticated parts are no longer obtainable from indigenous suppliers (Carr, 1990); for machine tools (Penn, 1992); furniture and clothing (Best, 1989; Zeitlin and Totterdill, 1989); and for the electronics industry, where only low-tech, heavy and bulky items are sourced in the UK (Sako, 1992: 95).

Where small firms are widely acknowledged to be innovative, such as in computer software or biotechnology, they are frequently taken over by larger firms (Saxenian, 1989; Walsh, 1991), or maintain more extensive relations with large foreign than British firms (Garnsey, 1993). To sum up this section, the industrial fabric needed to establish relational contracting simply no longer exist, in a number of British industries.

Even where British supplier relations are now closer and longer-term, there still exist many barriers to the establishment of relational contracting. Despite severe business problems, supplier firms are loath to accept those Japanese practices which would undermine their autonomy. Thus British suppliers in some industries actively resist the passing on to them of costs (Thoburn and Takashima, 1992: 71), as well as being not very amenable to the Japanese practice of constant cost reduction through efficiency improvement (Sako, 1992). Although single- or dual-sourcing is becoming more common for buyer firms, British suppliers, unlike their Japanese counterparts, are reluctant to become dependent on only one or two customers (Sako, 1992: 124; Thoburn and Takashima, 1992: 64). Conversely, a study of hi-tech firms in the Cambridge area (Alford and Garnsey, 1994) found that large buyer firms are often wary of single-sourcing because of the high rate of instability among new firms. Due to the low capitalization of many supplier firms, they enjoyed only low certainty that trading partners would be available for longer-term relationships (ibid.).

Stability and predictability are also hampered by other structural arrangements. The frequent reorganization of firms, due to acquisition and takeover, and the relatively high turnover of key managerial staff due to career and job mobility, form a strong impediment to stable, long-term relations (Franks and Mayer, 1990; Sako, 1992; Stewart *et al.*, 1994). Adverse consequences of instability for the development of trust can sometimes be overcome if there exist institutionalized means to signal competence as a trading partner. In this respect, the burgeoning system of general certifiable quality standards – BS5750 and ISO 9000 – has created better preconditions for the development of competence trust. But due to the remaining patchy development of the skill base of employees at all levels, lack of competence trust remains a serious problem. This is well illustrated by Sako's analysis of Japanese supplier networks in the electronics industry (1992: 90). Due to low confidence in the design capacity of British suppliers, Japanese buyer firms rarely involved them in the design process. An important precondition for mutual dependence is thus ruled out.

Despite widespread espousal of human resources management in order to improve employee relations and increase commitment, results are still seen to be patchy, particularly as far as *active* involvement is concerned (Storey and Sisson, 1990). There has been no acceptance of the notion of a 'works community' as in Germany, let alone of a 'community of fate' of the Japanese type. Lack of a cooperative ethos within firms finds a parallel in inter-firm relations. Cooperative supplier relations do not receive effective normative support from the wider institutional framework, such as from industry associations (Whitston, 1989; Penn, 1992). But some change in this respect is evident in the campaigning for partnership relations by the CBI, the DTI and the NEDC in the 1990s, although it is not clear how far such persuasion is backed up by actual support to smaller supplier firms.

There appears to be no uniform pattern on the use of written contracts or on whether or not they contribute to the building of trust. There is some evidence that informal agreements outweigh formal ones, and the latter largely cover short time-spans (Thoburn and Takashima, 1992: 68; Sako, 1992). Moreover, buyers and suppliers tend to each have their own terms and conditions, which sometimes creates 'a battle of forms' (Sako, 1992: 158). Given the lack of uniformity in the use of contracts, contractual trust is unlikely to flourish in Britain. The widespread flouting by buyer firms of payment rules and the refusal by the state to provide smaller firms with the necessary legal back-up to enforce payment is another instance of disdain for binding agreements.

In Germany, in contrast, the institutional environment generally provides much greater support for the development of trust and for relational contracting. Large-firm market strategy in most sectors is one of diversified quality production, backed up by commensurate investment behaviour, human resources strategies and production organization. Moreover, the long history in many industries of trading on technological sophistication and customer service has created an established tradition of extensive and close supplier relations (Porter, 1990: 374; Bannock and Albach, 1991: 19). This tradition has ensured the preservation of SMEs, well attuned to high demands from buyer firms (Doran, 1984; Hildebrandt and Seltz, 1989; Kotthoff and Reindl, 1990; Stoffaes, 1989; Vitols, 1994). Thus, just as in Japan, extensive use of suppliers in many industries and close relations with them is not a new feature in the German economic and social-institutional context, and contractual trust and competence trust have always existed in large measures.

Research in the industries of mining machinery and kitchen furniture in 1993 confirmed the virtual ubiquity of long-established and stable inter-firm relations (interview notes, 1993). The largely localized nature of outsourcing and the regional agglomeration of specialized supplier firms in both industries suggest the existence of specific industrial districts.[3] But, as pointed out by Grabher (1993), in the Ruhr mining machinery industry, close ties have led to functional and cognitive lock-in of supplier firms and have impeded innovative product diversification which would have permitted escape from a dying industry. To understand this phenomenon one needs to grasp the peculiar mix of trust and power relations in this industry. The presence of one quasi-monopoly buyer – Ruhrkohle, the German coal board – has engendered a paralysing dependence on the part of equipment manufacturers which has received further reinforcement from the state subsidy policy for coal. Dependence is, however, not a significant feature in relations of machinery producers with their own suppliers. Both sides have strenuously avoided dependence.

Empirical work on German supplier relations shows that relational contracting is not identical to Sako's Japanese-inspired obligational contracting and that trust can be built in a variety of ways. Different role understandings within Japanese and German firms have favoured the development of different forms of interaction between firms. The notions of dependency, particularism and lack of formality, which are part of Sako's OCR type, do not fit the German business context. Also diffuse relations, in which business and more informal social ties merge, are uncommon in German firms (interview notes, 1993). In addition, power relations need to be considered alongside trust relations. The German pattern of supplier relations shows substantial overlap with the Japanese in terms of support for stable and long-term relations and in providing fertile soil for the development of collectivity-oriented attitudes, conducive to cooperation and the development of trust. As in Japan, there is extensive technical cooperation between firms (Pohlmann *et al.*, 1992; field notes, 1993), and supplier relations between larger firms are often supplemented by other business ties, such as cross-shareholding and interlocking directorships. Trade associations and chambers of commerce encourage a rich flow of information and provide informal links between suppliers (*Beschaffung Aktuell*, various issues; interview notes, 1993).

But there are also important differences between German and Japanese supplier relations which bear particularly on the relation between market power and supplier autonomy and on the nature and extent of trust. Collectivism in Germany is of a more limited nature than in Japan, and social relations are less particularistic (Hampden-Turner and Trompenaars, 1994). A limited German communitarianism relies on formal, association-based regulation and on written contracts (Semlinger, 1989: 105; field notes, 1993) – a feature deemed incompatible with 'goodwill' trust by Sako (1992: 40). Personal ties between individual managers are also accorded great importance in Germany, but these tend to be mainly functionally oriented and supplement the more formal relations (field notes, 1993). The Japanese system, in contrast, is premised strongly on open-ended contracts and informal agreements, as well as on inter-firm dependence and obligation. In Germany, dependence is strongly frowned upon by both sides (Semlinger, 1991; field notes, 1993), and the Japanese value of permanent indebtedness is as alien to German as it is to British culture. The fundamentally different character of German SMEs and their stronger position relative to their larger buyer firms rules out such dependence and makes German SMEs more concerned with, and more able to attain, a degree of autonomy (Sengenberger and Loveman, 1988; Herrigel, 1989).

In the German context, power inequality is much less extreme and 'voluntary' interdependence is possible, whereas the Japanese pattern of obligational subcontracting frequently depends on pronounced power inequality and the customer's ability to dictate his definition of fairness. Despite Sako's protestations to the contrary, this power inequality leads to partial opportunism by large buyer firms, for example in the area of unilateral price determination or the injunction not to sell to other customers. Japanese SMEs cannot but tolerate this domination quietly, as they are too weak to change it. Trust, in this context, is of the paternalist sort, whereas in Germany it tends to be based on a more symmetrical, though by no means equal, relationship. But, as the example of the German mining machinery industry shows, extreme dependence cannot be ruled out even in the German industrial structure.

Supplier relations in both Britain and Germany do not uniformly correspond to the two polar types of contractual relations, and we need to consider variation within countries, as well as emergent trends and recent changes which have the potential to undermine important features of both types. The building of long-term trust relations, in both countries, is more compelling in industries of high technological complexity, whereas variation within industries depends on the degree of customization of outsourced parts or components. Change has been incited by factors in the global environment: the intensity of global competition and the adjustments in market strategy and production organization it demands; the emergence of Japan as the new economic hegemonic power; and the marketization of Eastern European countries. Industry and global influences are to some extent related, in that changes are most pronounced in industries affected by intense global competition – automobiles and electronics. These developments have acted as facilitators or stimulants of change, posing new challenges but also causing conflicts between established managerial roles and identities and new demands. They have caused shifts in power relations both within firms and between buyer and supplier firms, leading to new opportunities for, and constraints on, managerial choice.

In Britain, the car industry is now dominated by foreign multinationals, with the Japanese taking a dominant role in influencing managerial practice. The Japanese have a similarly dominant position in the electronics industry. Foreign penetration of both industries and the new hegemony of Japanese manufacturing policy have had a significant influence on supplier firms. The greatly increased demands in terms of price, quality, reliability and technical capability, requiring also much greater capital resources, together with the drastic reduction required in the number of suppliers, have eliminated large numbers of British suppliers in both industries and have led to the destruction of entire fields of specialization, particularly of the high value-added kind, among British-owned firms (Lane, 1992; Sako, 1992). But those supplier firms which remain, after a painful adjustment process, have moved away from many aspects of the ACR type. Supplier relations are no longer uniformly short-term, narrow, distant and adversarial, as some analysts proclaim. The number of suppliers invited to tender has been much reduced, price is no longer the only consideration, and quality standards have risen significantly. Frequent visiting of customers in the electronics industry also suggests a partial overcoming of the 'arm's-length' approach (Sako, 1992: 130), and British buyer companies (in engineering) were found willing to transfer technology and give other practical help although hardly any had a systematic policy of supplier development (Thoburn and Takashima, 1992: 62). In the more traditional industry of mining machinery, British managers were very much aware of the ideology of partnership, although the implementation of practices was still patchy (interview notes, 1994). But despite this picture of emergent change, most studies still show that managers have found it impossible to circumvent some of the cultural and structural constraints outlined above.

In Germany, neither the car industry nor the electronics industry are as heavily dominated by foreign multinationals, but the often indirect influence of the Japanese on supplier relations has nevertheless been strong. In the car industry, the intensity of global competition, together with a marked concentration process, have significantly changed the balance of power between buyer and supplier firms and facilitated a partial move away from relational contracting (Mendius and Wendeling-Schroeder, 1991; Deiss and Doehl, 1992). The introduction of Japanese-inspired techniques, such as JIT, has led to a much greater synchronization of production processes and methods between trading firms. It has introduced new dependencies and points of friction, and old-established trust relations have become severely strained (ibid.). There is concern among German analysts of subcontracting relations that the very autonomy and flexibility of SMEs, which has made them such desirable partner firms, may be destroyed by their increasing synchronization with large buyer firms and the more comprehensive control of all aspects of their business (Altmann and Sauer, 1989). But most of the above studies have been too wedded to theoretical interpretations, allowing only a 'zero-sum' approach to questions of power and autonomy. New approaches and further evidence will be needed to get a more balanced picture of supplier relations in the German car industry.

A comparative approach underlines the fact that, due to the stronger economic position and technological expertise of German supplier firms, and their continued ability to trade with indigenous final assemblers, change has been less drastic than in Britain. Although individual suppliers have been squeezed out in areas of lower value-added part production, more advanced specialisms have been retained, and the greater move to system production has brought closer technical cooperation (Deiss and Doehl, 1992). It is more accurate to speak of a complex mixture of domination and autonomy, of opportunism in certain circumstances and relations of trust in others (Pohlmann *et al.*, 1992; Semlinger, 1994).

It must be borne in mind that the car industry is still very exceptional and that it would be inappropriate to generalize from this industry to supplier relations elsewhere, as is often done in the literature on subcontracting. In other industries, relations have remained more cooperative (Pohlmann *et al.*, 1992; interview notes, 1993), and in traditional industries, such as engineering and kitchen furniture, Japanization, in the sense of close synchronization between processes in both firms, has so far had a negligible impact (ibid.). There were few differences between industries and firms in this respect, and managers showed little familiarity with the ideological notion of partnership along Japanese lines. But even in the more traditional industries there are emergent trends which, should they become more fully developed, would seriously undermine trust relations. The first trend is a general feeling that the high price of German products impairs competitiveness,[4] and that managerial preoccupation with quality, reliability and service now needs to be supplemented by a greater concern with price. In some cases, this has led to a reconsideration of the hitherto deeply entrenched practice in most industries to source in Germany alone, and frequently in the same region. In industries with a high division of labour and large-scale outsourcing of unskilled and standardized operations, as in the clothing industry, such outsourcing to lower-wage countries in Eastern Europe is now quite advanced (*Frankfurter Rundschau*, 2 May 1994). In other industries, such as mining machinery and kitchen furniture, firms are just beginning to source or invest in low-wage countries. This inclination has partly been stimulated by marketization in Eastern Europe, where there is reasonable geographical proximity (interview notes, 1993). Such a move would free managements not only from price constraints but also from other influences of the German industrial order which now push firms towards relational contracting. It would require change in managers' role identity, and there is some evidence that such change is already under way.

So far, SME supplier firms have been predominantly under family management, connected with a distinct entrepreneurial and familial management style. However, there is now talk of 'succession crisis' (Plasonig, 1994) brought about because more highly educated offspring either disdain succession or are more akin to professional managers, less beholden to traditional values and established German features of subcontracting.

Interviews in the mining machinery industry established that, because of business deterioration and the crisis in the industry, long-established adherence to family management is now being jettisoned in favour of professional management (field notes, 1993). However, the limited scale of existing evidence makes it is impossible to say whether, given the German emphasis on diversified quality production, such changes will become sufficiently prevalent to undermine crucial aspects of German industrial order.

CONCLUSIONS

The theoretical analysis of institutional determinants of the quality of supplier relations, supplemented by a review of empirical findings in the two countries, has established that national specificity of firms and inter-firm relations has remained far more striking than any convergence towards a universal pattern of supplier relations, as implied by the notion of Japanization. Institutional inertia has often undermined individual actors' efforts towards change, even when widespread attitudinal change and greater awareness of competitive weaknesses among managers and policy-makers is evident.

The reason for enduring national distinctiveness in patterns of supplier relations has been located in their embeddedness in social-institutional environments which influence managerial roles, goals, expectations and behaviour and, hence, also interaction between firms. These institutions have changed only very partially in recent decades: relevant features of state and financial systems, as well as of related associational and legal structures, have shown great stability in both countries, though more so in Germany than in Britain.

The different location of German and British patterns of supplier relations on the continuum between arms' length and relational contracting has, in turn, been connected with relations of power and trust, differentially shaped by institutional environments. This paper has sketched out a German pattern where power inequality between buyer and supplier firms is attenuated to a considerable extent and where various institutional mechanisms create stability and predictability, restrain opportunism and thus create a basis for the development of trust relations. It has counterposed a British pattern of greater polarization between large firms and SMEs, which amplifies power inequality, and a weakness of collective ties and binding regulatory norms which make opportunism tempting. This constellation of features is likely to impede the development of inter-firm trust relations. It has been shown that both trust and power relations are shaped by the very fabric of industrial structure – by the composition of firms in terms of size, factor endowment and technological expertise, and these factors are not very amenable to change by individual managerial actors. It has also been emphasized, however, that, in both countries, there is a constant tension between 'large firm' market power and a cooperative relation based on trust but that, in Germany, the tension is considerably less pronounced.

But this plea for continuing national divergence in vital aspects of supplier relations does not imply that industrial order is seen as an iron cage, making for complete uniformity within countries and blocking any kind of change. In both countries, there is some diversity in the nature of supplier relations, both between industries and between firms with different production paradigms, but the diversity is much less pronounced in Germany, due to the deeper embeddedness of German firms and markets. In both countries relational contracting is more prevalent in industries and firms that are committed to customization or a diversified quality production paradigm, particularly of technologically complex goods. Thus, in both countries, relational contracting has been found to be more common in the mining machinery industry than in the kitchen furniture industry. The difference is, however, much less pronounced in Germany than in Britain, due to the much wider adoption of diversified quality production in Germany. The lesser degree of embeddedness of British firms has allowed managers greater leeway in defining roles and role relationships. Whereas in large multinational corporations this may afford firms considerable autonomy in the way they conduct supplier relations in a large proportion of SME supplier firms, this autonomy is spurious. Lack of constraint equals lack of support from societal institutions and may lead to either strong dependency on large buyer firms or to bankruptcy. This is well illustrated by developments among British supplier firms in the car industry (Lane, 1992).

In both countries, the 1980s and 1990s have brought some changes in the organization of supplier relations, due to influences from the global environment, coupled to some transformations of national institutions. Greater instability and much intensified competition in many markets have affected British and German firms alike, the impact being particularly notable in highly internationalized industries such as the car and the electronics industries. But in Britain, exposure to global influences has been both more acute and more

direct. This has been due to greater decline of the indigenous manufacturing capacity, together with political changes which have 'freed'
firms and markets from regulation in a host of different respects
and have thus accelerated disembedding. The greater presence of
multinationals in general, and of Japanese firms in particular,
together with the almost complete loss of domestic capacity in some
industries, has also had a more marked impact on supplier relations.
Thus, a degree of Japanization has occurred in highly internationalized industries in both countries, but it seems to have gone further in
Britain. Although the differences between Japanese and traditional
British patterns of supplier relations are much greater than those
with German patterns, British firms have been more concerned, and
perhaps more obliged, to undergo Japanization than their German
counterparts. But, in addition to the stronger direct impact of
Japanese management practices, the lower degree of embeddedness
of firms leaves more leeway for organizational learning and the
redefinition of roles and behaviour. Thus, in these industries there
has emerged a new hybrid type of supplier relation which has moved
away from adversarial contracting without fully embracing obligational contracting.

Equivalent German industries have not been left untouched by
Japanese influence, but German industrial order has refracted and
modified this influence to a much higher degree. Also German
managers have remained more wedded to traditional German ways
of managing, displaying much less willingness to learn from foreign
examples than their British counterparts (Stewart *et al.*, 1994).
Although both German and Japanese firms tend to maintain close
and long-term relations with their suppliers, the mechanisms of trust
creation differ, as does the balance between trust and power. Due
to the greater competitive strength of German SMEs, there is no
parallel there of the high degree of power inequality between firms
and the extreme dependence of supplier firms in Japan. Furthermore, in German inter-firm relations trust creation depends much
more on formal institutional mechanisms and rarely relies on the
existence of particularistic and diffuse personal relations. Thus,
although the Japanese concept of 'lean production' has been enthusiastically embraced by many German managers (Grabher, 1993) the
greater German involvement of unions in its introduction and their
much stronger and more highly formalized role in the German
industrial order is sure to lead to very different final outcomes.

Japanization of supplier relations, particularly close synchronization between strategies and production processes, has made much

less impact in more traditional industries, but they have not been immune to the pressures of intensified competition. The latter has led to shifts in power between customer and supplier firms, with customers being able to dictate terms to a greater extent than in the past (interview notes, 1993 and 1994). Within firms, there has also been a shift in the balance of power between management and labour. Managers have experienced challenges to established identities and practices but have also had more scope on the shop floor for the implementation of new approaches. Buyers no longer demand either high quality or low price, but ask for both simultaneously. Thus British managers have had to develop greater sensitivity to quality problems, and their German counterparts have had to orient themselves much more to considerations of cost than in the past. Whether these new goals can be realized within existing industrial orders, or whether they will effect significant institutional reforms, remains to be seen.

Thus, to conclude, despite a highly turbulent environment for firms, stability of intra- and inter-firm role relations has been more striking than change, and the comparative analysis of supplier relations has shown that it is premature to talk of convergence. The continuing salience of divergent patterns of industrial organization, it has been argued, makes it inadvisable to develop theoretical tools which ignore this. Nevertheless, significant aspects of supplier relations are currently being reshaped. Here it is notable that change has been more evident in Britain than in Germany. Although this has been due partly to the weaker competitive position of British manufacturing industry, it has also been attributed to the peculiarities of the British industrial order, characterized by a much weaker social embeddedness of firms.

APPENDIX

Definitions of trust (Sako, 1992: 37–40)

Contractual trust   This implies that each party expects the other to adhere to specific oral or written agreements. A payment period may be agreed bilaterally, or may be an industry norm. This kind of trust may also entail the expectation that commercial secrets are kept. Reliance on oral agreements reflects more contractual trust than reliance on written contracts.

Competence trust   This concerns the expectation of a trading partner performing its role competently, in both technical and managerial terms. Competence trust is higher where quality checks are carried out by suppliers, and buyers do not inspect for quality on delivery of goods. Both contractual and competence trust rely mainly on reputation.

Goodwill trust   This type of trust is more diffuse and refers to mutual expectations of open commitment to each other. Commitment may be defined as the willingness to do more than is formally expected, i.e. to accede to the request from a trading partner, or to any observed opportunity that would improve performance over and beyond any specific agreements. The other party is given a high degree of discretion and can be trusted not to abuse it. Such trust is usually extended after satisfactory experience during a trial period, and it relies predominantly on a particularistic setting. There are shared principles of fairness and convergent mutual expectations about informal obligations.

NOTES

The support of the Economic and Social Research Council (ESRC) is gratefully acknowledged. The work is part of the ESRC Contracts and Competition Research Programme and is funded by ESRC award number 414 251016. The interviewing has been jointly carried out with colleagues on the programme: Reinhard Bachmann, Simon Deakin, Tom Goodwin and Frank Wilkinson.

1 These two banking sectors are able to provide long-term fixed rate and competitively priced loans because they have access to other banks and financial institutions which can procure such funds on capital markets and then relend them to an SME. Both the other banks (their own higher-tier regional and federal level banks) and the credit institutions (the Kreditanstalt für Wiederaufbau, the Deutsche Ausgleichsbank and the Industriekreditbank) are mainly publicly owned and are obliged to lend on favourable terms to SMEs, to guarantee portions of loans in certain circumstances, as well as to encourage business start-ups and restructuring. About 25 per cent of all long-term finance to industry has come from these credit institutes – channelled mainly through local house banks. (This account is based on Vitols, 1994.)

2 The two industries were chosen because they make complex multi-part products (which makes outsourcing likely) and to achieve a contrast between a technologically relatively simple and a technologically more advanced industry. In the German case, we are also contrasting a competitive industry – kitchen furniture – with a crisis industry – mining machinery. In Britain, both industries are in crisis.

3 In Germany, a large proportion of both buyer and supplier firms in the

mining machinery industry are concentrated in the Ruhr area of North Rhine Westphalia. The Ruhr area is seen by Grabher (1993) as a former industrial district which has lost its dynamism due to tight coupling between buyer and supplier firms, as well as between industrial actors and the state. In the kitchen furniture industry dispersion of firms is slightly greater, but even in this industry a high proportion of supplier firms are in the areas around Gütersloh and Herford in Eastern Westphalia. Thus, in the district (*Kreis*) of Herford, 29 per cent of those employed work in the furniture industry (*MM Maschinenmarkt*, 1 September 1993: 140).

4 According to the *Economic Bulletin* (31 January 1994: 10) of the German Economic Institute (DIW), German lack of international competitiveness due to high prices has not been borne out by a single empirical study, and this widely made claim is thus more a myth than reality. The related claim that German labour costs are too high is also not well founded, as unit wage costs have been below the average wage rates of Germany's trading partners (ibid.: 18).

REFERENCES

Alford, H. and Garnsey, E. (1994) 'Flexibility and specialization in supplier relations among new technology based firms', discussion paper of the Judge Institute of Management Studies, University of Cambridge.

Altmann, N. and Sauer, D. (eds) (1989) *Systemische Rationalisierung und Zulieferindustrie*, Frankfurt: Campus.

Bannock, G. and Albach, H. (1991) *Small Business Policy in Europe. Report for the Anglo-German Foundation*, London: Anglo-German Foundation.

Best, M. (1989), 'Sector strategies and industrial policy: the furniture industry and the Greater London Enterprise Board', in P. Hirst and J. Zeitlin (eds) *Reversing Industrial Decline?*, Oxford: Berg.

Carr, C. (1990) *Britain's Competitiveness. The Management of the Vehicle Components Industry*, London: Routledge.

CBI (1991) *Partnership Sourcing*, London: CBI.

Charkham, J. (1994) *Keeping Good Company. A study of corporate governance in five countries*, Oxford: Oxford University Press.

Deakin, S., Lane, C. and Wilkinson, F. (1993) 'Competition and cooperation in vertical contracts: an inter-disciplinary framework', in V. Corado-Simoes (ed.) *International Business and Europe after 1992. Proceedings of the 19th Annual Conference of the European International Business Association*, Lisbon: CEDE.

Deiss, M. and Doehl, V. (eds) (1992) *Vernetzte Produktion. Automobilzulieferer zwischen Kontrolle und Autonomie. ISF Muenchen*, Frankfurt: Campus.

Dellbridge, R., Turnbull, P. and Wilkinson, B. (1992) 'Pushing back the frontiers: management control and work intensification under JIT/TQM factory regimes', *New Technology, Work and Employment* 7(2): 97–106.

Doran, A. (1984) *Craft Enterprises in Britain and Germany*, London: Anglo-German Foundation.

DTI (1991) *Power in Partnership*, London: DTI.

Fox, A. (1985) *History and Heritage. The Social Origins of the British Industrial Relations System*, London: George Allen and Unwin.

Franks, J. and Mayer, C. (1990) 'Capital markets and corporate control: a study of France, Germany and the UK', *Economic Policy* April: 191–231.

Gambetta, D. (1988) 'Can we trust?', in D. Gambetta (ed.) *Trust: Making and Breaking Co-operative Relations*, Oxford: Basil Blackwell.

Garnsey, E. (1993) 'The "Cambridge Phenomenon" revisited: aggregate change among Cambridge high-technology companies since 1985', *Entrepreneurship and Regional Development* 5: 179–207.

Grabher, G. (1993) 'The weakness of strong ties: the lock-in of regional developments in the Ruhr area', in G. Grabher (ed.) *The Embedded Firm. On the Socio-economics of Industrial Networks*, London: Routledge.

Granovetter, M. (1985) 'Economic action and social structure: the problem of embeddedness', *American Journal of Sociology* 91: 481–510.

Hall, P. (1984) 'Patterns of economic policy: an organizational approach', in S. Bornstein, D. Held and J. Krieger (eds) *The State in Capitalist Europe*, London: Unwin Hyman.

—— (1986) *Governing the Economy*, Oxford: Oxford University Press.

Hampden-Turner, C. and Trompenaars, F. (1994) *The Seven Cultures of Capitalism*, London: Piatkus.

Herrigel, G. (1989) 'Industrial order and the politics of industrial change: mechanical engineering', in P. Katzenstein (ed.) *Industry and Politics in West Germany*, Ithaca, N.Y.: Cornell University Press.

Hildebrandt, E. and Seltz, R. (1989) *Wandel betrieblicher Sozialverfassung durch systemische Kontrolle? Die Einführung computergestützter Produktionsplanungs- und Steuerungssysteme im bundesdeutschen Maschinenbau*, Berlin: Rainer Bohn Verlag.

Hirst, P. and Thompson, G. (1992) 'The pattern of "globalization": international economic relations, national economic management and the formation of trading blocs', *Economy and Society* 21(4): 357–96.

—— and Zeitlin, J. (eds) (1989) *Reversing Industrial Decline?*, Oxford: Berg.

Hofstede, G. (1980) *Culture's Consequences*, Beverly Hills, Calif.: Sage.

—— (1993) 'Intercultural Conflict and Synergy in Europe', in D. Hickson (ed.) *Management in Western Europe*, Berlin: de Gruyter.

Hughes, A. (1990) 'Industrial concentration and the small business sector in the UK: the 1980s in historical perspective', Working Paper No. 6, Cambridge University: Small Business Research Centre.

Kotthoff, H. and Reindl, J. (1990) *Die soziale Welt kleiner Betriebe*, Goettingen: Otto Schwartz & Co.

Lane, C. (1989) *Management and Labour in Europe*, Aldershot: Edward Elgar.

—— (1991) 'Industrial Reorganization in Europe: Patterns of Convergence and Divergence in Germany, France and Britain', *Work, Employment and Society*, 5(4): 515–39.

Macfarlane, A. (1978) *The Origins of English Individualism*, Oxford: Basil Blackwell.

Marginson, P., Edwards, P. K., Martin, R. and Sisson, K. (1988) *Beyond the Workplace*, Oxford: Basil Blackwell.

Markesinis, B. (1990) 'Litigation-mania in England and Germany and the USA: are we so very different?', *Cambridge Law Journal* 49(2): 233–76.

Morris, J. and Imrie, R. (1991) *Transformations in the Buyer–Supplier Relationship*, London: Macmillan.

New, C. C. and Myers, A. (1986) *Managing Manufacturing Operations in the UK, 1975–85*, London: Institute of Manpower Studies.

O'Mahoney, M. and Wagner, K. (1994) 'Changing Fortunes: an industry study of British and German productivity growth over three decades', Discussion Paper FSI 304, Wissenschaftszentrum Berlin. Research Area: Labour Market and Employment. Berlin: WZB.

Penn, R. (1992) 'Contemporary relationships between firms in a classic industrial locality', *Work, Employment and Society*, 6(2): 209–27.

Piore, M. and Sabel, C. (1984) *The Second Industrial Divide. Possibilities for Prosperity*, New York: Basic Books.

Pohlmann, M., Apelt, M. and Martens, H., (1992) 'Autonomie und Abhängigkeit – die Voraussetzungen der Kooperation an der Schnittstelle Beschaffung-Zulieferung', in M. Deiss and V. Doehl (eds) *op. cit.*

Porter, M. (1990) *The Competitive Advantage of Nations*, London: Macmillan.

Powell, W. W. (1991) 'Neither market nor hierarchy: network forms of organization', in G. Thompson, J. Frances, R. Levacic and J. Mitchell (eds) *Markets, Hierarchies and Networks*, London: Sage, in cooperation with the Open University.

—— and DiMaggio, P. J. (eds) (1991) *The New Institutionalism in Organizational Analysis*, Chicago: Chicago University Press.

Prowse, S. (1994) *Corporate Governance in an International Perspective: a survey of corporate control mechanisms among large firms in the United States, the United Kingdom, Japan and Germany*, BIS Economic Papers, Basle: Bank for International Settlements.

Rainnie, A. (1993) 'The reorganization of large firm subcontracting: myth and reality', *Capital and Class* 49: 53–75.

Sabel, C. F. (1989) 'The reemergence of regional economies', discussion paper FSI 89-3, Research Unit Labour Market and Employment. Wissenschaftszentrum Berlin.

—— (1990) 'Skills without a place: the reorganization of the corporation and the experience of work', paper presented at the 1990 Conference of the British Sociological Association, Guildford.

Sako, M. (1992) *Prices, Quality and Trust. Inter-Firm Relations in Britain and Japan*, Cambridge: Cambridge University Press.

Saxenian, A. L. (1989) 'The Cheshire cat's grin: innovation, regional development and the Cambridge case', *Economy and Society*, 18(4).

Semlinger, K. (1989) 'Stellung und Probleme kleinbetrieblicher Zulieferer im Verhältnis zu grossen Abnehmern', in N. Altmann and D. Sauer (eds) *Systemische Rationalisierung und Zulieferindustrie*, Frankfurt: Campus.

—— (1991) 'New developments in subcontracting: mixing market and hierarchy', in A. Amin and M. Dietrich (eds) *Towards a New Europe*, Aldershot: Edward Elgar.

—— (1993) 'Small firms and outsourcing as flexibility reservoirs of large firms', in G. Grabher (ed.) *The Embedded Firm: On the socio-economics of embedded networks*, London: Routledge.

Sengenberger, W. and Loveman, G. (1988) *Smaller Units of Employment. A*

Synthesis Report on Industrial Reorganization in Industrialized Countries, Geneva: International Institute for Labour Studies.

—— and Pyke, F. (1990) 'Small firm industrial districts and local economic regeneration: research and policy issues', Paper No. 1 of the International Conference on Industrial Districts and Local Economic Regeneration, Geneva: International Institute for Labour Studies.

Stewart, R., Barsoux J.-L., Kieser, A., Ganter, H.-D. and Walgenbach, P. (1994) *Managing in Britain and Germany. Report for the Anglo-German Foundation*, London: AGF.

Stoffaes, C. (1989) 'Industrial policy and the state. From industry to enterprise' in P. Godt (ed.) *Policy Making in France*, London: Pinter.

Storey, J. and Sisson, K. (1990) 'Limits to transformation: human resource management in the British context', *Industrial Relations Journal* 21(1): 60–5.

Streeck, W. (1992) 'The logics of associative action and the territorial organization of interests: the case of German Handwerk', in W. Streeck, *Social Institutions and Economic Performance*, London: Sage.

Thelen, K. (1991) *Union of Parts. Labour Politics in Germany*, Ithaca, N.Y.: Cornell University Press.

Thoburn, J. T. and Takashima, M. (1992) *Industrial Subcontracting in the UK and Japan*, Aldershot: Avebury.

Turnbull, P. J. (1989) 'Buyer–supplier relations in the UK automotive industry', paper presented at the conference 'A Flexible Future?', Cardiff Business School.

Vitols, S. (1994) 'German banks and the modernization of the small firm sector: long-term finance in a comparative perspective', paper presented at the 9th International Conference of Europeanists, Chicago, March/April.

Walsh, V. (1991) 'Inter-firm technological alliances: a transient phenomenon or new structures in capitalist economies?', in A. Amin and M. Dietrich (eds) *Towards a New Europe*, Aldershot: Edward Elgar.

Whitston, C. (1989) 'Rationalizing foundries', in S. Tailby and C. Whitston (eds) *Manufacturing Change. Industrial Relations and Restructuring*, Oxford: Basil Blackwell.

Zeitlin, J. and Totterdill, P. (1989) 'Markets, technology and local intervention: the case of clothing', in P. Hirst and J. Zeitlin (eds) *op. cit.*

12 The Norwegian disconnection
Professional unity and industrial division

Tor Halvorsen, Olav Korsnes and Rune Sakslind

INTRODUCTION

To describe how the firm is socially constructed within a national economy involves an analysis not only of the so-called economic institutions, but also of many of the social relations within a country's civil society and politics. This applies particularly to peripheral economies such as that of Norway, in which at critical points in history most of the country's resources have had to be mobilized in order to make industrialization and capitalism merge into sustainable types of accumulation regimes.

The purpose of this article is not to describe all relevant processes for the construction of the firm, but to highlight some factors which, in our view, clearly contribute to the shaping of the Norwegian firm by defining its social integration, mode of reproduction and stabilization. In doing this we perceive the firm and its actors as socially constructed agencies, i.e. as actors embedded in particular social relations which at any point in history control their range of strategic choices. This approach requires that the strict dichotomy between external contingencies and the internal structures of the firm has to be overcome. Only through such an approach will it be possible to understand the social and industrial space that frames rational actions and indicates certain choices which move the firm towards specific 'national models', rather than towards a common model based on, for example, 'efficiency norms'.

THE ENGINEERING DIMENSION – PROFESSIONAL UNITY AND INDUSTRIAL FRAGMENTATION

In this article we will argue that the specificity of the Norwegian firm is closely related to the historical evolution of the engineering dimension of industrial activity. Perhaps to a greater degree than in any other country which has reached a comparable level of 'maturity' – including France, Germany and Japan – the engineering dimension in Norwegian industry has shaped the organization of the firm. Thus, an analysis of engineers and their construction as a profession is central to the understanding of how the Norwegian enterprise is organized, how it is managed, how ownership and management are related, how it relates to the market, how industrial relations are constituted, how products are shaped and finally how processes of production come about. Consequently, as an aspect of the analysis of firm strategies and the firm as an actor, we have to examine the professional *habitus* of the engineers.

Of course, the strategic orientation of business units has several other determinants, and the historical trajectory of the industrial system results from the interaction between various other factors pertaining to the business system as a whole. And the shaping of the engineering dimension results from the interaction between peculiarities of the profession and structures of the industrial sector itself.

A certain paradox emerges if we counterpose the social construction of engineering with patterns of industrial structure. By means of a collective project of professionalization based on the award of a diploma from the (single) Norwegian technical university (established in 1910), Norwegian engineers emerged as a socially homogeneous category (*Stand*), before the development of a modern Norwegian industrial sector proper. Thus, in important respects, the construction of an industrial cadre preceded the evolution of the industrial system and the consolidation of organized business interests. Quite possibly, compared to other industrializing countries, the firm was shaped by engineers in management more than the other way round. In contrast to this unified profile of the engineering profession, however, industry in Norway appears as a fragmented system of relatively autonomous sub-sectors, split according to branches and products, patterns of ownership and finance.

This 'asymmetry' between professional and industrial networks, between channels of knowledge and the conditions for its efficient application, appears as a distinct trait of the industrial system as a whole. And in fact, basic problems of industrial development in Norway have their origins in the discontinuities and lack of sectoral integration implied in this structure; discourses on industrial policy revolve around such issues. However, such debates rarely focus on the engineering dimension in a comprehensive fashion and its mode of articulation with industry, and the networking potentials and capacities of the profession are seldom exposed. If, as we think, the assumption is valid that the homogeneity of the engineering profession in a comparative perspective is something quite unique, this peculiarity is accompanied by a comparative uniqueness also in terms of a segmented industrial structure.

It is not possible here to lay out in detail the interrelations and interaction between the profession and industrial structure. However, our premise is that the historical fact of the coexistence of these domains for several decades justifies the assumption that there has been, and probably still exists, a specific logic of mutual reproduction between them. Peculiar to this mode of reproduction is the fact that the (relatively) homogeneous social and technological network represented by the profession has not, or has only to a limited degree, had any marked influence on the integration of industrial structures, e.g. in terms of the creation of interlinkages, industrial districts, or zones, clusters of firms, etc.

In what follows we briefly highlight some characteristics of the industrial sector. Then the focus is put on the engineering dimension, and on how this dimension is constituted at the firm level. By means of a general overview we try to indicate the role of the engineering profession. Several characteristic traits show a stable pattern, across cultural and economic conjunctures, to which a certain societal permanence and specific form of coherence between actors and institutions can be attributed (Sorge, 1991; Whitley, 1994). We discuss why the engineering professions have gained such relative importance, and why this element in the social construction of industrial firms is so crucial for understanding the specificity of the Norwegian firm. In the final part of the chapter we look at recent processes of industrial change and adjustment, and tentatively put forward a thesis on the role of the engineering profession in these processes.

INDUSTRIAL STRUCTURE AND THE BUSINESS SYSTEM

Fragmentation and compartmentalization

The industrialization of Norway has been the result of two relatively separate processes: the rapid, exogenous introduction of foreign capital and technology to exploit natural resources (hydroelectric power) in the production of standardized, intermediate goods for the world market; and the more gradual, endogenous process of development of various manufacturing industries based on the home market. While basic structures of the first development process were established in the first quarter of the century, the second process reached maturity only during the 1960s when, for instance the mechanical engineering sector emerged as an export industry. A pervasive attribute of the structures thus established has been the segmentation of industrial sectors and the existence of 'enclaves' or 'monocultures'. The producers of machinery and production equipment and services are only weakly linked to the producers of intermediate goods, and the various internally isolated parts of the power-intensive industry are themselves only to a small extent suppliers of inputs to Norwegian manufacturing industry. This picture of weak inter-industrial ties is also largely valid for the internal relations of the manufacturing industry, which depends considerably on imported goods and components. And even though the economy basically is populated by small firms, networks and strategic alliances between larger firms and subcontractors are scarce. Moreover, the Norwegian financial system has never developed a bank sector capable of serving as an integrative force in the processes of industrial and economic change.

In its basic traits, this structure of industrial segmentation appears to have been preserved until today. Perhaps the only real exception to this has been the case of the maritime sector. This industrial segment, which encompasses the producers of a wide range of equipment for maritime use, shipbuilders, shipping firms and ship-owners, has come through the crises since the mid-1970s and today represents a genuine industrial 'cluster', to use the terminology of the Porter studies (Reve *et al.*, 1992).

This fragmentation of the industrial sector is intertwined with a particular historical trend in the development of the Norwegian business system. In general terms, this development has been marked by tendencies of enclosure and compartmentalization. On the one hand, a combination of small industry and the local savings bank system with a common orientation towards market niches, can be identified (a segment with a strong regional, local attachment). The smaller firms, which dominate this segment, are not as strongly attached to industrial branches as larger firms. They are also little involved in the established R. & D. apparatuses, even though the R. & D. activity in regional networks may be of considerable importance. The size and region are probably more important for the identity of these firms, than what kind of industrial category they belong to, according to classification criteria established in official statistics. The industrial identity may be more important to such firms in other national systems, where subcontracting and tight links between larger and smaller firms within regions is more common. The fact that many of these firms have entered associations of small firms in Norway, which are organized in opposition to the originally predominant association for larger firms, indicates that such an identity is not yet well developed amongst these firms in Norway.

On the other hand, a segment can be identified which combines capital from the Norwegian investment banks and endogenous enterprises that historically have been owned by Norwegians. The firms in this internal segment have always been organized according to branch criteria, for example mechanical engineering industry, shipbuilding, textiles and garments (of which there are only remnants today), etc. Its market orientation has been towards both the national and the international markets, and most commonly consists in a strategic combination of these. The group of industrialists within this segment that have been most actively oriented towards international competition, have traditionally been strongly politically allied with the state.

There is a third important segment within the Norwegian business system, with a strong external basis and orientation. This segment consists of enterprises within various branches that could make use of Norwegian hydroelectric power and comparatively large amounts of foreign capital investment. These enterprises have been typically branch-specific in their industrial organization, although some were older firms with their own traditions. The individual firms were connected to an external industrial structure, usually both through market and product development and through ownership/ capital. These firms therefore had the greatest distance between ownership and control which, to a large degree, was exercised by engineering managers.

Another general trait of the Norwegian business system is that it is prominently dependent on the banking system for its finances, but that this financial system only to a minor extent tries to develop strategies for changing the way firms operate in markets. Actors in the internal and in the external segments, in particular, are more oriented towards technology and product development than market development, whereas actors in the local segment to a larger extent are both able and willing to adapt to changes in local demand. So, different logics for valuation of the productive versus the market-related functions may be found within the different types of business systems. Still, we may generally claim that the governance structures and promotional networks have given the engineers a strong position. Historical data show a clear division between industry, commerce and banking, a division which also has been clearly present within the professions (Amdam, 1994), leaving the industrial space for the engineers alone. The orientation towards product development and technology has been so strong in many Norwegian firms that the engineers only had to deal with economists or other professionals within the field of industrial administration at board level.

The fragmentation of the industrial structure, the compartmentalization of the business system, and its reliance on a banking system with low strategic capacity, reflect the low degree of integration between firms both within and across industrial sectors. In particular, firms in the local segment are weakly integrated within industries and national networks. Still, in some historical periods, firms in this segment have combined market and capital with industry in a way that has given rise to regional effects. Local industry has been able to create new lines of production that over time extend beyond the local market, but is constrained by its affiliation with the local savings bank system. It seems that these industries, more than industries within the other segments of the business system, combine a broad concept of engineering with '*gründer*' activities. The educational and qualifying institutions relating to technology have been of importance in shaping these firms and their relations to other firms, but within the firms the various technical qualifications relating to these institutions are not strongly differentiated. This tradition of entrepreneurialism of a more egalitarian kind within specific regions may have been generated by a host of factors, which we shall not go into here. The point is that they contribute to a type of general valuation of the engineering dimension which does not give a strong priority to a particular type of academic/scientific education. Engineering and practical activity are closely related. Given the importance of small industry in Norway and the strong social influence of this segment on the whole economy, we may talk of a development which affects the social fabric as a whole: structuring the firms within other segments of the business system, the educational system and finally shaping the general organization of the firm and its governing structure. The engineering dimension has become the managerial dimension, undercutting the importance of administrative techniques relating to competitive market strategies, such as accounting and business economics.

It is in relation to these traditions within the business system as a whole that the critique of the Norwegian business system as a system without market strategies is most appropriate. These structures, which were challenged as corporate governance strategies, both at an industrial and firm level, changed considerably during the 1960s and 1970s. A strong concentration of ownership within industrial branches was followed by a reduction of the number of firms within each line of production, as a result of concerted efforts by central political and economic actors. Venture capital and other types of capital mobilization became more normal. Yet the multi-unit manufacturing corporations remained with both feet (or at least one and a half) solidly planted within a particular product line and industry.

Attempts at establishing a business system oriented towards scale and scope were few, and in many cases unsuccessful. Among the first major ventures into such a strategy was Borregaard which aimed at divisionalization as early as 1950, but had to give up due to internal resistance. Norsk Hydro may be one of the few examples of successful diversification of production in independent divisions; a corporation which cuts across and combines traditions from internal (state) and external segments of the business system (Berg and Lange, 1989).

While the engineers as managers were strongly involved in the establishment of a new corporate structure between 1955 and 1975, they may have lost some of their grip over the business system as a whole in the 'decade of the economists', the 1980s. This may have been due to two processes: the attempt to divisionalize the corporations, and the attempt to combine this divisionalization with new market strategies. The market strategies represented an attempt to become multi-divisional 'conglomerates', i.e. to develop unrelated products for different types of markets (mass market, tailored, niches, etc.). In this period the engineers in management were to some degree replaced by economists in leading positions, the influence of the banks in the internal business system increased, and there was a movement towards the American general management ideal in Norwegian industry. But these attempts to introduce new governance principles have proved to be in conflict with fundamental tenets in the Norwegian value system, which give priority to egalitarianism, consensus-building and local self-government. Perhaps partly for this reason the trend of the 1980s was only moderately successful, the old system being reinstalled during the 1990s. The question is what may be the lasting effects of this; the business economists have certainly strengthened their position, the business system may have become more integrated and concentrated on the internal business-system tradition and, finally, financial interests also have gained in strength (Amdam, 1993; Gammelsæter, 1990; Simonsen, 1989; Berg and Lange, 1991), but the engineering dimension is still dominant.

The engineering dimension in the organization of the firm

The historical development and central position of the engineering dimension, and its importance for future attempts at restructuring Norwegian industry, must be seen against the background of this segmentation and compartmentalization of the industrial structure and the business system. Firms within both the local and the external segments seem to favour the engineering profession in strategic managerial positions. For reasons of simplicity we distinguish two engineering roles. First, the role of the 'innovator' doing technical work and, second, the role of the 'organizer' taking part in the general management of the firm. These roles are more or less separated in entrepreneurial types of activities, depending on the characteristics of firms and national economies. The point to be made here is that in all kinds of firms there is a tension between these roles, but in different ways within the different business systems. External capital seems to encourage a split between innovation and production, locating innovation separately and leaving the role of management and organization development to the engineer-managers. The internal segment of industry, on the other hand, tried after the Second World War to close this gap by developing institutions for technology development. Engineering representatives located within this segment were the driving force behind what today by many, particularly in smaller industries, is considered an oversized R. & D. sector.

Through this sector, the internal capital laid the foundation for the 'golden age' of the engineering profession in the 1960s and 1970s. Even so, the role of engineering innovation never seemed to develop successfully through this institutional structure. Processes of innovation within the firm did not easily connect to institution-based R. & D. Firm-based types of innovation seemed to dominate. The innovatory role of the engineer at the firm level was, therefore, given greater importance during the 1980s, when the R. & D. sector was reorganized and to a large degree privatized. The role of the engineer as innovator was now more strongly located to the firm, reducing the role of the autonomous external 'science'-based innovations (Halvorsen, 1984) which the OECD, for example, had advocated so strongly during the preceding decades. Firm-based technological development gained a stronger position through the upgrading of firms' departments for innovation. The overall effect was an increased emphasis on specialized technical knowledge developed within the higher educational and research-based institutions for the development of the firm and, on the other hand, a reduced autonomy for the comparatively huge external research sector. The shift of weight from the institutional sector to the firm as an arena for innovation represents a development which approaches the position of the local business system and types of organization of smaller firms, while the greater weight on higher education may be considered a process towards a closure of the engineering profession around higher educational positions, a development which seems to contradict organizational interests within smaller, locally based, industries.

The overall impression is that this industrial restructuring during the 1980s did not change the traditional composition of the engineering profession much. We may have had a change of balance between the two roles (innovator/organizer), and a change of influence within the engineering hierarchy, pushing the status hierarchy in the professional collective towards the academic civil engineer pole, but not to a degree that may make us talk of a fundamental change of the given 'engineering dimension'. So these recent developments did not fundamentally change the dominance of the role of organization over that of innovation.

Summary

What can be inferred so far is that the engineering dimension has provided a link in the Norwegian business system in the post-war period, and that the engineering profession has been important in organizational development and corporate governance at the industrial level. The engineers' entrenched position within R. & D. and in industrial administration may have had a conservative effect on business strategies, constraining managerial search processes in the market and making them stick to their traditional industrial branches and the well-known type of firm organization. But within the profession, as well as within industry, it is not the engineer as innovator, but as organizer that is most enhanced. It is this social aspect of the engineering dimension that contributes to what is to be considered a common profile within all segments of the business system: the strong position of production in the firm-internal status system in relation to finance and marketing. The engineering profession may thus have been more important in shaping the social relations within firms, than relations between firms. Therefore the paradox: unity of profession, but fragmentation within the industrial space.

One reason why the professional system is not as fragmented and subdivided as the industrial structure and the business system, may be its strong links with the state and the educational system. In nations with weaker states and stronger professional influence on the education system, other kinds of structuring principles may be important, for example leading to a greater division between industrial specialities, as in the USA where the engineering profession is split in several associations linked to industrial specialisms, or between academic specialisms, as in Great Britain. Such divisions are strongly played down in the social construction of the Norwegian engineering profession, which unifies industries on the basis of managerial roles relating to processes of organization. The agency for change, therefore, is to a high degree located at the firm level and in engineering managerial positions. The paradox is that the strong position of the engineering profession in Norway is not due to a high priority bestowed upon the production function as such – quite the contrary: traditionally, services and extractive industries, trade, shipping and now oil, represent the most respected activities in Norwegian culture, and the leadership purpose of industrial development is therefore not apparent. It is for this reason that the post-industrial idea that it does not matter what kind of activities we are involved in, as long as they are knowledge-intensive and not harmful to the environment, has gained such a strong influence in Norway (Byrkjeflot, 1990).

This socio-cultural aspect of Norwegian society means that the engineering profession did not face a major challenge by other prospective high-status professions, as improvement of professional standing by venturing into industry was not perceived to be a realistic strategy. Thus, the engineers have been able to develop a certain degree of autonomy, which has allowed them to develop a conception of innovation which integrates the tasks of organization. The engineers probably represent the only group that can establish the link between firms in the local and internal segments of the business system, which today is missing. During the 1980s the argument was that it might be difficult to continue to rely on engineers as the major link in industry, since the international system is increasingly driven by a financial logic (Fligstein, 1990). The engineers' strength is in product development and competent administration of production processes, and they might not be able to defend their position as their leadership purposes are undermined by financial and economic interests activated by the internationalization of the economy. The engineers' basic values – control and continuity – are not likely to be valued as highly in the future as they have been in the past. The engineering dimension may, then, not be an adequate defence strategy for Norwegian industry in a new international business environment, where the corporation is not a social system and a production unit, but a commodity having to face the constant challenge of buy-outs and mergers (Meyer, 1990). On the other hand, it may be argued that the strong domination of the engineering profession at all levels within the firm and within firm-related institutions may be a resource which has not yet been capitalized within strategies for industrial change.

THE FORMATION OF THE PROFESSIONAL SYSTEM FOR ENGINEERING

Its setting in firm and work organization

The particular kind of segmentation seen in the Norwegian business system, and the undervalued position of manufacturing in the Norwegian value system, assign a strong primacy to the engineering dimension within manufacturing industries. The topic in this section is how engineers and technical groups within industry are shaped and positioned within the education system, the firm and the work organization. Most positions with managerial responsibilities above the level of foreman are strongly dominated by one type of engineer or another. Even though engineers have to acquire new types of knowledge in order to improve their chances of advancement as managers, they seldom lose their primary industrial/technological identification. This is due to the engineers' historical status as the only educated groups in industry during industrialization – and to the way this heritage is currently being reproduced by established institutions. As we shall see below, there is a strong educational tradition for graduating and certifying polytechnically oriented engineers. This is considered a basic type of education, to which managerial types of knowledge must be added. Management and technology therefore seldom lose contact. In addition, the educational system is producing a hierarchy for all levels of administration within the firm. This hierarchy, however, does not create strong lines of demarcation between the different types of engineer, for example making the highest type of engineering education a type of management education. Managerial careers may also start from lower-level types of education, even though civil engineers dominate, and sooner or later more than half of these (perhaps as many as 70 per cent) become part of the executive function. As a general trend, we find within Norwegian firms a 'double professional effect'. The engineers of course more often recruit engineers than other professions, and engineers go through a hierarchy of managerial learning that produces professional trust. Each administrative level is contained in the next for two reasons: there is no closure between the educational categories, and most of the top executives are produced within the firm, and for the largest firms within the industry. Below, we shall try to illustrate some of the reasons for this strong organizational domination of the engineering profession and suggest how this is related to the industrial structure.

The technical education system

The educational system for engineers has been constituted as a fairly separate specialism in Norway. Particular vocational schools (*berufschulen*) or professional and semi-professional institutions have been developed parallel to and under the influence of the German tradition. Today there is a three-level system. At the highest level we have the Norwegian Institute of Technology (Norges Tekniske Høgskole, NTH), at the medium level twelve engineering colleges (*Ingeniørhøgskoler*) and at the lowest level about fifty schools of the technical disciplines (*Tekniske Fagskoler*). Until about 1970 the educational system was mainly divided in two, and what was below this was a less standardized variety of types of shorter education for technicians or 'technicians in the making'. After about 1970 the lowest level was brought into the national system of educational planning. This level educates 'technicians', its main source of recruitment being qualified workers. The standardization of these institutions gives the Norwegian system a character of 'duality'. The technicians may now advance within the educational system from *Tekniske Fagskole* and bypass the traditional entrance requirement for university studies: *artium (abitur)*, which historically has provided a sharp status distinction between technicians and engineers.

In a historical perspective, this new development is a counter-tendency to the predominant division between educational levels according to entrance criteria. To get into the one and only university-level technical school, NTH, which was established in 1910 with the same kind of diploma privileges as the German *Technische Hochschule*, you had to have the *artium*. With this education, an engineer was accepted as part of the educated middle classes (*Bildungsbürgertum*), although the educational system as such did not highly value industrially oriented activities. Neither did industry particularly value education as such, as we shall see, as a precondition for engineering work. Gradually this system was dissolved through an 'academic drift' at the secondary level, adopting the *artium* as the entrance criterion for semi-skilled jobs during the 1960s, and by the standardization of lower-level technical education. From being a strictly compartmentalized system, the system of education for industrial activities now changed into a system that allowed for vertical mobility. Another recent important change is that the NTH's monopoly at the highest level of technical education was broken. During the 1980s the universities were also allowed to qualify engineers. The numbers are still marginal, but indicate a change in the rather pronounced distinction between engineering and science and the low esteem of 'science' (i.e. university-based education) within industry.

The only level within the educational system which seems to be able easily to create new types of disciplines and to combine them in new ways is the third level, the *Tekniske Fagskole*. This training gives technicians a head-start on their way to become engineers. The two other levels have up to now proved to be conservative, sticking to the 'polytechnical tradition' (i.e. general education) as a precondition for specialization. Both the general and the special educational track is provided by the same school. Each *Ingeniørhøgskole* is more or less the same as the other, and all of them are shaped in the image of NTH. In this sense the educational system creates a strong common engineering identification around subject-oriented types of specialization. It has not been possible to create special schools for special branches of industry, as in France. The degree of horizontal differentiation in technical education is low. The identities are primarily based on level of education, not specialism or academic discipline. The differentiation into disciplines at the higher level is also moderate, primarily centred on the 'traditional' industries. So to sum up: the educational system produces a loosely coupled hierarchy, which gives scope for upward mobility within the firm into the managerial positions for, in principle, all types of engineers. This creates a strong internal trust-relation in the firm between types of technical work and types of managerial responsibility that goes with the technical work. Management and staff functions relating to development of technology are not separated by the educational system and the firm as different career paths. This is only slightly modified when we look at how the educational categories are restructured within the work organization, after having been given an educational certificate or title.

The engineer status and the system of professions

The titles that engineers use (*siv.ing., ing.* and *tekn.*) indicate that the status system is even less hierarchical than the three-level nature of the educational system might lead us to believe. Status group identifications seem to be broken down quickly by a common engineering identification in everyday working life. The title 'engineer' is common for the two top levels, and carries with it something of the meaning of what in France are called industrial 'cadres', i.e. a class of people educated to take leadership functions in the state and industry. The difference is that Norwegian engineers are not organized in the same way as the French cadres, but in two strongly related professional organizations that also function as trade unions. The title system of the firm does not systematically reflect the educational titles, this being only one indication of how the differing educational groups overlap in the work-organization. Even though the engineers are organized within national unions primarily according to educational level, this differentiation neither penetrates the work organization in industries, nor the public sphere. This tendency is even more apparent if we consider the status of the technicians. Their status is hard to separate from that of engineers, and usually they soon acquire engineering jobs due to their knowledge of practical problem-solving. On the whole, even though the educational system is primarily hierarchically differentiated, this does not structure the status system, a system that due to both social/cultural and work organization traditions and practices primarily values the engineering collective. The relations within the organization recreate a strong alliance between engineers around the dual role structure discussed earlier: technology and management. The tendency, therefore (also given the domination of small firms), is that both the execution of work tasks and the execution of orders follow the line, i.e. technology and authority are closely connected. The staff developed in support of this line, seem, on the other hand primarily to be of a mercantile and accounting type. The recruitment of engineers, therefore, is really of a more general kind: following an organizational logic rather than a professional logic linked to staff functions (Perrow, 1986).

Recruitment

The recruitment of engineers shows that firms have a rather broad attitude to the engineering profession. Firms usually ask for individual qualifications, rather than a particular educational background – advertisements usually specify individual capacities; the necessary educational qualifications listed are not overly specific. The most common requirement is a general engineering title, sometimes there is a preference for a 'civil engineer' (i.e. engineer with a diploma). There are also openings for other types of engineers if their practical background is more suitable, or if more highly educated engineers cannot be found. On the other hand there seems to be little opening for combinations of disciplines or for recruitment of alternative disciplines to the ones within which the jobs are placed. This confirms the strong branch structure, the tendency to use the internal labour market for recruitment to management, and the tendency for engineers to remain within their specialism even after they reach higher levels of management and start to move between firms. There seems, generally speaking, to be a relatively close correlation between how jobs are constructed and the different engineering specialisms. In this sense the recruitment of younger engineers in particular, who still have more educational than managerial identity, confirms their potential innovative role (or appeals to their expectations of acquiring a professional identity as a technologist). The recruitment of civil engineers with experience therefore seems to be associated either with their capacities as experts who have specialized within their subject field (research) or as generalists who have abandoned their role as active creators of technology and have become 'engineering managers' (i.e. with responsibility for and knowledge of rationalization and organization). The crucial point, perhaps, is that within each of the recruitment systems (research and management) both types of engineers, and even technicians (who often acquire the engineering title through direct employment in engineering jobs) may get positions. Where the educational level seems to have strongest influence is on the recruitment to research-related jobs, while managerial jobs usually demand a mixture of qualifications that may more easily be attained by all types of engineers. In other words, the relationship between educational path and career pattern is more consistent in technology and research than in management.

This of course also works the other way around: when the demand for technical education is downplayed in recruitment, the school system will increasingly develop more management-oriented subjects. In other words, the ideal that education first of all must produce a proper professional technologist is embedded in the way the work organization is structured. First you have to prove that you have the proper technological knowledge, then you may eventually develop into a manager through organizational learning, a learning process which starts after the school has delivered its finished product. There is, then, no sharp break between a technological professional and an organizational career as manager or leader, and subsequently no sharp distinction between professionalism and bureaucracy within industry in Norway. In this respect Norway seems to resemble Germany rather than France (Maurice *et al.*, 1986).

Entry into working life

There is a long tradition within engineering education for combining school-based education with practical training. Gradually, however, practical training has been reduced, and engineers now acquire their final degrees without any kind of work practice. Today, engineers entering employment and starting work within a firm are considered more 'finished products' than before, since they have acquired their educational titles and are not expected to go back to school for further learning. The so-called 'educational revolution' in Norway during the latter part of the 1960s, represented types of 'academic drift' which also emptied education of its practical training. On the other hand, since the emphasis today is considered to be largely educational/theoretical, which is not highly valued by industry, newly educated engineers are considered to be in need of work-place socialization for quite some time. They may be individually selected for specific jobs, but in actual work practice they are collectively socialized within a system of high flexibility and mobility, until 'real qualifications' are crystallized. As the social construction of the 'finished engineer' gradually became more educationally based, which means that the educational and professional titles increasingly overlap, the division of labour became more blurred due to the lack of relevance of theory to work ability. On the job, people got a chance to prove themselves no matter what social status they had been infused with through education. Even though the level of entrance job, to some degree, particularly within research fields, might correlate with level of education, the different types of engineers are no longer considered ready for specific jobs and career patterns. Internal processes of qualification in the firm lead differently educated engineers into overlapping job positions, combining authority, conception and execution in the same jobs. There seems to be only a general differentiation in entrance criteria between those who are supposedly going into manual and more conceptual and authority-based jobs. The engineering identities that emerge from internal careers tend to erode these criteria of differentiation. Organizational and professional learning go hand in hand: professionalization is a precondition for successful bureaucratization.

Career progression and mobility

The engineering labour market seems to have developed a balance between internal and external mobility. The average engineer changes jobs through the external labour market about five times during his working lifetime. The normal extent of internal promotion is, of course, harder to verify, but is perhaps of about the same magnitude. The most highly educated seem to use the external labour market far more extensively than the less educated. In other words, the chances of promotion for the less-educated are greater within firms than through the external labour market. This may be connected to the fact that the external labour market is more strongly dominated by the big firms, which also are the firms that are most heavily engaged in R. & D. The greater external mobility of civil engineers is also an indication of a more penetrating split of career-orientation between the role of research and that of management. The civil engineers are also younger than other engineers when they have to make their career choice and the orientation towards higher management is also an orientation towards 'job-hopping'. Again, the managerial labour market is constructed by the needs of the bigger firms. Although we may say that the blurring of career patterns between types of engineers is most strongly associated with the internal labour market, it may be reproduced by the external market, primarily because this market is more shaped by the needs of the bigger firms. But rarely do we see managers cross the lines between industries or branches. The management-oriented type of engineer – until recently, probably the predominant type in the profession (and, among the civil engineers, by far) – seems to stick to the same type of industry throughout his/her entire career. In other words, the engineering profession as a recruitment-pool for management subdivides the management market along industrial branches. Only a few get into general management and become leading figures in an epistemological fight for and social development of a 'new profession' around ideas of 'general management'.

The professional organizations reinforce this pattern. Within the Norwegian *Sonderweg*, which is characterized by a strong relationship between the politics in the firm and the politics at national level, the professional unions have developed their distinctive shape. They combine economic bargaining power with professional knowledge strategies, and they combine strategies for change of the work organization with collective strategies at a national level. The individual engineer has a strong influence on his/her career prospects through personal contract negotiation. But these individual bargaining procedures are always aided by the national unions, and the individual contract cannot deviate greatly from the minimum standards set by the professional unions. There is a dialectic between individual and collective agreements; progress on the individual level creates improvement of the collective standards that all the engineers benefit from. Individuals who do not promote themselves will in other words be promoted by the system of collective agreements. This system seems to be reinforcing types of careers that combine rationalization and organizational knowledge with technological knowledge within the same jobs. The professional unions, which in Norway combine qualification bargaining with wage bargaining, will not permit the development of a separate hierarchy for 'managers' as a field of identification outside the professional space. Competences and skills are not easily split apart.

Organizational competence and skills

Norwegian engineers may, therefore, as far as their competences and skills are concerned, be considered as being shaped by a combination of professional and organizational processes that reinforce the common engineering dimension across levels and positions. The organizationally and professionally shaped engineer represents the filter for managerial work. The primacy of the common title of 'engineer', to any type of subtitle, shows that the professional identification is more shaped by 'equalizing' processes in the firm than by the type of differentiations that follow from the educational hierarchy or from the distinction between intellectual versus manual work reproduced by R. & D. institutions. The important institutions and relations for valuing the engineering competences and skills are not those that promote the role of the innovator as such (the research-oriented engineer), but the type of engineering that is involved in the combined development of technology and organization. In this sense we might say that the primacy of the work organization, as far as the total identification of the engineers is concerned, creates a continuity in the engineering dimension that enhances the engineering hierarchy as such more than particular levels, or particular roles within this hierarchy. R. & D. staff, for example, are closely connected to the processes of organizational change and rationalization. They seem to be only mildly diversified internally by the more important position of the highly educated within this type of work. In other words, the internal engineering dimension is more homogeneous than in most other countries, and even more so than what could be expected when considering the educational system. Even the rather autonomous and relatively extensive R. & D. sector does not seem to be creating staff for R. & D. internally in the firm. When engineers are 'constructed' within the work organization along with the jobs their capacities are meant for, the emphasis is on competence and skills that we might, in honour of the Norwegian tradition, call 'socio-technical'.

So to sum up briefly, the managerial and technical skills are combined at many levels, giving all the educational groups access to the types of competencies that are highly valued in the firm. The division of labour within the technical-engineering collective and the field of knowledge which constitutes the frame for this division of labour, are closely associated to the firm and its work organization. The engineering dimension becomes reproduced through the value structure of the firm, which reproduces a close internal bond between all kinds of technical/engineering work. The relatively huge external sector for technology development does not dominate the engineering dimension. The relationship between 'technology' as the work of expertise, external to the firm or within clearly defined categories of staff, and the firm organization does not take the shape of a conflict or a cooperation between two parts. This engineering role is mediated by the firm and therefore integrated in a common engineering identification. Potential conflicts between profession and organizations are again played down. The later reforms within the educational system seem to support such a development. The large external institutional R. & D. sector, which had the support, particularly during the 1970s and early 1980s, of a statist industrial strategy to create a concentration around so-called 'science-based' industry, did not become a strong enough alternative to transform the engineering role into one of science-based highly educated technological expertise. Neither did the over-sized external R. & D. sector produce alternative types of industrial integration. Rather, the research sector reinforced the autonomy of the firm, through the role of the firm as the most important consumer of R. & D. services.

TOWARDS A NEW TYPE OF INDUSTRIAL INTEGRATION?

We have argued that the social construction of the engineering dimension in Norwegian industry diverges from that of most other national cases treated in the literature on industry and its societal embeddedness. The peculiarities of this configuration of actors and institutions are epitomized in its specific mode of articulating technology and organization, and the way these factors themselves are defined and shaped by the culture of engineering and industrial traditions in this country. In general, its effects are to lend a certain unity and homogeneity to engineering as a precondition for industrial activity, across firms, industries and subdivisions within the business system. The efficient management of a firm or company presupposes the enactment of such generic, cultural and institutional traits and its strengths, that is the mobilization of technology and organization as resources for transformation.

In contrast to the French case, the culture of 'technology' does not mean a predominating rationalist leaning and prejudice towards its 'scientific' elements, but rather technology as pragmatism and the art of making useful objects. And 'organization' does not imply elements of Taylorism or élitist management but, instead, sociotechnical optimization, compromise and negotiation. Compared to the policy proposed by the Finniston Committee as a cure for English industry (HMSO, 1980), the Norwegian system appears as an ideal type of the embodiment of the engineering dimension. While this surely means a central position for engineering in the strategies of the firm, its function differs from the unifying place of *technik* in German production. Due to the discontinuities in qualification between engineers, foremen and workers, the key to establishing consensus on the shop floor is less technology than organization and negotiated change. Continuous innovation is therefore hampered by the recurring need to create agreement by means of bargaining. Innovations in production technology and attempts to achieve increased flexibility in production and polyvalence among workers not only encounter problems arising from the existing structure of qualifications and competences, but also confront routinely the 'tariff system' of agreements as essentials of the system of industrial relations. Hence, initiating change in the technical domain presupposes often quite considerable efforts to mobilize or neutralize actors in the social domain. This configuration probably also explains a good part of the frequent complaints expressed by managers that innovation in Norwegian firms is too greatly characterized by the mentality of 'all-out effort' (*skippertak*) and investment in extraordinary energy, to the detriment of more permanent efforts to modernize.[1]

In spite of their specificity, such structures in themselves are, of course, compatible with more than one type of business strategy. Nevertheless, they appear to have a certain general potential in the explanation of recent processes of change and 'deindustrialization'. A look at the trends, in particular the mode of readjustment in the mechanical engineering industry since the mid-1970s, shows us a picture of processes driven by strategies of 'numerical' rationalization; cut-backs in workforce and the narrowing of activities and structures, curtailing costs and investments, dropping unprofitable products and departments, externalizing functions, etc. Contrary to the English case, for instance, the strategic direction appears not simply to be the strengthening of price competitiveness, but the amplification or reconsolidation of strategies of niche-production, and thus away from standardized products. If this is correct, it is still fairly compatible with the traditional 'product conservatism' in the industry, where company culture and the identity of actors are defined by a specific product more than a range of capacities for marketing and production. The result, thus, is not so much 'diversified quality production' (Sorge, 1991), but quality production according to niches, where product design and innovation are important. Thus, diversification may be a trait of industry and branches as sectors, although it is not a characteristic central to the single, 'readjusted' firm. Moreover, such a picture is consistent with the observed priority placed, in this period, on capital rationalization and projects of organizational restructuring, including increasing the efficiency in logistics, in Norwegian firms. The result is a noticeable enhancement of cost-efficiency alongside organizational flexibility, that is responsiveness to changes in demand and optimum management of production flows, but perhaps to a lesser degree the creation of 'scope-efficiency' or increased capacities for product-diversification in rapidly changing markets. Apparently, engineering still holds a position of centrality, and there has been no radical departure from the firm-based safeguarding of products reflecting the dominance of the profession. Products become, so to speak, the symbol of the common business culture and the integrated engineering hierarchy within the firm. Attempts at industrial reorientation seems to be enacting the generic cultural and institutional traits of the profession and its strengths: technology within and through organization.

Whilst recent tendencies of change appear to reproduce the composite structure of unity and division in Norwegian industry, the state of affairs is increasingly judged by the actors themselves as inappropriate for the demands of the future. Types of integration within industry must come about, including new types of linkages between and within branches, in order to cope with market uncertainties and rapid technological change, and to engender a process of reindustrialization. Today, such a policy for regeneration and integration is summarized in the widespread concern for construction of 'networks' and the making of strategic alliances. Although the forces behind such attempts do not always appear very strong, one may expect them to have noticeable effects, for example on the relationships between firms and subcontractors and between the R. & D. agents and the SME sector.

However, the structural factors implied in the historical pattern of industrial segmentation will evidently be effective also in the future. It remains to be seen how the social relations of the engineering profession will shape such processes of industrial readjustment, and whether circumstances will animate the networking capabilities of engineers in novel ways. The question, therefore, is not so much whether basic traits are recreated, but their specific mode of reproduction and the precise direction of industrial change.

NOTE

1 This implies that contrary to, for example, the Danish case, Norwegian engineers in management do not confront an industry-wide 'craft complex', embodying technical and industrial dynamism in its own right, but rather local, enterprise-specific groups of workers with a narrower skill profile (cf. Kristensen, 1992).

REFERENCES

Abbott, A. L (1988) *The System of Professions*, Chicago, Ill.: University of Chicago Press.

Amdam, R. P. (1993) *For egen regning. BI og den økonomis-administrative utdanningen*, Oslo: Universitetsforlaget.

—— (1994) 'Foreign influences on the education of Norwegian business managers before World War II', *Business History* 36(4).

—— and Bjarnar, O. (1989) *En bedrift i norsk skole. NKS og fjernundervisningen i Norge 1914–1989*, NKS-Forlaget.

Bergh, T. and Lange, E. (1989) *Foredlet virke. Historien om Borregaard 1889–1989*, Oslo: AdNotam Forlag.

Boltanski, L. (1987) *The Making of a Class: Cadres in French Society*, Cambridge: Cambridge University Press.

Campbell, J. L., Hollingsworth, R. J. and Lindberg, L. (1991) *Governance of the American Economy*, Cambridge: Cambridge University Press.

Chisholm, A. W. J. (1975) *Education and Training of Engineers on the Continent of Europe, with Special Reference to Courses in Total Technology*, Manchester: Engineering Education and Training Project, Dept. of Mechanical Engineering, University of Salford.

Fligstein, N. (1990) *Transformation of Corporate Control*.

Fores, M. (1982) 'Technical change and "Technology" myth', *The Scandinavian Economic History Review and Economic History* XXX(3): 167–88.

—— and Pratt, J. (1980) 'Engineering: our last change', *Higher Education Review* 12(3): 5–26.

—— and Rey, L. (1979) 'Technik: the relevance of a missing concept', *Higher Education Review* II, Spring: 43–57.

—— Glover, I. and Lawrence, P. (1991) 'Professionalism and rationality: A study in misapprehension', *Sociology* 25(1): 79–100.

Gammelsæter, H. (1990) *Organisasjonsendringer gjennom generasjoner av ledere*, Molde: Møreforskning.

Glover, I. and Kelley, M. P. (1987) *Engineers in Britain. A Sociological Study of the Engineering Dimension*, London: Allen and Unwin.

Halvorsen, T. (1982) 'Profesjonalisering – Taylorisering. Ingeniørar mellom leiing og arbeidarmotstand'. Hovedfagsoppgave. Institutt for Administrasjon og Organisasjonsvitskap, Bergen University.

—— (1983) 'Kunnskapsformer og profesjonelle yrker i vitskapleggjeringa av norsk foretaksorganisasjon', *Moralprosjektets skriftserie*, no. 6, Bergen University.

—— (1984) 'Tayloringeniøren og foretaksorganizering i norsk mellomkrigstid', *Moralprosjektets skriftserie*, no. 8, Bergen University.

—— (1984) 'Teknologipolitikk og ingeniørdimensjonen i den industripolitiske omstilling', *Statsviteren* 4.

—— and Sakslind, R. (1984) 'Produksjonens politikk. Om utdanning og profesjoner ifremveksten av moderne bedriftsorganisasjon', *Forskningsnytt* 3: 21–5.

HMSO (1980) *Engineering Our Future*, Report of the Committee of Inquiry into the Engineering Profession, Chairman: Sir Montague Finniston, FRS, London: HMSO.

Jordan A. G. and Richardson, J. J. (1984) 'Engineering a consensus: from the Finniston Report to the Engineering Council', *Public Administration* 62: 383–400.

—— (1990a) *On the Social Construction of the Skilled Industrial Worker*, Bergen: Gruppe for flerfaglig arbeidslivsforskning. Bergen University.

—— (1990b) *Hva kan vi lære av den historisk-sosiologiske arbeidslivsforskningen?* Bergen: Bergen University, Sociology Institute.

—— (1993) *Lærlingeordningas sosio-strukturelle betingelser. Et framlegg til et forskningsprogram*, Bergen: Bergen University.

Kristensen, P. H. (1992) 'Strategies against structure. Institutions and economic organization in Denmark', in R. Whitley (ed.) *European Business Systems. Firms and Markets in their National Context*, London: Sage.

Maurice, M. (1986) 'La qualification comme rapport social à propos de la "qualification" comme "mise en forme du travail" ', in R. Salais and L. Thévenot (eds) *Le travail, marché, règles, conventions*, Paris: INSEE, Economica.

—— (1989) *For en sosiologi om foretaket i samfunnet. Kritisk blikk på en debatt og et framlegg til forskning*, Bergen: University of Bergen, AHS series B, 1989: 5.

—— Selliers, F. and Silvestre, J.-J. (1986) *The Social Foundation of Industrial Power. A Comparison of France and Germany*, Cambridge, Mass.: MIT Press.

Meyer, M. W. (1990) 'The Weberian tradition in organization research', in C. Calhoun *et al.* (eds) *Structures of Power and Constraint*, Cambridge: Cambridge University Press.

Myklebust, S. (1990) *Arbeidsmarkedet i 90–årene. Teknologisk endring og nye kvalifikasjonskrav i tjenestesektoren*, Oslo: Oslo University.

Perrow, C. (1986) *Complex Organizations. A critical essay*, New York: Random House.

Reve, T., Lensberg, T. and Grønhaug, T. (1992) *Et konkurransedyktig Norge*, Oslo: Tano.

Sakslind, R. (1989) 'Social relations and use of NC-technology in manufacturing. Transformations in Norwegian mechanical-engineering enterprises', mimeo, Bergen University, Sociology Institute.

—— (1990) *Flexible Technology and Social Relations in Industry. Adaptation to NC-technology in Norwegian Mechanical-Engineering Enterprises*, Bergen: University of Bergen, AHS series B, 1990–3.

Simonsen, H. (1989) *Sivilingeniøren vrakes som toppleder*, Ledelse.

Sorge, A. (1981/82) 'Culture and organization', *Journal of General Management* 7(2): 62–80.

—— (1985) *Informationstechnik und Arbeit im sozialen Prozess*, Frankfurt/ New York: Campus Verlag.

—— (1991) 'Strategic fit and the societal effect: interpreting cross-national comparisons of technology. Organizations and human resources', *Organization Studies* 12(2): 161–90.

—— and Warner, M. (1989) *Comparative Factory Organization*, Gower: WZB Publications.

Whitley, R. (ed.) (1992) *European Business Systems*, London: Sage.

Index

330   *Index*